UNIVERSITY CASEBOOK SERIES®

2021 CASE, STATUTE, AND RULE SUPPLEMENT TO

ADMIRALTY

CASES AND MATERIALS

RANDALL D. SCHMIDT
Clinical Professor of Law
University of Chicago

FOUNDATION
PRESS

© 1987, 1991, 1996, 2003 By FOUNDATION PRESS
© 2009, 2012 By THOMSON REUTERS/FOUNDATION PRESS
© 2021 LEG, Inc. d/b/a West Academic
    444 Cedar Street, Suite 700
    St. Paul, MN 55101
    1-877-888-1330

Printed in the United States of America

ISBN: 978-1-63659-104-9

TABLE OF CONTENTS

TABLE OF CASES

The principal cases are in bold type.

UNIVERSITY CASEBOOK SERIES®

2021 CASE, STATUTE, AND RULE SUPPLEMENT TO

ADMIRALTY

CASES AND MATERIALS

I. CONSTITUTION OF THE UNITED STATES

ARTICLE III

Section 1. The judicial Power of the United States, shall be vested in one supreme Court, and in such inferior Courts as the Congress may from time to time ordain and establish. The Judges, both of the supreme and inferior Courts, shall hold their Offices during good Behavior, and shall, at stated Times, receive for their Services, a Compensation, which shall not be diminished during their Continuance in Office.

Section 2. The judicial Power shall extend to all Cases, in Law and Equity, arising under this Constitution, the Laws of the United States, and Treaties made, or which shall be made, under their Authority;—to all Cases affecting Ambassadors, other public Ministers and Consuls;—to all Cases of admiralty, and maritime Jurisdiction;—to Controversies to which the United States shall be a Party;—to Controversies between two or more States;—between a State and Citizens of another State;—between Citizens of different States;—between Citizens of the same State claiming Lands under Grants of different States, and between a State, or the Citizens thereof, and foreign States, Citizens or Subjects.

In all Cases affecting Ambassadors, other public Ministers and Consuls, and those in which a State shall be Party, the supreme Court shall have original Jurisdiction. In all the other Cases before mentioned, the supreme Court shall have appellate Jurisdiction, both as to Law and Fact, with such Exceptions, and under such Regulations as the Congress shall make.

The Trial of all Crimes, except in Cases of Impeachment, shall be by Jury; and such Trial shall be held in the State where the said Crimes shall have been committed; but when not committed within any State, the Trial shall be at such Place or Places as the Congress may by Law have directed.

Section 3. Treason against the United States, shall consist only in levying War against them, or in adhering to their Enemies, giving them Aid and Comfort. No Person shall be convicted of Treason unless on the Testimony of two Witnesses to the same overt Act, or on Confession in open Court.

The Congress shall have Power to declare the Punishment of Treason, but no Attainder of Treason shall work Corruption of Blood, or Forfeiture except during the Life of the Person attainted.

II. SELECTED CURRENT PROVISIONS OF THE UNITED STATES CODE

TITLE 1
GENERAL PROVISIONS

§ 3. **"VESSEL" AS INCLUDING ALL MEANS OF WATER TRANSPORTATION**

The word "vessel" includes every description of watercraft or other artificial contrivance used, or capable of being used, as a means of transportation on water.

TITLE 10
ARMED SERVICES
SUBTITLE C
NAVY AND MARINE CORPS
CHAPTER 883.   PRIZE

§ 8851. **SCOPE OF CHAPTER**

(a) This chapter applies to all captures of vessels as prize during war by authority of the United States or adopted and ratified by the President. However, this chapter does not affect the right of the Army or the Air Force, while engaged in hostilities, to capture wherever found and without prize procedure—

(1) enemy property; or

(2) neutral property used or transported in violation of the obligations of neutrals under international law.

(b) As used in this chapter—

(1) "vessel" includes aircraft; and

(2) "master" includes the pilot or other person in command of an aircraft.

(c) Property seized or taken upon the inland waters of the United States by its naval forces is not maritime prize. All such property shall be delivered promptly to the proper officers of the courts.

(d) Nothing in this chapter may be construed as contravening any treaty of the United States.

§ 8852. **JURISDICTION**

(a) The United States district courts have original jurisdiction, exclusive of the courts of the States, of each prize and each proceeding for the condemnation of property taken as prize, if the prize is—

(1) brought into the United States, or the Commonwealths or possessions;

(2) brought into the territorial waters of a cobelligerent;

(3) brought into a locality in the temporary or permanent possession of, or occupied by, the armed forces of the United States; or

(4) appropriated for the use of the United States.

(b) The United States district courts, exclusive of the courts of the States, also have original jurisdiction of a prize cause in which the prize property—

(1) is lost or entirely destroyed; or

(2) cannot be brought in for adjudication because of its condition.

(c) The jurisdiction conferred by this section of prizes brought into the territorial waters of a cobelligerent may not be exercised, nor may prizes be appropriated for the use of the United States within those territorial waters, unless the government having jurisdiction over those waters consents to the exercise of the jurisdiction or to the appropriation.

[Procedure in prize cases is set out in §§ 8853–8881]

CHAPTER 885.   STAY OF PROCEEDINGS

§ 8891. SCOPE OF CHAPTER

(a) This chapter applies to any suit against the United States under Chapter 311 of Title 46—

(1) damage caused by a vessel in the naval service; or

(2) compensation for towage or salvage services, including contract salvage, rendered to a vessel in the naval service.

(b) In this chapter the term "vessel in the naval service" means—

(1) any vessel of the Navy, manned by the Navy, or chartered on bareboat charter to the Navy; or

(2) when the Coast Guard is operating as a service in the Navy, any vessel of the Coast Guard, or chartered on bareboat charter to the Coast Guard.

§ 8892. STAY OF SUIT

(a) Whenever in time of war the Secretary of the Navy certifies to a court, or to a judge of a court, in which a suit described in section 7721 of this title is pending, that the prosecution of the suit would tend to endanger the security of naval operations in the war, or would tend to interfere with those operations, all further proceedings in the suit shall be stayed.

(b) A stay under this section does not suspend the issue of process to take or preserve evidence to be used in the trial or prevent the completion of action under similar process issued before the stay.

TITLE 18

CRIMES AND CRIMINAL PROCEDURE

PART I.   CRIMES

CHAPTER I.   GENERAL PROVISIONS

§ 7.   SPECIAL MARITIME AND TERRITORIAL JURISDICTION OF THE UNITED STATES DEFINED

The term "special maritime and territorial jurisdiction of the United States," as used in this title, includes:

(1)   The high seas, any other waters within the admiralty and maritime jurisdiction of the United States and out of the jurisdiction of any particular State, and any vessel belonging in whole or in part to the United States or any citizen thereof, or to any corporation created by or under the laws of the United States, or of any State, Territory, District, or possession thereof, when such vessel is within the admiralty and maritime jurisdiction of the United States and out of the jurisdiction of any particular State.

(2)   Any vessel registered, licensed, or enrolled under the laws of the United States, and being on a voyage upon the waters of any of the Great Lakes, or any of the waters connecting them, or upon the Saint Lawrence River where the same constitutes the International Boundary Line.

(3)   * * *

(4)   * * *

(5)   * * *

(6)   * * *

(7)   * * *

(8)   To the extent permitted by international law, any foreign vessel during a voyage having a scheduled departure or arrival in the United States with respect to an offense committed by or against a national of the United States.

(9)   * * *

TITLE 28

JUDICIARY AND JUDICIAL PROCEDURE

PART IV.   JURISDICTION AND VENUE

CHAPTER 83.   COURT OF APPEALS

§ 1292. INTERLOCUTORY DECISIONS

(a)   Except as provided in subsections (c) and (d) of this section, the courts of appeals shall have jurisdiction of appeals from:

(1)   Interlocutory orders of the district courts of the United States, the United States District Court for the District of the Canal Zone, the District Court of Guam, and the District Court of the

Virgin Islands, or of the judges thereof, granting, continuing, modifying, refusing or dissolving injunctions, or refusing to dissolve or modify injunctions, except where a direct review may be had in the Supreme Court;

(2) Interlocutory orders appointing receivers, or refusing orders to wind up receiverships or to take steps to accomplish the purposes thereof, such as directing sales or other disposals of property;

(3) Interlocutory decrees of such district courts or the judges thereof determining the rights and liabilities of the parties to admiralty cases in which appeals from final decrees are allowed.

(b) When a district judge, in making in a civil action an order not otherwise appealable under this section, shall be of the opinion that such order involves a controlling question of law as to which there is substantial ground for difference of opinion and that an immediate appeal from the order may materially advance the ultimate termination of the litigation, he shall so state in writing in such order. The Court of Appeals which would have jurisdiction of an appeal of such action may, thereupon, in its discretion, permit an appeal to be taken from such order, if application is made to it within ten days after the entry of the order: *Provided, however,* That application for an appeal hereunder shall not stay proceedings in the district court unless the district judge or the Court of Appeals or a judge thereof shall so order.

(c) * * *

(d) * * *

(e) The Supreme Court may prescribe rules, in accordance with section 2072 of this title, to provide for an appeal of an interlocutory decision to the courts of appeals that is not otherwise provided for under subsection (a), (b), (c), or (d).

CHAPTER 85. DISTRICT COURTS; JURISDICTION

§ 1330. ACTIONS AGAINST FOREIGN STATES

(a) The district courts shall have original jurisdiction without regard to amount in controversy of any nonjury civil action against a foreign state as defined in section 1603(a) of this title as to any claim for relief in personam with respect to which the foreign state is not entitled to immunity either under sections 1605–1607 of this title or under any applicable international agreement.

(b) Personal jurisdiction over a foreign state shall exist as to every claim for relief over which the district courts have jurisdiction under subsection (a) where service has been made under section 1608 of this title.

(c) For purposes of subsection (b), an appearance by a foreign state does not confer personal jurisdiction with respect to any claim for relief not arising out of any transaction or occurrence enumerated in sections 1605–1607 of this title.

§ 1331. FEDERAL QUESTION; AMOUNT IN CONTROVERSY; COSTS

The district courts shall have original jurisdiction of all civil actions arising under the Constitution, laws or treaties of the United States.

§ 1332. DIVERSITY OF CITIZENSHIP; AMOUNT IN CONTROVERSY; COSTS

(a) The district courts shall have original jurisdiction of all civil actions where the matter in controversy exceeds the sum or value of $75,000, exclusive of interest and costs, and is between—

    (1) citizens of different States;

    (2) citizens of a State and citizens or subjects of a foreign state, except that the district courts shall not have original jurisdiction under this subsection of an action between citizens of a State and citizens or subjects of a foreign state who are lawfully admitted for permanent residence in the United States and are domiciled in the same State;

    (3) citizens of different States and in which citizens or subjects of a foreign state are additional parties; and

    (4) a foreign state, defined in Section 1603(a) of this title, as plaintiff and citizens of a State or of different States.

(b) Except when express provision therefor is otherwise made in a statute of the United States, where the plaintiff who files the case originally in the Federal courts is finally adjudged to be entitled to recover less than the sum or value of $75,000, computed without regard to any setoff or counterclaim to which the defendant may be adjudged to be entitled, and exclusive of interests and costs, the district court may deny costs to the plaintiff and, in addition, may impose costs on the plaintiff.

(c) For the purposes of this section and section 1441 of this title—

    (1) a corporation shall be deemed to be a citizen of every State and foreign state by which it has been incorporated and of the State or foreign state where it has its principal place of business, except that in any direct action against the insurer of a policy or contract of liability insurance, whether incorporated or unincorporated, to which action the insured is not joined as a party-defendant, such insurer shall be deemed a citizen of—

        (A) every State and foreign state of which the insured is a citizen;

        (B) every State and foreign state by which the insurer has been incorporated; and

        (C) the State or foreign state where the insurer has its principal place of business; and

(2) the legal representative of the estate of a decedent shall be deemed to be a citizen only of the same State as the decedent, and the legal representative of an infant or incompetent shall be deemed to be a citizen only of the same State as the infant or incompetent.

§ 1333. ADMIRALTY, MARITIME AND PRIZE CASES

The district courts shall have original jurisdiction, exclusive of the courts of the States, of:

(1) Any civil case of admiralty or maritime jurisdiction, saving to suitors in all cases all other remedies to which they are otherwise entitled.

(2) Any prize brought into the United States and all proceedings for the condemnation of property taken as prize.

§ 1345. UNITED STATES AS PLAINTIFF

Except as otherwise provided by Act of Congress, the district courts shall have original jurisdiction of all civil actions, suits or proceedings commenced by the United States, or by any agency or officer thereof expressly authorized to sue by Act of Congress.

§ 1346. UNITED STATES AS DEFENDANT

(a) The district courts shall have original jurisdiction, concurrent with the United States Court of Federal Claims, of:

(1) Any civil action against the United States for the recovery of any internal-revenue tax alleged to have been erroneously or illegally assessed or collected, or any penalty claimed to have been collected without authority or any sum alleged to have been excessive or in any manner wrongfully collected under the internal-revenue laws;

(2) Any other civil action or claim against the United States, not exceeding $10,000 in amount, founded either upon the Constitution, or any Act of Congress, or any regulation of an executive department, or upon any express or implied contract with the United States, or for liquidated or unliquidated damages in cases not sounding in tort, except that the district courts shall not have jurisdiction of any civil action or claim against the United States founded upon any express or implied contract with the United States or for liquidated or unliquidated damages in cases not sounding in tort which are subject to sections 7104(b)(1) and 7107(a)(1) of title 41. For the purpose of this paragraph, an express or implied contract with the Army and Air Force Exchange Service, Navy Exchanges, Marine Corps Exchanges, Coast Guard Exchanges, or Exchange Councils of the National Aeronautics and Space Administration shall be considered an express or implied contract with the United States.

(b)(1) Subject to the provisions of chapter 171 of this title, the district courts, together with the United States District Court for the

District of the Canal Zone and the District Court of the Virgin Islands, shall have exclusive jurisdiction of civil actions on claims against the United States, for money damages, accruing on and after January 1, 1945, for injury or loss of property, or personal injury or death caused by the negligent or wrongful act or omission of any employee of the Government while acting within the scope of his office or employment, under circumstances where the United States, if a private person, would be liable to the claimant in accordance with the law of the place where the act or omission occurred.

(2)   No person convicted of a felony who is incarcerated while awaiting sentencing or while serving a sentence may bring a civil action against the United States or an agency, officer, or employee of the government for mental or emotional injury suffered while in custody without a prior showing of physical injury.

(c)   The jurisdiction conferred by this section includes jurisdiction of any set-off, counterclaim, or other claim or demand whatever on the part of the United States against any plaintiff commencing an action under this section.

(d)   The district courts shall not have jurisdiction under this section of any civil action or claim for a pension.

(e)   The district courts shall have original jurisdiction of any civil action against the United States provided in section 6226, 6228(a), 7426, or 7428 (in the case of the United States district court for the District of Columbia) or section 7429 of the Internal Revenue Code of 1986.

(f)   The district courts shall have exclusive original jurisdiction of civil actions under section 2409a to quiet title to an estate or interest in real property in which an interest is claimed by the United States.

(g)   Subject to the provisions of chapter 179, the district courts of the United States shall have exclusive jurisdiction over any civil action commenced under section 453(2) of title 3 by a covered employee under chapter 5 of such title.

§ 1367. SUPPLEMENTAL JURISDICTION

(a)   Except as provided in subsections (b) and (c) or as expressly provided otherwise by Federal statute, in any civil action of which the district courts have original jurisdiction, the district courts shall have supplemental jurisdiction over all other claims that are so related to claims in the action within such original jurisdiction that they form part of the same case or controversy under Article III of the United States Constitution. Such supplemental jurisdiction shall include claims that involve the joinder or intervention of additional parties.

(b)   In any civil action of which the district courts have original jurisdiction founded solely on section 1332 of this title, the district courts shall not have supplemental jurisdiction under subsection (a) over claims by plaintiffs against persons made parties under Rule 14, 19, 20, or 24 of the Federal Rules of Civil Procedure, or over claims by persons proposed to be joined as plaintiffs under Rule 19 of such rules, or seeking to intervene as plaintiffs under Rule 24 of such rules, when exercising supplemental jurisdiction over such claims would be inconsistent with the jurisdictional requirements of section 1332.

(c) The district courts may decline to exercise supplemental jurisdiction over a claim under subsection (a) if—

(1) the claim raises a novel or complex issue of State law,

(2) the claim substantially predominates over claims over which the district court has original jurisdiction,

(3) the district court has dismissed all claims over which it has original jurisdiction, or

(4) in exceptional circumstances, there are other compelling reasons for declining jurisdiction.

(d) The period of limitations for any claim asserted under subsection (a), and for any other claim in the same action that is voluntarily dismissed at the same time as or after the dismissal of the claim under section (a), shall be tolled while the claim is pending and for a period of 30 days after it is dismissed unless State law provides for a longer tolling period.

(e) As used in this section, the term "State" includes the District of Columbia, the Commonwealth of Puerto Rico, and any territory or possession of the United States.

CHAPTER 87. DISTRICT COURTS; VENUE

§ 1391. VENUE GENERALLY

(a) Applicability of section.—Except as otherwise provided by law—

(1) this section shall govern the venue of all civil actions brought in district courts of the United States; and

(2) the proper venue for a civil action shall be determined without regard to whether the action is local or transitory in nature.

(b) Venue in general.—A civil action may be brought in—

(1) a judicial district in which any defendant resides, if all defendants are residents of the State in which the district is located;

(2) a judicial district in which a substantial part of the events or omissions giving rise to the claim occurred, or a substantial part of property that is the subject of the action is situated; or

(3) if there is no district in which an action may otherwise be brought as provided in this section, any judicial district in which any defendant is subject to the court's personal jurisdiction with respect to such action.

(c) Residency.—For all venue purposes—

(1) a natural person, including an alien lawfully admitted for permanent residence in the United States, shall be deemed to reside in the judicial district in which that person is domiciled;

(2) an entity with the capacity to sue and be sued in its common name under applicable law, whether or not incorporated, shall be deemed to reside, if a defendant, in any judicial district in which such defendant is subject to the court's personal jurisdiction with respect to the civil action in question and, if a plaintiff, only in the judicial district in which it maintains its principal place of business; and

(3) a defendant not resident in the United States may be sued in any judicial district, and the joinder of such a defendant shall be disregarded in determining where the action may be brought with respect to other defendants.

(d) Residency of corporations in States with multiple districts.—For purposes of venue under this chapter, in a State which has more than one judicial district and in which a defendant that is a corporation is subject to personal jurisdiction at the time an action is commenced, such corporation shall be deemed to reside in any district in that State within which its contacts would be sufficient to subject it to personal jurisdiction if that district were a separate State, and, if there is no such district, the corporation shall be deemed to reside in the district within which it has the most significant contacts.

(e) Actions where defendant is officer or employee of the United States—

(1) In general.—A civil action in which a defendant is an officer or employee of the United States or any agency thereof acting in his official capacity or under color of legal authority, or an agency of the United States, or the United States, may, except as otherwise provided by law, be brought in any judicial district in which (A) a defendant in the action resides, (B) a substantial part of the events or omissions giving rise to the claim occurred, or a substantial part of property that is the subject of the action is situated, or (C) the plaintiff resides if no real property is involved in the action. Additional persons may be joined as parties to any such action in accordance with the Federal Rules of Civil Procedure and with such other venue requirements as would be applicable if the United States or one of its officers, employees, or agencies were not a party.

(2) Service.—The summons and complaint in such an action shall be served as provided by the Federal Rules of Civil Procedure except that the delivery of the summons and complaint to the officer or agency as required by the rules may be made by certified mail beyond the territorial limits of the district in which the action is brought.

(f) Civil actions against a foreign state—A civil action against a foreign state as defined in section 1603(a) of this title may be brought—

(1) in any judicial district in which a substantial part of the events or omissions giving rise to the claim occurred, or a substantial part of property that is the subject of the action is situated;

(2) in any judicial district in which the vessel or cargo of a foreign state is situated, if the claim is asserted under section 1605(b) of this title;

(3) in any judicial district in which the agency or instrumentality is licensed to do business or is doing business, if the action is brought against an agency or instrumentality of a foreign state as defined in section 1603(b) of this title; or

(4) in the United States District Court for the District of Columbia if the action is brought against a foreign state or political subdivision thereof.

(g) Multiparty, multiforum litigation—A civil action in which jurisdiction of the district court is based upon section 1369 of this title may be brought in any district in which any defendant resides or in which a substantial part of the accident giving rise to the action took place.

§ 1395. FINE, PENALTY OR FORFEITURE

(a) A civil proceeding for the recovery of a pecuniary fine, penalty or forfeiture may be prosecuted in the district where it accrues or the defendant is found.

(b) A civil proceeding for the forfeiture of property may be prosecuted in any district where such property is found.

(c) A civil proceeding for the forfeiture of property seized outside any judicial district may be prosecuted in any district into which the property is brought.

(d) A proceeding in admiralty for the enforcement of fines, penalties and forfeitures against a vessel may be brought in any district in which the vessel is arrested.

(e) Any proceeding for the forfeiture of a vessel or cargo entering a port of entry closed by the President in pursuance of law, or of goods and chattels coming from a State or section declared by proclamation of the President to be in insurrection, or of any vessel or vehicle conveying persons or property to or from such State or section or belonging in whole or in part to a resident thereof, may be prosecuted in any district into which the property is taken and in which the proceeding is instituted.

§ 1404. CHANGE OF VENUE

(a) For the convenience of parties and witnesses, in the interest of justice, a district court may transfer any civil action to any other district or division where it might have been brought.

(b) Upon motion, consent or stipulation of all parties, any action, suit or proceeding of a civil nature or any motion or hearing thereof, may be transferred, in the discretion of the court, from the division in which pending to any other division in the same district. Transfer of proceedings in rem brought by or on behalf of the United States may be transferred under this section without the consent of the United States where all other parties request transfer.

(c) A district court may order any civil action to be tried at any place within the division in which it is pending.

(d) Transfers from a district court of the United States to the District Court of Guam, the District Court for the Northern Mariana Islands, or the District Court of the Virgin Islands shall not be permitted under this section. As otherwise used in this section, the term "district court" includes the District Court of Guam, the District Court for the Northern Mariana Islands, and the District Court of the Virgin Islands, and the term "district" includes the territorial jurisdiction of each such court.

CHAPTER 89. DISTRICT COURTS; REMOVAL OF ACTIONS FROM STATE COURTS

§ 1441. REMOVAL OF CIVIL ACTIONS

(a) Generally.—Except as otherwise expressly provided by Act of Congress, any civil action brought in a State court of which the district courts of the United States have original jurisdiction, may be removed by the defendant or the defendants, to the district court of the United States for the district and division embracing the place where such action is pending.

(b) Removal based on diversity of citizenship.—(1) In determining whether a civil action is removable on the basis of the jurisdiction under section 1332(a) of this title, the citizenship of defendants sued under fictitious names shall be disregarded.

(2) A civil action otherwise removable solely on the basis of the jurisdiction under section 1332(a) of this title may not be removed if any of the parties in interest properly joined and served as defendants is a citizen of the State in which such action is brought.

(c) Joinder of Federal law claims and State law claims.—(1) If a civil action includes—

(A) a claim arising under the Constitution, laws, or treaties of the United States (within the meaning of section 1331 of this title), and

(B) a claim not within the original or supplemental jurisdiction of the district court or a claim that has been made nonremovable by statute,

the entire action may be removed if the action would be removable without the inclusion of the claim described in subparagraph (B).

(2) Upon removal of an action described in paragraph (1), the district court shall sever from the action all claims described in

paragraph (1)(B) and shall remand the severed claims to the State court from which the action was removed. Only defendants against whom a claim described in paragraph (1)(A) has been asserted are required to join in or consent to the removal under paragraph (1).

(d) Actions against foreign States.—Any civil action brought in a State court against a foreign state as defined in section 1603(a) of this title may be removed by the foreign state to the district court of the United States for the district and division embracing the place where such action is pending. Upon removal the action shall be tried by the court without jury. Where removal is based upon this subsection, the time limitations of section 1446(b) of this chapter may be enlarged at any time for cause shown.

(e)   * * *

(f) Derivative removal jurisdiction.—The court to which a civil action is removed under this section is not precluded from hearing and determining any claim in such civil action because the State court from which such civil action is removed did not have jurisdiction over that claim.

§ 1445. NONREMOVABLE ACTIONS

(a) A civil action in any State court against a railroad or its receivers or trustees, arising under sections 1–4 and 3–10 of the Act of April 22, 1908 (45 U.S.C. 51–54, 55–60) may not be removed to any district court of the United States.

(b) A civil action in any State court against a carrier or its receivers or trustees to recover damages for delay, loss, or injury of shipments, arising under section 11706 or 14706 of Title 49, may not be removed to any district court of the United States unless the matter in controversy exceeds $10,000, exclusive of interest and costs.

(c) A civil action in any State court arising under the workmen's compensation laws of such state may not be removed to any district court of the United States.

(d) A civil action in any State court arising under section 40302 of the Violence against Women Act of 1994 may not be removed to any district court of the United States.

CHAPTER 97.   JURISDICTIONAL IMMUNITIES
OF FOREIGN STATES

§ 1603. DEFINITIONS

For purposes of this chapter—

(a) A "foreign state", except as used in section 1608 of this title, includes a political subdivision of a foreign state or an agency or instrumentality of a foreign state as defined in subsection (b).

(b) An "agency or instrumentality of a foreign state" means any entity—

(1)   which is a separate legal person, corporate or otherwise, and

(2)   which is an organ of a foreign state or political subdivision thereof, or a majority of whose shares or other ownership interest is owned by a foreign state or political subdivision thereof, and

(3)   which is neither a citizen of a State of the United States as defined in section 1332(c) and (e) of this title, nor created under the laws of any third country.

(c)   The United States includes all territory and waters, continental or insular, subject to the jurisdiction of the United States.

(d)   A "commercial activity" means either a regular course of commercial conduct or a particular commercial transaction or act. The commercial character of an activity shall be determined by reference to the nature of the course of conduct or particular transaction or act, rather than by reference to its purpose.

(e)   A "commercial activity carried on in the United States by a foreign state" means commercial activity carried on by such state and having substantial contact with the United States.

§ 1604. IMMUNITY OF A FOREIGN STATE FROM JURISDICTION

Subject to existing international agreements to which the United States is a party at the time of enactment of this Act a foreign state shall be immune from the jurisdiction of the courts of the United States and of the States except as provided in sections 1605 to 1607 of this chapter.

§ 1605. GENERAL EXCEPTIONS TO THE JURISDICTIONAL IMMUNITY OF A FOREIGN STATE

(a)   A foreign state shall not be immune from the jurisdiction of courts of the United States or of the States in any case—

(1)   in which the foreign state has waived its immunity either explicitly or by implication, notwithstanding any withdrawal of the waiver which the foreign state may purport to effect except in accordance with the terms of the waiver;

(2)   in which the action is based upon a commercial activity carried on in the United States by the foreign state; or upon an act performed in the United States in connection with a commercial activity of the foreign state elsewhere; or upon an act outside the territory of the United States in connection with a commercial activity of the foreign state elsewhere and that act causes a direct effect in the United States;

(3)   in which rights in property taken in violation of international law are in issue and that property or any property exchanged for such property is present in the United States in connection with a commercial activity carried on in the United States by the foreign state; or that property or any property

exchanged for such property is owned or operated by an agency or instrumentality of the foreign state and that agency or instrumentality is engaged in a commercial activity in the United States;

(4) in which rights in property in the United States acquired by succession or gift or rights in immovable property situated in the United States are in issue;

(5) not otherwise encompassed in paragraph (2) above, in which money damages are sought against a foreign state for personal injury or death, or damage to or loss of property, occurring in the United States and caused by the tortious act or omission of that foreign state or of any official or employee of that foreign state while acting within the scope of his office or employment; except this paragraph shall not apply to—

(A) any claim based upon the exercise or performance or the failure to exercise or perform a discretionary function regardless of whether the discretion be abused, or

(B) any claim arising out of malicious prosecution, abuse of process, libel, slander, misrepresentation, deceit, or interference with contract rights; or

(6) in which the action is brought, either to enforce an agreement made by the foreign state with or for the benefit of a private party to submit to arbitration all or any differences which have arisen or which may arise between the parties with respect to a defined legal relationship, whether contractual or not, concerning a subject matter capable of settlement by arbitration under the laws of the United States, or to confirm an award made pursuant to such an agreement to arbitrate, if

(A) the arbitration takes place or is intended to take place in the United States,

(B) the agreement or award is or may be governed by a treaty or other international agreement in force for the United States calling for the recognition and enforcement of arbitral awards,

(C) the underlying claim, save for the agreement to arbitrate, could have been brought in a United States court under this section or section 1607, or

(D) paragraph (1) of this subsection is otherwise applicable.

(b) A foreign state shall not be immune from the jurisdiction of the courts of the United States in any case in which a suit in admiralty is brought to enforce a maritime lien against a vessel or cargo of the foreign state, which maritime lien is based upon a commercial activity of the foreign state: *Provided,* That—

(1) notice of the suit is given by delivery of a copy of the summons and of the complaint to the person, or his agent, having possession of the vessel or cargo against which the maritime lien is asserted; and if the vessel or cargo is arrested pursuant to process obtained on behalf of the party bringing the suit, the service of process of arrest shall be deemed to constitute valid delivery of such notice, but the party bringing the suit shall be liable for any damages sustained by the foreign state as a result of the arrest if the party bringing the suit had actual or constructive knowledge that the vessel or cargo of a foreign state was involved; and

(2) notice to the foreign state of the commencement of suit as provided in section 1608 of this title is initiated within ten days either of the delivery of notice as provided in paragraph (1) of this subsection or, in the case of a party who was unaware that the vessel or cargo of a foreign state was involved, of the date such party determined the existence of the foreign state's interest.

(c) Whenever notice is delivered under subsection (b)(1), the suit to enforce a maritime lien shall thereafter proceed and shall be heard and determined according to the principles of law and rules of practice of suits in rem whenever it appears that, had the vessel been privately owned and possessed, a suit in rem might have been maintained. A decree against the foreign state may include costs of the suit and, if the decree is for a money judgment, interest as ordered by the court, except that the court may not award judgment against the foreign state in an amount greater than the value of the vessel or cargo upon which the maritime lien arose. Such value shall be determined as of the time notice is served under subsection (b)(1). Decrees shall be subject to appeal and revision as provided in other cases of admiralty and maritime jurisdiction. Nothing shall preclude the plaintiff in any proper case from seeking relief in personam in the same action brought to enforce a maritime lien as provided in this section.

(d) A foreign state shall not be immune from the jurisdiction of the courts of the United States in any action brought to foreclose a preferred mortgage, as defined in section 31301 of title 46. Such action shall be brought, heard, and determined in accordance with the provisions of chapter 313 of title 46 and in accordance with the principles of law and rules of practice of suits in rem, whenever it appears that had the vessel been privately owned and possessed a suit in rem might have been maintained.

[(e), (f) Repealed. * * *]

(g) Limitation on discovery.

(1) In general.

(A) Subject to paragraph (2), if an action is filed that would otherwise be barred by section 1604, but for section 1605A, the court, upon request of the Attorney General, shall stay any request, demand, or order for discovery on the United States that the Attorney General certifies would significantly interfere with a criminal investigation or prosecution, or a national security operation, related to the incident that gave rise to the cause of action, until such time as the Attorney General advises the court that such request, demand, or order will no longer so interfere.

(B) A stay under this paragraph shall be in effect during the 12-month period beginning on the date on which the court issues the order to stay discovery. The court shall renew the order to stay discovery for additional 12-month periods upon motion by the United States if the Attorney General certifies that discovery would significantly interfere with a criminal investigation or prosecution, or a national security operation, related to the incident that gave rise to the cause of action.

(2) Sunset.—(A) Subject to subparagraph (B), no stay shall be granted or continued in effect under paragraph (1) after the date that is 10 years after the date on which the incident that gave rise to the cause of action occurred.

(B) After the period referred to in subparagraph (A), the court, upon request of the Attorney General, may stay any request, demand, or order for discovery on the United States that the court finds a substantial likelihood would—

(i) create a serious threat of death or serious bodily injury to any person;

(ii) adversely affect the ability of the United States to work in cooperation with foreign and international law enforcement agencies in investigating violations of United States law; or

(iii) obstruct the criminal case related to the incident that gave rise to the cause of action or undermine the potential for a conviction in such case.

(3) Evaluation of evidence. The court's evaluation of any request for a stay under this subsection filed by the Attorney General shall be conducted ex parte and in camera.

(4) Bar on motions to dismiss. A stay of discovery under this subsection shall constitute a bar to the granting of a motion to dismiss under rules 12(b)(6) and 56 of the Federal Rules of Civil Procedure.

(5) Construction. Nothing in this subsection shall prevent the United States from seeking protective orders or asserting privileges ordinarily available to the United States.

(h) * * *

§ 1605A.   TERRORISM EXCEPTION TO THE JURISDICTIONAL IMMUNITY OF A FOREIGN STATE

(a)   In general.

(1)   No immunity. A foreign state shall not be immune from the jurisdiction of courts of the United States or of the States in any case not otherwise covered by this chapter in which money damages are sought against a foreign state for personal injury or death that was caused by an act of torture, extrajudicial killing, aircraft sabotage, hostage taking, or the provision of material support or resources for such an act if such act or provision of material support or resources is engaged in by an official, employee, or agent of such foreign state while acting within the scope of his or her office, employment, or agency.

(2)   Claim heard. The court shall hear a claim under this section if—

(A)(i)(I) the foreign state was designated as a state sponsor of terrorism at the time the act described in paragraph (1) occurred, or was so designated as a result of such act, and, subject to subclause (II), either remains so designated when the claim is filed under this section or was so designated within the 6-month period before the claim is filed under this section; or

(II)   in the case of an action that is refiled under this section by reason of section 1083(c)(2)(A) of the National Defense Authorization Act for Fiscal Year 2008 [note to this section] or is filed under this section by reason of section 1083(c)(3) of that Act [note to this section], the foreign state was designated as a state sponsor of terrorism when the original action or the related action under section 1605(a)(7) (as in effect before the enactment of this section [enacted Jan. 28, 2008]) or section 589 of the Foreign Operations, Export Financing, and Related Programs Appropriations Act, 1997 (as contained in section 101(c) of division A of Public Law 104–208) was filed;

(ii)   the claimant or the victim was, at the time the act described in paragraph (1) occurred—

(I)   a national of the United States;

(II)   a member of the armed forces; or

(III) otherwise an employee of the Government of the United States, or of an individual performing a contract awarded by the United States Government, acting within the scope of the employee's employment; and

(iii) in a case in which the act occurred in the foreign state against which the claim has been brought, the claimant has afforded the foreign state a reasonable opportunity to arbitrate the claim in accordance with the accepted international rules of arbitration; or

(B) the act described in paragraph (1) is related to Case Number 1:00CV03110 (EGS) in the United States District Court for the District of Columbia.

(b) Limitations. An action may be brought or maintained under this section if the action is commenced, or a related action was commenced under section 1605(a)(7) (before the date of the enactment of this section) or section 589 of the Foreign Operations, Export Financing, and Related Programs Appropriations Act, 1997 (as contained in section 101(c) of division A of Public Law 104–208) not later than the latter of—

(1) 10 years after April 24, 1996; or

(2) 10 years after the date on which the cause of action arose.

(c) Private right of action. A foreign state that is or was a state sponsor of terrorism as described in subsection (a)(2)(A)(i), and any official, employee, or agent of that foreign state while acting within the scope of his or her office, employment, or agency, shall be liable to—

(1) a national of the United States,

(2) a member of the armed forces,

(3) an employee of the Government of the United States, or of an individual performing a contract awarded by the United States Government, acting within the scope of the employee's employment, or

(4) the legal representative of a person described in paragraph (1), (2), or (3),

for personal injury or death caused by acts described in subsection (a)(1) of that foreign state, or of an official, employee, or agent of that foreign state, for which the courts of the United States may maintain jurisdiction under this section for money damages. In any such action, damages may include economic damages, solatium, pain and suffering, and punitive damages. In any such action, a foreign state shall be vicariously liable for the acts of its officials, employees, or agents.

(d) Additional damages. After an action has been brought under subsection (c), actions may also be brought for reasonably foreseeable property loss, whether insured or uninsured, third party liability, and loss claims under life and property insurance policies, by reason of the same acts on which the action under subsection (c) is based.

(e) Special masters.

(1) In general. The courts of the United States may appoint special masters to hear damage claims brought under this section.

(2) Transfer of funds. The Attorney General shall transfer, from funds available for the program under section 1404C of the Victims of Crime Act of 1984 (42 U.S.C. 10603c), to the Administrator of the United States district court in which any case is pending which has been brought or maintained under this section such funds as may be required to cover the costs of special masters appointed under paragraph (1). Any amount paid in compensation to any such special master shall constitute an item of court costs.

(f) Appeal. In an action brought under this section, appeals from orders not conclusively ending the litigation may only be taken pursuant to section 1292(b) of this title.

(g) Property disposition.

(1) In general. In every action filed in a United States district court in which jurisdiction is alleged under this section, the filing of a notice of pending action pursuant to this section, to which is attached a copy of the complaint filed in the action, shall have the effect of establishing a lien of lis pendens upon any real property or tangible personal property that is—

(A) subject to attachment in aid of execution, or execution, under section 1610;

(B) located within that judicial district; and

(C) titled in the name of any defendant, or titled in the name of any entity controlled by any defendant if such notice contains a statement listing such controlled entity.

(2) Notice. A notice of pending action pursuant to this section shall be filed by the clerk of the district court in the same manner as any pending action and shall be indexed by listing as defendants all named defendants and all entities listed as controlled by any defendant.

(3) Enforceability. Liens established by reason of this subsection shall be enforceable as provided in chapter 111 of this title.

(h) Definitions. For purposes of this section—

(1) the term "aircraft sabotage" has the meaning given that term in Article 1 of the Convention for the Suppression of Unlawful Acts Against the Safety of Civil Aviation;

(2) the term "hostage taking" has the meaning given that term in Article 1 of the International Convention Against the Taking of Hostages;

(3) the term "material support or resources" has the meaning given that term in section 2339A of title 18;

(4) the term "armed forces" has the meaning given that term in section 101 of title 10;

(5)　the term "national of the United States" has the meaning given that term in section 101(a)(22) of the Immigration and Nationality Act (8 U.S.C. 1101(a)(22));

(6)　the term "state sponsor of terrorism" means a country the government of which the Secretary of State has determined, for purposes of section 6(j) of the Export Administration Act of 1979 (50 U.S.C. App. 2405(j)), section 620A of the Foreign Assistance Act of 1961 (22 U.S.C. 2371), section 40 of the Arms Export Control Act (22 U.S.C. 2780), or any other provision of law, is a government that has repeatedly provided support for acts of international terrorism; and

(7)　the terms "torture" and "extrajudicial killing" have the meaning given those terms in section 3 of the Torture Victim Protection Act of 1991 (28 U.S.C. 1350 note).

§ 1606. EXTENT OF LIABILITY

As to any claim for relief with respect to which a foreign state is not entitled to immunity under section 1605 or 1607 of this chapter, the foreign state shall be liable in the same manner and to the same extent as a private individual under like circumstances; but a foreign state except for an agency or instrumentality thereof shall not be liable for punitive damages; if, however, in any case where death was caused, the law of the place where the act or omission occurred provides, or has been construed to provide, for damages only punitive in nature, the foreign state shall be liable for actual or compensatory damages measured by the pecuniary injuries resulting from such death which were incurred by the persons for whose benefit the action was brought.

§ 1607. COUNTERCLAIMS

In any action brought by a foreign state, or in which a foreign state intervenes, in a court of the United States or of a State, the foreign state shall not be accorded immunity with respect to any counterclaim—

(a)　for which the foreign state would not be entitled to immunity under section 1605 or 1605A of this chapter had such claim been brought in a separate action against the foreign state; or

(b)　arising out of the transaction or occurrence that is the subject matter of the claim of the foreign state; or

(c)　to the extent that the counterclaim does not seek relief exceeding in amount or differing in kind from that sought by the foreign state.

§ 1608. SERVICE; TIME TO ANSWER; DEFAULT

(a)　Service in the courts of the United States and of the States shall be made upon a foreign state or political subdivision of a foreign state:

(1)　by delivery of a copy of the summons and complaint in accordance with any special arrangement for service between the plaintiff and the foreign state or political subdivision; or

(2) if no special arrangement exists, by delivery of a copy of the summons and complaint in accordance with an applicable international convention on service of judicial documents; or

(3) if service cannot be made under paragraphs (1) or (2), by sending a copy of the summons and complaint and a notice of suit, together with a translation of each into the official language of the foreign state, by any form of mail requiring a signed receipt, to be addressed or dispatched by the clerk of the court to the head of the ministry of foreign affairs of the foreign state concerned, or

(4) if service cannot be made within 30 days under paragraph (3), by sending two copies of the summons and complaint and a notice of suit, together with a translation of each into the official language of the foreign state, by any form of mail requiring a signed receipt, to be addressed and dispatched by the clerk of the court to the Secretary of State in Washington, District of Columbia, to the attention of the Director of Special Consular Services—and the Secretary shall transmit one copy of the papers through diplomatic channels to the foreign state and shall send to the clerk of the court a certified copy of the diplomatic note indicating when the papers were transmitted.

As used in this subsection, a "notice of suit" shall mean a notice addressed to a foreign state and in a form prescribed by the Secretary of State by regulation.

(b) Service in the courts of the United States and of the States shall be made upon an agency or instrumentality of a foreign state:

(1) by delivery of a copy of the summons and complaint in accordance with any special arrangement for service between the plaintiff and the agency or instrumentality; or

(2) if no special arrangement exists, by delivery of a copy of the summons and complaint either to an officer, a managing or general agent, or to any other agent authorized by appointment or by law to receive service of process in the United States; or in accordance with an applicable international convention on service of judicial documents; or

(3) if service cannot be made under paragraphs (1) or (2), and if reasonably calculated to give actual notice, by delivery of a copy of the summons and complaint, together with a translation of each into the official language of the foreign state—

(A) as directed by an authority of the foreign state or political subdivision in response to a letter rogatory or request or

(B) by any form of mail requiring a signed receipt, to be addressed and dispatched by the clerk of the court to the agency or instrumentality to be served, or

(C) as directed by order of the court consistent with the law of the place where the service is to be made.

(c) Service shall be deemed to have been made—

(1) in the case of service under subsection (a)(4), as of the date of transmittal indicated in a certified copy of the diplomatic note; and

(2) in any other case under this section, as of the date of receipt indicated in the certification, signed and returned postal receipt, or other proof of service applicable to the method of service employed.

(d) In any action brought in a court of the United States or of a State, a foreign state, a political subdivision thereof, or an agency or instrumentality of a foreign state shall serve an answer or other responsive pleading to the complaint within sixty days after service has been made under this section.

(e) No judgment by default shall be entered by a court of the United States or of a State against a foreign state, a political subdivision thereof, or an agency or instrumentality of a foreign state, unless the claimant establishes his claim or right to relief by evidence satisfactory to the court. A copy of any such default judgment shall be sent to the foreign state or political subdivision in the manner prescribed for service in this section.

§ 1609. IMMUNITY FROM ATTACHMENT AND EXECUTION AND EXECUTION OF PROPERTY OF A FOREIGN STATE

Subject to existing international agreements to which the United States is a party at the time of enactment of this Act the property in the United States of a foreign state shall be immune from attachment arrest and execution except as provided in sections 1610 and 1611 of this chapter.

§ 1610. EXCEPTIONS TO THE IMMUNITY FROM ATTACHMENT OR EXECUTION

(a) The property in the United States of a foreign state, as defined in section 1603(a) of this chapter, used for a commercial activity in the United States, shall not be immune from attachment in aid of execution, or from execution, upon a judgment entered by a court of the United States or of a State after the effective date of this Act, if—

(1) the foreign state has waived its immunity from attachment in aid of execution or from execution either explicitly or by implication, notwithstanding any withdrawal of the waiver the foreign state may purport to effect except in accordance with the terms of the waiver, or

(2) the property is or was used for the commercial activity upon which the claim is based, or

(3) the execution relates to a judgment establishing rights in property which has been taken in violation of international law or which has been exchanged for property taken in violation of international law, or

(4) the execution relates to a judgment establishing rights in property—

    (A) which is acquired by succession or gift, or

    (B) which is immovable and situated in the United States: *Provided:* That such property is not used for purposes of maintaining a diplomatic or consular mission or the residence of the Chief of such mission, or

(5) the property consists of any contractual obligation or any proceeds from such a contractual obligation to indemnify or hold harmless the foreign state or its employees under a policy of automobile or other liability or casualty insurance covering the claim which merged into the judgment, or

(6) the judgment is based on an order confirming an arbitral award rendered against the foreign state, provided that attachment in aid of execution, or execution, would not be inconsistent with any provision in the arbitral agreement, or

(7) the judgment relates to a claim for which the foreign state is not immune under section 1605A, or section 1605(a)(7) (as such section was in effect on January 27, 2008) regardless of whether the property is or was involved with the act upon which the claim is based.

(b) In addition to subsection (a), any property in the United States of an agency or instrumentality of a foreign state engaged in commercial activity in the United States shall not be immune from attachment in aid of execution, or from execution, upon a judgment entered by a court of the United States or of a State after the effective date of this Act, if—

(1) the agency or instrumentality has waived its immunity from attachment in aid of execution or from execution either explicitly or implicitly, notwithstanding any withdrawal of the waiver the agency or instrumentality may purport to effect except in accordance with the terms of the waiver, or

(2) the judgment relates to a claim for which the agency or instrumentality is not immune by virtue of section 1605(a)(2), (3), or (5), or 1605(b), or 1605A of this chapter, regardless of whether the property is or was involved in the act upon which the claim is based, or

(3) the judgment relates to a claim for which the agency or instrumentality is not limited by virtue of section 1605A of this chapter or section 1605(a)(7) of this chapter (as such section was in

effect on January 27, 2008), regardless of whether the property is or was involved in the act upon which the claim is based.

(c) No attachment or execution referred to in subsections (a) and (b) of this section shall be permitted until the court has ordered such attachment and execution after having determined that a reasonable period of time has elapsed following the entry of judgment and the giving of any notice required under section 1608(e) of this chapter.

(d) The property of a foreign state, as defined in section 1603(a) of this chapter, used for a commercial activity in the United States, shall not be immune from attachment prior to the entry of judgment in any action brought in a court of the United States or of a State, or prior to the elapse of the period of time provided in subsection (c) of this section, if—

    (1) the foreign state has explicitly waived its immunity from attachment prior to judgment, notwithstanding any withdrawal of the waiver the foreign state may purport to effect except in accordance with the terms of the waiver, and

    (2) the purpose of the attachment is to secure satisfaction of a judgment that has been or may ultimately be entered against the foreign state, and not to obtain jurisdiction.

(e) The vessels of a foreign state shall not be immune from arrest in rem, interlocutory sale, and execution in actions brought to foreclose a preferred mortgage as provided in section 1605(d).

(f)(1)(A) Notwithstanding any other provision of law, including but not limited to section 208(f) of the Foreign Missions Act (22 U.S.C. 4308(f)), and except as provided in subparagraph (B), any property with respect to which financial transactions are prohibited or regulated pursuant to section 5(b) of the Trading with the Enemy Act (50 U.S.C. App. 5(b)), section 620(a) of the Foreign Assistance Act of 1961 (22 U.S.C. § 2370(a)), sections 202 and 203 of the International Emergency Economic Powers Act (50 U.S.C. 1701–1702) or any other proclamation, order, regulation, or license issued pursuant thereto, shall be subject to execution or attachment relating to a claim for which a foreign state (including any agency or instrumentality or such state) is not immune under section 1605(a)(7) (as in effect before the enactment of section 1605A) or section 1605A.

    (B) Subparagraph (A) shall not apply if, at the time the property is expropriated or seized by the foreign state, the property has been held in title by a natural person, or if held in trust, has been held for the benefit of a natural person or persons.

    (2)(A) At the request of any party in whose favor a judgment has been issued with respect to a claim for which the foreign state is not immune under section 1606(a)(7) (as in effect before the enactment of section 1605A) or section 1605A, the Secretary of the Treasury and the Secretary of State should make every effort to fully, promptly, and effectively assist any judgment creditor or any court that has issued any such judgment in identifying, locating, and executing against the property of that foreign state or any agency or instrumentality of such state.

(B) In providing such assistance, the Secretaries—

(i) may provide such information to the court under seal; and

(ii) should make every effort to provide the information in a manner sufficient to allow the court to direct the United States Marshal's office to promptly execute against that property.

(3) Waiver.—The President may waive any provision of paragraph (1) in the interest of national security.

(g) Property in certain actions.—

(1) In general.—Subject to paragraph (3), the property of a foreign state against which a judgment is entered under section 1605A, and the property of an agency or instrumentality of such a state, including property that is a separate juridical entity or is an interest held directly or indirectly in a separate juridical entity, is subject to attachment in aid of execution, and execution, upon that judgment as provided in this section, regardless of—

(A) the level of economic control over the property by the government of the foreign state;

(B) whether the profits of the property go to that government;

(C) the degree to which officials of that government manage the property or otherwise control its daily affairs;

(D) whether that government is the sole beneficiary in interest of the property; or

(E) whether establishing the property as a separate entity would entitle the foreign state to benefits in United States courts while avoiding its obligations.

(2) United States sovereign immunity inapplicable.—Any property of a foreign state, or agency or instrumentality of a foreign state, to which paragraph (1) applies shall not be immune from attachment in aid of execution, or execution, upon a judgment entered under section 1605A because the property is regulated by the United States Government by reason of action taken against that foreign state under the Trading With the Enemy Act or the International Emergency Economic Powers Act.

(3) Third-party joint property holders.—Nothing in this subsection shall be construed to supersede the authority of a court to prevent appropriately the impairment of an interest held by a

person who is not liable in the action giving rise to a judgment in property subject to attachment in aid of execution, or execution, upon such judgment.

§ 1611. CERTAIN TYPES OF PROPERTY IMMUNE FROM EXECUTION

(a) Notwithstanding the provisions of section 1610 of this chapter, the property of those organizations designated by the President as being entitled to enjoy the privileges, exemptions, and immunities provided by the International Organizations Immunities Act shall not be subject to attachment or any other judicial process impeding the disbursement of funds to, or on the order of, a foreign state as a result of an action brought in the courts of the United States or of the States.

(b) Notwithstanding the provisions of section 1610 of this chapter, the property of a foreign state shall be immune from attachment and from execution, if—

(1) the property is that of a foreign central bank or monetary authority held for its own account, unless such bank or authority, or its parent foreign government, has explicitly waived its immunity from attachment in aid of execution, or from execution, not withstanding any withdrawal of the waiver which the bank, authority or government may purport to effect except in accordance with the terms of the waiver; or

(2) the property is, or is intended to be, used in connection with a military activity and

(A) is of a military character, or

(B) is under the control of a military authority or defense agency.

(c) Notwithstanding the provisions of section 1610 of this chapter, the property of a foreign state shall be immune from attachment and from execution in an action brought under section 302 of the Cuban Liberty and Solidarity (LIBERTAD) Act of 1996 [22 U.S.C. § 6082] to the extent that the property is a facility or installation used by an accredited diplomatic mission for official purposes.

CHAPTER 99. GENERAL PROVISIONS

§ 1631. TRANSFER TO CURE WANT OF JURISDICTION

Whenever a civil action is filed in a court as defined in section 610 of this title or an appeal, including a petition for review of administrative action, is noticed for or filed with such a court and that court finds that there is a want of jurisdiction, the court shall, if it is in the interest of justice, transfer such action or appeal to any other such court (or, for cases within the jurisdiction of the United States Tax Court, to that court) in which the action or appeal could have been brought at the time it was filed or noticed, and the action or appeal shall proceed as if it had been filed in or noticed for the court to which it is transferred on the date upon which it was actually filed in or noticed for the court from which it is transferred.

PART V.   PROCEDURE

CHAPTER 111.   GENERAL PROVISIONS

§ 1658. TIME LIMITATION ON THE COMMENCEMENT OF CIVIL ACTIONS ARISING UNDER ACTS OF CONGRESS

(a) Except as otherwise provided by law, a civil action arising under an Act of Congress enacted after the date of the enactment of this section may not be commenced later than 4 years after the cause of action accrues.

(b)   * * *

CHAPTER 121.   JURIES; TRIAL BY JURY

§ 1873. ADMIRALTY AND MARITIME CASES

In any case of admiralty and maritime jurisdiction relating to any matter of contract or tort arising upon or concerning any vessel of twenty tons or upward, enrolled and licensed for the coasting trade, and employed in the business of commerce and navigation between places in different states upon the lakes and navigable waters connecting said lakes, the trial of all issues of fact shall be by jury if either party demands it.

TITLE 33
NAVIGABLE WATERS

CHAPTER 7. REGULATIONS FOR THE SUPPRESSION OF PIRACY

§ 381.   USE OF PUBLIC VESSELS TO SUPPRESS PIRACY

The President is authorized to employ so many of the public armed vessels as in his judgment the service may require, with suitable instructions to the commanders thereof, in protecting the merchant vessels of the United States and their crews from piratical aggressions and depredations.

§ 382.   SEIZURE OF PIRATICAL VESSELS GENERALLY

The President is authorized to instruct the commanders of the public armed vessels of the United States to subdue, seize, take, and send into any port of the United States, any armed vessel or boat, or any vessel or boat, the crew whereof shall be armed, and which shall have attempted or committed any piratical aggression, search, restraint, depredation, or seizure, upon any vessel of the United States, or of the citizens thereof, or upon any other vessel; and also to retake any vessel of the United States, or its citizens, which may have been unlawfully captured upon the high seas.

§ 383.   RESISTANCE OF PIRATES BY MERCHANT VESSELS

The commander and crew of any merchant vessel of the United States, owned wholly, or in part, by a citizen thereof, may oppose and defend against any aggression, search, restraint, depredation, or seizure, which shall be attempted upon such vessel, or upon any other vessel so owned, by the commander or crew of any armed vessel whatsoever, not being a public armed vessel of some nation in amity with the United States, and may subdue and capture the same; and may also retake any vessel so owned which may have been captured by the commander or crew of any such armed vessel, and send the same into any port of the United States.

§ 384.   CONDEMNATION OF PIRATICAL VESSELS

Whenever any vessel, which shall have been built, purchased, fitted out in whole or in part, or held for the purpose of being employed in the commission of any piratical aggression, search, restraint, depredation, or seizure, or in the commission of any other act of piracy as defined by the law of nations, or from which any piratical aggression, search, restraint, depredation, or seizure shall have been first attempted or made, is captured and brought into or captured in any port of the United States, the same shall be adjudged and condemned to their use, and that of the captors after due process and trial in any court having admiralty jurisdiction, and which shall be holden for the district into which such captured vessel shall be brought; and the same court shall thereupon order a sale and distribution thereof accordingly, and at its discretion.

§ 385.   SEIZURE AND CONDEMNATION OF VESSELS FITTED OUT FOR PIRACY

Any vessel built, purchased, fitted out in whole or in part, or held for the purpose of being employed in the commission of any piratical aggression, search, restraint, depredation, or seizure, or in the commission of any other act of piracy, as defined by the law of nations, shall be liable to be captured and brought into any port of the United States if found upon the high seas, or to be seized if found in any port or place within the United States, whether the same shall have actually sailed upon any piratical expedition or not, and whether any act of piracy shall have been committed or attempted upon or from such vessel or not; and any such vessel may be adjudged and condemned, if captured by a vessel authorized as mentioned in section 386 of this title to the use of the United States, and to that of the captors, and if seized by a collector, surveyor, or marshal, then to the use of the United States.

§ 386.   COMMISSIONING PRIVATE VESSELS FOR SEIZURE OF PIRATICAL VESSELS

The President is authorized to instruct the commanders of the public-armed vessels of the United States, and to authorize the commanders of any other armed vessels sailing under the authority of any letters of marque and reprisal granted by Congress, or the commanders of any other suitable vessels, to subdue, seize, take, and, if on the high seas, to send into any port of the United States, any vessel or boat built, purchased, fitted out, or held as mentioned in section 385 of this title.

§ 387. DUTIES OF OFFICERS OF CUSTOMS AND MARSHALS AS TO SEIZURE

The collectors of the several ports of entry, the surveyors of the several ports of delivery, and the marshals of the several judicial districts within the United States, shall seize any vessel or boat built, purchased, fitted out, or held as mentioned in section 385 of this title, which may be found within their respective ports or districts, and to cause the same to be proceeded against and disposed of as provided by that section.

CHAPTER 8. SUMMARY TRIALS FOR CERTAIN OFFENSES AGAINST NAVIGATION LAWS

§ 391. SUMMARY TRIALS AUTHORIZED

Whenever a complaint shall be made against any master, officer, or seaman of any vessel belonging, in whole or in part, to any citizen of the United States, of the commission of any offense, not capital or otherwise infamous, against any law of the United States made for the protection of persons or property engaged in commerce or navigation, it shall be the duty of the United States attorney to investigate the same, and the general nature thereof, and if, in his opinion, the case is such as should be summarily tried, he shall report the same to the district judge, and the judge shall forthwith, or as soon as the ordinary business of the court will permit, proceed to try the cause, and for that purpose may, if necessary, hold a special session of the court, either in term time or vacation.

§ 392. COMPLAINT AND ANSWER; JURY TRIAL

At the summary trial of offenses against the laws for the protection of persons or property engaged in commerce or navigation, it shall not be necessary that the accused shall have been previously indicted, but a statement of complaint, verified by oath in writing, shall be presented to the court, setting out the offense in such manner as clearly to apprise the accused of the character of the offense complained of, and to enable him to answer the complaint. The complaint or statement shall be read to the accused, who may plead to or answer the same, or make a counterstatement. The trial shall thereupon be proceeded with in a summary manner, and the case shall be decided by the court, unless, at the time for pleading or answering, the accused shall demand a jury, in which case the trial shall be upon the complaint and plea of not guilty.

§ 393. AMENDMENTS OF COMPLAINT AND ADJOURNMENTS

It shall be lawful for the court to allow the United States attorney to amend his statement of complaint at any stage of the proceedings, before verdict, if, in the opinion of the court, such amendment will work no injustice to the accused; and if it appears to the court that the accused is unprepared to meet the charge as amended, and that an adjournment of the cause will promote the ends of justice, such adjournment shall be made, until a further day, to be fixed by the court.

§ 394.   CHALLENGE TO JURORS

At the trial in summary cases, if by jury, the United States and the accused shall each be entitled to three peremptory challenges. Challenges for cause, in such cases, shall be tried by the court without the aid of triers.

§ 395.   LIMIT OF SENTENCE

It shall not be lawful for the court to sentence any person convicted in such trial to any greater punishment than imprisonment in jail for one year, or to a fine exceeding $500, or both, in its discretion, in those cases where the laws of the United States authorize such imprisonment and fine.

§ 396.   RECOVERY OF PENALTIES AND FORFEITURES GENERALLY

All the penalties and forfeitures which may be incurred for offenses against title 48 of the Revised Statutes may be sued for, prosecuted, and recovered in such court, and be disposed of in such manner, as any penalties and forfeitures which may be incurred for offenses against the laws relating to the collection of duties, except when otherwise expressly prescribed.

CHAPTER 9.   PROTECTION OF NAVIGABLE WATER AND HARBORS AND RIVER IMPROVEMENTS GENERALLY

§ 409.   OBSTRUCTION OF NAVIGABLE WATERS BY VESSELS; FLOATING TIMBER; MARKING AND REMOVAL OF SUNKEN VESSELS

It shall not be lawful to tie up or anchor vessels or other craft in navigable channels in such a manner as to prevent or obstruct the passage of other vessels or craft; or to sink, or permit or cause to be sunk, vessels or other craft in navigable channels; or to float loose timber and logs, or to float what is known as "sack rafts of timber and logs" in streams or channels actually navigated by steamboats in such manner as to obstruct, impede, or endanger navigation. And whenever a vessel, raft, or other craft is wrecked and sunk in a navigable channel, it shall be the duty of the owner, lessee, or operator of such sunken craft to immediately mark it with a buoy or beacon during the day and, unless otherwise granted a waiver by the Commandant of the Coast Guard, a light at night, and to maintain such marks until the sunken craft is removed or abandoned, and the neglect or failure of the said owner, lessee, or operator so to do shall be unlawful; and it shall be the duty of the owner, lessee, or operator of such sunken craft to commence the immediate removal of the same, and prosecute such removal diligently, and failure to do so shall be considered as an abandonment of such craft, and subject the same to removal by the United States as provided for in sections 411 to 416, 418, and 502 of this title. The Commandant of the Coast Guard may waive the requirement to mask a wrecked vessel, raft, or other craft with a light at night if the Commandant determines that placing a light would be impractical and granting such a waiver would not create an undue hazard to navigation.

§ 414. REMOVAL BY SECRETARY OF ARMY OF SUNKEN WATER CRAFT GENERALLY; LIABILITY OF OWNER, LESSEE, OR OPERATOR

(a) Whenever the navigation of any river, lake, harbor, sound, bay, canal, or other navigable waters of the United States shall be obstructed or endangered by any sunken vessel, boat, water craft, raft, or other similar obstruction, and such obstruction has existed for a longer period than thirty days, or whenever the abandonment of such obstruction can be legally established in a less space of time, the sunken vessel, boat, water craft, raft, or other obstruction shall be subject to be broken up, removed, sold, or otherwise disposed of by the Secretary of the Army at his discretion, without liability for any damage to the owners of the same: *Provided,* That in his discretion, the Secretary of the Army may cause reasonable notice of such obstruction of not less than thirty days, unless the legal abandonment of the obstruction can be established in a less time, to be given by publication, addressed "To whom it may concern," in a newspaper published nearest to the locality of the obstruction, requiring the removal thereof: *And Provided also,* That the Secretary of the Army may, in his discretion, at or after the time of giving such notice, cause sealed proposals to be solicited by public advertisement, giving reasonable notice of not less than ten days, for the removal of such obstruction as soon as possible after the expiration of the above specified thirty days' notice, in case it has not in the meantime been so removed, these proposals and contracts, at his discretion, to be conditioned that such vessel, boat, water craft, raft, or other obstruction, and all cargo and property contained therein, shall become the property of the contractor, and the contract shall be awarded to the bidder making the proposition most advantageous to the United States: *Provided,* That such bidder shall give satisfactory security to execute the work: *Provided further,* That any money received from the sale of any such wreck, or from any contractor for the removal of wrecks, under this paragraph shall be covered into the Treasury of the United States.

(b) The owner, lessee, or operator of such vessel, boat, water craft, raft, or other obstruction as described in this section shall be liable to the United States for the cost of removal or destruction and disposal as described which exceeds the costs recovered under subsection (a) of this section. Any amount recovered from the owner, lessee, or operator of such vessel pursuant to this subsection to recover costs in excess of the proceeds from the sale or disposition of such of the Treasury of the United States.

§ 415. SUMMARY REMOVAL OF WATER CRAFT OBSTRUCTING NAVIGATION

(a) Removal authority

Under emergency, in the case of any vessel, boat, water craft, or raft, or other similar obstruction, sinking or grounding, or being unnecessarily delayed in any Government canal or lock, or in any navigable waters mentioned in section 414 of this title, in such manner as to stop, seriously interfere with, or specially endanger navigation, in the opinion of the Secretary of the Army, or any agent of the United States to whom the Secretary may delegate proper authority, the Secretary of the Army or any such agent shall have the right to take immediate possession of such boat, vessel, or other water craft, or raft, so far as to remove or to destroy it and to clear immediately the canal, lock, or navigable waters aforesaid of the obstruction thereby caused, using his best judgment to prevent any unnecessary injury; and no one shall interfere with or prevent such removal or destruction: *Provided,* That the officer or agent charged with the removal or destruction of an obstruction under this section may in his discretion give notice in writing to the owners of any such obstruction requiring them to remove it: *And provided further,* That the actual expense, including administrative expenses, of removing any such obstruction as aforesaid shall be a charge against such craft and cargo; and if the owners thereof fail or refuse to reimburse the United States for such expenses within thirty days after notification, then the officer or agent aforesaid may sell the craft or cargo, or any part thereof that may not have been destroyed in removal, and the proceeds of such sale shall be covered into the treasury of the United States.

(b) Removal Requirement

Not later than 24 hours after the Secretary of the Department in which the Coast Guard is operating issues an order to stop or delay navigation in any navigable waters of the United States because of conditions related to the sinking or grounding of a vessel, the owner or operator of the vessel, with the approval of the Secretary of the Army, shall begin the removal of the vessel using the most expeditious removal method available or, if appropriate, secure the vessel pending removal to allow navigation to resume. If the owner or operator fails to begin removal or to secure the vessel pending removal on an expedited basis, the Secretary of the Army shall remove or destroy the vessel using the summary removal procedures under subsection (a) of this section.

(c) Liability of owner, lessee, or operator

The owner, lessee, or operator of such vessel, boat, water craft, raft, or other obstruction as described in this section shall be liable to the United States for the cost, including administrative cost, of removal or destruction and disposal as described which exceeds the costs recovered under subsection (a) of this section. Any amount recovered from the owner, lessee, or operator of such vessel pursuant to this subsection to recover costs in excess of the proceeds from the sale or disposition of such vessel shall be deposited in the general fund of the Treasury of the United States.

CHAPTER 18. LONGSHORE AND HARBOR WORKERS' COMPENSATION ACT

§ 902. DEFINITIONS

When used in this chapter—

(1) The term "person" means individual, partnership, corporation, or association.

(2) The term "injury" means accidental injury or death arising out of and in the course of employment, and such occupational disease or infection as arises naturally out of such employment or as naturally or unavoidably results from such accidental injury, and includes an injury caused by the willful act of a third person directed against an employee because of his employment.

(3) The term "employee" means any person engaged in maritime employment, including any longshoreman or other person engaged in longshoring operations, and any harbor-worker including a ship repairman, shipbuilder, and ship-breaker, but such term does not include—

(A) individuals employed exclusively to perform office clerical, secretarial, security, or data processing work;

(B) individuals employed by a club, camp, recreational operation, restaurant, museum, or retail outlet;

(C) individuals employed by a marina and who are not engaged in construction, replacement, or expansion of such marina (except for routine maintenance);

(D) individuals who (i) are employed by suppliers, transporters, or vendors, (ii) are temporarily doing business on the premises of an employer described in paragraph (4), and (iii) are not engaged in work normally performed by employees of that employer under this chapter;

(E) aquaculture workers;

(F) individuals employed to build any recreational vessel under sixty-five feet in length, or individuals employed to repair any recreational vessel, or to dismantle any part of a recreational vessel in connection with the repair of such vessel;

(G) a master or member of a crew of any vessel; or

(H) any person engaged by a master to load or unload or repair any small vessel under eighteen tons net;

if individuals described in clauses (A) through (F) are subject to coverage under a State workers' compensation law.

(4) The term "employer" means an employer any of whose employees are employed in maritime employment, in whole or in part, upon the navigable waters of the United States (including any adjoining pier, wharf, dry dock, terminal, building way, marine railway, or other adjoining area customarily used by an employer in loading, unloading, repairing, or building a vessel).

(5) The term "carrier" means any person or fund authorized under section 932 of this title to insure under this chapter and includes self-insurers.

(6) The term "Secretary" means the Secretary of Labor.

(7) The term "deputy commissioner" means the deputy commissioner having jurisdiction in respect of an injury or death.

(8) The term "State" includes a Territory and the District of Columbia.

(9) The term "United States" when used in a geographical sense means the several States and Territories and the District of Columbia, including the territorial waters thereof.

(10) "Disability" means incapacity because of injury to earn the wages which the employee was receiving at the time of injury in the same or any other employment; but such term shall mean permanent impairment, determined (to the extent covered thereby) under the guides to the evaluation of permanent impairment promulgated and modified from time to time by the American Medical Association, in the case of an individual whose claim is described in section 910(d)(2) of this title.

(11) "Death" as a basis for a right to compensation means only death resulting from an injury.

(12) "Compensation" means the money allowance payable to an employee or to his dependents as provided for in this chapter, and includes funeral benefits provided therein.

(13) The term "wages" means the money rate at which the service rendered by an employee is compensated by an employer under the contract of hiring in force at the time of the injury, including the reasonable value of any advantage which is received from the employer and included for purposes of any withholding of tax under subtitle C of title 26 (relating to employment taxes). The term wages does not include fringe benefits, including (but not limited to) employer payments for or contributions to a retirement, pension, health and welfare, life insurance, training, social security or other employee or dependent benefit plan for the employee's or dependent's benefit, or any other employee's dependent entitlement.

(14) "Child" shall include a posthumous child, a child legally adopted prior to the injury of the employee, a child in relation to whom the deceased employee stood in loco parentis for at least one year prior to the time of injury, and a stepchild or acknowledged illegitimate child

dependent upon the deceased, but does not include married children unless wholly dependent on him. "Grandchild" means a child as above defined of a child as above defined. "Brother" and "sister" includes stepbrothers and stepsisters, half brothers and half sisters, and brothers and sisters by adoption, but does not include married brothers nor married sisters unless wholly dependent on the employee. "Child", "grandchild", "brother", and "sister" include only a person who is under eighteen years of age, or who, though eighteen years of age or over, is (1) wholly dependent upon the employee and incapable of self-support by reason of mental or physical disability, or (2) a student as defined in paragraph (19) of this section.

(15) The term "parent" includes step-parents and parents by adoption, parents-in-law, and any person who for more than three years prior to the death of the deceased employee stood in the place of a parent to him, if dependent on the injured employee.

(16) The terms "widow or widower" includes only the decedent's wife or husband living with or dependent for support upon him or her at the time of his or her death; or living apart for justifiable cause or by reason of his or her desertion at such time.

(17) The terms "adoption" or "adopted" mean legal adoption prior to the time of the injury.

(18) The term "student" means a person regularly pursuing a full-time course of study or training at an institution which is—

    (A) a school or college or university operated or directly supported by the United States, or by any State or local government or political subdivision thereof,

    (B) a school or college or university which has been accredited by a State or by a State recognized or nationally recognized accrediting agency or body,

    (C) a school or college or university not so accredited but whose credits are accepted, on transfer, by not less than three institutions which are so accredited, for credit on the same basis as if transferred from an institution so accredited, or

    (D) an additional type of educational or training institution as defined by the Secretary,

but not after he reaches the age of twenty-three or has completed four years of education beyond the high school level, except that, where his twenty-third birthday occurs during a semester or other enrollment period, he shall continue to be considered a student until the end of such semester or other enrollment period. A child shall not be deemed to have ceased to be a student during any interim between school years if the interim does not exceed five months and if he shows to the satisfaction of the Secretary that he has a bona fide intention of continuing to pursue a full-time course of education or training during the semester or other enrollment period immediately following the interim or during periods of reasonable duration during which, in the judgment of the Secretary, he is prevented by factors beyond his control from pursuing his education. A child shall not be deemed to be a student under this chapter during a period of service in the Armed Forces of the United States.

(19) The term "national average weekly wage" means the national average weekly earnings of production or nonsupervisory workers on private nonagricultural payrolls.

(20) The term "Board" shall mean the Benefits Review Board.

(21) Unless the context requires otherwise, the term "vessel" means any vessel upon which or in connection with which any person entitled to benefits under this chapter suffers injury or death arising out of or in the course of his employment, and said vessel's owner, owner pro hac vice, agent, operator, charter or bare boat charterer, master, officer, or crew member.

(22) The singular includes the plural and the masculine includes the feminine and neuter.

§ 903. COVERAGE

(a) Disability or death; injuries occurring upon navigable waters of United States

Except as otherwise provided in this section, compensation shall be payable under this chapter in respect of disability or death of an employee, but only if the disability or death results from an injury occurring upon the navigable waters of the United States (including any adjoining pier, wharf, dry dock, terminal, building way, marine railway, or other adjoining area customarily used by an employer in loading, unloading, repairing, dismantling, or building a vessel).

(b) Governmental officers and employees

No compensation shall be payable in respect of the disability or death of an officer or employee of the United States, or any agency thereof, or of any State or foreign government, or any subdivision thereof.

(c) Intoxication; willful intention to kill

No compensation shall be payable if the injury was occasioned solely by the intoxication of the employee or by the willful intention of the employee to injure or kill himself or another.

(d) Small vessels

(1) No compensation shall be payable to an employee employed at a facility of an employer if, as certified by the Secretary, the facility is engaged in the business of building, repairing, or dismantling exclusively small vessels (as defined in paragraph (3) of this subsection), unless the injury occurs while upon the navigable waters of the United States or while upon any adjoining pier, wharf,

dock, facility over land for launching vessels, or facility over land for hauling, lifting, or drydocking vessels.

(2) Notwithstanding paragraph (1), compensation shall be payable to an employee—

(A) who is employed at a facility which is used in the business of building, repairing, or dismantling small vessels if such facility receives Federal maritime subsidies; or

(B) if the employee is not subject to coverage under a State workers' compensation law.

(3) For purposes of this subsection, a small vessel means—

(A) a commercial barge which is under 900 lightship displacement tons; or

(B) a commercial tugboat, towboat, crew boat, supply boat, fishing vessel, or other work vessel which is under 1,600 tons gross as measured under section 14502 of title 46, or an alternate tonnage measured under section 14302 of that title as prescribed by the Secretary under section 14104 of that title.

(e) Credit for benefits paid under other laws

Notwithstanding any other provision of law, any amounts paid to an employee for the same injury, disability, or death for which benefits are claimed under this chapter pursuant to any other workers' compensation law or section 30104 of title 46 shall be credited against any liability imposed by this chapter.

§ 904. LIABILITY FOR COMPENSATION

(a) Every employer shall be liable for and shall secure the payment to his employees of the compensation payable under sections 907, 908, and 909 of this title. In the case of an employer who is a subcontractor, only if such subcontractor fails to secure the payment of compensation shall the contractor be liable for and be required to secure the payment of compensation. A subcontractor shall not be deemed to have failed to secure the payment of compensation if the contractor has provided insurance for such compensation for the benefit of the subcontractor.

(b) Compensation shall be payable irrespective of fault as a cause for the injury.

§ 905. EXCLUSIVENESS OF LIABILITY

(a) Employer liability; failure of employer to secure payment of compensation

The liability of an employer prescribed in section 904 of this title shall be exclusive and in place of all other liability of such employer to the employee, his legal representative, husband or wife, parents, dependents, next of kin, and anyone otherwise entitled to recover damages from such employer at law or in admiralty on account of such injury or death, except that if an employer fails to secure payment of compensation as required by this chapter, an injured employee, or his legal representative in case death results from the injury, may elect to claim compensation under the chapter, or to maintain an action at law or in admiralty for damages on account of such injury or death. In such action the defendant may not plead as a defense that the injury was caused by the negligence of a fellow servant, or that the employee assumed the risk of his employment, or that the injury was due to the contributory negligence of the employee. For purposes of this subsection, a contractor shall be deemed the employer of a subcontractor's employees only if the subcontractor fails to secure the payment of compensation as required by section 904 of this title.

(b)   Negligence of vessel

In the event of injury to a person covered under this chapter caused by the negligence of a vessel, then such person, or anyone otherwise entitled to recover damages by reason thereof, may bring an action against such vessel as a third party in accordance with the provisions of section 933 of this title, and the employer shall not be liable to the vessel for such damages directly or indirectly and any agreements or warranties to the contrary shall be void. If such person was employed by the vessel to provide stevedoring services, no such action shall be permitted if the injury was caused by the negligence of persons engaged in providing stevedoring services to the vessel. If such person was employed to provide shipbuilding, repairing, or breaking services and such person's employer was the owner, owner pro hac vice, agent, operator, or charterer of the vessel, no such action shall be permitted, in whole or in part or directly or indirectly, against the injured person's employer (in any capacity, including as the vessel's owner, owner pro hac vice, agent, operator, or charterer) or against the employees of the employer. The liability of the vessel under this subsection shall not be based upon the warranty of seaworthiness or a breach thereof at the time the injury occurred. The remedy provided in this subsection shall be exclusive of all other remedies against the vessel except remedies available under this chapter.

(c)   Outer Continental Shelf

In the event that the negligence of a vessel causes injury to a person entitled to receive benefits under this chapter by virtue of section 1333 of title 43, then such person, or anyone otherwise entitled to recover damages by reason thereof, may bring an action against such vessel in accordance with the provisions of subsection (b) of this section. Nothing contained in subsection (b) of this section shall preclude the enforcement according to its terms of any reciprocal indemnity provision whereby the employer of a person entitled to receive benefits under this chapter by virtue of section 1333 of title 43 and the vessel agree to defend and indemnify the other for cost of defense and loss or liability for damages arising out of or resulting from death or bodily injury to their employees.

§ 919. PROCEDURE IN RESPECT OF CLAIMS

(a) Filing of claim

Subject to the provisions of section 913 of this title a claim for compensation may be filed with the deputy commissioner in accordance with regulations prescribed by the Secretary at any time after the first seven days of disability following any injury, or at any time after death, and the deputy commissioner shall have full power and authority to hear and determine all questions in respect of such claim.

(b) Notice of claim

Within ten days after such claim is filed the deputy commissioner, in accordance with regulations prescribed by the Secretary, shall notify the employer and any other person (other than the claimant), whom the deputy commissioner considers an interested party, that a claim has been filed. Such notice may be served personally upon the employer or other person, or sent to such employer or person by registered mail.

(c) Investigations; order for hearing; notice; rejection or award

The deputy commissioner shall make or cause to be made such investigations as he considers necessary in respect of the claim, and upon application of any interested party shall order a hearing thereon. If a hearing on such claim is ordered the deputy commissioner shall give the claimant and other interested parties at least ten days' notice of such hearing, served personally upon the claimant and other interested parties or sent to such claimant and other interested parties by registered mail or by certified mail, and shall within twenty days after such hearing is had, by order, reject the claim or make an award in respect of the claim. If no hearing is ordered within twenty days after notice is given as provided in subdivision (b) of this section, the deputy commissioner shall, by order, reject the claim or make an award in respect of the claim.

(d) Provisions governing conduct of hearing; administrative law judges

Notwithstanding any other provisions of this chapter, any hearing held under this chapter shall be conducted in accordance with the provisions of section 554 of title 5. Any such hearing shall be conducted by an administrative law judge qualified under section 3105 of that title. All powers, duties, and responsibilities vested by this chapter, on October 27, 1972, in the deputy commissioners with respect to such hearings shall be vested in such administrative law judges.

(e) Filing and mailing of order rejecting claim or making award

The order rejecting the claim or making the award (referred to in this chapter as a compensation order) shall be filed in the office of the deputy commissioner, and a copy thereof shall be sent by registered mail or by certified mail to the claimant and to the employer at the last known address of each.

(f)   Awards after death of employee

An award of compensation for disability may be made after the death of an injured employee.

(g)   Transfer of case

At any time after a claim has been filed with him, the deputy commissioner may, with the approval of the Secretary, transfer such case to any other deputy commissioner for the purpose of making investigation, taking testimony, making physical examinations or taking such other necessary action therein as may be directed.

(h)   Physical examination of injured employee

An injured employee claiming or entitled to compensation shall submit to such physical examination by a medical officer of the United States or by a duly qualified physician designated or approved by the Secretary as the deputy commissioner may require. The place or places shall be reasonably convenient for the employee. Such physician or physicians as the employee, employer, or carrier may select and pay for may participate in an examination if the employee, employer, or carrier so requests. Proceedings shall be suspended and no compensation be payable for any period during which the employee may refuse to submit to examination.

§ 920.   PRESUMPTIONS

In any proceeding for the enforcement of a claim for compensation under this chapter it shall be presumed, in the absence of substantial evidence to the contrary—

(a)   That the claim comes within the provisions of this chapter.

(b)   That sufficient notice of such claim has been given.

(c)   That the injury was not occasioned solely by the intoxication of the injured employee.

(d)   That the injury was not occasioned by the willful intention of the injured employee to injure or kill himself or another.

§ 921.   REVIEW OF COMPENSATION ORDERS

(a)   Effectiveness and finality of orders

A compensation order shall become effective when filed in the office of the deputy commissioner as provided in section 919 of this title, and, unless proceedings for the suspension or setting aside of such order are instituted as provided in subdivision (b) of this section, shall become final at the expiration of the thirtieth day thereafter.

(b)   Benefits Review Board; establishment; members; chairman; quorum; voting; questions reviewable; record; conclusiveness of findings; stay of payments; remand

(1)   There is hereby established a Benefits Review Board which shall be composed of five members appointed by the Secretary from

among individuals who are especially qualified to serve on such Board. The Secretary shall designate one of the members of the Board to serve as chairman. The Chairman shall have the authority, as delegated by the Secretary, to exercise all administrative functions necessary to operate the Board.

(2) For the purpose of carrying out its functions under this chapter, three members of the Board shall constitute a quorum and official action can be taken only on the affirmative vote of at least three members.

(3) The Board shall be authorized to hear and determine appeals raising a substantial question of law or fact taken by any party in interest from decisions with respect to claims of employees under this chapter and the extensions thereof. The Board's orders shall be based upon the hearing record. The findings of fact in the decision under review by the Board shall be conclusive if supported by substantial evidence in the record considered as a whole. The payment of the amounts required by an award shall not be stayed pending final decision in any such proceeding unless ordered by the Board. No stay shall be issued unless irreparable injury would otherwise ensue to the employer or carrier.

(4) The Board may, on its own motion or at the request of the Secretary, remand a case to the administrative law judge for further appropriate action. The consent of the parties in interest shall not be a prerequisite to a remand by the Board.

(5) Notwithstanding paragraphs (1) through (4), upon application of the Chairman of the Board, the Secretary may designate up to four Department of Labor administrative law judges to serve on the Board temporarily, for not more than one year. The Board is authorized to delegate to panels of three members any or all of the powers which the Board may exercise. Each such panel shall have no more than one temporary member. Two members shall constitute a quorum of a panel. Official adjudicative action may be taken only on the affirmative vote of at least two members of a panel. Any party aggrieved by a decision of a panel of the Board may, within thirty days after the date of entry of the decision, petition the entire permanent Board for review of the panel's decision. Upon affirmative vote of the majority of the permanent members of the Board, the petition shall be granted. The Board shall amend its Rules of Practice to conform with this paragraph. Temporary members, while serving as members of the Board, shall be compensated at the same rate of compensation as regular members.

(c) Court of appeals; jurisdiction; persons entitled to review; petition; record; determination and enforcement; service of process; stay of payments

Any person adversely affected or aggrieved by a final order of the Board may obtain a review of that order in the United States court of appeals for the circuit in which the injury occurred, by filing in such court within sixty days following the issuance of such Board order a written petition praying that the order be modified or set aside. A copy of such petition shall be forthwith transmitted by the clerk of the court, to the Board, and to the other parties, and thereupon the Board shall file in the court the record in the proceedings as provided in section 2112 of title 28. Upon such filing, the court shall have jurisdiction of the proceeding and shall have the power to give a decree affirming, modifying, or setting aside, in whole or in part, the order of the Board and enforcing same to the extent that such order is affirmed or modified. The orders, writs, and processes of the court in such proceedings may run, be served, and be returnable anywhere in the United States. The payment of the amounts required by an award shall not be stayed pending final decision in any such proceeding unless ordered by the court. No stay shall be issued unless irreparable injury would otherwise ensue to the employer or carrier. The order of the court allowing any stay shall contain a specific finding, based upon evidence submitted to the court and identified by reference thereto, that irreparable damage would result to the employer, and specifying the nature of the damage.

(d)   District court; jurisdiction; enforcement of orders; application of beneficiaries of awards or deputy commissioner; process for compliance with orders

If any employer or his officers or agents fails to comply with a compensation order making an award, that has become final, any beneficiary of such award or the deputy commissioner making the order, may apply for the enforcement of the order to the Federal district court for the judicial district in which the injury occurred (or to the United States District Court for the District of Columbia if the injury occurred in the District). If the court determines that the order was made and served in accordance with law, and that such employer or his officers or agents have failed to comply therewith, the court shall enforce obedience to the order by writ of injunction or by other proper process, mandatory or otherwise, to enjoin upon such person and his officers and agents compliance with the order.

(e) Institution of proceedings for suspension, setting aside, or enforcement of compensation orders.

Proceedings for suspending, setting aside, or enforcing a compensation order, whether rejecting a claim or making an award, shall not be instituted otherwise than as provided in this section and section 918 of this title.

§ 922. MODIFICATION OF AWARDS

Upon his own initiative, or upon the application of any party in interest (including an employer or carrier which has been granted relief under section 908(f) of this title), on the ground of a change in conditions or because of a mistake in a determination of fact by the deputy commissioner, the deputy commissioner may, at any time prior to one year after the date of the last payment of compensation, whether or not a compensation order has been issued, or at any time prior to one year after the rejection of a claim, review a compensation case (including a case under which payments are made pursuant to section 944(i) of this title) in accordance with the procedure prescribed in respect of claims in section 919 of this title, and in accordance with such section issue a new compensation order which may terminate, continue, reinstate, increase, or decrease such compensation, or award compensation. Such new order shall not affect any compensation previously paid, except that an award increasing the compensation rate may be made effective from the date of the injury, and if any part of the compensation due or to become due is unpaid, an award decreasing the compensation rate may be made effective from the date of the injury, and any payment made prior thereto in excess of such decreased rate shall be deducted from any unpaid compensation, in such manner and by such method as may be determined by the deputy commissioner with the approval of the Secretary. This section does not authorize the modification of settlements.

§ 933. COMPENSATION FOR INJURIES WHERE THIRD PERSONS ARE LIABLE

(a) Election of remedies

If on account of a disability or death for which compensation is payable under this chapter the person entitled to such compensation determines that some person other than the employer or a person or persons in his employ is liable in damages, he need not elect whether to receive such compensation or to recover damages against such third person.

(b) Acceptance of compensation operating as assignment

Acceptance of compensation under an award in a compensation order filed by the deputy commissioner, an administrative law judge, or the Board shall operate as an assignment to the employer of all rights of the person entitled to compensation to recover damages against such third person unless such person shall commence an action against such third person within six months after such acceptance. If the employer fails to commence an action against such third person within ninety days after the cause of action is assigned under this section, the right to bring such action shall revert to the person entitled to compensation. For the purpose of this subsection, the term "award" with respect to a compensation order means a formal order issued by the deputy commissioner, an administrative law judge, or Board.

(c) Payment into section 944 fund operating as assignment

The payment of such compensation into the fund established in section 944 of this title shall operate as an assignment to the employer of all right of the legal representative of the deceased (hereinafter referred to as "representative") to recover damages against such third person.

(d)   Institution of proceedings or compromise by assignee

Such employer on account of such assignment may either institute proceedings for the recovery of such damages or may compromise with such third person either without or after instituting such proceeding.

(e)   Recoveries by assignee

Any amount recovered by such employer on account of such assignment, whether or not as the result of a compromise, shall be distributed as follows:

(1)   The employer shall retain an amount equal to—

(A) the expenses incurred by him in respect to such proceedings or compromise (including a reasonable attorney's fee as determined by the deputy commissioner or Board);

(B) the cost of all benefits actually furnished by him to the employee under section 907 of this title;

(C) all amounts paid as compensation;

(D) the present value of all amounts thereafter payable as compensation, such present value to be computed in accordance with a schedule prepared by the Secretary, and the present value of the cost of all benefits thereafter to be furnished under section 907 of this title, to be estimated by the deputy commissioner, and the amounts so computed and estimated to be retained by the employer as a trust fund to pay such compensation and the cost of such benefits as they become due, and to pay any sum finally remaining in excess thereof to the person entitled to compensation or to the representative; and

(2)   The employer shall pay any excess to the person entitled to compensation or to the representative.

(f)   Institution of proceedings by person entitled to compensation

If the person entitled to compensation institutes proceedings within the period prescribed in subsection (b) of this section the employer shall be required to pay as compensation under this chapter a sum equal to the excess of the amount which the Secretary determines is payable on account of such injury or death over the net amount recovered against such third person. Such net amount shall be equal to the actual amount recovered less the expenses reasonably incurred by such person in respect to such proceedings (including reasonable attorneys' fees).

(g)   Compromise obtained by person entitled to compensation

(1) If the person entitled to compensation (or the person's representative) enters into a settlement with a third person referred to in subsection (a) of this section for an amount less than the compensation to which the person (or the person's representative)

would be entitled under this chapter, the employer shall be liable for compensation as determined under subsection (f) of this section only if written approval of the settlement is obtained from the employer and the employer's carrier, before the settlement is executed, and by the person entitled to compensation (or the person's representative). The approval shall be made on a form provided by the Secretary and shall be filed in the office of the deputy commissioner within thirty days after the settlement is entered into.

(2) If no written approval of the settlement is obtained and filed as required by paragraph (1), or if the employee fails to notify the employer of any settlement obtained from or judgment rendered against a third person, all rights to compensation and medical benefits under this chapter shall be terminated, regardless of whether the employer or the employer's insurer has made payments or acknowledged entitlement to benefits under this chapter.

(3) Any payments by the special fund established under section 944 of this title shall be a lien upon the proceeds of any settlement obtained from or judgment rendered against a third person referred to under subsection (a) of this section. Notwithstanding any other provision of law, such lien shall be enforceable against such proceeds, regardless of whether the Secretary on behalf of the special fund has agreed to or has received actual notice of the settlement or judgment.

(4) Any payments by a trust fund described in section 917 of this title shall be a lien upon the proceeds of any settlement obtained from or judgment recorded against a third person referred to under subsection (a) of this section. Such lien shall have priority over a lien under paragraph (3) of this subsection.

(h) Subrogation

Where the employer is insured and the insurance carrier has assumed the payment of the compensation, the insurance carrier shall be subrogated to all the rights of the employer under this section.

(i) Right to compensation as exclusive remedy

The right to compensation or benefits under this chapter shall be the exclusive remedy to an employee when he is injured, or to his eligible survivors or legal representatives if he is killed, by the negligence or wrong of any other person or persons in the same employ: *Provided,* That this provision shall not affect the liability of a person other than an officer or employee of the employer.

§ 938. PENALTIES

(a) Failure to secure payment of compensation

Any employer required to secure the payment of compensation under this chapter who fails to secure such compensation shall be guilty of a misdemeanor and, upon conviction thereof, shall be punished by a fine of not more than $10,000, or by imprisonment for not more than one year, or by both such fine and imprisonment; and in any case where such employer is a corporation, the president, secretary, and treasurer thereof shall be also severally liable to such fine or imprisonment as herein provided for the failure of such corporation to secure the payment of compensation; and such president, secretary, and treasurer shall be severally personally liable, jointly with such corporation, for any compensation or other benefit which may accrue under the said chapter in respect to any injury which may occur to any employee of such corporation while it shall so fail to secure the payment of compensation as required by section 932 of this title.

(b)   Avoiding payment of compensation

Any employer who knowingly transfers, sells, encumbers, assigns, or in any manner disposes of, conceals, secretes, or destroys any property belonging to such employer, after one of his employees has been injured within the purview of this chapter, and with intent to avoid the payment of compensation under this chapter to such employee or his dependents, shall be guilty of a misdemeanor and, upon conviction thereof, shall be punished by a fine of not more than $10,000, or by imprisonment for not more than one year, or by both such fine and imprisonment; and in any case where such employer is a corporation, the president, secretary, and treasurer thereof shall be also severally liable to such penalty of imprisonment as well as jointly liable with such corporation for such fine.

(c)   Effect on other liability of employer

This section shall not affect any other liability of the employer under this chapter.

TITLE 45
RAILROADS

CHAPTER 2. LIABILITY FOR INJURIES TO EMPLOYEES

"Federal Employers' Liability Act"

§ 51.   LIABILITY OF COMMON CARRIERS BY RAILROAD, IN INTERSTATE OR FOREIGN COMMERCE, FOR INJURIES TO EMPLOYEES FROM NEGLIGENCE; EMPLOYEE DEFINED

Every common carrier by railroad while engaging in commerce between any of the several States or Territories, or between any of the States and Territories, or between the District of Columbia and any of the States or Territories, or between the District of Columbia or any of the States or Territories and any foreign nation or nations, shall be liable in damages to any person suffering injury while he is employed by such carrier in such commerce, or, in case of the death of such employee, to his or her personal representative, for the benefit of the surviving widow or husband and children of such employee; and, if none, then of such employee's parents; and, if none, then of the next of kin dependent upon such employee, for such injury or death resulting in whole or in part from the negligence of any of the officers, agents, or employees of such carrier, or by reason of any defect of insufficiency, due to its negligence, in its cars, engines, appliances, machinery, track, roadbed, works, boats, wharves, or other equipment.

Any employee of a carrier, any part of whose duties as such employee shall be the furtherance of interstate or foreign commerce; or shall, in any way directly or closely and substantially, affect such commerce as above set forth shall, for the purposes of this chapter, be considered as being employed by such carrier in such commerce and shall be considered as entitled to the benefits of this chapter.

§ 53. CONTRIBUTORY NEGLIGENCE; DIMINUTION OF DAMAGES

In all actions hereafter brought against any such common carrier by railroad under or by virtue of any of the provisions of this chapter to recover damages for personal injuries to an employee, or where such injuries have resulted in his death, the fact that the employee may have been guilty of contributory negligence shall not bar a recovery, but the damages shall be diminished by the jury in proportion to the amount of negligence attributable to such employee: *Provided,* That no such employee who may be injured or killed shall be held to have been guilty of contributory negligence in any case where the violation by such common carrier of any statute enacted for the safety of employees contributed to the injury or death of such employee.

§ 54. ASSUMPTION OF RISKS OF EMPLOYMENT

In any action brought against any common carrier under or by virtue of any of the provisions of this chapter to recover damages for injuries to, or the death of, any of its employees, such employee shall not be held to have assumed the risks of his employment in any case where such injury or death resulted in whole or in part from the negligence of any of the officers, agents, or employees of such carrier; and no employee shall be held to have assumed the risks of his employment in any case where the violation by such common carrier of any statute enacted for the safety of employees contributed to the injury or death of such employee.

§ 56. ACTIONS; LIMITATIONS; CONCURRENT JURISDICTION OF COURTS

No action shall be maintained under this chapter unless commenced within three years from the day the cause of action accrued.

Under this chapter an action may be brought in a district court of the United States, in the district of the residence of the defendant, or in which the cause of action arose, or in which the defendant shall be doing business at the time of commencing such action. The jurisdiction of the courts of the United States under this chapter shall be concurrent with that of the courts of the several States.

§ 59.   SURVIVAL OF RIGHT OF ACTION OF PERSON INJURED

Any right of action given by this chapter to a person suffering injury shall survive to his or her personal representative, for the benefit of the surviving widow or husband and children of such employee, and, if none, then of such employee's parents; and, if none, then of the next of kin dependent upon such employee, but in such cases there shall be only one recovery for the same injury.

TITLE 46
SHIPPING
SUBTITLE II
VESSELS AND SEAMEN
PART A.   GENERAL PROVISIONS
CHAPTER 23.   OPERATION OF VESSELS GENERALLY

§ 2303.   DUTIES RELATED TO MARINE CASUALTY ASSISTANCE AND INFORMATION

(a)   The master or individual in charge of a vessel involved in a marine casualty shall—

(1)   render necessary assistance to each individual affected to save that affected individual from danger caused by the marine casualty, so far as the master or individual in charge can do so without serious danger to the master's or individual's vessel or to individuals on board; and

(2)   give the master's or individual's name and address and identification of the vessel to the master or individual in charge of any other vessel involved in the casualty, to any individual injured, and to the owner of any property damaged.

(b)   An individual violating this section or a regulation prescribed under this section shall be fined not more than $1,000 or imprisoned for not more than 2 years. The vessel also is liable in rem to the United States Government for the fine.

(c)   An individual complying with subsection (a) of this section or gratuitously and in good faith rendering assistance at the scene of a marine casualty without objection by an individual assisted, is not liable for damages as a result of rendering assistance or for an act or omission in providing or arranging salvage, towage, medical treatment, or other assistance when the individual acts as an ordinary, reasonable, and prudent individual would have acted under the circumstances.

§ 2304.   DUTY TO PROVIDE ASSISTANCE AT SEA

(a)(1)   A master or individual in charge of a vessel shall render assistance to any individual found at sea in danger of being lost, so far as the master or individual in charge can do so without serious danger to the master's or individual's vessel or individuals on board.

(2) Paragraph (1) does not apply to a vessel of war or a vessel owned by the United States Government appropriated only to a public service.

(b) A master or individual violating this section shall be fined not more than $1,000, imprisoned for not more than 2 years, or both.

PART G. MERCHANT SEAMEN PROTECTION AND RELIEF

CHAPTER 103. FOREIGN AND INTERCOASTAL VOYAGES

§ 10313. WAGES

(a) A seaman's entitlement to wages and provisions begins when the seaman begins work or when specified in the agreement required by section 10302 of this title for the seaman to begin work or be present on board, whichever is earlier.

(b) Wages are not dependent on the earning of freight by the vessel. When the loss or wreck of the vessel ends the service of a seaman before the end of the period contemplated in the agreement, the seaman is entitled to wages for the period of time actually served. The seaman shall be deemed a destitute seaman under section 11104 of this title. This subsection applies to a fishing or whaling vessel but not a yacht.

(c) When a seaman who has signed an agreement is discharged improperly before the beginning of the voyage or before one month's wages are earned, without the seaman's consent and without the seaman's fault justifying discharge, the seaman is entitled to receive from the master or owner, in addition to wages earned, one month's wages as compensation.

(d) A seaman is not entitled to wages for a period during which the seaman—

    (1) unlawfully failed to work when required, after the time fixed by the agreement for the seaman to begin work; or

    (2) lawfully was imprisoned for an offense, unless a court hearing the case otherwise directs.

(e) After the beginning of the voyage, a seaman is entitled to receive from the master, on demand, one-half of the balance of wages earned and unpaid at each port at which the vessel loads or delivers cargo during the voyage. A demand may not be made before the expiration of 5 days from the beginning of the voyage, not more than once in 5 days, and not more than once in the same port on the same entry. If a master does not comply with this subsection, the seaman is released from the agreement and is entitled to payment of all wages earned. Notwithstanding a release signed by a seaman under section 10312 of this title, a court having jurisdiction may set aside, for good cause shown, the release and take action that justice requires. This subsection does not apply to a fishing or whaling vessel or a yacht.

(f)   At the end of a voyage, the master shall pay each seaman the balance of wages due the seaman within 24 hours after the cargo has been discharged or within 4 days after the seaman is discharged, whichever is earlier. When a seaman is discharged and final payment of wages is delayed for the period permitted by this subsection, the seaman is entitled at the time of discharge to one-third of the wages due the seaman.

(g)(1)   Subject to paragraph (2), when payment is not made as provided under subsection (f) of this section without sufficient cause, the master or owner shall pay to the seaman 2 days' wages for each day payment is delayed.

(2)   The total amount required to be paid under paragraph (1) with respect to all claims in a class action suit by seamen on a passenger vessel capable of carrying more than 500 passengers for wages under this section against a vessel master, owner, or operator or the employer of the seamen shall not exceed ten times the unpaid wages that are the subject of the claims.

(3)   A class action suit for wages under this subsection must be commenced within three years after the later of—

(A)   the date of the end of the last voyage for which the wages are claimed; or

(B)   the receipt, by a seaman who is a claimant in the suit, of a payment of wages that are the subject of the suit that is made in the ordinary course of employment.

(h)   Subsections (f) and (g) of this section do not apply to a fishing or whaling vessel or a yacht.

(i)   This section applies to a seaman on a foreign vessel when in a harbor of the United States. The courts are available to the seaman for the enforcement of this section.

§ 10317.   LOSS OF LIEN AND RIGHT TO WAGES

A master or seaman by any agreement other than one provided for in this chapter may not forfeit the master's or seaman's lien on the vessel or be deprived of a remedy to which the master or seaman otherwise would be entitled for the recovery of wages. A stipulation in an agreement inconsistent with this chapter, or a stipulation by which a seaman consents to abandon a right to wages if the vessel is lost, or to abandon a right the seaman may have or obtain in the nature of salvage, is void.

CHAPTER 111.   PROTECTION AND RELIEF

§ 11109.   ATTACHMENT OF WAGES

(a)   Wages due or accruing to a master or seaman are not subject to attachment or arrestment from any court, except for an order of a court about the payment by a master or seaman of any part of the master's or seaman's wages for the support and maintenance of the spouse or minor children of the master or seaman, or both. A payment of wages to a master or seaman is valid, notwithstanding any prior sale or assignment of wages or any attachment, encumbrance, or arrestment of the wages.

(b) An assignment or sale of wages or salvage made before the payment of wages does not bind the party making it, except allotments authorized by section 10315 of this title.

(c) This section applies to an individual employed on a fishing vessel or any fish processing vessel.

SUBTITLE III

MARITIME LIABILITY

CHAPTER 301.   GENERAL LIABILITY PROVISIONS

§ 30101. EXTENSION OF JURISDICTION TO CASES OF DAMAGE OR INJURY ON LAND

(a) In general.—The admiralty and maritime jurisdiction of the United States extends to and includes cases of injury or damage, to person or property, caused by a vessel on navigable waters, even though the injury or damage is done or consummated on land.

(b) Procedure.—A civil action in a case under subsection (a) may be brought in rem or in personam according to the principles of law and the rules of practice applicable in cases where the injury or damage has been done and consummated on navigable waters.

(c) Actions against United States.—

(1) Exclusive remedy.—In a civil action against the United States for injury or damage done or consummated on land by a vessel on navigable waters, chapter 309 or 311 of this title, as appropriate, provides the exclusive remedy.

(2) Administrative claim.—A civil action described in paragraph (1) may not be brought until the expiration of the 6-month period after the claim has been presented in writing to the agency owning or operating the vessel causing the injury or damage.

§ 30102. LIABILITY TO PASSENGERS

(a) Liability.—The owner and master of a vessel, and the vessel, are liable for personal injury to a passenger or damage to a passenger's baggage caused by—

(1) a neglect or failure to comply with part B or F of subtitle II of this title; or

(2) a known defect in the steaming apparatus or hull of the vessel.

(b) Not subject to limitation.—A liability imposed under this section is not subject to limitation under chapter 305 of this title.

§ 30103.   LIABILITY OF MASTER, MATE, ENGINEER, AND PILOT

A person may bring a civil action against a master, mate, engineer, or pilot of a vessel, and recover damages, for personal injury or loss caused by the master's, mate's, engineer's, or pilot's—

     (1)   negligence or willful misconduct; or

     (2)   neglect or refusal to obey the laws governing the navigation of vessels.

§ 30104.   PERSONAL INJURY TO OR DEATH OF SEAMEN

A seaman injured in the course of employment or, if the seaman dies from the injury, the personal representative of the seaman may elect to bring a civil action at law, with the right of trial by jury, against the employer. Laws of the United States regulating recovery for personal injury to, or death of, a railway employee apply to an action under this section.

§ 30105.   RESTRICTION ON RECOVERY BY NON-CITIZENS AND NONRESIDENT ALIENS FOR INCIDENTS IN WATERS OF OTHER COUNTRIES

(a) Definition.—In this section, the term "continental shelf" has the meaning given that term in article I of the 1958 Convention on the Continental Shelf.

(b) Restriction.—Except as provided in subsection (c), a civil action for maintenance and cure or for damages for personal injury or death may not be brought under a maritime law of the United States if—

     (1)   the individual suffering the injury or death was not a citizen or permanent resident alien of the United States at the time of the incident giving rise to the action;

     (2)   the incident occurred in the territorial waters or waters overlaying the continental shelf of a country other than the United States; and

     (3)   the individual suffering the injury or death was employed at the time of the incident by a person engaged in the exploration, development, or production of offshore mineral or energy resources, including drilling, mapping, surveying, diving, pipelaying, maintaining, repairing, constructing, or transporting supplies, equipment, or personnel, but not including transporting those resources by a vessel constructed or adapted primarily to carry oil in bulk in the cargo spaces.

(c) Nonapplication.—Subsection (b) does not apply if the individual bringing the action establishes that a remedy is not available under the laws of—

     (1)   the country asserting jurisdiction over the area in which the incident occurred; or

(2) the country in which the individual suffering the injury or death maintained citizenship or residency at the time of the incident.

§ 30106.   Time Limit on Bringing Maritime Action for Personal Injury or Death

Except as otherwise provided by law, a civil action for damages for personal injury or death arising out of a maritime tort must be brought within 3 years after the cause of action arose.

Chapter 303.   Death on the High Seas

§ 30301.   Short Title

This chapter may be cited as the "Death on the High Seas Act".

§ 30302.   Cause of Action

When the death of an individual is caused by wrongful act, neglect, or default occurring on the high seas beyond 3 nautical miles from the shore of the United States, the personal representative of the decedent may bring a civil action in admiralty against the person or vessel responsible. The action shall be for the exclusive benefit of the decedent's spouse, parent, child, or dependent relative.

§ 30303.   Amount and Apportionment of Recovery

The recovery in an action under this chapter shall be a fair compensation for the pecuniary loss sustained by the individuals for whose benefit the action is brought. The court shall apportion the recovery among those individuals in proportion to the loss each has sustained.

§ 30304.   Contributory negligence

In an action under this chapter, contributory negligence of the decedent is not a bar to recovery. The court shall consider the degree of negligence of the decedent and reduce the recovery accordingly.

§ 30305.   Death of plaintiff in pending action

If a civil action in admiralty is pending in a court of the United States to recover for personal injury caused by wrongful act, neglect, or default described in section 30302 of this title, and the individual dies during the action as a result of the wrongful act, neglect, or default, the personal representative of the decedent may be substituted as the plaintiff and the action may proceed under this chapter for the recovery authorized by this chapter.

§ 30306.   Foreign cause of action

When a cause of action exists under the law of a foreign country for death by wrongful act, neglect, or default on the high seas, a civil action in admiralty may be brought in a court of the United States based on the foreign cause of action, without abatement of the amount for which recovery is authorized.

§ 30307.   COMMERCIAL AVIATION ACCIDENTS

(a)   Definition.—In this section, the term "nonpecuniary damages" means damages for loss of care, comfort, and companionship.

(b)   Beyond 12 Nautical Miles.—In an action under this chapter, if the death resulted from a commercial aviation accident occurring on the high seas beyond 12 nautical miles from the shore of the United States, additional compensation is recoverable for nonpecuniary damages, but punitive damages are not recoverable.

(c)   Within 12 Nautical Miles.—This chapter does not apply if the death resulted from a commercial aviation accident occurring on the high seas 12 nautical miles or less from the shore of the United States.

§ 30308.   NONAPPLICATION

(a)   State Law.—This chapter does not affect the law of a State regulating the right to recover for death.

(b)   Internal Waters.—This chapter does not apply to the Great Lakes or waters within the territorial limits of a State.

CHAPTER 305.   EXONERATION AND LIMITATION OF LIABILITY

§ 30501.   DEFINITION

In this chapter, the term "owner" includes a charterer that mans, supplies, and navigates a vessel at the charterer's own expense or by the charterer's own procurement.

§ 30502.   APPLICATION

Except as otherwise provided, this chapter (except section 30503) applies to seagoing vessels and vessels used on lakes or rivers or in inland navigation, including canal boats, barges, and lighters.

§ 30503.   DECLARATION OF NATURE AND VALUE OF GOODS

(a)   In general.—If a shipper of an item named in subsection (b), contained in a parcel, package, or trunk, loads the item as freight or baggage on a vessel, without at the time of loading giving to the person receiving the item a written notice of the true character and value of the item and having that information entered on the bill of lading, the owner and master of the vessel are not liable as carriers. The owner and master are not liable beyond the value entered on the bill of lading.

(b)   Items.—The items referred to in subsection (a) are precious metals, gold or silver plated articles, precious stones, jewelry, trinkets, watches, clocks, glass, china, coins, bills, securities, printings, engravings, pictures, stamps, maps, papers, silks, furs, lace, and similar items of high value and small size.

§ 30504.   LOSS BY FIRE

The owner of a vessel is not liable for loss or damage to merchandise on the vessel caused by a fire on the vessel unless the fire resulted from the design or neglect of the owner.

§ 30505.   General Limit of Liability

(a) In General.—Except as provided in section 30506 of this title, the liability of the owner of a vessel for any claim, debt, or liability described in subsection (b) shall not exceed the value of the vessel and pending freight. If the vessel has more than one owner, the proportionate share of the liability of any one owner shall not exceed that owner's proportionate interest in the vessel and pending freight.

(b) Claims Subject to Limitation.—Unless otherwise excluded by law, claims, debts, and liabilities subject to limitation under subsection (a) are those arising from any embezzlement, loss, or destruction of any property, goods, or merchandise shipped or put on board the vessel, any loss, damage, or injury by collision, or any act, matter, or thing, loss, damage, or forfeiture, done, occasioned, or incurred, without the privity or knowledge of the owner.

(c) Wages.—Subsection (a) does not apply to a claim for wages.

§ 30506.   Limit of Liability for Personal Injury or Death

(a) Application.—This section applies only to seagoing vessels, but does not apply to pleasure yachts, tugs, towboats, towing vessels, tank vessels, fishing vessels, fish tender vessels, canal boats, scows, car floats, barges, lighters, or nondescript vessels.

(b) Minimum Liability.—If the amount of the vessel owner's liability determined under section 30505 of this title is insufficient to pay all losses in full, and the portion available to pay claims for personal injury or death is less than $420 times the tonnage of the vessel, that portion shall be increased to $420 times the tonnage of the vessel. That portion may be used only to pay claims for personal injury or death.

(c) Calculation of Tonnage.—Under subsection (b), the tonnage of a self-propelled vessel is the gross tonnage without deduction for engine room, and the tonnage of a sailing vessel is the tonnage for documentation. However, space for the use of seamen is excluded.

(d) Claims Arising on Distinct Occasions.—Separate limits of liability apply to claims for personal injury or death arising on distinct occasions.

(e) Privity or Knowledge.—In a claim for personal injury or death, the privity or knowledge of the master or the owner's superintendent or managing agent, at or before the beginning of each voyage, is imputed to the owner.

§ 30507.   Apportionment of Losses

If the amounts determined under sections 30505 and 30506 of this title are insufficient to pay all claims—

(1) all claimants shall be paid in proportion to their respective losses out of the amount determined under section 30505 of this title; and

(2) personal injury and death claimants, if any, shall be paid an additional amount in proportion to their respective losses out of the additional amount determined under section 30506(b) of this title.

§ 30508. PROVISIONS REQUIRING NOTICE OF CLAIM OR LIMITING TIME FOR BRINGING ACTION

(a) Application.—This section applies only to seagoing vessels, but does not apply to pleasure yachts, tugs, towboats, towing vessels, tank vessels, fishing vessels, fish tender vessels, canal boats, scows, car floats, barges, lighters, or nondescript vessels.

(b) Minimum Time Limits.—The owner, master, manager, or agent of a vessel transporting passengers or property between ports in the United States, or between a port in the United States and a port in a foreign country, may not limit by regulation, contract, or otherwise the period for—

(1) giving notice of, or filing a claim for, personal injury or death to less than 6 months after the date of the injury or death; or

(2) bringing a civil action for personal injury or death to less than one year after the date of the injury or death.

(c) Effect of Failure to Give Notice.—When notice of a claim for personal injury or death is required by a contract, the failure to give the notice is not a bar to recovery if—

(1) the court finds that the owner, master, or agent of the vessel had knowledge of the injury or death and the owner has not been prejudiced by the failure;

(2) the court finds there was a satisfactory reason why the notice could not have been given; or

(3) the owner of the vessel fails to object to the failure to give the notice.

(d) Tolling of Period to Give Notice.—If a claimant is a minor or mental incompetent, or if a claim is for wrongful death, any period provided by a contract for giving notice of the claim is tolled until the earlier of—

(1) the date a legal representative is appointed for the minor, incompetent, or decedent's estate; or

(2) 3 years after the injury or death.

§ 30509. PROVISIONS LIMITING LIABILITY FOR PERSONAL INJURY OR DEATH

(a) Prohibition.—

(1) In general.—The owner, master, manager, or agent of a vessel transporting passengers between ports in the United States, or between a port in the United States and a port in a foreign

country, may not include in a regulation or contract a provision limiting—

> (A) the liability of the owner, master, or agent for personal injury or death caused by the negligence or fault of the owner or the owner's employees or agents; or

> (B) the right of a claimant for personal injury or death to a trial by court of competent jurisdiction.

> (2) Voidness.—A provision described in paragraph (1) is void.

(b) Emotional distress, mental suffering, and psychological injury.—

> (1) In general.—Subsection (a) does not prohibit a provision in a contract or in ticket conditions of carriage with a passenger that relieves an owner, master, manager, agent, operator, or crewmember of a vessel from liability for infliction of emotional distress, mental suffering, or psychological injury so long as the provision does not limit such liability when the emotional distress, mental suffering, or psychological injury is—

> > (A) the result of physical injury to the claimant caused by the negligence or fault of a crewmember or the owner, master, manager, agent, or operator;

> > (B) the result of the claimant having been at actual risk of physical injury, and the risk was caused by the negligence or fault of a crewmember or the owner, master, manager, agent, or operator; or

> > (C) intentionally inflicted by a crewmember or the owner, master, manager, agent, or operator.

> (2) Sexual offenses.—This subsection does not limit the liability of a crewmember or the owner, master, manager, agent, or operator of a vessel in a case involving sexual harassment, sexual assault, or rape.

§ 30510. VICARIOUS LIABILITY FOR MEDICAL MALPRACTICE WITH REGARD TO CREW

In a civil action by any person in which the owner or operator of a vessel or employer of a crewmember is claimed to have vicarious liability for medical malpractice with regard to a crewmember occurring at a shoreside facility, and to the extent the damages resulted from the conduct of any shoreside doctor, hospital, medical facility, or other health care provider, the owner, operator, or employer is entitled to rely on any statutory limitations of liability applicable to the doctor, hospital, medical facility, or other health care provider in the State of the United States in which the shoreside medical care was provided.

§ 30511.   ACTION BY OWNER FOR LIMITATION

(a) In general.—The owner of a vessel may bring a civil action in a district court of the United States for limitation of liability under this chapter. The action must be brought within 6 months after a claimant gives the owner written notice of a claim.

(b) Creation of Fund.—When the action is brought, the owner (at the owner's option) shall—

(1) deposit with the court, for the benefit of claimants—

(A) an amount equal to the value of the owner's interest in the vessel and pending freight, or approved security; and

(B) an amount, or approved security, that the court may fix from time to time as necessary to carry out this chapter; or

(2) transfer to a trustee appointed by the court, for the benefit of claimants—

(A) the owner's interest in the vessel and pending freight; and

(B) an amount, or approved security, that the court may fix from time to time as necessary to carry out this chapter.

(c) Cessation of Other Actions.—When an action has been brought under this section and the owner has complied with subsection (b), all claims and proceedings against the owner related to the matter in question shall cease.

CHAPTER 307. LIABILITY OF WATER CARRIERS

The Carriage of Goods by Sea Act

§ 30701   NOTE

[The Carriage of Goods by Sea Act was not incorporated into the 2006 Revision of Title 46 but was not repealed nor amended. The text of the Act is reproduced in a reviser's note to § 30701.]

Carriage of Goods by Sea

Act April 16, 1936, ch. 229, 49 Stat. 1207; Aug. 6, 1981, P.L. 97–31, § 12(146), 95 Stat. 166, provided that:

Bills of lading subject to chapter [note]

"Every bill of lading or similar document of title which is evidence of a contract for the carriage of goods by sea to or from ports of the United States, in foreign trade, shall have effect subject to the provisions of this Act.

"Section 1. When used in this chapter [this note]—

"(a) The term 'carrier' includes the owner or the charterer who enters into a contract of carriage with a shipper.

"(b) The term 'contract of carriage' applies only to contracts of carriage covered by a bill of lading or any similar document of title, insofar as such document relates to the carriage of goods by sea, including any bill of lading or any similar document as aforesaid issued under or pursuant to a charter party from the moment at which such bill of lading or similar document of title regulates the relations between a carrier and a holder of the same.

"(c) The term 'goods' includes goods, wares, merchandise, and articles of every kind, whatsoever, except live animals and cargo which by the contract of carriage is stated as being carried on deck and is so carried.

"(d) The term 'ship' means any vessel used for the carriage of goods by sea.

"(e) The term 'carriage of goods' covers the period from the time when the goods are loaded on to the time when they are discharged from the ship.

"Sec. 2. Duties and rights of carrier

"Subject to the provisions of section 6, under every contract of carriage of goods by sea, the carrier in relation to the loading, handling, stowage, carriage, custody, care, and discharge of such goods, shall be subject to the responsibilities and liabilities and entitled to the rights and immunities hereinafter set forth.

"Sec. 3. Responsibilities and liabilities of carrier and ship

"(1) Seaworthiness

The carrier shall be bound, before and at the beginning of the voyage, to exercise due diligence to—

"(a) Make the ship seaworthy;

"(b) Properly man, equip, and supply the ship;

"(c) Make the holds, refrigerating and cooling chambers, and all other parts of the ship in which goods are carried, fit and safe for their reception, carriage, and preservation.

"(2) Cargo

"The carrier shall properly and carefully load, handle, stow, carry, keep, care for, and discharge the goods carried.

"(3) Contents of bill

"After receiving the goods into his charge the carrier, or the master or agent of the carrier, shall, on demand of the shipper, issue to the shipper a bill of lading showing among other things—

"(a) The leading marks necessary for identification of the goods as the same are furnished in writing by the shipper before the loading of such goods starts, provided such marks are stamped or otherwise shown clearly upon the goods if uncovered, or on the cases or coverings in which such goods are contained, in such a manner as should ordinarily remain legible until the end of the voyage.

"(b) Either the number of packages or pieces, or the quantity or weight, as the case may be, as furnished in writing by the shipper.

"(c) The apparent order and condition of the goods: Provided, That no carrier, master, or agent of the carrier, shall be bound to state or show in the bill of lading any marks, number, quantity, or weight which he has reasonable ground for suspecting not accurately to represent the goods actually received, or which he has had no reasonable means of checking.

"(4) Bill as prima facie evidence

"Such a bill of lading shall be prima facie evidence of the receipt by the carrier of the goods as therein described in accordance with paragraphs (3)(a), (b), and (c), of this section: *Provided,* That nothing in this chapter [this note] shall be construed as repealing or limiting the application of any part of chapter 801 of Title 49.

"(5) Guaranty of statements

"The shipper shall be deemed to have guaranteed to the carrier the accuracy at the time of shipment of the marks, number, quantity, and weight, as furnished by him; and the shipper shall indemnify the carrier against all loss, damages, and expenses arising or resulting from inaccuracies in such particulars. The right of the carrier to such indemnity shall in no way limit his responsibility and liability under the contract of carriage to any person other than the shipper.

"(6) Notice of loss or damage; limitation of actions

"Unless notice of loss or damage and the general nature of such loss or damage be given in writing to the carrier or his agent at the port of discharge before or at the time of the removal of the goods into the custody of the person entitled to delivery thereof under the contract of carriage, such removal shall be prima facie evidence of the delivery by the carrier of the goods as described in the bill of lading. If the loss or damage is not apparent, the notice must be given within three days of the delivery.

"Said notice of loss or damage may be endorsed upon the receipt for the goods given by the person taking delivery thereof.

"The notice in writing need not be given if the state of the goods has at the time of their receipt been the subject of joint survey or inspection.

"In any event the carrier and the ship shall be discharged from all liability in respect of loss or damage unless suit is brought within one year after delivery of the goods or the date when the goods should have been delivered: *Provided,* That if a notice of loss or damage, either apparent or concealed, is not given as provided for in this section, that fact shall not affect or prejudice the right of the shipper to bring suit within one year after the delivery of the goods or the date when the goods should have been delivered.

"In the case of any actual or apprehended loss or damage the carrier and the receiver shall give all reasonable facilities to each other for inspecting and tallying the goods.

"(7) 'Shipped' bill of lading

"After the goods are loaded the bill of lading to be issued by the carrier, master, or agent of the carrier to the shipper shall, if the shipper so demands, be a 'shipped' bill of lading: *Provided,* That if the shipper shall have previously taken up any document of title to such goods, he shall surrender the same as against the issue of the "shipped" bill of lading, but at the option of the carrier such document of title may be noted at the port of shipment by the carrier, master, or agent with the name or names of the ship or ships upon which the goods have been shipped and the date or dates of shipment, and when so noted the same shall for the purpose of this section be deemed to constitute a 'shipped' bill of lading.

"(8) Limitation of liability for negligence

"Any clause, covenant, or agreement in a contract of carriage relieving the carrier or the ship from liability for loss or damage to or in connection with the goods, arising from negligence, fault, or failure in the duties and obligations provided in this section, or lessening such liability otherwise than as provided in this Act, shall be null and void and of no effect. A benefit of insurance in favor of the carrier, or similar clause, shall be deemed to be a clause relieving the carrier from liability.

[In par. (4), "chapter 801 of title 49" substituted for "the Act of August 29, 1916, commonly known as 'Pomerene Bills of Lading Act' [49 App. U.S.C.A. § 81 et seq.]" on authority of Pub.L. 103–272, § 6(b), July 5, 1994, 108 Stat. 1378, the first section of which enacted subtitles II, III, and IV to X of Title 49, Transportation.]

"Sec. 4. Rights and immunities of carrier and ship

"(1) Unseaworthiness

"Neither the carrier nor the ship shall be liable for loss or damage arising or resulting from unseaworthiness unless caused by want of due diligence on the part of the carrier to make the ship seaworthy, and to secure that the ship is properly manned, equipped, and supplied, and to make the holds, refrigerating and cool chambers, and all other parts of the ship in which goods are carried fit and safe for their reception, carriage, and preservation in accordance with the provisions of paragraph (1) of section 3. Whenever loss or damage has resulted from unseaworthiness, the burden of proving the exercise of due diligence shall be on the carrier or other persons claiming exemption under this section.

"(2) Uncontrollable causes of loss

"Neither the carrier nor the ship shall be responsible for loss or damage arising or resulting from—

"(a) Act, neglect, or default of the master, mariner, pilot, or the servants of the carrier in the navigation or in the management of the ship;

"(b) Fire, unless caused by the actual fault or privity of the carrier;

"(c) Perils, dangers, and accidents of the sea or other navigable waters;

"(d) Act of God;

"(e) Act of war;

"(f) Act of public enemies;

"(g) Arrest or restraint of princes, rulers, or people, or seizure under legal process;

"(h) Quarantine restrictions;

"(i) Act or omission of the shipper or owner of the goods, his agent or representative;

"(j) Strikes or lockouts or stoppage or restraint of labor from whatever cause, whether partial or general: Provided, that nothing herein contained shall be construed to relieve a carrier from responsibility for the carrier's own acts;

"(k) Riots and civil commotions;

"(*l*) Saving or attempting to save life or property at sea;

"(m)Wastage in bulk or weight or any other loss or damage arising from inherent defect, quality, or vice of the goods;

"(n) Insufficiency of packing;

"(*o*) Insufficiency or inadequacy of marks;

"(p) Latent defects not discoverable by due diligence; and

"(q) Any other cause arising without the actual fault and privity of the carrier and without the fault or neglect of the agents or servants of the carrier, but the burden of proof shall be on the person claiming the benefit of this exception to show that neither the actual fault or privity of the carrier nor the fault or neglect of the agents or servants of the carrier contributed to the loss or damage.

"(3) Freedom from negligence

"The shipper shall not be responsible for loss or damage sustained by the carrier or the ship arising or resulting from any cause without the act, fault, or neglect of the shipper, his agents, or his servants.

"(4) Deviations

"Any deviation in saving or attempting to save life or property at sea, or any reasonable deviation shall not be deemed to be an infringement or breach of this Act or of the contract of carriage, and the carrier shall not be liable for any loss or damage resulting therefrom: *Provided, however,*

That if the deviation is for the purpose of loading or unloading cargo or passengers it shall, prima facie, be regarded as unreasonable.

"(5) Amount of liability; valuation of cargo

"Neither the carrier nor the ship shall in any event be or become liable for any loss or damage to or in connection with the transportation of goods in an amount exceeding $500 per package lawful money of the United States, or in case of goods not shipped in packages, per customary freight unit, or the equivalent of that sum in other currency, unless the nature and value of such goods have been declared by the shipper before shipment and inserted in the bill of lading. This declaration, if embodied in the bill of lading, shall be prima facie evidence, but shall not be conclusive on the carrier.

"By agreement between the carrier, master, or agent of the carrier, and the shipper another maximum amount than that mentioned in this paragraph may be fixed: *Provided,* That such maximum shall not be less than the figure above named. In no event shall the carrier be liable for more than the amount of damage actually sustained.

"Neither the carrier nor the ship shall be responsible in any event for loss or damage to or in connection with the transportation of the goods if the nature or value thereof has been knowingly and fraudulently misstated by the shipper in the bill of lading.

"(6) Inflammable, explosive, or dangerous cargo

"Goods of an inflammable, explosive, or dangerous nature to the shipment whereof the carrier, master or agent of the carrier, has not consented with knowledge of their nature and character, may at any time before discharge be landed at any place or destroyed or rendered innocuous by the carrier without compensation, and the shipper of such goods shall be liable for all damages and expenses directly or indirectly arising out of or resulting from such shipment. If any such goods shipped with such knowledge and consent shall become a danger to the ship or cargo, they may in like manner be landed at any place, or destroyed or rendered innocuous by the carrier without liability on the part of the carrier except to general average, if any.

"Sec. 5. Surrender of rights; increase of liabilities; charter parties; general average

"A carrier shall be at liberty to surrender in whole or in part all or any of his rights and immunities or to increase any of his responsibilities and liabilities under this chapter [this note], provided such surrender or increase shall be embodied in the bill of lading issued to the shipper.

"The provisions of this chapter [this note] shall not be applicable to charter parties; but if bills of lading are issued in the case of a ship under a charter party, they shall comply with the terms of this Act. Nothing in this chapter [this note] shall be held to prevent the insertion in a bill of lading of any lawful provision regarding general average.

"Sec. 6. Special agreement as to particular goods

"Notwithstanding the provisions of the preceding sections, a carrier, master or agent of the carrier, and a shipper shall, in regard to any particular goods be at liberty to enter into any agreement in any terms as to the responsibility and liability of the carrier for such goods, and as to the rights and immunities of the carrier in respect of such goods, or his obligation as to seaworthiness (so far as the stipulation regarding seaworthiness is not contrary to public policy), or the care or diligence of his servants or agents in regard to the loading, handling, stowage, carriage, custody, care, and discharge of the goods carried by sea: *Provided,* That in this case no bill of lading has been or shall be issued and that the terms agreed shall be embodied in a receipt which shall be a nonnegotiable document and shall be marked as such.

"Any agreement so entered into shall have full legal effect: *Provided,* That this section shall not apply to ordinary commercial shipments made in the ordinary course of trade but only to other shipments where the character or condition of the property to be carried or the circumstances, terms, and conditions under which the carriage is to be performed are such as reasonably to justify a special agreement.

"Sec. 7. Agreement as to liability prior to loading or after discharge

"Nothing contained in this chapter [this note] shall prevent a carrier or a shipper from entering into any agreement, stipulation, condition, reservation, or exemption as to the responsibility and liability of the carrier or the ship for the loss or damage to or in connection with the custody and care and handling of goods prior to the loading on and subsequent to the discharge from the ship on which the goods are carried by sea.

"Sec. 8. Rights and liabilities under other provisions

"The provisions of this chapter [this note] shall not affect the rights and obligations of the carrier under the provisions of the Shipping Act, 1916, or under the provisions of sections 4281 to 4289, inclusive, of the Revised Statutes of the United States [46 U.S.C. §§ 30501 et seq.], or of any amendments thereto; or under the provisions of any other enactment for the time being in force relating to the limitation of the liability of the owners of seagoing vessels.

"Sec. 9. Discrimination between competing shippers

"Nothing contained in this chapter [this note] shall be construed as permitting a common carrier by water to discriminate between competing shippers similarly placed in time and circumstances, either (a) with respect to their right to demand and receive bills of lading subject to the provisions of this chapter [this note]; or (b) when issuing such bills of lading, either in the surrender of any of the carrier's rights and immunities or in the increase of any of the carrier's responsibilities and liabilities pursuant to section 1305 of this title [section 5 of this note]; or (c) in any other way prohibited by the Shipping Act, 1916, as amended.

"Sec. 10. [Formerly set out as 49 App. U.S.C.A. § 25, and repealed by Sept. 18, 1940, c. 722, T. I, § 14(a), 54 Stat. 919.]

"Sec. 11. Weight of bulk cargo

"Where under the customs of any trade the weight of any bulk cargo inserted in the bill of lading is a weight ascertained or accepted by a third party other than the carrier or the shipper, and the fact that the weight is so ascertained or accepted is stated in the bill of lading, then, notwithstanding anything in this chapter [this note], the bill of lading shall not be deemed to be prima facie evidence against the carrier of the receipt of goods of the weight so inserted in the bill of lading, and the accuracy thereof at the time of shipment shall not be deemed to have been guaranteed by the shipper.

"Sec. 12. Liabilities before loading and after discharge, effect on other laws

"Nothing in this chapter [this note] shall be construed as superseding any part of sections 190 to 196 of this title, or of any other law which would be applicable in the absence of this chapter [this note], insofar as they relate to the duties, responsibilities, and liabilities of the ship or carrier prior to the time when the goods are loaded on or after the time they are discharged from the ship.

"Sec. 13. Scope of chapter [note]; 'United States'; 'foreign trade'

"This chapter [this note] shall apply to all contracts for carriage of goods by sea to or from ports of the United States in foreign trade. As used in this chapter [this note] the term 'United States' includes its districts, territories, and possessions. The term 'foreign trade' means the transportation of goods between the ports of the United States and ports of foreign countries. Nothing in this chapter [this note] shall be held to apply to contracts for carriage of goods by sea between any port of the United States or its possessions, and any other port of the United States or its possessions: *Provided, however,* That any bill of lading or similar document of title which is evidence of a contract for the carriage of goods by sea between such ports, containing an express statement that it shall be subject to the provisions of this chapter [this note], shall be subjected hereto as fully as if subject hereto by the express provisions of this Act: *Provided further,* That every bill of lading or similar document of title which is evidence of a contract for the carriage of goods by sea from ports of the United States, in foreign trade, shall contain a statement that it shall have effect subject to the provisions of this chapter [this note].

[A proviso in the second sentence that the Philippine Legislature might by law exclude its application to transportation to or from parts in the Philippine Islands was omitted in view of Proc. No. 2695, set out as a note under § 1394 of Title 22, Foreign Relations and Intercourse, which proclaimed the independence of the Philippines.]

"Sec. 14. Suspension of provisions by President

"Upon the certification of the Secretary of Transportation that the foreign commerce of the United States in its competition with that of foreign nations is prejudiced by the provisions, or any of them, of sections 1301 to 1308 of this title [sections 1 to 8 of this note], or by the laws of any foreign country or countries relating to the carriage of goods by sea, the President of the United States may, from time to time, by proclamation, suspend any or all provisions of said sections for such periods of time or indefinitely as may be designated in the proclamation. The President may at any time rescind such suspension of said sections, and any provisions thereof which may have been suspended shall thereby be reinstated and again apply to contracts thereafter made for the carriage of goods by sea. Any proclamation of suspension or rescission of any such suspension shall take effect on a date named therein, which date shall be not less than ten days from the issue of the proclamation.

"Any contract for the carriage of goods by sea, subject to the provisions of this chapter [note], effective during any period when sections 1301 to 1308 of this title [sections 1 to 8 of this note], or any part thereof, are suspended, shall be subject to all provisions of law now or hereafter applicable to that part of said sections which may have thus been suspended.

"Sec. 15. Effective date; retroactive effect

"This chapter [this note] shall take effect ninety days after April 16, 1936; but nothing in this chapter [this note] shall apply during a period not to exceed one year following April 16, 1936, to any contract for the carriage of goods by sea, made before April 16, 1936, nor to any bill of lading or similar document of title issued, whether before or after such date in pursuance of any such contract as aforesaid.

"Sec. 16. Short title

"This chapter [this note] may be cited as the 'Carriage of Goods by Sea Act' ".

The Harter Act of 1893

§ 30701.   DEFINITION

In this chapter, the term "carrier" means the owner, manager, charterer, agent, or master of a vessel.

§ 30702.   APPLICATION

(a) In general—Except as otherwise provided, this chapter applies to a carrier engaged in the carriage of goods to or from any port in the United States.

(b) Live animals—Sections 30703 and 30704 of this title do not apply to the carriage of live animals.

§ 30703.   BILLS OF LADING

(a) Issuance—On demand of a shipper, the carrier shall issue a bill of lading or shipping document.

(b) Contents—The bill of lading or shipping document shall include a statement of—

(1) the marks necessary to identify the goods;

(2) the number of packages, or the quantity or weight, and whether it is carrier's or shipper's weight; and

(3) the apparent condition of the goods.

(c) Prima Facie Evidence of Receipt—A bill of lading or shipping document issued under this section is prima facie evidence of receipt of the goods described.

§ 30704.   LOADING, STORAGE, CUSTODY, CARE, AND DELIVERY

A carrier may not assert in a bill of lading or shipping document a provision avoiding its liability for loss or damage arising from negligence or fault in loading, stowage, custody, care, or proper delivery. Any such provision is void.

§ 30705.   SEAWORTHINESS

(a) Prohibition.—A carrier may not insert in a bill of lading or shipping document a provision lessening or avoiding its obligation to exercise due diligence to—

(1) make the vessel seaworthy, and

(2) properly man, equip, and supply the vessel.

(b) Voidness.—A provision described in subsection (a) is void.

§ 30706.   DEFENSES

(a) Due Diligence.—If a carrier has exercised due diligence to make the vessel in all respects seaworthy and to properly man, equip, and supply the vessel, the carrier and the vessel are not liable for loss or damage arising from an error in the navigation and management vessel.

(b) Other Defenses.—A carrier and the vessel are not liable for loss or damage arising from—

(1) dangers of the sea or other navigable waters;

(2) acts of God;

(3) public enemies;

(4) seizure under legal process;

(5) inherent defect, quality, or vice of the goods;

(6) insufficiency of package;

(7) act or omission of the shipper or owner of the goods or their agent; or

(8) saving or attempting to save life or property at sea, including a deviation in rendering such a service.

§ 30707. CRIMINAL PENALTY

(a) In General—A carrier that violates this chapter shall be fined under title 18.

(b) Lien.—The amount of the fine and costs for the violation constitute a lien on the vessel engaged in the carriage. A civil action in rem to enforce the lien may be brought in the district court of the United States for any district in which the vessel is found.

(c) Disposition of Fine.—Half of the fine shall go to the person injured by the violation and half to the United States Government.

CHAPTER 309. SUITS IN ADMIRALTY AGAINST THE UNITED STATES

§ 30901. SHORT TITLE

This chapter may be cited as the "Suits in Admiralty Act".

§ 30902. DEFINITION

In this chapter, the term "federally-owned corporation" means a corporation in which the United States owns all the outstanding capital stock.

§ 30903. WAIVER OF IMMUNITY

(a) In General.—In a case in which, if a vessel were privately owned or operated, or if cargo were privately owned or possessed, or if a private person or property were involved, a civil action in admiralty could be maintained, a civil action in admiralty in personam may be brought against the United States or a federally owned corporation. In a civil action in admiralty brought by the United States or a federally-owned corporation, an admiralty claim in personam may be filed or a setoff claimed against the United States or corporation.

(b) Non-Jury.—A claim against the United States or a federally-owned corporation under this section shall be tried without a jury.

§ 30904. EXCLUSIVE REMEDY

If a remedy is provided by this chapter, it shall be exclusive of any other action arising out of the same subject matter against the officer, employee, or agent of the United States or the federally owned corporation whose act or omission gave rise to the claim.

§ 30905. PERIOD FOR BRINGING ACTION

A civil action under this chapter must be brought within 2 years after the cause of action arose.

§ 30906. VENUE

(a) In General.—A civil action under this chapter shall be brought in the district court of the United States for the district in which—

(1) any plaintiff resides or has its principal place of business; or

(2) the vessel or cargo is found.

(b) Transfer.—On a motion by a party, the court may transfer the action to any other district court of the United States.

§ 30907. PROCEDURE FOR HEARING AND DETERMINATION

(a) In General.—A civil action under this chapter shall proceed and be heard and determined according to the principles of law and the rules of practice applicable in like cases between private parties.

(b) In Rem.—

(1) Requirements.—The action may proceed according to the principles of an action in rem if—

(A) the plaintiff elects in the complaint; and

(B) it appears that an action in rem could have been maintained had the vessel or cargo been privately owned and possessed.

(2) Effect on relief in Personam.—An election under paragraph (1) does not prevent the plaintiff from seeking relief in personam in the same action.

§ 30908. EXEMPTION FROM ARREST OR SEIZURE

The following are not subject to arrest or seizure by judicial process in the United States:

(1) A vessel owned by, possessed by, or operated by or for the United States or a federally-owned corporation.

(2) Cargo owned or possessed by the United States or a federally-owned corporation.

§ 30909. SECURITY

Neither the United States nor a federally-owned corporation may be required to give a bond or admiralty stipulation in a civil action under this chapter.

§ 30910. EXONERATION AND LIMITATION

The United States is entitled to the exemptions from and limitations of liability provided by law to an owner, charterer, operator, or agent of a vessel.

§ 30911. COSTS AND INTEREST

(a) In general.—A judgment against the United States or a federally-owned corporation under this chapter may include costs and interest at the rate of 4 percent per year until satisfied. Interest shall run as ordered by the court, except that interest is not allowable for the period before the action is filed.

(b) Contract providing for interest.—Notwithstanding subsection (a), if the claim is based on a contract providing for interest, interest may be awarded at the rate and for the period provided in the contract.

§ 30912. ARBITRATION, COMPROMISE, OR SETTLEMENT

The Secretary of a department of the United States Government, or the board of trustees of a federally-owned corporation, may arbitrate, compromise, or settle a claim under this chapter.

§ 30913. PAYMENT OF JUDGMENT OR SETTLEMENT

(a) In general.—The proper accounting officer of the United States shall pay a final judgment, arbitration award, or settlement under this chapter on presentation of an authenticated copy.

(b) Source of payment.—Payment shall be made from an appropriation or fund available specifically for the purpose. If no appropriation or fund is specifically available, there is hereby appropriated, out of money in the Treasury not otherwise appropriated, an amount sufficient to pay the judgment, award, or settlement.

§ 30914. RELEASE OF PRIVATELY OWNED VESSEL AFTER ARREST OR ATTACHMENT

If a privately owned vessel not in the possession of the United States or a federally-owned corporation is arrested or attached in a civil action arising or alleged to have arisen from prior ownership, possession, or operation by the United States or corporation, the vessel shall be released without bond or stipulation on a statement by the United States, through the Attorney General or other authorized law officer, that the United States is interested in the action, desires release of the vessel, and assumes liability for the satisfaction of any judgment obtained by the plaintiff. After the vessel is released, the action shall proceed against the United States in accordance with this chapter.

§ 30915. SEIZURES AND OTHER PROCEEDINGS IN FOREIGN JURISDICTIONS

(a) In general.—If a vessel or cargo described in section 30908 or 30914 of this title is arrested, attached, or otherwise seized by judicial process in a foreign country, or if an action is brought in a court of a foreign country against the master of such a vessel for a claim arising from the ownership, possession, or operation of the vessel, or the ownership, possession, or carriage of such cargo, the Secretary of State, on request of the Attorney General or another officer authorized by the Attorney General, may direct the United States consul residing at or nearest the place at which the action was brought—

(1) to claim the vessel or cargo as immune from arrest, attachment, or other seizure, and to execute an agreement, stipulation, bond, or undertaking, for the United States or federally-owned corporation, for the release of the vessel or cargo and the prosecution of any appeal; or

(2) if an action has been brought against the master of such a vessel, to enter the appearance of the United States or corporation and to pledge the credit of the United States or corporation to the payment of any judgment and costs in the action.

(b) Arranging bond or stipulation.—The Attorney General may—

(1) arrange with a bank, surety company, or other person, whether in the United States or a foreign country, to execute a bond or stipulation; and

(2) pledge the credit of the United States to secure the bond or stipulation.

(c) Payment of judgment.—The appropriate accounting officer of the United States or corporation may pay a judgment in an action described in subsection (a) on presentation of a copy of the judgment if certified by the clerk of the court and authenticated by—

(1) the certificate and seal of the United States consul claiming the vessel or cargo, or by the consul's successor; and

(2) the certificate of the Secretary as to the official capacity of the consul.

(d) Right to claim immunity not affected.—This section does not affect the right of the United States to claim immunity of a vessel or cargo from foreign jurisdiction.

§ 30916. RECOVERY BY THE UNITED STATES FOR SALVAGE SERVICES

(a) Civil action.—The United States, and the crew of a merchant vessel owned or operated by the United States, or a federally owned corporation, may bring a civil action to recover for salvage services provided by the vessel and crew.

(b) Deposit of amounts recovered.—Any amount recovered under this section by the United States for its own benefit, and not for the benefit of the crew, shall be deposited in the Treasury to the credit of the department of the United States Government, or the corporation, having control of the possession or operation of the vessel.

§ 30917. DISPOSITION OF AMOUNTS RECOVERED BY THE UNITED STATES

Amounts recovered in a civil action brought by the United States on a claim arising from the ownership, possession, or operation of a merchant vessel, or the ownership, possession, or carriage of cargo, shall be deposited in the Treasury to the credit of the department of the United States Government, or the federally owned corporation, having control of the vessel or cargo, for reimbursement of the appropriation, insurance fund, or other fund from which the compensation for which the judgment was recovered was or will be paid.

§ 30918.   REPORTS

The Secretary of each department of the United States Government, and the board of trustees of each federally-owned corporation, shall report to Congress at each session thereof all arbitration awards and settlements agreed to under this chapter since the previous session, for which the time to appeal has expired or been waived.

CHAPTER 311.   SUITS INVOLVING PUBLIC VESSELS

§ 31101.   SHORT TITLE

This chapter may be cited as the "Public Vessels Act".

§ 31102.   WAIVER OF IMMUNITY

(a) In general.—A civil action in personam in admiralty may be brought, or an impleader filed, against the United States for—

(1) damages caused by a public vessel of the United States; or

(2) compensation for towage and salvage services, including contract salvage, rendered to a public vessel of the United States.

(b) Counterclaim or setoff.—If the United States brings a civil action in admiralty for damages caused by a privately owned vessel, the owner of the vessel, or the successor in interest, may file a counterclaim in personam, or claim a setoff, against the United States for damages arising out of the same subject matter.

§ 31103.   APPLICABLE PROCEDURE

A civil action under this chapter is subject to the provisions of chapter 309 of this title except to the extent inconsistent with this chapter.

§ 31104.   VENUE

(a) In general.—A civil action under this chapter shall be brought in the district court of the United States for the district in which the vessel or cargo is found within the United States.

(b) Vessel or cargo outside territorial waters.—If the vessel or cargo is outside the territorial waters of the United States—

(1) the action shall be brought in the district court of the United States for any district in which any plaintiff resides or has an office for the transaction of business; or Public Vessels Act.

(2) if no plaintiff resides or has an office for the transaction of business in the United States, the action may be brought in the district court of the United States for any district.

§ 31105.   SECURITY WHEN COUNTERCLAIM FILED

If a counterclaim is filed for a cause of action for which the original action is filed under this chapter, the respondent to the counterclaim shall give security in the usual amount and form to respond to the counterclaim, unless the court for cause shown orders otherwise. The proceedings in the original action shall be stayed until the security is given.

§ 31106.   EXONERATION AND LIMITATION

The United States is entitled to the exemptions from and limitations of liability provided by law to an owner, charterer, operator, or agent of a vessel.

§ 31107.   INTEREST

A judgment in a civil action under this chapter may not include interest for the period before the judgment is issued unless the claim is based on a contract providing for interest.

§ 31108.   ARBITRATION, COMPROMISE, OR SETTLEMENT

The Attorney General may arbitrate, compromise, or settle a claim under this chapter if a civil action based on the claim has been commenced.

§ 31109.   PAYMENT OF JUDGMENT OR SETTLEMENT

The proper accounting officer of the United States shall pay a final judgment, arbitration award, or settlement under this chapter on presentation of an authenticated copy. Payment shall be made from any money in the Treasury appropriated for the purpose.

§ 31110.   SUBPOENAS TO OFFICERS OR MEMBERS OF CREW

An officer or member of the crew of a public vessel may not be subpoenaed in a civil action under this chapter without the consent of—

> (1) the Secretary of the department or the head of the independent establishment having control of the vessel at the time the cause of action arose; or

> (2) the master or commanding officer of the vessel at the time the subpoena is issued.

§ 31111.   CLAIMS BY NATIONALS OF FOREIGN COUNTRIES

A national of a foreign country may not maintain a civil action under this chapter unless it appears to the satisfaction of the court in which the action is brought that the government of that country, in similar circumstances, allows nationals of the United States to sue in its courts.

§ 31112.   LIEN NOT RECOGNIZED OR CREATED

This chapter shall not be construed as recognizing the existence of or as creating a lien against a public vessel of the United States.

§ 31113.   REPORTS

The Attorney General shall report to Congress at each session thereof all claims settled under this chapter.

CHAPTER 313.   COMMERCIAL INSTRUMENTS
AND MARITIME LIENS

SUBCHAPTER I.   GENERAL

§ 31301.   DEFINITIONS

In this chapter—

(1) "acknowledge" means making—

(A) an acknowledgment or notarization before a notary public or other official authorized by a law of the United States or a State to take acknowledgments of deeds; or

(B) a certificate issued under the Hague Convention Abolishing the Requirement of Legislation for Foreign Public Documents, 1961;

(2) "district court" means—

(A) a district court of the United States (as defined in section 451 of title 28);

(B) the District Court of Guam;

(C) the District Court of the Virgin Islands;

(D) the District Court for the Northern Mariana Islands;

(E) the High Court of American Samoa; and

(F) any other court of original jurisdiction of a territory or possession of the United States;

(3) "mortgagee" means—

(A) a person to whom property is mortgaged; or

(B) when a mortgage on a vessel involves a trust, the trustee that is designated in the trust agreement;

(4) "necessaries" includes repairs, supplies, towage, and the use of a dry dock or marine railway;

(5) "preferred maritime lien" means a maritime lien on a vessel—

(A) arising before a preferred mortgage was filed under section 31321 of this title;

(B) for damage arising out of maritime tort;

(C) for wages of a stevedore when employed directly by a person listed in section 31341 of this title;

(D) for wages of the crew of the vessel;

(E) for general average; or

(F) for salvage, including contract salvage; and

(6) "preferred mortgage"—

(A) means a mortgage that is a preferred mortgage under section 31322 of this title; and

(B) also means in sections 31325 and 31326 of this title, a mortgage, hypothecation, or similar charge that is established as a security on a foreign vessel if the mortgage, hypothecation, or similar charge was executed under the laws of the foreign country under whose laws the ownership of the vessel is documented and has been registered under those laws in a public register at the port of registry of the vessel or at a central office.

(7) "Secretary" means the Secretary of the Department of Homeland Security, unless otherwise noted.

§ 31302. AVAILABILITY OF INSTRUMENTS, COPIES, AND INFORMATION

The Secretary shall—

(1) make any instrument filed or recorded with the Secretary under this chapter available for public inspection;

(2) on request, provide a copy, including a certified copy, of any instrument made available for public inspection under this chapter; and

(3) on request, provide a certificate containing information included in an instrument filed or recorded under this chapter.

§ 31303. CERTAIN CIVIL ACTIONS NOT AUTHORIZED

If a mortgage covers a vessel and additional property that is not a vessel, this chapter does not authorize a civil action in rem to enforce the rights of the mortgagee under the mortgage against the additional property.

§ 31304. LIABILITY FOR NONCOMPLIANCE

(a) If a person makes a contract secured by, or on the credit of, a vessel covered by a mortgage filed or recorded under this chapter and sustains a monetary loss because the mortgagor or the master or other individual in charge of the vessel does not comply with a requirement imposed on the mortgagor, master, or individual under this chapter, the mortgagor is liable for the loss.

(b) A civil action may be brought to recover for losses referred to in subsection (a) of this section. The district courts have original jurisdiction of the action, regardless of the amount in controversy or the citizenship of the parties. If the plaintiff prevails, the court shall award costs and attorney fees to the plaintiff.

§ 31305. WAIVER OF LIEN RIGHTS

This chapter does not prevent a mortgagee or other lien holder from waiving or subordinating at any time by agreement or otherwise the lien holder's right to a lien, the priority or, if a preferred mortgage lien, the preferred status of the lien.

§ 31306.   DECLARATION OF CITIZENSHIP

(a) Except as provided by the Secretary of Transportation, when an instrument transferring an interest in a vessel is presented to the Secretary for filing or recording, the transferee shall file with the instrument a declaration, in the form the Secretary may prescribe by regulation, stating information about citizenship and other information the Secretary may require to show the transaction involved does not violate section 56102 or 56103 of this title.

(b) A declaration under this section filed by a corporation must be signed by its president, secretary, treasurer, or other official authorized by the corporation to execute the declaration.

(c) Except as provided by the Secretary, an instrument transferring an interest in a vessel is not valid against any person until the declaration required by this section has been filed.

(d) A person knowingly making a false statement of a material fact in a declaration filed under this section shall be fined under title 18, imprisoned for not more than 5 years, or both.

§ 31307.   STATE STATUTES SUPERSEDED

This chapter supersedes any State statute conferring a lien on a vessel to the extent the statute establishes a claim to be enforced by a civil action in rem against the vessel for necessaries.

§ 31308.   SECRETARY OF COMMERCE OF TRANSPORTATION AS MORTGAGEE

When the Secretary of Commerce or Transportation is a mortgagee under this chapter, the Secretary may foreclose on a lien arising from a right established under a mortgage under chapter 537 of this title, subject to section 362(b) of title 11.

§ 31309.   GENERAL CIVIL PENALTY

Except as otherwise provided in this chapter, a person violating this chapter or a regulation prescribed under this chapter is liable to the United States Government for a civil penalty of not more than $10,000.

SUBCHAPTER II. COMMERCIAL INSTRUMENTS

§ 31321.   FILING, RECORDING, AND DISCHARGE

(a)(1) A bill of sale, conveyance, mortgage, assignment, or related instrument, whenever made, that includes any part of a documented vessel or a vessel for which an application for documentation is filed, must be filed with the Secretary of Transportation to be valid, to the extent the vessel is involved, against any person except—

(A) the grantor, mortgagor, or assignor;

(B) the heir or devisee of the grantor, mortgagor, or assignor; and

(C) a person having actual notice of the sale, conveyance, mortgage, assignment, or related instrument.

(2) Each bill of sale, conveyance, mortgage, assignment, or related instrument that is filed in substantial compliance with this section is valid against any person from the time it is filed with the Secretary.

(3) The parties to an instrument or an application for documentation shall use diligence to ensure that the parts of the instrument or application for which they are responsible are in substantial compliance with the filing and documentation requirements.

(4) A bill of sale, conveyance, mortgage, assignment, or related instrument may be filed electronically under regulations prescribed by the Secretary.

(b) To be filed, a bill of sale, conveyance, mortgage, assignment, or related instrument must—

(1) identify the vessel;

(2) state the name and address of each party to the instrument;

(3) state, if a mortgage, the amount of the direct or contingent obligations (in one or more units of account as agreed to by the parties) that is or may become secured by the mortgage, excluding interest, expenses, and fees;

(4) state the interest of the grantor, mortgagor, or assignor in the vessel;

(5) state the interest sold, conveyed, mortgaged, or assigned; and

(6) be signed and acknowledged.

(c) If a bill of sale, conveyance, mortgage, assignment, or related document is filed that involves a vessel for which an application for documentation is filed, and the Secretary decides that the vessel cannot be documented by an applicant—

(1) the Secretary shall send notice of the Secretary's decision, including reasons for the decision, to each interested party to the instrument filed for recording; and

(2) 90 days after sending the notice as provided under clause (1) of this subsection, the Secretary—

(A) may terminate the filing; and

(B) may return the instrument filed without recording it under subsection (e) of this section.

(d) A person may withdraw an application for documentation of a vessel for which a mortgage has been filed under this section only if the mortgagee consents.

(e) The Secretary shall—

(1) record the bills of sale, conveyances, mortgages, assignments, and related instruments of a documented vessel complying with subsection (b) of this section in the order they are filed; and

(2) maintain appropriate indexes, for use by the public, of instruments filed or recorded, or both.

(f) On full and final discharge of the indebtedness under a mortgage recorded under subsection (e)(1) of this section, a mortgagee, on request of the Secretary or mortgagor, shall provide the Secretary with an acknowledged certificate of discharge of the indebtedness in a form prescribed by the Secretary. The Secretary shall record the certificate.

(g) The mortgage or related instrument of a vessel covered by a preferred mortgage under section 31322(d) of this title, that is later filed under this section at the time an application for documentation is filed, is valid under this section from the time the mortgage or instrument representing financing became a preferred mortgage under section 31322(d).

(h) On full and final discharge of the indebtedness under a mortgage deemed to be a preferred mortgage under section 31322(d) of this title, a mortgagee, on request of the Secretary, a State, or mortgagor, shall provide the Secretary or the State, as appropriate, with an acknowledged certificate of discharge of the indebtedness in a form prescribed by the Secretary or the State, as applicable. If filed with the Secretary, the Secretary shall enter that information in the vessel identification system under chapter 125 of this title.

§ 31322.   PREFERRED MORTGAGES

(a) A preferred mortgage is a mortgage, whenever made, that—

(1) includes the whole of the vessel;

(2) is filed in substantial compliance with section 31321 of this title;

(3)(A)   covers a documented vessel; or

(B) covers a vessel for which an application for documentation is filed that is in substantial compliance with the requirements of chapter 121 of this title and the regulations prescribed under that chapter; and

(4) with respect to a vessel with a fishery endorsement that is 100 feet or greater in registered length, has as the mortgagee—

     (A) a person eligible to own a vessel with a fishery endorsement under section 12113(c) of this title;

     (B) State or federally chartered financial institution that is insured by the Federal Deposit Insurance Corporation;

     (C) a farm credit lender established under title 12, chapter 23 of the United States Code;

     (D) a commercial fishing and agriculture bank established pursuant to State law;

     (E) a commercial lender organized under the laws of the United States or of a State and eligible to own a vessel for purposes of documentation under section 12103 of this title; or

     (F) a mortgage trustee under subsection (f) of this section.

  (b) Any indebtedness secured by a preferred mortgage that is filed or recorded under this chapter, or that is subject to a mortgage, security agreement, or instruments granting a security interest that is deemed to be a preferred mortgage under subsection (d) of this section, may have any rate of interest to which the parties agree.

  (c)(1) If a preferred mortgage includes more than one vessel or property that is not a vessel, the mortgage may provide for the separate discharge of each vessel and all property not a vessel by the payment of a part of the mortgage indebtedness.

     (2) If a vessel covered by a preferred mortgage that includes more than one vessel or property that is not a vessel is to be sold on the order of a district court in a civil action in rem, and the mortgage does not provide for separate discharge as provided under paragraph (1) of this subsection—

     (A) the mortgage constitutes a lien on that vessel in the full amount of the outstanding mortgage indebtedness; and

     (B) an allocation of mortgage indebtedness for purposes of separate discharge may not be made among the vessel and other property covered by the mortgage.

  (d)(1) A mortgage, security agreement, or instrument granting a security interest perfected under State law covering the whole of a vessel titled in a State is deemed to be a preferred mortgage if—

     (A) the Secretary certifies that the State titling system complies with the Secretary's guidelines for a titling system under section 13107(b)(8) of this title; and

     (B) information on the vessel covered by the mortgage, security agreement, or instrument is made available to the Secretary under chapter 125 of this title.

     (2) This subsection applies to mortgages, security agreements, or instruments covering vessels titled in a State after—

(A) the Secretary's certification under paragraph (1)(A) of this subsection; and

(B) the State begins making information available to the Secretary under chapter 125 of this title.

(3) A preferred mortgage under this subsection continues be a preferred mortgage even if the vessel is no longer titled in the State where the mortgage, security agreement, or instrument granting a security interest became a preferred mortgage under this subsection.

(e) If a vessel is already covered by a preferred mortgage when application for titling or documentation is filed—

(1) the status of the preferred mortgage covering the vessel to be titled in the State is determined by the law of the jurisdiction where the vessel is currently titled or documented; and

(2) the status of the preferred mortgage covering the vessel to be documented under chapter 121 is determined by subsection (a) of this section.

(f)(1) A mortgage trustee may hold in trust, for an individual or entity, an instrument or evidence of indebtedness, secured by a mortgage of the vessel to the mortgage trustee, provided that the mortgage trustee—

(A) is eligible to be a preferred mortgagee under subsection (a)(4), subparagraphs (A)–(E) of this section;

(B) is organized as a corporation, and is doing business, under the laws of the United States or of a State;

(C) is authorized under those laws to exercise corporate trust powers;

(D) is subject to supervision or examination by an official of the United States Government or a State;

(E) has a combined capital and surplus (as stated in its most recent published report of condition) of at least $3,000,000; and

(F) meets any other requirements prescribed by the Secretary.

(2) If the beneficiary under the trust arrangement is not a commercial lender, a lender syndicate or eligible to be a preferred mortgagee under subsection (a)(4), subparagraphs (A)–(E) of this section, the Secretary must determine that the issuance, assignment, transfer, or trust arrangement does not result in an impermissible transfer of control of the vessel to a person not eligible to own a vessel with a fishery endorsement under section 12113(c) of this title.

(3) A vessel with a fishery endorsement may be operated by a mortgage trustee only with the approval of the Secretary.

(4) A right under a mortgage of a vessel with a fishery endorsement may be issued, assigned, or transferred to a person not eligible to be a mortgagee of that vessel under this section only with the approval of the Secretary.

(5) The issuance, assignment, or transfer of an instrument or evidence of indebtedness contrary to this subsection is voidable by the Secretary.

(g) For purposes of this section a "commercial lender" means an entity primarily engaged in the business of lending and other financing transactions with a loan portfolio in excess of $100,000,000, of which not more than 50 per centum in dollar amount consists of loans to borrowers in the commercial fishing industry, as certified to the Secretary by such lender.

(h) For purposes of this section a "lender syndicate" means an arrangement established for the combined extension of credit of not less than $20,000,000 made up of four or more entities that each have a beneficial interest, held through an agent, under a trust arrangement established pursuant to subsection (f), no one of which may exercise powers thereunder without the concurrence of at least one other unaffiliated beneficiary.

§ 31323. DISCLOSING AND INCURRING OBLIGATIONS BEFORE EXECUTING PREFERRED MORTGAGES

(a) On request of the mortgagee and before executing a preferred mortgage, the mortgagor shall disclose in writing to the mortgagee the existence of any obligation known to the mortgagor on the vessel to be mortgaged.

(b) After executing a preferred mortgage and before the mortgagee has had a reasonable time to file the mortgage, the mortgagor may not incur, without the consent of the mortgagee, any contractual obligation establishing a lien on the vessel except a lien for—

(1) wages of a stevedore when employed directly by a person listed in section 31341 of this title;

(2) wages for the crew of the vessel;

(3) general average; or

(4) salvage, including contract salvage.

(c) On conviction of a mortgagor under section 31330(a)(1)(A) or (B) of this title for violating this section, the mortgage indebtedness, at the option of the mortgagee, is payable immediately.

§ 31324. RETENTION AND EXAMINATION OF MORTGAGES OF VESSELS COVERED BY PREFERRED MORTGAGES

(a) On request, the owner, master, or individual in charge of a vessel covered by a preferred mortgage shall permit a person to examine the mortgage if the person has business with the vessel that may give rise to a maritime lien or the sale, conveyance, mortgage, or assignment of a mortgage of the vessel.

(b) A mortgagor of a preferred mortgage covering a self-propelled vessel shall use diligence in keeping a certified copy of the mortgage on the vessel.

§ 31325.   PREFERRED MORTGAGE LIENS AND ENFORCEMENT

(a) A preferred mortgage is a lien on the mortgaged vessel in the amount of the outstanding mortgage indebtedness secured by the vessel.

(b) On default of any term of the preferred mortgage, the mortgagee may—

(1) enforce the preferred mortgage lien in a civil action in rem for a documented vessel, a vessel to be documented under chapter 121 of this title, a vessel titled in a State, or a foreign vessel; and

(2) enforce a claim for the outstanding indebtedness secured by the mortgaged vessel in—

(A) a civil action in personam in admiralty against the mortgagor, maker, comaker, or guarantor for the amount of the outstanding indebtedness or any deficiency in full payment of that indebtedness; and

(B) a civil action against the mortgagor, maker, comaker, or guarantor for the amount of the outstanding indebtedness or any deficiency in full payment of that indebtedness; and

(3) enforce the preferred mortgage lien or a claim for the outstanding indebtedness secured by the mortgaged vessel, or by exercising any other remedy (including an extrajudicial remedy) against a documented vessel, a vessel for which an application for documentation is filed under chapter 121 of this title, a vessel titled in a State, a foreign vessel, or a mortgagor, maker, co-maker or guarantor for the amount of the outstanding indebtedness of any deficiency in full payment of that indebtedness, if—

(A) the remedy is allowed under applicable law; and

(B) the exercise of the remedy will not result in a violation of Section 56101 or 56102 of this title.

(c) The district courts have original jurisdiction of a civil action brought under subsection (b)(1) or (2) of this section. However, for a documented vessel, a vessel to be documented under chapter 121 of this title, a vessel titled in a State, or a foreign vessel, this jurisdiction is exclusive of the courts of the States for a civil action brought under subsection (b)(1) of this section.

(d)(1) Actual notice of a civil action brought under subsection (b)(1) of this section, or to enforce a maritime lien, must be given in the manner directed by the court to—

(A) the master or individual in charge of the vessel;

(B) any person that recorded under section 31343(a) or (d) of this title an unexpired notice of a claim of an undischarged lien on the vessel; and

(C) a mortgagee of a mortgage filed or recorded under section 31321 of this title that is an undischarged mortgage on the vessel.

(2) Notice under paragraph (1) of this subsection is not required if, after search satisfactory to the court, the person entitled to the notice has not been found in the United States.

(3) Failure to give notice required by this subsection does not affect the jurisdiction of the court in which the civil action is brought. However, unless notice is not required under paragraph (2) of this subsection, the party required to give notice is liable to the person not notified for damages in the amount of that person's interest in the vessel terminated by the action brought under subsection (b)(1) of this section. A civil action may be brought to recover the amount of the terminated interest. The district courts have original jurisdiction of the action, regardless of the amount in controversy or the citizenship of the parties. If the plaintiff prevails, the court may award costs and attorney fees to the plaintiff.

(e) In a civil action brought under subsection (b)(1) of this section—

(1) the court may appoint a receiver and authorize the receiver to operate the mortgaged vessel and shall retain in rem jurisdiction over the vessel even if the receiver operates the vessel outside the district in which the court is located; and

(2) when directed by the court, a United States marshal may take possession of a mortgaged vessel even if the vessel is in the possession or under the control of a person claiming a possessory common law lien.

(f)(1) Before title to the documented vessel or vessel for which application for documentation is filed under chapter 121 is transferred by an extrajudicial remedy, the person exercising the remedy shall give notice of the proposed transfer to the Secretary, to the mortgagee of any mortgage on the vessel in substantial compliance with § 31321 of this title before notice of the proposed transfer is given to the Secretary, and to any person that recorded an unexpired notice of a claim of an undischarged lien on the vessel under section 31343(a) or (d) of this title before notice of the proposed transfer is given to the Secretary.

(2) Failure to give notice as required by this subsection shall not affect the transfer of title to a vessel. However, the rights of any holder of a maritime lien or a preferred mortgage on the vessel shall not be affected by transfer of title by an extrajudicial remedy exercised under this section, regardless whether notice is required by this subsection or not.

(3) The Secretary shall prescribe regulations establishing the time and manner of providing notice under this subsection.

§ 31326.   COURT SALES TO ENFORCE PREFERRED MORTGAGE LIENS AND MARITIME LIENS AND PRIORITY OF CLAIMS

(a) When a vessel is sold by order of a district court in a civil action in rem brought to enforce a preferred mortgage lien or a maritime lien, any claim in the vessel existing on the date of sale is terminated, including a possessory common law lien of which a person is deprived under section 31325(e)(2) of this title, and the vessel is sold free of all those claims.

(b) Each of the claims terminated under subsection (a) of this section attaches, in the same amount and in accordance with their priorities to the proceeds of the sale, except that—

(1) the preferred mortgage lien, including a preferred mortgage lien on a foreign vessel whose mortgage has been guaranteed under chapter 537 of this title et seq., has priority over all claims against the vessel (except for expenses and fees allowed by the court, costs imposed by the court, and preferred maritime liens); and

(2) for a foreign vessel whose mortgage has not been guaranteed under chapter 537 of this title, the preferred mortgage lien is subordinate to a maritime lien for necessaries provided in the United States.

§ 31327.   FORFEITURE OF MORTGAGEE INTEREST

The interest of a mortgagee in a documented vessel or a vessel covered by a preferred mortgage under section 31322(d) of this title may be terminated by a forfeiture of the vessel for a violation of a law of the United States only if the mortgagee authorized, consented, or conspired to do the act, failure, or omission that is the basis of the violation.

§ 31329.   COURT SALES OF DOCUMENTED VESSELS

(a) A documented vessel may be sold by order of a district court only to—

(1) a person eligible to own a documented vessel under section 12102 of this title; or

(2) a mortgagee of that vessel.

(b) When a vessel is sold to a mortgagee not eligible to own a documented vessel—

(1) the vessel must be held by the mortgagee for resale;

(2) the vessel held by the mortgagee is subject to chapter 563 of this title;

(3) the sale of the vessel to the mortgagee is not a sale to a person not a citizen of the United States under Section 12132 of this title.

(c) Unless waived by the Secretary of Transportation, a person purchasing a vessel by court order under subsection (a)(1) of this section or from a mortgagee under subsection (a)(2) of this section must document the vessel under chapter 121 of this title.

(d) The vessel may be operated by the mortgagee not eligible to own a documented vessel only with the approval of the Secretary of Transportation.

(e) A sale of a vessel contrary to this section is void.

(f) This section does not apply to a documented vessel that has been operated only for pleasure.

§ 31330. PENALTIES

(a)(1) A mortgagor shall be fined under title 18, imprisoned for not more than 2 years, or both, if the mortgagor—

(A) with intent to defraud, does not disclose an obligation on a vessel as required by section 31323(a) of this title;

(B) with intent to defraud, incurs a contractual obligation in violation of section 31323(b) of this title; or

(C) with intent to hinder or defraud an existing or future creditor of the mortgagor or a lienor of the vessel, files a mortgage with the Secretary.

(2) A mortgagor is liable to the United States Government for a civil penalty of not more than $10,000 if the mortgagor—

(A) does not disclose an obligation on a vessel as required by section 31323(a) of this title;

(B) incurs a contractual obligation in violation of section 31323(b) of this title; or

(C) files with the Secretary a mortgage made not in good faith.

(b)(1) A person that knowingly violates section 31329 of this title shall be fined under title 18, imprisoned for not more than 3 years, or both.

(2) A person violating section 31329 of this title is liable to the Government for a civil penalty of not more than $25,000.

(3) A vessel involved in a violation under section 31329 of this title and its equipment may be seized by, and forfeited to, the Government.

(c) If a person not an individual violates this section, the president or chief executive of the person also is subject to any penalty provided under this section.

SUBCHAPTER III. MARITIME LIENS

§ 31341. PERSONS PRESUMED TO HAVE AUTHORITY TO PROCURE NECESSARIES

(a) The following persons are presumed to have authority to procure necessaries for a vessel:

(1) the owner;

(2) the master;

(3) a person entrusted with the management of the vessel at the port of supply; or

(4) an officer or agent appointed by—

(A) the owner;

(B) a charterer;

(C) an owner pro hac vice; or

(D) an agreed buyer in possession of the vessel.

(b) A person tortiously or unlawfully in possession or charge of a vessel has no authority to procure necessaries for the vessel.

§ 31342. ESTABLISHING MARITIME LIENS

(a) Except as provided in subsection (b) of this section, a person providing necessaries to a vessel on the order of the owner or a person authorized by the owner—

(1) has a maritime lien on the vessel;

(2) may bring a civil action in rem to enforce the lien; and

(3) is not required to allege or prove in the action that credit was given to the vessel.

(b) This section does not apply to a public vessel.

§ 31343. RECORDING AND DISCHARGING NOTICES OF CLAIM OF MARITIME LIEN

(a) Except as provided under subsection (d) of this section, a person claiming a lien on a vessel covered by a preferred mortgage filed or recorded under this chapter may record with the Secretary a notice of that person's lien claim on the vessel. To be recordable, the notice must—

(1) state the nature of the lien;

(2) state the date the lien was established;

(3) state the amount of the lien;

(4) state the name and address of the person; and

(5) be signed and acknowledged.

(b)(1) The Secretary shall record a notice complying with subsection (a) of this section if, when the notice is presented to the

Secretary for recording, the person having the claim files with the notice a declaration stating the following:

    (A) The information in the notice is true and correct to the best of the knowledge, information, and belief of the individual who signed it.

    (B) A copy of the notice, as presented for recordation, has been sent to each of the following:

        (i) The owner of the vessel.

        (ii) Each person that recorded under subsection (a) of this section an unexpired notice of a claim of an undischarged lien on the vessel.

        (iii) The mortgagee of each mortgage filed or recorded under section 31321 of this title that is an undischarged mortgage on the vessel.

  (2) A declaration under this subsection filed by a person that is not an individual must be signed by the president, member, partner, trustee, or other individual authorized to execute the declaration on behalf of the person.

(c)(1) On full and final discharge of the indebtedness that is the basis for a notice of claim of lien recorded under subsection (b) of this section, the person having the claim shall provide the Secretary with an acknowledged certificate of discharge of the indebtedness. The Secretary shall record the certificate.

  (2) The district courts of the United States shall have jurisdiction over a civil action in Admiralty to declare that a vessel is not subject to a lien claimed under subsection (b) of this section, or that the vessel is not subject to the notice of claim of lien, or both, regardless of the amount in controversy or the citizenship of the parties. Venue in such an action shall be in the district where the vessel is found or where the claimant resides or where the notice of claim of lien is recorded. The court may award costs and attorneys fees to the prevailing party, unless the court finds that the position of the other party was substantially justified or other circumstances make an award of costs and attorneys fees unjust. The Secretary shall record any such declaratory order.

(d) A person claiming a lien on a vessel covered by a preferred mortgage under section 31322(d) of this title must record and discharge the lien as provided by the law of the State in which the vessel is titled.

(e) A notice of claim of lien recorded under subsection (b) of this section shall expire 3 years after the date the lien was established, as such date is stated in the notice under subsection (a) of this section.

(f) This section does not alter in any respect the law pertaining to the establishment of a maritime lien, the remedy provided by such a lien, or the defenses thereto, including any defense under the doctrine of laches.

SUBTITLE VII

MISCELLANEOUS

CHAPTER 801.   WRECKS AND SALVAGE

§ 80107.   SALVORS OF LIFE TO SHARE IN REMUNERATION

(a) Entitlement of Salvors.—A salvor of human life, who gave aid following an accident giving rise to salvage, is entitled to a fair share of the payment awarded to the salvor for salvaging the vessel or other property or preventing or minimizing damage to the environment.

(b) Common Ownership of Vessels.—The right to remuneration for aid or salvage services is not affected by common ownership of the vessels giving and receiving the aid or salvage services.

(c) Time Limit on Bringing Actions.—A civil action to recover remuneration for giving aid or salvage services must be brought within 2 years after the date the aid or salvage services were given, unless the court in which the action is brought is satisfied that during that 2-year period there had not been a reasonable opportunity to seize the aided or salvaged vessel within the jurisdiction of the court or within the territorial waters of the country of the plaintiff's residence or principal place of business.

(d) Nonapplication.—This section does not apply to a vessel of war or a vessel owned by the United States Government appropriated only to a public service.

III. INTERNATIONAL AGREEMENTS

A. CARRIAGE OF GOODS

INTERNATIONAL CONVENTION FOR THE UNIFICATION OF CERTAIN RULES OF LAW RELATING TO BILLS OF LADING

("Hague Rules")

Brussels, 25 August 1924

Article 1

In this Convention the following words are employed with the meanings set out below:

(a) "Carrier" includes the owner or the charterer who enters into a contract of carriage with a shipper.

(b) "Contract of carriage" applies only to contracts of carriage covered by a bill of lading or any similar document of title, in so far as such document relates to the carriage of goods by sea, including any bill of lading or any similar document as aforesaid issued under or pursuant to a charter party from the moment at which such bill of lading or similar document of title regulates the relations between a carrier and a holder of the same.

(c) "Goods" includes goods, wares, merchandise and articles of every kind whatsoever except live animals and cargo which by the contract of carriage in stated as being carried on deck and is so carried.

(d) "Ship" means any vessel used for the carriage of goods by sea.

(e) "Carriage of goods" covers the period from the time when the goods are loaded on to the time they are discharged from the ship.

Article 2

Subject to the provisions of Article 6, under every contract of carriage of goods by sea the carrier, in relation to the loading, handling, stowage, carriage, custody, care and discharge of such goods, shall be subject to the responsibilities and liabilities, and entitled to the rights and immunities hereinafter set forth.

Article 3

1. The carrier shall be bound before and at the beginning of the voyage to exercise due diligence to:

(a) Make the ship seaworthy.

(b) Properly man, equip and supply the ship.

(c) Make the holds, refrigerating and cool chambers, and all other parts of the ship in which goods are carried, fit and safe for their reception, carriage and preservation.

2. Subject to the provisions of Article 4, the carrier shall properly and carefully load, handle, stow, carry, keep, care for, and discharge the goods carried.

3. After receiving the goods into his charge the carrier or the master or agent of the carrier shall, on demand of the shipper, issue to the shipper a bill of lading showing among other things:

(a) The leading marks necessary for identification of the goods as the same are furnished in writing by the shipper before the loading of such goods starts, provided such marks are stamped or otherwise shown clearly upon the goods if uncovered, or on the cases or coverings in which such goods are contained, in such a manner as should ordinarily remain legible until the end of the voyage.

(b) Either the number of packages or pieces, or the quantity, or weight, as the case may be, as furnished in writing by the shipper.

(c) The apparent order and condition of the goods.

Provided that no carrier, master or agent of the carrier shall be bound to state or show in the bill of lading any marks, number, quantity, or weight which he has reasonable ground for suspecting not accurately to represent the goods actually received, or which he has had no reasonable means of checking.

4. Such a bill of lading shall be *prima facie* evidence of the receipt by the carrier of the goods as therein described in accordance with paragraph 3(a), (b) and (c).

5. The shipper shall be deemed to have guaranteed to the carrier the accuracy at the time of shipment of the marks, number, quantity and weight, as furnished by him, and the shipper shall indemnity the carrier against all loss, damages and expenses arising or resulting from inaccuracies in such particulars. The right of the carrier to such indemnity shall in no way limit his responsibility and liability under the contract of carriage to any person other than the shipper.

6. Unless notice of loss or damage and the general nature of such loss or damage be given in writing to the carrier or his agent at the port of discharge before or at the time of the removal of the goods into the custody of the person entitled to delivery thereof under the contract of carriage, or, if the loss or damage be not apparent, within three days, such removal shall be *prima facie* evidence of the delivery by the carrier of the goods as described in the bill of lading.

If the loss or damage is not apparent, the notice must be given within three days of the delivery of the goods.

The notice in writing need not be given if the state of the goods has, at the time of their receipt, been the subject of joint survey or inspection.

In any event the carrier and the ship shall be discharged from all liability in respect of loss or damage unless suit is brought within one year after delivery of the goods or the date when the goods should have been delivered.

In the case of any actual or apprehended loss or damage the carrier and the receiver shall give all reasonable facilities to each other for inspecting and tallying the goods.

7. After the goods are loaded the bill of lading to be issued by the carrier, master, or agent of the carrier, to the shipper shall, if the shipper so demands, be a "shipped" bill of lading, provided that if the shipper shall have previously taken up any document of title to such goods, he shall surrender the same as against the issue of the "shipped" bill of lading, but at the option of the carrier such document of title may be noted at the port of shipment by the carrier, master, or agent with the name or names of the ship or ships upon which the goods have been shipped and the date or dates of shipment, and when so noted, if it shows the particulars mentioned in paragraph 3 of Article 3, shall for the purpose of this Article be deemed to constitute a "shipped" bill of lading.

8. Any clause, covenant, or agreement in a contract of carriage relieving the carrier or the ship from liability for loss or damage to, or in connexion with, goods arising from negligence, fault, or failure in the duties and obligations provided in this Article or lessening such liability otherwise than as provided in this Convention, shall be null and void and of no effect. A benefit of insurance in favour of the carrier or similar clause shall be deemed to be a clause relieving the carrier from liability.

Article 4

1. Neither the carrier nor the ship shall be liable for loss or damage arising or resulting from unseaworthiness unless caused by want of due diligence on the part of the carrier to make the ship seaworthy and to secure that the ship is properly manned, equipped and supplied, and to make the holds, refrigerating and cool chambers and all other parts of the ship in which goods are carried fit and safe for their reception, carriage and preservation in accordance with the provisions of paragraph 1 of Article 3. Whenever loss or damage has resulted from unseaworthiness the burden of proving the exercise of due diligence shall be on the carrier or other person claiming exemption under this Article.

2. Neither the carrier nor the ship shall be responsible for loss or damage arising or resulting from:

(a) Act, neglect, or default of the master, mariner, pilot, or the servants of the carrier in the navigation or in the management of the ship.

(b) Fire, unless caused by the actual fault or privity of the carrier.

(c)   Perils, dangers and accidents of the sea or other navigable waters.

(d)   Act of God.

(e)   Act of war.

(f)   Act of public enemies.

(g)   Arrest or restraint or princes, rulers or people, or seizure under legal process.

(h)   Quarantine restrictions.

(i)   Act or omission of the shipper or owner of the goods, his agent or representative.

(j)   Strikes or lockouts or stoppage or restraint of labour from whatever cause, whether partial or general.

(k)   Riots and civil commotions.

(*l*)   Saving or attempting to save life or property at sea.

(m) Wastage in bulk or weight or any other loss or damage arising from inherent defect, quality or vice of the goods.

(n)   Insufficiency of packing.

(o)   Insufficiency or inadequacy of marks.

(p)   Latent defects not discoverable by due diligence.

(q)   Any other cause arising without the actual fault or privity of the carrier, or without the actual fault or neglect of the agents or servants of the carrier, but the burden of proof shall be on the person claiming the benefit of this exception to show that neither the actual fault or privity of the carrier nor the fault or neglect of the agents or servants of the carrier contributed to the loss or damage.

3.   The shipper shall not be responsible for loss or damage sustained by the carrier or the ship arising or resulting from any cause without the act, fault or neglect of the shipper, his agents or his servants.

4.   Any deviation in saving or attempting to save life or property at sea or any reasonable deviation shall not be deemed to be an infringement or breach of this Convention or of the contract of carriage, and the carrier shall not be liable for any loss or damage resulting therefrom.

5.   Neither the carrier nor the ship shall in any event be or become liable for any loss or damage to or in connexion with goods in an amount exceeding 100 pounds sterling per package or unit, or the equivalent of that sum in other currency unless the nature and value of such goods have been declared by the shipper before shipment and inserted in the bill of lading.

This declaration if embodied in the bill of lading shall be *prima facie* evidence, but shall not be binding or conclusive on the carrier.

By agreement between the carrier, master or agent of the carrier and the shipper another maximum amount than that mentioned in this paragraph may be fixed, provided that such maximum shall not be less than the figure above named.

Neither the carrier nor the ship shall be responsible in any event for loss or damage to, or in connexion with, goods if the nature or value thereof has been knowingly misstated by the shipper in the bill of lading.

6. Goods of an inflammable, explosive or dangerous nature to the shipment whereof the carrier, master or agent of the carrier has not consented with knowledge of their nature and character, may at any time before discharge be landed at any place, or destroyed or rendered innocuous by the carrier without compensation and the shipper of such goods shall be liable for all damage and expenses directly or indirectly arising out of or resulting from such shipment. If any such goods shipped with such knowledge and consent shall become a danger to the ship or cargo, they may in like manner be landed at any place, or destroyed or rendered innocuous by the carrier without liability on the part of the carrier except to general average, if any.

Article 5

A carrier shall be at liberty to surrender in whole or in part all or any of his rights and immunities or to increase any of his responsibilities and obligations under this Convention, provided such surrender or increase shall be embodied in the bill of lading issued to the shipper.

The provisions of this Convention shall not be applicable to charter parties, but if bills of lading are issued in the case of a ship under a charter party they shall comply with the terms of this Convention. Nothing in these rules shall be held to prevent the insertion in a bill of lading of any lawful provision regarding general average.

Article 6

Notwithstanding the provisions of the preceding Articles, a carrier, master or agent of the carrier and a shipper shall in regard to any particular goods be at liberty to enter into any agreement in any terms as to the responsibility and liability of the carrier for such goods, and as to the rights and immunities of the carrier in respect of such goods, or his obligation as to seaworthiness, so far as this stipulation is not contrary to public policy, or the care or diligence of his servants or agents in regard to the loading, handling, stowage, carriage, custody, care and discharge of the goods carried by sea, provided that in this case no bill of lading has been or shall be issued and that the terms agreed shall be embodied in a receipt which shall be a non-negotiable document and shall be marked as such.

Any agreement so entered into shall have full legal effect.

Provided that this Article shall not apply to ordinary commercial shipments made in the ordinary course of trade, but only to other shipments where the character or condition of the property to be carried or the circumstances, terms and conditions under which the carriage is to be performed are such as reasonably to justify a special agreement.

Article 7

Nothing herein contained shall prevent a carrier or a shipper from entering into any agreement, stipulation, condition, reservation or exemption as to the responsibility and liability of the carrier or the ship for the loss or damage to, or in connexion with, the custody and care and handling of goods prior to the loading on, and subsequent to, the discharge from the ship on which the goods are carried by sea

Article 8

The provisions of this Convention shall not affect the rights and obligations of the carrier under any statute for the time being in force relating to the limitation of the liability of owners of sea-going vessels.

Article 9

The monetary units mentioned in this Convention are to be taken to be gold value.

Those contracting States in which the pound sterling is not a monetary unit reserve to themselves the right of translating the sums indicated in this Convention in terms of pound sterling into terms of their own monetary system in round figures.

The national laws may reserve to the debtor the right of discharging his debt in national currency according to the rate of exchange prevailing on the day of the arrival of the ship at the port of discharge of the goods concerned.

Article 10

The provisions of this Convention shall apply to all bills of lading issued in any of the contracting States.

Article 11

After an interval of not more than two years from the day on which the Convention is signed, the Belgian Government shall place itself in communication with the Governments of the High Contracting Parties which have declared themselves prepared to ratify the Convention, with a view to deciding whether it shall be put into force. The ratifications shall be deposited at Brussels at a date to be fixed by agreement among the said Governments. The first deposit of ratifications shall be recorded in a *procès-verbal* signed by the representatives of the Powers which take part therein and by the Belgian Minister of Foreign Affairs.

The subsequent deposit of ratifications shall be made by means of a written notification, addressed to the Belgian Government and accompanied by the instrument of ratification.

A duly certified copy of the *procès-verbal* relating to the first deposit of ratifications, of the notifications referred to in the previous paragraph, and also of the instruments of ratification accompanying them, shall be immediately sent by the Belgian Government through the diplomatic channel to the Powers who have signed this Convention or who have acceded to it. In the cases contemplated in the preceding paragraph, the said Government shall inform them at the same time of the date on which it received the notification.

Article 12

Non-signatory States may accede to the present Convention whether or not they have been represented at the International Conference at Brussels.

A State which desires to accede shall notify its intention in writing to the Belgian Government, forwarding to it the document of accession, which shall be deposited in the archives of the said Government.

The Belgian Government shall immediately forward to all the States which have signed or acceded to the Convention a duly certified copy of the notification and of the act of accession, mentioning the date on which it received the notification.

Article 13

The High Contracting Parties may at the time of signature, ratification or accession declare that their acceptance of the present Convention does not include any or all of the self-governing dominions, or of the colonies, overseas possessions, protectorates or territories under their sovereignty or authority, and they may subsequently accede separately on behalf of any self-governing dominion, colony, overseas possession, protectorate or territory excluded in their declaration. They may also denounce the Convention separately in accordance with its provisions in respect of any self-governing dominion, or any colony, overseas possession, protectorate or territory under their sovereignty or authority.

Article 14

The present Convention shall take effect, in the case of the States which have taken part in the first deposit of ratifications, one year after the date of the protocol recording such deposit.

As respects the States which ratify subsequently or which accede, and also in cases in which the Convention is subsequently put into effect in accordance with Article 13, it shall take effect six months after the notifications specified in paragraph 2 of Article 11 and paragraph 2 of Article 12 have been received by the Belgian Government.

Article 15

In the event of one of the contracting States wishing to denounce the present Convention, the denunciation shall be notified in writing to the Belgian Government, which shall immediately communicate a duly certified copy of the notification to all the other States, informing them of the date on which it was received.

The denunciation shall only operate in respect of the State which made the notification, and on the expiry of one year after the notification has reached the Belgian Government.

Article 16

Any one of the contracting States shall have the right to call for a fresh conference with a view to considering possible amendments.

A State which would exercise this right should notify its intention to the other States through the Belgian Government, which would make arrangements for convening the Conference.

THE HAGUE RULES AS AMENDED BY THE BRUSSELS PROTOCOL 1968

("The Hague-Visby Rules")

Brussels, February 23, 1968

Article I

In these Rules the following words are employed, with the meanings set out below:

(a) "Carrier" includes the owner or the charterer who enters into a contract of carriage with a shipper.

(b) "Contract of carriage" applies only to contracts of carriage covered by a bill of lading or any similar document of title, in so far as such document relates to the carriage of goods by sea, including any bill of lading or any similar document as aforesaid issued under or pursuant to a charter party from the moment at which such bill of lading or similar document of title regulates the relations between a carrier and a holder of the same.

(c) "Goods" includes goods, wares, merchandise, and articles of every kind whatsoever except live animals and cargo which by the contract of carriage is stated as being carried on deck and is so carried.

(d) "Ship" means any vessel used for the carriage of goods by sea.

(e) "Carriage of goods" covers the period from the time when the goods are loaded on to the time they are discharged from the ship.

Article II

Subject to the provisions of Article VI, under every contract of carriage of goods by sea the carrier, in relation to the loading, handling, stowage, carriage, custody, care and discharge of such goods, shall be subject to the responsibilities and liabilities and entitled to the rights and immunities hereinafter set forth.

Article III

1. The carrier shall be bound before and at the beginning of the voyage to exercise due diligence to:

(a)   Make the ship seaworthy;

(b)   Properly man, equip and supply the ship;

(c)   Make the holds, refrigerating and cool chambers, and all other parts of the ship in which goods are carried, fit and safe for their reception, carriage and preservation.

2.   Subject to the provisions of Article IV, the carrier shall properly and carefully load, handle, stow, carry, keep, care for, and discharge the goods carried.

3.   After receiving the goods into his charge the carrier or the master or agent of the carrier shall, on demand of the shipper, issue to the shipper a bill of lading showing among other things:

(a)   The leading marks necessary for identification of the goods as the same are furnished in writing by the shipper before the loading of such goods starts, provided such marks are stamped or otherwise shown clearly upon the goods if uncovered, or on the cases or coverings in which such goods are contained, in such a manner as should ordinarily remain legible until the end of the voyage.

(b)   Either the number of packages or pieces, or the quantity, or weight, as the case may be, as furnished in writing by the shipper.

(c)   The apparent order and condition of the goods.

Provided that no carrier, master or agent of the carrier shall be bound to state or show in the bill of lading any marks, number, quantity or weight which he has reasonable ground for suspecting not accurately to represent the goods actually received, or which he has had no reasonable means of checking.

4.   Such a bill of lading shall be prima facie evidence of the receipt by the carrier of the goods as therein described in accordance with paragraph 3 (a), (b) and (c). However, proof to the contrary shall not be admissible when the bill of lading has been transferred to a third party acting in good faith.

5.   The shipper shall be deemed to have guaranteed to the carrier the accuracy at the time of shipment of the marks, number, quantity and weight, as furnished by him, and the shipper shall indemnify the carrier against all loss, damages and expenses arising or resulting from inaccuracies in such particulars. The right of the carrier to such indemnity shall in no way limit his responsibility and liability under the contract of carriage to any person other than the shipper.

6.   Unless notice of loss or damage and the general nature of such loss or damage be given in writing to the carrier or his agent at the port of discharge before or at the time of the removal of the goods into the custody of the person entitled to delivery thereof under the contract of carriage, or, if the loss or damage be not apparent, within three days, such removal shall be prima facie evidence of the delivery by the carrier of the goods as described in the bill of lading.

The notice in writing need not be given if the state of the goods has, at the time of their receipt, been the subject of joint survey or inspection.

Subject to paragraph 6bis the carrier and the ship shall in any event be discharged from all liability whatsoever in respect of the goods, unless suit is brought within one year of their delivery or of the date when they should have been delivered. This period, may however, be extended if the parties so agree after the cause of action has arisen.

In the case of any actual or apprehended loss or damage the carrier and the receiver shall give all reasonable facilities to each other for inspecting and tallying the goods.

6 *bis*. An action for indemnity against a third person may be brought even after the expiration of the year provided for in the preceding paragraph if brought within the time allowed by the law of the Court seized of the case. However, the time allowed shall be not less than three months, commencing from the day when the person bringing such action for indemnity has settled the claim or has been served with process in the action against himself.

7.   After the goods are loaded the bill of lading to be issued by the carrier, master, or agent of the carrier, to the shipper shall, if the shipper so demands be a 'shipped' bill of lading, provided that if the shipper shall have previously taken up any document of title to such goods, he shall surrender the same as against the issue of the 'shipped' bill of lading, but at the option of the carrier such document of title may be noted at the port of shipment by the carrier, master, or agent with the name or names of the ship or ships upon which the goods have been shipped and the date or dates of shipment, and when so noted, if it shows the particulars mentioned in paragraph 3 of Article III, shall for the purpose of this article be deemed to constitute a 'shipped' bill of lading.

8.   Any clause, covenant, or agreement in a contract of carriage relieving the carrier or the ship from liability for loss or damage to, or in connection with, goods arising from negligence, fault, or failure in the duties and obligations provided in this article or lessening such liability otherwise than as provided in these Rules, shall be null and void and of no effect. A benefit of insurance in favour of the carrier or similar clause shall be deemed to be a clause relieving the carrier from liability.

Article IV

1.   Neither the carrier nor the ship shall be liable for loss or damage arising or resulting from unseaworthiness unless caused by want of due diligence on the part of the carrier to make the ship seaworthy, and to secure that the ship is properly manned, equipped and supplied, and to make the holds, refrigerating and cool chambers and all other parts of the ship in which goods are carried fit and safe for their reception, carriage and preservation in accordance with the provisions of paragraph 1 of Article III. Whenever loss or damage has resulted from

unseaworthiness the burden of proving the exercise of due diligence shall be on the carrier or other person claiming exemption under this article.

2.   Neither the carrier nor the ship shall be responsible for loss or damage arising or resulting from:

(a)   Act, neglect, or default of the master, mariner, pilot, or the servants of the carrier in the navigation or in the management of the ship.

(b)   Fire, unless caused by the actual fault or privity of the carrier.

(c)   Perils, dangers and accidents of the sea or other navigable waters.

(d)   Act of God.

(e)   Act of war.

(f)   Act of public enemies.

(g)   Arrest or restraint of princes, rulers or people, or seizure under legal process.

(h)   Quarantine restrictions.

(i)   Act or omission of the shipper or owner of the goods, his agent or representative.

(j)   Strikes or lockouts or stoppage or restraint of labour from whatever cause, whether partial or general.

(k)   Riots and civil commotions.

(*l*)   Saving or attempting to save life or property at sea.

(m) Wastage in bulk of weight or any other loss or damage arising from inherent defect, quality or vice of the goods.

(n)   Insufficiency of packing.

(*o*)   Insufficiency or inadequacy of marks.

(p)   Latent defects not discoverable by due diligence.

(q)   Any other cause arising without the actual fault or privity of the carrier, or without the fault or neglect of the agents or servants of the carrier, but the burden of proof shall be on the person claiming the benefit of this exception to show that neither the actual fault or privity of the carrier nor the fault or neglect of the agents or servants of the carrier contributed to the loss or damage.

3.   The shipper shall not be responsible for loss or damage sustained by the carrier or the ship arising or resulting from any cause without the act, fault or neglect of the shipper, his agents or his servants.

4.   Any deviation in saving or attempting to save life or property at sea or any reasonable deviation shall not be deemed to be an infringement or breach of these Rules or of the contract of carriage, and the carrier shall not be liable for any loss or damage resulting therefrom.

5. (a) Unless the nature and value of such goods have been declared by the shipper before shipment and inserted in the bill of lading, neither the carrier nor the ship shall in any event be or become liable for any loss or damage to or in connection with the goods in an amount exceeding the equivalent of 666.67 units of account per package or unit or units of account per kilo of gross weight of the goods lost or damaged, whichever is the higher.

(b) The total amount recoverable shall be calculated by reference to the value of such goods at the place and time at which the goods are discharged from the ship in accordance with the contract or should have been so discharged.

The value of the goods shall be fixed according to the commodity exchange price, or, if there be no such price, according to the current market price, or, if there be no commodity exchange price or current market price, by reference to the normal value of goods of the same kind and quality.

(c) Where a container, pallet or similar article of transport is used to consolidate goods, the number of packages or units enumerated in the bill of lading as packed in such article of transport shall be deemed the number of packages or units for the purpose of this paragraph as far as these packages or units are concerned. Except as aforesaid such article of transport shall be considered the package or unit.

(d) The unit of account mentioned in this Article is the special drawing right as defined by the International Monetary Fund. The amounts mentioned in . . . sub-paragraph (a) of this paragraph shall be converted into national currency on the basis of the value of that currency on a date to be determined by the law of the Court seized of the case.

(e) Neither the carrier nor the ship shall be entitled to the benefit of the limitation of liability provided for in this paragraph if it is proved that the damage resulted from an act or omission of the carrier done with intent to cause damage, or recklessly and with knowledge that damage would probably result.

(f) The declaration mentioned in sub-paragraph (a) of this paragraph, if embodied in the bill of lading, shall be prima facie evidence, but shall not be binding or conclusive on the carrier.

(g) By agreement between the carrier, master or agent of the carrier and the shipper other maximum amounts than those mentioned in sub-paragraph (a) of this paragraph may be fixed, provided that no maximum amount so fixed shall be less than the appropriate maximum mentioned in that sub-paragraph.

(h) Neither the carrier nor the ship shall be responsible in any event for loss or damage to, or in connection with, goods if the nature or value thereof has been knowingly mis-stated by the shipper in the bill of lading.

6. Goods of an inflammable, explosive or dangerous nature to the shipment whereof the carrier, master or agent of the carrier has not consented with knowledge of their nature and character, may at any time before discharge be landed at any place, or destroyed or rendered innocuous by the carrier without compensation and the shipper of such goods shall be liable for all damages and expenses directly or indirectly arising out of or resulting from such shipment. If any such goods shipped with such knowledge and consent shall become a danger to the ship or cargo, they may in like manner be landed at any place, or destroyed or rendered innocuous by the carrier without liability on the part of the carrier except to general average, if any.

Article IV bis

1. The defences and limits of liability provided for in these Rules shall apply in any action against the carrier in respect of loss or damage to goods covered by a contract of carriage whether the action be founded in contract or in tort.

2. If such an action is brought against a servant or agent of the carrier (such servant or agent not being an independent contractor), such servant or agent shall be entitled to avail himself of the defences and limits of liability which the carrier is entitled to invoke under these Rules.

3. The aggregate of the amounts recoverable from the carrier, and such servants and agents, shall in no case exceed the limit provided for in these Rules.

4. Nevertheless, a servant or agent of the carrier shall not be entitled to avail himself of the provisions of this article, if it is proved that the damage resulted from an act or omission of the servant or agent done with intent to cause damage or recklessly and with knowledge that damage would probably result.

Article V

A carrier shall be at liberty to surrender in whole or in part all or any of his rights and immunities or to increase any of his responsibilities and obligations under these Rules, provided such surrender or increase shall be embodied in the bill of lading issued to the shipper. The provisions of these Rules shall not be applicable to charter parties, but if bills of lading are issued in the case of a ship under a charter party they shall comply with the terms of these Rules. Nothing in these Rules shall be held to prevent the insertion in a bill of lading of any lawful provision regarding general average.

Article VI

Notwithstanding the provisions of the preceding articles, a carrier, master or agent of the carrier and a shipper shall in regard to any particular goods be at liberty to enter into any agreement in any terms as to the responsibility and liability of the carrier for such goods, and as to the rights and immunities of the carrier in respect of such goods, or his obligation as to seaworthiness, so far as this stipulation is not contrary to public policy, or the care or diligence of his servants or agents in regard to the loading, handling, stowage, carriage, custody, care and discharge of the goods carried by sea, provided that in this case no bill of lading has been or shall be issued and that the terms agreed shall be embodied in a receipt which shall be a non-negotiable document and shall be marked as such.

An agreement so entered into shall have full legal effect.

Provided that this article shall not apply to ordinary commercial shipments made in the ordinary course of trade, but only to other shipments where the character or condition of the property to be carried or the circumstances, terms and conditions under which the carriage is to be performed are such as reasonably to justify a special agreement.

Article VII

Nothing herein contained shall prevent a carrier or a shipper from entering into any agreement, stipulation, condition, reservation or exemption as to the responsibility and liability of the carrier or the ship for the loss or damage to, or in connection with, the custody and care and handling of goods prior to the loading on, and subsequent to the discharge from, the ship on which the goods are carried by sea.

Article VIII

The provisions of these Rules shall not affect the rights and obligations of the carrier under any statute for the time being in force relating to the limitation of the liability of owners of sea-going vessels.

Article IX

These Rules shall not affect the provisions of any international Convention or national law governing liability for nuclear damage.

Article X

The provisions of these Rules shall apply to every bill of lading relating to the carriage of goods between ports in two different States if

(a)   the bill of lading is issued in a contracting State, or

(b)   the carriage is from a port in a contracting State, or

(c)   the contract contained in or evidenced by the bill of lading provides that these Rules or legislation of any State giving effect to them are to govern the contract;

whatever may be the nationality of the ship, the carrier, the shipper, the consignee, or any other interested person.

UNITED NATIONS CONVENTION ON THE CARRIAGE OF GOODS BY SEA

("Hamburg Rules")

Hamburg, March 31, 1978

[PREAMBLE OMITTED.]

PART I. GENERAL PROVISIONS

Article 1

Definitions

In this Convention:

1.   "Carrier" means any person by whom or in whose name a contract of carriage of goods by sea has been concluded with a shipper.

2.   "Actual carrier" means any person to whom the performance of the carriage of the goods, or of part of the carriage, has been entrusted by the carrier, and includes any other person to whom such performance has been entrusted.

3.   "Shipper" means any person by whom or in whose name or on whose behalf a contract of carriage of goods by sea has been concluded with a carrier, or any person by whom or in whose name or on whose behalf the goods are actually delivered to the carrier in relation to the contract of carriage by sea.

4.   "Consignee" means the person entitled to take delivery of the goods.

5.   "Goods" includes live animals; where the goods are consolidated in a container, pallet or similar article of transport or where they are packed, "goods" includes such article of transport or packaging if supplied by the shipper.

6.   "Contract of carriage by sea" means any contract whereby the carrier undertakes against payment of freight to carry goods by sea from one port to another; however, a contract which involves carriage by sea and also carriage by some other means is deemed to be a contract of carriage by sea for the purpose of this Convention only in so far as it relates to the carriage by sea.

7.   "Bill of lading" means a document which evidences a contract of carriage by sea and the taking over or loading of the goods by the carrier, and by which the carrier undertakes to deliver the goods against surrender of the document. A provision in the document that the goods are to be delivered to the order of a named person, or to order, or to bearer, constitutes such an undertaking.

8.   "Writing" includes, *inter alia,* telegram and telex.

Article 2

1.   The provisions of this Convention are applicable to all contracts of carriage by sea between two different States, if:

(a) the port of loading as provided for in the contract of carriage by sea is located in a Contracting State, or

(b) the port of discharge as provided for in the contract of carriage by sea is located in a Contracting State, or

(c) one of the optional ports of discharge provided for in the contract of carriage by sea is the actual port of discharge and such port is located in a Contracting State, or

(d) the bill of lading or other document evidencing the contract of carriage by sea is issued in a Contracting State, or

(e) the bill of lading or other document evidencing the contract of carriage by sea provides that the provisions of this Convention or the legislation of any State giving effect to them are to govern the contract.

2.   The provisions of this Convention are applicable without regard to the nationality of the ship, the carrier, the actual carrier, the shipper, the consignee or any other interested person.

3.   The provisions of this Convention are not applicable to charter-parties. However, where a bill of lading is issued pursuant to a charter-party, the provisions of the Convention apply to such a bill of lading if it governs the relation between the carrier and the holder of the bill of lading, not being the charterer.

4.   If a contract provides for future carriage of goods in a series of shipments during an agreed period, the provisions of this Convention apply to each shipment. However, where a shipment is made under a charter-party, the provisions of paragraph 3 of this article apply.

Article 3

In the interpretation and application of the provisions of this Convention regard shall be had to its international character and to the need to promote uniformity.

PART II.   LIABILITY OF THE CARRIER

Article 4

Period of Responsibility

1.   The responsibility of the carrier for the goods under this Convention covers the period during which the carrier is in charge of the goods at the port of loading, during the carriage and at the port of discharge.

2.   For the purpose of paragraph 1 of this article, the carrier is deemed to be in charge of the goods:

(a) from the time he has taken over the goods from:

(i)   the shipper, or a person acting on his behalf; or

(ii)   an authority or other third party to whom, pursuant to law or regulations applicable at the port of loading, the goods must be handed over for shipment;

(b)   until the time he has delivered the goods:

(i)   by handing over the goods to the consignee; or

(ii)   in cases where the consignee does not receive the goods from the carrier, by placing them at the disposal of the consignee in accordance with the contract or with the law or with the usage of the particular trade, applicable at the port of discharge; or

(iii) by handing over the goods to an authority or other third party to whom, pursuant to law or regulations applicable at the port of discharge, the goods must be handed over.

3.   In paragraphs 1 and 2 of this article, reference to the carrier or to the consignee means, in addition to the carrier or the consignee, the servants or agents, respectively of the carrier or the consignee.

Article 5

Basis of Liability

1.   The carrier is liable for loss resulting from loss of or damage to the goods, as well as from delay in delivery, if the occurrence which caused the loss, damage or delay took place while the goods were in his charge as defined in article 4, unless the carrier proves that he, his servants or agents took all measures that could reasonably be required to avoid the occurrence and its consequences.

2.   Delay in delivery occurs when the goods have not been delivered at the port of discharge provided for in the contract of carriage by sea within the time expressly agreed upon or, in the absence of such agreement, within the time which it would be reasonable to require of a diligent carrier, having regard to the circumstances of the case.

3.   The person entitled to make a claim for the loss of goods may treat the goods as lost if they have not been delivered as required by article 4 within 60 consecutive days following the expiry of the time for delivery according to paragraph 2 of this article.

4.   (a) The carrier is liable

(i)   for loss of or damage to the goods or delay in delivery caused by fire, if the claimant proves that the fire arose from fault or neglect on the part of the carrier, his servants or agents;

(ii) for such loss, damage or delay in delivery which is proved by the claimant to have resulted from the fault or neglect of the carrier, his servants or agents, in taking all measures that could reasonably be required to put out the fire and avoid or mitigate its consequences.

(b)   In case of fire on board the ship affecting the goods, if the claimant or the carrier so desires, a survey in accordance with shipping practices must be held into the cause and circumstances of the fire, and a copy of the surveyor's report shall be made available on demand to the carrier and the claimant.

5.   With respect to live animals, the carrier is not liable for loss, damage or delay in delivery resulting from any special risks inherent in that kind of carriage. If the carrier proves that he has complied with any special instructions given to him by the shipper respecting the animals and that, in the circumstances of the case, the loss, damage or delay in delivery could be attributed to such risks, it is presumed that the loss, damage or delay in delivery was so caused, unless there is proof that all or a part of the loss, damage or delay in delivery resulted from fault or neglect on the part of the carrier, his servants or agents.

6.   The carrier is not liable, except in general average, where loss, damage or delay in delivery resulted from measures to save life or from reasonable measures to save property at sea.

7.   Where fault or neglect on the part of the carrier, his servants or agents combines with another cause to produce loss, damage, or delay in delivery is attributable to such fault or neglect, provided that the carrier proves the amount of the loss, damage or delay in delivery not attributable thereto.

Article 6

Limits of Liability

1.   (a) The liability of the carrier for loss resulting from loss of or damage of goods according to the provision of article 5 is limited to an amount equivalent to 835 units of account per package or other shipping unit or 2.5 units of account per kilogramme of gross weight of the goods lost or damaged, whichever is the higher.

(b)   The liability of the carrier for delay in delivery according to the provisions of article 5 is limited to an amount equivalent to two and a half times the freight payable for the goods delayed, but not exceeding the total freight payable under the contract of carriage of goods by sea.

(c)   In no case shall the aggregate liability of the carrier, under both subparagraphs (a) and (b) of this paragraph, exceed the limitation which would be established under subparagraph (a) of this paragraph for total loss of the goods with respect to which such liability was incurred.

2.   For the purpose of calculating which amount is the higher in accordance with paragraph 1(a) of this article, the following rules apply:

(a)   Where a container, pallet or similar article of transport is used to consolidate goods, the package or other shipping units enumerated in the bill of lading, if issued, or otherwise in any other document evidencing the contract of carriage by sea, as packed in such article of transport are deemed packages or shipping units.

Except as aforesaid the goods in such article of transport are deemed one shipping unit.

(b) In cases where the article of transport itself has been lost or damaged, that article of transport, if now owned or otherwise supplied by the carrier, is considered one separate shipping unit.

3. Unit of account means the unit of account mentioned in article 26.

4. By agreement between the carrier and the shipper, limits of liability exceeding those provided for in paragraph 1 may be fixed.

Article 7

Application to Non-Contractual Claims

1. The defences and limits of liability provided for in this Convention apply in any action against the carrier in respect of loss or damage to the goods covered by the contract of carriage by sea, as well as of delay in delivery whether the action is founded in contract, in tort or otherwise.

2. If such an action is brought against a servant or agent of the carrier, such servant or agent, if he proves that he acted within the scope of his employment, is entitled to avail himself of the defences and limits of liability which the carrier is entitled to invoke under this Convention.

3. Except as provided in article 8, the aggregate of the amounts recoverable from the carrier and from any persons referred to in paragraph 2 of this article shall not exceed the limits of liability provided for in this Convention.

Article 8

Loss of Right to Limit Responsibility

1. The carrier is not entitled to the benefit of the limitation of liability provided for in article 6 if it is proved that the loss, damage or delay in delivery resulted from an act or omission of the carrier done with the intent to cause such loss, damage or delay, or recklessly and with knowledge that such loss, damage or delay would probably result.

2. Notwithstanding the provisions of paragraph 2 of article 7, a servant or agent of the carrier is not entitled to the benefit of the limitation of liability provided for in article 6 if it is proved that the loss, damage or delay in delivery resulted from an act or omission of such servant or agent, done with the intent to cause such loss, damage or delay, or recklessly and with knowledge that such loss, damage or delay would probably result.

Article 9

Deck Cargo

1. The carrier is entitled to carry the goods on deck only if such carriage is in accordance with an agreement with the shipper or with the

usage of the particular trade or is required by statutory rules or regulations.

2.   If the carrier and the shipper have agreed that the goods shall or may be carried on deck, the carrier must insert in the bill of lading or other document evidencing the contract of carriage by sea a statement to that effect. In the absence of such a statement the carrier has the burden of proving that an agreement for carriage on deck has been entered into; however, the carrier is not entitled to invoke such an agreement against a third party, including a consignee, who has acquired the bill of lading in good faith.

3.   Where the goods have been carried on deck contrary to the provisions of paragraph 1 of this article or where the carrier may not under paragraph 2 of this article invoke an agreement for carriage on deck, the carrier, notwithstanding the provisions of paragraph 1 of article 5, is liable for loss of or damage to the goods, as well as for delay in delivery, resulting solely from the carriage on deck, and the extent of his liability is to be determined in accordance with the provisions of article 6 or article 8 of this Convention, as the case may be.

4.   Carriage of goods on deck contrary to express agreement for carriage under deck is deemed to be an act or omission of the carrier within the meaning of article 8.

Article 10

Liability of the Carrier and Actual Carrier

1.   Where the performance of the carriage or part thereof has been entrusted to an actual carrier, whether or not in pursuance of a liberty under the contract of carriage by sea to do so, the carrier nevertheless remains responsible for the entire carriage according to the provisions of this Convention. The carrier is responsible, in relation to the carriage performed by the actual carrier, for the acts and omissions of the actual carrier and of his servants and agents acting within the scope of their employment.

2.   All the provisions of this Convention governing the responsibility of the carrier also apply to the responsibility of the actual carrier for the carriage performed by him. The provisions of paragraphs 2 and 3 of article 7 of paragraph 2 of article 8 apply if an action is brought against a servant or agent of the actual carrier.

3.   Any special agreement under which the carrier assumes obligations not imposed by this Convention or waives rights conferred by this Convention affects the actual carrier only if agreed to by him expressly and in writing. Whether or not the actual carrier has so agreed, the carrier nevertheless remains bound by the obligations or waivers resulting from such special agreement.

4.   Where and to the extent that both the carrier and the actual carrier are liable, their liability is joint and several.

5. The aggregate of the amounts recoverable from the carrier, the actual carrier and their servants and agents shall not exceed the limits of liability provided for in this Convention.

6. Nothing in this article shall prejudice any right of recourse as between the carrier and the actual carrier.

Article 11

Through Carriage

1. Notwithstanding the provisions of paragraph 1 of article 10, where a contract of carriage by sea provides explicitly that a specified part of the carriage covered by the said contract is to be performed by a named person other than the carrier, the contract may also provide that the carrier is not liable for loss, damage or delay in delivery caused by an occurrence which takes place while the goods are in the charge of the actual carrier during such part of the carriage. Nevertheless, any stipulation limiting or excluding such liability is without effect if no judicial proceedings can be instituted against the actual carrier in a court competent under paragraph 1 or 2 of article 21. The burden of proving that any loss, damage or delay in delivery has been caused by such an occurrence rests upon the carrier.

2. The actual carrier is responsible in accordance with the provisions of paragraph 2 of article 10 for loss, damage or delay in delivery caused by an occurrence which takes place while the goods are in his charge.

PART III.   LIABILITY OF THE SHIPPER

Article 12

General Rule

The shipper is not liable for loss sustained by the carrier or the actual carrier, or for damage sustained by the ship, unless such loss or damage was caused by the fault or neglect of the shipper, his servants or agents. Nor is any servant or agent of the shipper liable for such loss or damage unless the loss or damage was caused by fault or neglect on his part.

Article 13

Special Rules on Dangerous Goods

1. The shipper must mark or label in a suitable manner dangerous goods as dangerous.

2. Where the shipper hands over dangerous goods to the carrier or an actual carrier, as the case may be, the shipper must inform him of the dangerous character of the goods and, if necessary, of the precautions to be taken. If the shipper fails to do so and such carrier or actual carrier does not otherwise have knowledge of their dangerous character:

(a) the shipper is liable to the carrier and any actual carrier for the loss resulting from the shipment of such goods, and

(b) the goods may at any time be unloaded, destroyed or rendered innocuous, as the circumstances may require, without payment of compensation.

3.   The provisions of paragraph 2 of this article may not be invoked by any person if during the carriage he has taken the goods in his charge with knowledge of their dangerous character.

4.   If, in cases where the provisions of paragraph 2, subparagraph (b), of this article do not apply or may not be invoked, dangerous goods become an actual danger to life or property, they may be unloaded, destroyed or rendered innocuous, as the circumstances may require, without payment of compensation except where there is an obligation to contribute in general average or where the carrier is liable in accordance with the provisions of article 5.

PART IV.   TRANSPORT DOCUMENTS

Article 14

Issue of Bill of Lading

1.   When the carrier or the actual carrier takes the goods in his charge, the carrier must, on demand of the shipper, issue to the shipper a bill of lading.

2.   The bill of lading may be signed by a person having authority from the carrier. A bill of lading signed by the master of the ship carrying the goods is deemed to have been signed on behalf of the carrier.

3.   The signature on the bill of lading may be in handwriting, printed in facsimile, perforated, stamped, in symbols, or made by any other mechanical or electronic means, if not inconsistent with the law of the country where the bill of lading issued.

Article 15

Contents of Bill of Lading

1.   The bill of lading must include, inter alia, the following particulars:

(a) the general nature of the goods, the leading marks necessary for identification of the goods, and express statement, if applicable, as to the dangerous character of the goods, the number of packages or pieces, and the weight of the goods or their quantity otherwise expressed, all such particulars as furnished by the shipper;

(b)   the apparent condition of the goods;

(c)   the name and principal place of business of the carrier;

(d)   the name of the shipper;

(e)   the consignee if named by the shipper;

(f) the port of loading under the contract of carriage by sea and the date on which the goods were taken over by the carrier at the port of loading;

(g) the port of discharge under the contract of carriage by sea;

(h) the number of originals of the bill of lading, if more than one;

(i) the place of issuance of the bill of lading;

(j) the signature of the carrier or a person acting on his behalf;

(k) the freight to the extent payable by the consignee or other indication that freight is payable to him;

(*l*) the statement referred to in paragraph 3 of article 23;

(m) the statement, if applicable, that the goods shall or may be carried on deck;

(n) the date or the period of delivery of the goods at the port of discharge if expressly agreed upon between the parties; and

(o) any increased limit or limits of liability where agreed in accordance with paragraph 4 of article 6.

2. After the goods have been loaded on board, if the shipper so demands the carrier must issue to the shipper a "shipped" bill of lading which, in addition to the particulars required under paragraph 1 of this article, must state that the goods are on board a named ship or ships, and the date or dates of loading. If the carrier has previously issued to the shipper a bill of lading or other document of title with respect to any of such goods, on request of the carrier, the shipper must surrender such document in exchange for a "shipped" bill of lading. The carrier may amend any previously issued document in order to meet the shipper's demand for a "shipped" bill of lading if, as amended, such document includes all the information required to be contained in a "shipped" bill of lading.

3. The absence in the bill of lading of one or more particulars referred to in this article does not affect the legal character of the document as a bill of lading provided that it nevertheless meets the requirements set out in paragraph 7 of article 1.

Article 16

Bills of Lading: Reservations and Evidentiary Effect

1. If the bill of lading contains particulars concerning the general nature, leading marks, number of packages or pieces, weight or quantity of the goods which the carrier or other person issuing the bill of lading on his behalf knows or has reasonable grounds to suspect do not accurately represent the goods actually taken over or, where a "shipped" bill of lading is issued, loaded, or if he had no reasonable means of checking such particulars, the carrier or such other person must insert in the bill

of lading a reservation specifying these inaccuracies, grounds of suspicion or the absence of reasonable means of checking.

2.   If the carrier or other person issuing the bill of lading on his behalf fails to note on the bill of lading the apparent condition of the goods, he is deemed to have noted on the bill of lading that the goods were in apparent good condition.

3.   Except for particulars in respect of which and to the extent to which a reservation permitted under paragraph 1 of this article has been entered:

   (a)   the bill of lading is *prima facie* evidence of the taking over or, where a "shipped" bill of lading is issued, loading, by the carrier of the goods as described in the bill of lading; and

   (b)   proof to the contrary by the carrier is not admissible if the bill of lading has been transferred to a third party, including a consignee, who in good faith has acted in reliance on the description of the goods therein.

4.   A bill of lading which does not, as provided in paragraph 1, subparagraph (k) of article 15, set forth the freight or otherwise indicate that freight is payable by the consignee or does not set forth demurrage incurred at the port of loading payable by the consignee, is *prima facie* evidence that no freight or such demurrage is payable by him. However, proof to the contrary by the carrier is not admissible when the bill of lading has been transferred to a third party, including a consignee, who in good faith has acted in reliance on the absence in the bill of lading of any such indication.

Article 17

Guarantees by the Shipper

1.   The shipper is deemed to have guaranteed to the carrier the accuracy of particulars relating to the general nature of the goods, their marks, number, weight and quantity as furnished by him for insertion in the bill of lading. The shipper must indemnify the carrier against the loss resulting from inaccuracies in such particulars. The shipper remains liable even if the bill of lading has been transferred by him. The right of the carrier to such indemnity in no way limits his liability under the contract of carriage by sea to any person other than the shipper.

2.   Any letter of guarantee or agreement by which the shipper undertakes to indemnify the carrier against loss resulting from the issuance of the bill of lading by the carrier, or by a person acting on his behalf, without entering a reservation relating to particulars furnished by the shipper for insertion in the bill of lading, or to the apparent condition of the goods, is void and of no effect as against any third party, including a consignee, to whom the bill of lading has been transferred.

3.   Such letter of guarantee or agreement is valid as against the shipper unless the carrier or the person acting on his behalf, by omitting

the reservation referred to in paragraph 2 of this article, intends to defraud a third party, including a consignee, who acts in reliance on the description of the goods in the bill of lading. In the latter case, if the reservation omitted relates to particulars furnished by the shipper for insertion in the bill of lading, the carrier has no right of indemnity from the shipper pursuant to paragraph 1 of this article.

4.   In the case of intended fraud referred to in paragraph 3 of this article the carrier is liable, without the benefit of the limitation of liability provided for in this convention, for the loss incurred by a third party, including a consignee, because he has acted in reliance on the description of the goods in the bill of lading.

Article 18

Documents other than Bills of Lading

Where a carrier issues a document other than a bill of lading to evidence the receipt of the goods to be carried, such a document is *prima facie* evidence of the conclusion of the contract of carriage by sea and the taking over by the carrier of the goods as therein described.

PART V. CLAIMS AND ACTIONS

Article 19

Notice of Loss, Damage or Delay

1.   Unless notice of loss or damage, specifying the general nature of such loss or damage, is given in writing by the consignee to the carrier not later than the working day after the day when the goods were handed over to the consignee, such handing over is *prima facie* evidence of the delivery by the carrier of the goods as described in the document of transport or, if no such document has been issued, in good condition.

2.   Where the loss damage is not apparent, the provisions of paragraph 1 of this article apply correspondingly if notice in writing is not given within 15 consecutive days after the day when the goods were handed over to the consignee.

3.   If the state of the goods at the time they were handed over to the consignee has been the subject of a joint survey or inspection by the parties, notice in writing need not be given of loss or damage ascertained during such survey or inspection.

4.   In the case of any actual or apprehended loss or damage the carrier and the consignee must give all reasonable facilities to each other for inspecting and tallying the goods.

5.   No compensation shall be payable for loss resulting from delay in delivery unless a notice has been given in writing to the carrier within 60 consecutive days after the day when the goods were handed over to the consignee.

6.   If the goods have been delivered by an actual carrier, any notice given under this article to him shall have the same effect as if it had been

115

given to the carrier, and any notice given to the carrier shall have effect as is given to such actual carrier.

7. Unless notice of loss or damage, specifying the general nature of the loss or damage, is given in writing by the carrier or actual carrier to the shipper not later than 90 consecutive days after the occurrence of such loss or damage or after the delivery of the goods in accordance with paragraph 2 of article 4, whichever is later, the failure to give such notice is *prima facie* evidence that the carrier or the actual carrier has sustained no loss or damage due to the fault or neglect of the shipper, his servants or agents.

8. For the purpose of this article, notice given to a person acting on the carrier's or the actual carrier's behalf, including the master or the officer in charge of the ship, or to a person acting on the shipper's behalf is deemed to have been to the carrier, to the actual carrier or the shipper, respectively.

Article 20

Limitation of Actions

1. Any action relating to carriage of goods under this Convention is time-barred if judicial or arbitral proceedings have not been instituted within a period of two years.

2. The limitation period commences on the day on which the carrier has delivered the goods or part thereof or, in cases where no goods have been delivered, on the last day on which the goods should have been delivered.

3. The day on which the limitation period commences is not included in the period.

4. The person against whom a claim is made may at any time during the running of the limitation period extend that period by a declaration in writing to the claimant. This period may be further extended by another declaration or declarations.

5. An action for indemnity by a person held liable may be instituted even after the expiration of the limitation period provided for in the preceding paragraphs if instituted within the time allowed by the law of the State where proceedings are instituted. However, the time allowed shall not be less than 90 days commencing from the day when the person instituting such action for indemnity has settled the claim or has been served with process in the action against himself.

Article 21

Jurisdiction

1. In judicial proceedings relating to carriage of goods under this Convention the plaintiff, at his option, may institute an action in a court which, according to the law of the State where the court is situated, is

competent and within the jurisdiction of which is situated one of the following places:

(a) the principal place of business or, in the absence thereof, the habitual residence of the defendant; or

(b) the place where the contract was made provided that the defendant has there a place of business, branch or agency through which the contract was made; or

(c) the port of loading or the port of discharge; or

(d) any additional place designated for that purpose in the contract of carriage by sea.

2.   (a) Notwithstanding the preceding provisions of this article, an action may be instituted in the courts of any port or place in a Contracting State at which the carrying vessel or any other vessel of the same ownership may have been arrested in accordance with applicable rules of the law of that State and of international law. However, in such a case, at the petition of the defendant, the claimant must remove the action, at his choice, to one of the jurisdictions referred to in paragraph 1 of this article for the determination of the claim, but before such removal the defendant must furnish security sufficient to ensure payment of any judgment that may subsequently be awarded to the claimant in the action.

(b) All questions relating to the sufficiency or otherwise of the security shall be determined by the court of the port or place of the arrest.

3.   No judicial proceedings relating to carriage of goods under this Convention may be instituted in a place not specified in paragraph 1 or 2 of this article. The provisions of this paragraph do not constitute an obstacle to the jurisdiction of the Contracting States for provisional or protective measures.

4.   (a) Where an action has been instituted in a court competent under paragraph 1 or 2 of this article or where judgment has been delivered by such a court, no new action may be started between the same parties on the same grounds unless the judgment of the court before which the first action was instituted is not enforceable in the country in which the new proceedings are instituted;

(b) for the purpose of this article the institution of measures with a view to obtaining enforcement of a judgment is not to be considered as the starting of a new action;

(c) for the purpose of this article, the removal of an action to a different court within the same country, or to a court in another country, in accordance with paragraph 2(a) of this article, is not to be considered as the starting of a new action.

5.   Notwithstanding the provisions of the preceding paragraphs, an agreement made by the parties, after a claim under the contract of

carriage by sea has arisen, which designates the place where the claimant may institute an action, is effective.

Article 22

Arbitration

1. Subject to the provisions of this article, parties may provide by agreement evidenced in writing that any dispute that may rise relating to carriage of goods under this convention shall be referred to arbitration.

2. Where a charter-party contains a provision that disputes arising thereunder shall be referred to arbitration and a bill of lading issued pursuant to the charter-party does not contain a special annotation providing that such provision shall be binding upon the holder of the bill of lading, the carrier may not invoke such provision as against a holder having acquired the bill of lading good faith.

3. The arbitration proceedings shall, at the option of the claimant, be instituted at one of the following places:

(a) a place in a State within whose territory is situated:

(i) the principal place of business of the defendant or, in the absence thereof, the habitual residence of the defendant; or

(ii) the place where the contract was made, provided that the defendant has there a place of business, branch or agency through which the contract was made; or

(iii) the port of loading or the port of discharge; or

(b) any place designated for that purpose in the arbitration clause or agreement.

4. The arbitrator or arbitration tribunal shall apply the rules of this Convention.

5. The provisions of paragraphs 3 and 4 of this article are deemed to be part of every arbitration clause or agreement, and any term of such clause or agreement which is inconsistent therewith is null and void.

6. Nothing in this article affects the validity of an agreement relating to arbitration made by the parties after the claim under the contract of carriage by sea has arisen.

PART VI.   SUPPLEMENTARY PROVISIONS

Article 23

Contractual Stipulations

1. Any stipulation in a contract of carriage by sea, in a bill of lading, or in any other document evidencing the contract of carriage by sea is null and void to the extent that it derogates, directly or indirectly, from the provisions of this Convention. The nullity of such a stipulation does not affect the validity of the other provisions of the contract or document of which it forms a part. A clause assigning benefit of insurance

of the goods in favour of the carrier, or any similar clause, is null and void.

2. Notwithstanding the provisions of paragraph 1 of this article, a carrier may increase his responsibilities and obligations under this Convention.

3. Where a bill of lading or any other document evidencing the contract of carriage by sea is issued, it must contain a statement that the carriage is subject to the provisions of this Convention which nullify any stipulation derogating therefrom to the detriment of the shipper or the consignee.

4. Where the claimant in respect of the goods has incurred loss as a result of a stipulation which is null and void by virtue of the present article, or as a result of the omission of the statement referred to in paragraph 3 of this article, the carrier must pay compensation to the extent required in order to give the claimant compensation in accordance with the provisions of this Convention for any loss of or damage to the goods as well as for delay in delivery. The carrier must, in addition, pay compensation for costs incurred by the claimant for the purpose of exercising his right, provided that costs incurred in the action where the foregoing provision is invoked are to be determined in accordance with the law of the State where proceedings are instituted.

Article 24

General Average

1. Nothing in this Convention shall prevent the application of provisions in the contract of carriage by sea or national law regarding the adjustment of general average.

2. With the exception of article 20, the provisions of this Convention relating to the liability of the carrier for loss of or damage to the goods also determine whether the consignee may refuse contribution in general average and the liability of the carrier to indemnify the consignee in respect of any such contribution made or any salvage paid.

Article 25

Other Conventions

1. This Convention does not modify the rights or duties of the carrier, the actual carrier and their servants and agents, provided for in international conventions or national law relating to the limitation of liability of owners of seagoing ships.

2. The provisions of articles 21 and 22 of this Convention do not prevent the application of the mandatory provisions of any other multilateral convention already in force at the date of this Convention relating to matters dealt with in the said articles, provided that the dispute arises exclusively between parties having their principal place of business in States members of such other convention. However, this

paragraph does not affect the application of paragraph 4 of article 22 of this Convention.

3.   No liability shall arise under the provisions of this Convention for damage caused by a nuclear incident if the operator of a nuclear installation is liable for such damage:

(a)   under either the Paris Convention of 29 July 1960 on Third Party Liability in the Field of Nuclear Energy as amended by the Additional Protocol of 28 January 1964 or the Vienna Convention of 21 May 1963 on Civil Liability for Nuclear Damage, or

(b)   by virtue of national law governing the liability for such damage, provided that such law is in all respects as favourable to persons who may suffer damage as either the Pairs or Vienna Conventions.

4.   No liability shall arise under the provisions of this Convention for any loss of or damage to or delay in delivery of luggage for which the carrier is responsible under any international convention or national law relating to the carriage of passengers and their luggage by sea.

5.   Nothing contained in this Convention prevents a Contracting State from applying any other international convention which is already in force at the date of this Convention and which applies mandatorily to contracts of carriage of goods primarily by a mode of transport other than transport by sea. This provision also applies to any subsequent revision or amendment of such international convention.

Article 26

Unit of Account

1.   The unit of account referred to in article 6 of this Convention is the Special Drawing Right as defined by the International Monetary Fund. The amounts mentioned in article 6 are to be converted into the national currency of a State according to the value of such currency at the date of judgment or the date agreed upon by the parties. The value of a national currency, in terms of the Special Drawing Right, of a Contracting State which is a member of the International Monetary Fund is to be calculated in accordance with the method of valuation applied by the International Monetary Fund in effect at the date in question for its operation and transactions. The value of a national currency in terms of the Special Drawing Right of a Contracting State which is not a member of the International Monetary Fund is to be calculated in a manner determined by that State.

2.   Nevertheless, those States which are not members of the International Monetary Fund and whose law does not permit the application of the provisions of paragraph 1 of this article may, at the time of signature, or at the time of ratification, acceptance, approval or accession or at any time thereafter, declare that the limits of liability

provided for in this Convention to be applied in their territories shall be fixed as:

> 12,500 monetary units per package or other shipping unit or 37.5 monetary units per kilogramme of gross weight of the goods.

3.   The monetary unit referred to in paragraph 2 of this article corresponds to sixty-five and a half milligrammes of gold of millesimal fineness nine hundred. The conversion of the amounts referred to in paragraph 2 into the national currency is to be made according to the law of the State concerned.

4.   The calculation mentioned in the last sentence of paragraph 1 and the conversion mentioned in paragraph 3 of this article is to be made in such a manner as to express in the national currency of the Contracting State as far as possible the same real value for the amounts in article 6 as is expressed there in units of account. Contracting States must communicate to the depositary the manner of calculation pursuant to paragraph 1 of this article, or the result of the conversion mentioned in paragraph 3 of this article, as the case may be, at the time of signature or when depositing their instruments of ratification, acceptance, approval or accession, or when availing themselves of the option provided for in paragraph 2 of this article and whenever there is a change in the manner of such calculation or in the result of such conversion.

PART VII.   FINAL CLAUSES

* * *

UNITED NATIONS CONVENTION ON CONTRACTS FOR THE INTERNATIONAL CARRIAGE OF GOODS WHOLLY OR PARTLY BY THE SEA

("Rotterdam Rules")

Drafted by the United Nations Commission on International Trade Law and adopted by the General Assembly of the United Nations on December 11, 2008.

The States Parties to this Convention,

Reaffirming their belief that international trade on the basis of equality and mutual benefit is an important element in promoting friendly relations among States,

Convinced that the progressive harmonization and unification of international trade law, in reducing or removing legal obstacles to the flow of international trade, significantly contributes to universal economic cooperation among all States on a basis of equality, equity and common interest, and to the well-being of all peoples,

Recognizing the significant contribution of the International Convention for the Unification of Certain Rules of Law relating to Bills of Lading, signed in Brussels on 25 August 1924, and its Protocols, and of the United Nations Convention on the Carriage of Goods by Sea, signed in Hamburg on 31 March 1978, to the harmonization of the law governing the carriage of goods by sea,

Mindful of the technological and commercial developments that have taken place since the adoption of those conventions and of the need to consolidate and modernize them,

Noting that shippers and carriers do not have the benefit of a binding universal regime to support the operation of contracts of maritime carriage involving other modes of transport,

Believing that the adoption of uniform rules to govern international contracts of carriage wholly or partly by sea will promote legal certainty, improve the efficiency of international carriage of goods and facilitate new access opportunities for previously remote parties and markets, thus playing a fundamental role in promoting trade and economic development, both domestically and internationally,

Have agreed as follows:

Chapter 1
General provisions
Article 1
Definitions

For the purposes of this Convention:

1.   "Contract of carriage" means a contract in which a carrier, against the payment of freight, undertakes to carry goods from one place to another. The contract shall provide for carriage by sea and may provide for carriage by other modes of transport in addition to the sea carriage.

2.   "Volume contract" means a contract of carriage that provides for the carriage of a specified quantity of goods in a series of shipments during an agreed period of time. The specification of the quantity may include a minimum, a maximum or a certain range.

3.   "Liner transportation" means a transportation service that is offered to the public through publication or similar means and includes transportation by ships operating on a regular schedule between specified ports in accordance with publicly available timetables of sailing dates.

4.   "Non-liner transportation" means any transportation that is not liner transportation.

5.   "Carrier" means a person that enters into a contract of carriage with a shipper.

6.   (a) "Performing party" means a person other than the carrier that performs or undertakes to perform any of the carrier's obligations under a contract of carriage with respect to the receipt, loading, handling, stowage, carriage, care, unloading or delivery of the goods, to the extent

that such person acts, either directly or indirectly, at the carrier's request or under the carrier's supervision or control.

(b) "Performing party" does not include any person that is retained, directly or indirectly, by a shipper, by a documentary shipper, by the controlling party or by the consignee instead of by the carrier.

7. "Maritime performing party" means a performing party to the extent that it performs or undertakes to perform any of the carrier's obligations during the period between the arrival of the goods at the port of loading of a ship and their departure from the port of discharge of a ship. An inland carrier is a maritime performing party only if it performs or undertakes to perform its services exclusively within a port area.

8. "Shipper" means a person that enters into a contract of carriage with a carrier.

9. "Documentary shipper" means a person, other than the shipper, that accepts to be named as "shipper" in the transport document or electronic transport record.

10. "Holder" means:

(a) A person that is in possession of a negotiable transport document; and (I) if the document is an order document, is identified in it as the shipper or the consignee, or is the person to which the document is duly endorsed; or (ii) if the document is a blank endorsed order document or bearer document, is the bearer thereof; or

(b) The person to which a negotiable electronic transport record has been issued or transferred in accordance with the procedures referred to in article 9, paragraph 1.

11. "Consignee" means a person entitled to delivery of the goods under a contract of carriage or a transport document or electronic transport record.

12. "Right of control" of the goods means the right under the contract of carriage to give the carrier instructions in respect of the goods in accordance with chapter 10.

13. "Controlling party" means the person that pursuant to article 51 is entitled to exercise the right of control.

14. "Transport document" means a document issued under a contract of carriage by the carrier that:

(a) Evidences the carrier's or a performing party's receipt of goods under a contract of carriage; and

(b) Evidences or contains a contract of carriage.

15. "Negotiable transport document" means a transport document that indicates, by wording such as "to order" or "negotiable" or other appropriate wording recognized as having the same effect by the law applicable to the document, that the goods have been consigned to the

order of the shipper, to the order of the consignee, or to bearer, and is not explicitly stated as being "non-negotiable" or "not negotiable".

16. "Non-negotiable transport document" means a transport document that is not a negotiable transport document.

17. "Electronic communication" means information generated, sent, received or stored by electronic, optical, digital or similar means with the result that the information communicated is accessible so as to be usable for subsequent reference.

18. "Electronic transport record" means information in one or more messages issued by electronic communication under a contract of carriage by a carrier, including information logically associated with the electronic transport record by attachments or otherwise linked to the electronic transport record contemporaneously with or subsequent to its issue by the carrier, so as to become part of the electronic transport record, that:

(a) Evidences the carrier's or a performing party's receipt of goods under a contract of carriage; and

(b) Evidences or contains a contract of carriage.

19. "Negotiable electronic transport record" means an electronic transport record:

(a) That indicates, by wording such as "to order", or "negotiable", or other appropriate wording recognized as having the same effect by the law applicable to the record, that the goods have been consigned to the order of the shipper or to the order of the consignee, and is not explicitly stated as being "non-negotiable" or "not negotiable"; and

(b) The use of which meets the requirements of article 9, paragraph 1.

20. "Non-negotiable electronic transport record" means an electronic transport record that is not a negotiable electronic transport record.

21. The "issuance" of a negotiable electronic transport record means the issuance of the record in accordance with procedures that ensure that the record is subject to exclusive control from its creation until it ceases to have any effect or validity.

22. The "transfer" of a negotiable electronic transport record means the transfer of exclusive control over the record.

23. "Contract particulars" means any information relating to the contract of carriage or to the goods (including terms, notations, signatures and endorsements) that is in a transport document or an electronic transport record.

24. "Goods" means the wares, merchandise, and articles of every kind whatsoever that a carrier undertakes to carry under a contract of

carriage and includes the packing and any equipment and container not supplied by or on behalf of the carrier.

25. "Ship" means any vessel used to carry goods by sea.

26. "Container" means any type of container, transportable tank or flat, swapbody, or any similar unit load used to consolidate goods, and any equipment ancillary to such unit load.

27. "Vehicle" means a road or railroad cargo vehicle.

28. "Freight" means the remuneration payable to the carrier for the carriage of goods under a contract of carriage.

29. "Domicile" means (*a*) a place where a company or other legal person or association of natural or legal persons has its (i) statutory seat or place of incorporation or central registered office, whichever is applicable, (ii) central administration or (iii) principal place of business, and (*b*) the habitual residence of a natural person.

30. "Competent court" means a court in a Contracting State that, according to the rules on the internal allocation of jurisdiction among the courts of that State, may exercise jurisdiction over the dispute.

Article 2

Interpretation of this Convention

In the interpretation of this Convention, regard is to be had to its international character and to the need to promote uniformity in its application and the observance of good faith in international trade.

Article 3

Form requirements

The notices, confirmation, consent, agreement, declaration and other communications referred to in articles 19, paragraph 2; 23, paragraphs 1 to 4; 36, subparagraphs 1 (*b*), (*c*) and (*d*); 40, subparagraph 4 (*b*); 44; 48, paragraph 3; 51, subparagraph 1 (*b*); 59, paragraph 1; 63; 66; 67, paragraph 2; 75, paragraph 4; and 80, paragraphs 2 and 5, shall be in writing. Electronic communications may be used for these purposes, provided that the use of such means is with the consent of the person by which it is communicated and of the person to which it is communicated.

Article 4

Applicability of defences and limits of liability

1. Any provision of this Convention that may provide a defence for, or limit the liability of, the carrier applies in any judicial or arbitral proceeding, whether founded in contract, in tort, or otherwise, that is instituted in respect of loss of, damage to, or delay in delivery of goods covered by a contract of carriage or for the breach of any other obligation under this Convention against:

(a)   The carrier or a maritime performing party;

(b) The master, crew or any other person that performs services on board the ship; or

(c) Employees of the carrier or a maritime performing party.

2. Any provision of this Convention that may provide a defence for the shipper or the documentary shipper applies in any judicial or arbitral proceeding, whether founded in contract, in tort, or otherwise, that is instituted against the shipper, the documentary shipper, or their subcontractors, agents or employees.

Chapter 2

Scope of application

Article 5

General scope of application

1. Subject to article 6, this Convention applies to contracts of carriage in which the place of receipt and the place of delivery are in different States, and the port of loading of a sea carriage and the port of discharge of the same sea carriage are in different States, if, according to the contract of carriage, any one of the following places is located in a Contracting State:

(a) The place of receipt;

(b) The port of loading;

(c) The place of delivery; or

(d) The port of discharge.

2. This Convention applies without regard to the nationality of the vessel, the carrier, the performing parties, the shipper, the consignee, or any other interested parties.

Article 6

Specific exclusions

1. This Convention does not apply to the following contracts in liner transportation:

(a) Charter parties; and

(b) Other contracts for the use of a ship or of any space thereon.

2. This Convention does not apply to contracts of carriage in non-liner transportation except when:

(a) There is no charter party or other contract between the parties for the use of a ship or of any space thereon; and

(b) A transport document or an electronic transport record is issued.

Article 7

Application to certain parties

Notwithstanding article 6, this Convention applies as between the carrier and the consignee, controlling party or holder that is not an original party to the charter party or other contract of carriage excluded from the application of this Convention. However, this Convention does not apply as between the original parties to a contract of carriage excluded pursuant to article 6.

Chapter 3

Electronic transport records

Article 8

Use and effect of electronic transport records

Subject to the requirements set out in this Convention:

(a) Anything that is to be in or on a transport document under this Convention may be recorded in an electronic transport record, provided the issuance and subsequent use of an electronic transport record is with the consent of the carrier and the shipper; and

(b) The issuance, exclusive control, or transfer of an electronic transport record has the same effect as the issuance, possession, or transfer of a transport document.

Article 9

Procedures for use of negotiable electronic transport records

1. The use of a negotiable electronic transport record shall be subject to procedures that provide for:

(a) The method for the issuance and the transfer of that record to an intended holder;

(b) An assurance that the negotiable electronic transport record retains its integrity;

(c) The manner in which the holder is able to demonstrate that it is the holder; and

(d) The manner of providing confirmation that delivery to the holder has been effected, or that, pursuant to articles 10, paragraph 2, or 47, subparagraphs 1 (a) (ii) and (c), the electronic transport record has ceased to have any effect or validity.

2. The procedures in paragraph 1 of this article shall be referred to in the contract particulars and be readily ascertainable.

Article 10

Replacement of negotiable transport document or
negotiable electronic transport record

1.   If a negotiable transport document has been issued and the carrier and the holder agree to replace that document by a negotiable electronic transport record:

(a) The holder shall surrender the negotiable transport document, or all of them if more than one has been issued, to the carrier;

(b) The carrier shall issue to the holder a negotiable electronic transport record that includes a statement that it replaces the negotiable transport document; and

(c) The negotiable transport document ceases thereafter to have any effect or validity.

2.   If a negotiable electronic transport record has been issued and the carrier and the holder agree to replace that electronic transport record by a negotiable transport document:

(a) The carrier shall issue to the holder, in place of the electronic transport record, a negotiable transport document that includes a statement that it replaces the negotiable electronic transport record; and

(b) The electronic transport record ceases thereafter to have any effect or validity.

Chapter 4

Obligations of the carrier

Article 11

Carriage and delivery of the goods

The carrier shall, subject to this Convention and in accordance with the terms of the contract of carriage, carry the goods to the place of destination and deliver them to the consignee.

Article 12

Period of responsibility of the carrier

1.   The period of responsibility of the carrier for the goods under this Convention begins when the carrier or a performing party receives the goods for carriage and ends when the goods are delivered.

2.   (a) If the law or regulations of the place of receipt require the goods to be handed over to an authority or other third party from which the carrier may collect them, the period of responsibility of the carrier begins when the carrier collects the goods from the authority or other third party.

(b) If the law or regulations of the place of delivery require the carrier to hand over the goods to an authority or other third party from which the consignee may collect them, the period of responsibility of the carrier ends when the carrier hands the goods over to the authority or other third party.

3.   For the purpose of determining the carrier's period of responsibility, the parties may agree on the time and location of receipt and delivery of the goods, but a provision in a contract of carriage is void to the extent that it provides that:

(a)   The time of receipt of the goods is subsequent to the beginning of their initial loading under the contract of carriage; or

(b)   The time of delivery of the goods is prior to the completion of their final unloading under the contract of carriage.

Article 13

Specific obligations

1.   The carrier shall during the period of its responsibility as defined in article 12, and subject to article 26, properly and carefully receive, load, handle, stow, carry, keep, care for, unload and deliver the goods.

2.   Notwithstanding paragraph 1 of this article, and without prejudice to the other provisions in chapter 4 and to chapters 5 to 7, the carrier and the shipper may agree that the loading, handling, stowing or unloading of the goods is to be performed by the shipper, the documentary shipper or the consignee. Such an agreement shall be referred to in the contract particulars.

Article 14

Specific obligations applicable to the voyage by sea

The carrier is bound before, at the beginning of, and during the voyage by sea to exercise due diligence to:

(a)   Make and keep the ship seaworthy;

(b)   Properly crew, equip and supply the ship and keep the ship so crewed, equipped and supplied throughout the voyage; and

(c)   Make and keep the holds and all other parts of the ship in which the goods are carried, and any containers supplied by the carrier in or upon which the goods are carried, fit and safe for their reception, carriage and preservation.

Article 15

Goods that may become a danger

Notwithstanding articles 11 and 13, the carrier or a performing party may decline to receive or to load, and may take such other measures as are reasonable, including unloading, destroying, or rendering goods harmless, if the goods are, or reasonably appear likely to become during the carrier's period of responsibility, an actual danger to persons, property or the environment.

Article 16

Sacrifice of the goods during the voyage by sea

Notwithstanding articles 11, 13, and 14, the carrier or a performing party may sacrifice goods at sea when the sacrifice is reasonably made for the common safety or for the purpose of preserving from peril human life or other property involved in the common adventure.

Chapter 5

Liability of the carrier for loss, damage or delay

Article 17

Basis of liability

1.   The carrier is liable for loss of or damage to the goods, as well as for delay in delivery, if the claimant proves that the loss, damage, or delay, or the event or circumstance that caused or contributed to it took place during the period of the carrier's responsibility as defined in chapter 4.

2.   The carrier is relieved of all or part of its liability pursuant to paragraph 1 of this article if it proves that the cause or one of the causes of the loss, damage, or delay is not attributable to its fault or to the fault of any person referred to in article 18.

3.   The carrier is also relieved of all or part of its liability pursuant to paragraph 1 of this article if, alternatively to proving the absence of fault as provided in paragraph 2 of this article, it proves that one or more of the following events or circumstances caused or contributed to the loss, damage, or delay:

(a) Act of God;

(b) Perils, dangers, and accidents of the sea or other navigable waters;

(c) War, hostilities, armed conflict, piracy, terrorism, riots, and civil commotions;

(d) Quarantine restrictions; interference by or impediments created by governments, public authorities, rulers, or people including detention, arrest, or seizure not attributable to the carrier or any person referred to in article 18;

(e) Strikes, lockouts, stoppages, or restraints of labour;

(f) Fire on the ship;

(g) Latent defects not discoverable by due diligence;

(h) Act or omission of the shipper, the documentary shipper, the controlling party, or any other person for whose acts the shipper or the documentary shipper is liable pursuant to article 33 or 34;

(i) Loading, handling, stowing, or unloading of the goods performed pursuant to an agreement in accordance with article 13, paragraph 2, unless the carrier or a performing party performs such activity on behalf of the shipper, the documentary shipper or the consignee;

(j) Wastage in bulk or weight or any other loss or damage arising from inherent defect, quality, or vice of the goods;

(k) Insufficiency or defective condition of packing or marking not performed by or on behalf of the carrier;

(l) Saving or attempting to save life at sea;

(m) Reasonable measures to save or attempt to save property at sea;

(n) Reasonable measures to avoid or attempt to avoid damage to the environment; or

(o) Acts of the carrier in pursuance of the powers conferred by articles 15 and 16.

4. Notwithstanding paragraph 3 of this article, the carrier is liable for all or part of the loss, damage, or delay:

(a) If the claimant proves that the fault of the carrier or of a person referred to in article 18 caused or contributed to the event or circumstance on which the carrier relies; or

(b) If the claimant proves that an event or circumstance not listed in paragraph 3 of this article contributed to the loss, damage, or delay, and the carrier cannot prove that this event or circumstance is not attributable to its fault or to the fault of any person referred to in article 18.

5. The carrier is also liable, notwithstanding paragraph 3 of this article, for all or part of the loss, damage, or delay if:

(a) The claimant proves that the loss, damage, or delay was or was probably caused by or contributed to by (I) the unseaworthiness of the ship; (ii) the improper crewing, equipping, and supplying of the ship; or (iii) the fact that the holds or other parts of the ship in which the goods are carried, or any containers supplied by the carrier in or upon which the goods are carried, were not fit and safe for reception, carriage, and preservation of the goods; and

(b) The carrier is unable to prove either that: (I) none of the events or circumstances referred to in subparagraph 5 (a) of this article caused the loss, damage, or delay; or (ii) it complied with its obligation to exercise due diligence pursuant to article 14.

6. When the carrier is relieved of part of its liability pursuant to this article, the carrier is liable only for that part of the loss, damage or delay that is attributable to the event or circumstance for which it is liable pursuant to this article.

Article 18

Liability of the carrier for other persons

The carrier is liable for the breach of its obligations under this Convention caused by the acts or omissions of:

(a) Any performing party;

(b) The master or crew of the ship;

(c) Employees of the carrier or a performing party; or

(d) Any other person that performs or undertakes to perform any of the carrier's obligations under the contract of carriage, to the extent that the person acts, either directly or indirectly, at the carrier's request or under the carrier's supervision or control.

Article 19

Liability of maritime performing parties

1. A maritime performing party is subject to the obligations and liabilities imposed on the carrier under this Convention and is entitled to the carrier's defences and limits of liability as provided for in this Convention if:

(a) The maritime performing party received the goods for carriage in a Contracting State, or delivered them in a Contracting State, or performed its activities with respect to the goods in a port in a Contracting State; and

(b) The occurrence that caused the loss, damage or delay took place: (i) during the period between the arrival of the goods at the port of loading of the ship and their departure from the port of discharge from the ship; (ii) while the maritime performing party had custody of the goods; or (iii) at any other time to the extent that it was participating in the performance of any of the activities contemplated by the contract of carriage.

2. If the carrier agrees to assume obligations other than those imposed on the carrier under this Convention, or agrees that the limits of its liability are higher than the limits specified under this Convention, a maritime performing party is not bound by this agreement unless it expressly agrees to accept such obligations or such higher limits.

3. A maritime performing party is liable for the breach of its obligations under this Convention caused by the acts or omissions of any person to which it has entrusted the performance of any of the carrier's obligations under the contract of carriage under the conditions set out in paragraph 1 of this article.

4. Nothing in this Convention imposes liability on the master or crew of the ship or on an employee of the carrier or of a maritime performing party.

Article 20

Joint and several liability

1.   If the carrier and one or more maritime performing parties are liable for the loss of, damage to, or delay in delivery of the goods, their liability is joint and several but only up to the limits provided for under this Convention.

2.   Without prejudice to article 61, the aggregate liability of all such persons shall not exceed the overall limits of liability under this Convention.

Article 21

Delay

Delay in delivery occurs when the goods are not delivered at the place of destination provided for in the contract of carriage within the time agreed.

Article 22

Calculation of compensation

Subject to article 59, the compensation payable by the carrier for loss of or damage to the goods is calculated by reference to the value of such goods at the place and time of delivery established in accordance with article 43.

The value of the goods is fixed according to the commodity exchange price or, if there is no such price, according to their market price or, if there is no commodity exchange price or market price, by reference to the normal value of the goods of the same kind and quality at the place of delivery.

In case of loss of or damage to the goods, the carrier is not liable for payment of any compensation beyond what is provided for in paragraphs 1 and 2 of this article except when the carrier and the shipper have agreed to calculate compensation in a different manner within the limits of chapter 16.

Article 23

Notice in case of loss, damage or delay

1.   The carrier is presumed, in absence of proof to the contrary, to have delivered the goods according to their description in the contract particulars unless notice of loss of or damage to the goods, indicating the general nature of such loss or damage, was given to the carrier or the performing party that delivered the goods before or at the time of the delivery, or, if the loss or damage is not apparent, within seven working days at the place of delivery after the delivery of the goods.

2.   Failure to provide the notice referred to in this article to the carrier or the performing party shall not affect the right to claim compensation for loss of or damage to the goods under this Convention,

nor shall it affect the allocation of the burden of proof set out in article 17.

3. The notice referred to in this article is not required in respect of loss or damage that is ascertained in a joint inspection of the goods by the person to which they have been delivered and the carrier or the maritime performing party against which liability is being asserted.

4. No compensation in respect of delay is payable unless notice of loss due to delay was given to the carrier within twenty-one consecutive days of delivery of the goods.

5. When the notice referred to in this article is given to the performing party that delivered the goods, it has the same effect as if that notice was given to the carrier, and notice given to the carrier has the same effect as a notice given to a maritime performing party.

6. In the case of any actual or apprehended loss or damage, the parties to the dispute shall give all reasonable facilities to each other for inspecting and tallying the goods and shall provide access to records and documents relevant to the carriage of the goods.

Chapter 6

Additional provisions relating to particular stages of carriage

Article 24

Deviation

When pursuant to applicable law a deviation constitutes a breach of the carrier's obligations, such deviation of itself shall not deprive the carrier or a maritime performing party of any defence or limitation of this Convention, except to the extent provided in article 61.

Article 25

Deck cargo on ships

1. Goods may be carried on the deck of a ship only if:

(a) Such carriage is required by law;

(b) They are carried in or on containers or vehicles that are fit for deck carriage, and the decks are specially fitted to carry such containers or vehicles; or

(c) The carriage on deck is in accordance with the contract of carriage, or the customs, usages or practices of the trade in question.

2. The provisions of this Convention relating to the liability of the carrier apply to the loss of, damage to or delay in the delivery of goods carried on deck pursuant to paragraph 1 of this article, but the carrier is not liable for loss of or damage to such goods, or delay in their delivery, caused by the special risks involved in their carriage on deck when the goods are carried in accordance with subparagraphs 1 (*a*) or (*c*) of this article.

3.   If the goods have been carried on deck in cases other than those permitted pursuant to paragraph 1 of this article, the carrier is liable for loss of or damage to the goods or delay in their delivery that is exclusively caused by their carriage on deck, and is not entitled to the defences provided for in article 17.

4.   The carrier is not entitled to invoke subparagraph 1 © of this article against a third party that has acquired a negotiable transport document or a negotiable electronic transport record in good faith, unless the contract particulars state that the goods may be carried on deck.

5.   If the carrier and shipper expressly agreed that the goods would be carried under deck, the carrier is not entitled to the benefit of the limitation of liability for any loss of, damage to or delay in the delivery of the goods to the extent that such loss, damage, or delay resulted from their carriage on deck.

Article 26

Carriage preceding or subsequent to sea carriage

When loss of or damage to goods, or an event or circumstance causing a delay in their delivery, occurs during the carrier's period of responsibility but solely before their loading onto the ship or solely after their discharge from the ship, the provisions of this Convention do not prevail over those provisions of another international instrument that, at the time of such loss, damage or event or circumstance causing delay:

(a)   Pursuant to the provisions of such international instrument would have applied to all or any of the carrier's activities if the shipper had made a separate and direct contract with the carrier in respect of the particular stage of carriage where the loss of, or damage to goods, or an event or circumstance causing delay in their delivery occurred;

(b)   Specifically provide for the carrier's liability, limitation of liability, or time for suit; and

(c)   Cannot be departed from by contract either at all or to the detriment of the shipper under that instrument.

Chapter 7

Obligations of the shipper to the carrier

Article 27

Delivery for carriage

1.   Unless otherwise agreed in the contract of carriage, the shipper shall deliver the goods ready for carriage. In any event, the shipper shall deliver the goods in such condition that they will withstand the intended carriage, including their loading, handling, stowing, lashing and securing, and unloading, and that they will not cause harm to persons or property.

2.   The shipper shall properly and carefully perform any obligation assumed under an agreement made pursuant to article 13, paragraph 2.

3.   When a container is packed or a vehicle is loaded by the shipper, the shipper shall properly and carefully stow, lash and secure the contents in or on the container or vehicle, and in such a way that they will not cause harm to persons or property.

Article 28

Cooperation of the shipper and the carrier in providing information and instructions

The carrier and the shipper shall respond to requests from each other to provide information and instructions required for the proper handling and carriage of the goods if the information is in the requested party's possession or the instructions are within the requested party's reasonable ability to provide and they are not otherwise reasonably available to the requesting party.

Article 29

Shipper's obligation to provide information, instructions and documents

1.   The shipper shall provide to the carrier in a timely manner such information, instructions and documents relating to the goods that are not otherwise reasonably available to the carrier, and that are reasonably necessary:

(a)   For the proper handling and carriage of the goods, including precautions to be taken by the carrier or a performing party; and

(b)   For the carrier to comply with law, regulations or other requirements of public authorities in connection with the intended carriage, provided that the carrier notifies the shipper in a timely manner of the information, instructions and documents it requires.

2.   Nothing in this article affects any specific obligation to provide certain information, instructions and documents related to the goods pursuant to law, regulations or other requirements of public authorities in connection with the intended carriage.

Article 30

Basis of shipper's liability to the carrier

1.   The shipper is liable for loss or damage sustained by the carrier if the carrier proves that such loss or damage was caused by a breach of the shipper's obligations under this Convention.

2.   Except in respect of loss or damage caused by a breach by the shipper of its obligations pursuant to articles 31, paragraph 2, and 32, the shipper is relieved of all or part of its liability if the cause or one of the causes of the loss or damage is not attributable to its fault or to the fault of any person referred to in article 34.

3.   When the shipper is relieved of part of its liability pursuant to this article, the shipper is liable only for that part of the loss or damage that is attributable to its fault or to the fault of any person referred to in article 34.

Article 31

Information for compilation of contract particulars

1.   The shipper shall provide to the carrier, in a timely manner, accurate information required for the compilation of the contract particulars and the issuance of the transport documents or electronic transport records, including the particulars referred to in article 36, paragraph 1; the name of the party to be identified as the shipper in the contract particulars; the name of the consignee, if any; and the name of the person to whose order the transport document or electronic transport record is to be issued, if any.

2.   The shipper is deemed to have guaranteed the accuracy at the time of receipt by the carrier of the information that is provided according to paragraph 1 of this article. The shipper shall indemnify the carrier against loss or damage resulting from the inaccuracy of such information.

Article 32

Special rules on dangerous goods

When goods by their nature or character are, or reasonably appear likely to become, a danger to persons, property or the environment:

(a) The shipper shall inform the carrier of the dangerous nature or character of the goods in a timely manner before they are delivered to the carrier or a performing party. If the shipper fails to do so and the carrier or performing party does not otherwise have knowledge of their dangerous nature or character, the shipper is liable to the carrier for loss or damage resulting from such failure to inform; and

(b) The shipper shall mark or label dangerous goods in accordance with any law, regulations or other requirements of public authorities that apply during any stage of the intended carriage of the goods. If the shipper fails to do so, it is liable to the carrier for loss or damage resulting from such failure.

Article 33

Assumption of shipper's rights and obligations
by the documentary shipper

1.   A documentary shipper is subject to the obligations and liabilities imposed on the shipper pursuant to this chapter and pursuant to article 55, and is entitled to the shipper's rights and defences provided by this chapter and by chapter 13.

2.   Paragraph 1 of this article does not affect the obligations, liabilities, rights or defences of the shipper.

Article 34

Liability of the shipper for other persons

The shipper is liable for the breach of its obligations under this Convention caused by the acts or omissions of any person, including employees, agents and subcontractors, to which it has entrusted the performance of any of its obligations, but the shipper is not liable for acts or omissions of the carrier or a performing party acting on behalf of the carrier, to which the shipper has entrusted the performance of its obligations.

Chapter 8

Transport documents and electronic transport records

Article 35

Issuance of the transport document or the electronic transport record

Unless the shipper and the carrier have agreed not to use a transport document or an electronic transport record, or it is the custom, usage or practice of the trade not to use one, upon delivery of the goods for carriage to the carrier or performing party, the shipper or, if the shipper consents, the documentary shipper, is entitled to obtain from the carrier, at the shipper's option:

(a) A non-negotiable transport document or, subject to article 8, subparagraph (a), a non-negotiable electronic transport record; or

(b) An appropriate negotiable transport document or, subject to article 8, subparagraph (a), a negotiable electronic transport record, unless the shipper and the carrier have agreed not to use a negotiable transport document or negotiable electronic transport record, or it is the custom, usage or practice of the trade not to use one.

Article 36

Contract particulars

1. The contract particulars in the transport document or electronic transport record referred to in article 35 shall include the following information, as furnished by the shipper:

(a) A description of the goods as appropriate for the transport;

(b) The leading marks necessary for identification of the goods;

(c) The number of packages or pieces, or the quantity of goods; and

(d) The weight of the goods, if furnished by the shipper.

2. The contract particulars in the transport document or electronic transport record referred to in article 35 shall also include:

138

(a) A statement of the apparent order and condition of the goods at the time the carrier or a performing party receives them for carriage;

(b) The name and address of the carrier;

(c) The date on which the carrier or a performing party received the goods, or on which the goods were loaded on board the ship, or on which the transport document or electronic transport record was issued; and

(d) If the transport document is negotiable, the number of originals of the negotiable transport document, when more than one original is issued.

3.   The contract particulars in the transport document or electronic transport record referred to in article 35 shall further include:

(a) The name and address of the consignee, if named by the shipper;

(b) The name of a ship, if specified in the contract of carriage;

(c) The place of receipt and, if known to the carrier, the place of delivery; and

(d) The port of loading and the port of discharge, if specified in the contract of carriage.

4.   For the purposes of this article, the phrase "apparent order and condition of the goods" in subparagraph 2 (a) of this article refers to the order and condition of the goods based on:

(a) A reasonable external inspection of the goods as packaged at the time the shipper delivers them to the carrier or a performing party; and

(b) Any additional inspection that the carrier or a performing party actually performs before issuing the transport document or electronic transport record.

Article 37

Identity of the carrier

1.   If a carrier is identified by name in the contract particulars, any other information in the transport document or electronic transport record relating to the identity of the carrier shall have no effect to the extent that it is inconsistent with that identification.

2.   If no person is identified in the contract particulars as the carrier as required pursuant to article 36, subparagraph 2 (b), but the contract particulars indicate that the goods have been loaded on board a named ship, the registered owner of that ship is presumed to be the carrier, unless it proves that the ship was under a bareboat charter at the time of the carriage and it identifies this bareboat charterer and indicates its address, in which case this bareboat charterer is presumed to be the carrier. Alternatively, the registered owner may rebut the

presumption of being the carrier by identifying the carrier and indicating its address. The bareboat charterer may rebut any presumption of being the carrier in the same manner.

3.   Nothing in this article prevents the claimant from proving that any person other than a person identified in the contract particulars or pursuant to paragraph 2 of this article is the carrier.

Article 38

Signature

1.   A transport document shall be signed by the carrier or a person acting on its behalf.

2.   An electronic transport record shall include the electronic signature of the carrier or a person acting on its behalf. Such electronic signature shall identify the signatory in relation to the electronic transport record and indicate the carrier's authorization of the electronic transport record.

Article 39

Deficiencies in the contract particulars

1.   The absence or inaccuracy of one or more of the contract particulars referred to in article 36, paragraphs 1, 2 or 3, does not of itself affect the legal character or validity of the transport document or of the electronic transport record.

2.   If the contract particulars include the date but fail to indicate its significance, the date is deemed to be:

(a)   The date on which all of the goods indicated in the transport document or electronic transport record were loaded on board the ship, if the contract particulars indicate that the goods have been loaded on board a ship; or

(b)   The date on which the carrier or a performing party received the goods, if the contract particulars do not indicate that the goods have been loaded on board a ship.

3.   If the contract particulars fail to state the apparent order and condition of the goods at the time the carrier or a performing party receives them, the contract particulars are deemed to have stated that the goods were in apparent good order and condition at the time the carrier or a performing party received them.

Article 40

Qualifying the information relating to the goods in the contract particulars

1.   The carrier shall qualify the information referred to in article 36, paragraph 1, to indicate that the carrier does not assume responsibility for the accuracy of the information furnished by the shipper if:

(a) The carrier has actual knowledge that any material statement in the transport document or electronic transport record is false or misleading; or

(b) The carrier has reasonable grounds to believe that a material statement in the transport document or electronic transport record is false or misleading.

2.   Without prejudice to paragraph 1 of this article, the carrier may qualify the information referred to in article 36, paragraph 1, in the circumstances and in the manner set out in paragraphs 3 and 4 of this article to indicate that the carrier does not assume responsibility for the accuracy of the information furnished by the shipper.

3.   When the goods are not delivered for carriage to the carrier or a performing party in a closed container or vehicle, or when they are delivered in a closed container or vehicle and the carrier or a performing party actually inspects them, the carrier may qualify the information referred to in article 36, paragraph 1, if:

(a) The carrier had no physically practicable or commercially reasonable means of checking the information furnished by the shipper, in which case it may indicate which information it was unable to check; or

(b) The carrier has reasonable grounds to believe the information furnished by the shipper to be inaccurate, in which case it may include a clause providing what it reasonably considers accurate information.

4.   When the goods are delivered for carriage to the carrier or a performing party in a closed container or vehicle, the carrier may qualify the information referred to in:

(a) Article 36, subparagraphs 1 (a), (b), or (c), if:

(i)   The goods inside the container or vehicle have not actually been inspected by the carrier or a performing party; and

(ii) Neither the carrier nor a performing party otherwise has actual knowledge of its contents before issuing the transport document or the electronic transport record; and

(b) Article 36, subparagraph 1 (d), if:

(i)   Neither the carrier nor a performing party weighed the container or vehicle, and the shipper and the carrier had not agreed prior to the shipment that the container or vehicle would be weighed and the weight would be included in the contract particulars; or

(ii) There was no physically practicable or commercially reasonable means of checking the weight of the container or vehicle.

Article 41

Evidentiary effect of the contract particulars

Except to the extent that the contract particulars have been qualified in the circumstances and in the manner set out in article 40:

(a) A transport document or an electronic transport record is prima facie evidence of the carrier's receipt of the goods as stated in the contract particulars;

(b) Proof to the contrary by the carrier in respect of any contract particulars shall not be admissible, when such contract particulars are included in:

(i) A negotiable transport document or a negotiable electronic transport record that is transferred to a third party acting in good faith; or

(ii) A non-negotiable transport document that indicates that it must be surrendered in order to obtain delivery of the goods and is transferred to the consignee acting in good faith;

(c) Proof to the contrary by the carrier shall not be admissible against a consignee that in good faith has acted in reliance on any of the following contract particulars included in a non-negotiable transport document or a non-negotiable electronic transport record:

(i) The contract particulars referred to in article 36, paragraph 1, when such contract particulars are furnished by the carrier;

(ii) The number, type and identifying numbers of the containers, but not the identifying numbers of the container seals; and

(iii) The contract particulars referred to in article 36, paragraph 2.

Article 42

"Freight prepaid"

If the contract particulars contain the statement "freight prepaid" or a statement of a similar nature, the carrier cannot assert against the holder or the consignee the fact that the freight has not been paid. This article does not apply if the holder or the consignee is also the shipper.

Chapter 9

Delivery of the goods

Article 43

Obligation to accept delivery

When the goods have arrived at their destination, the consignee that demands delivery of the goods under the contract of carriage shall accept delivery of the goods at the time or within the time period and at the location agreed in the contract of carriage or, failing such agreement, at the time and location at which, having regard to the terms of the contract, the customs, usages or practices of the trade and the circumstances of the carriage, delivery could reasonably be expected.

Article 44

Obligation to acknowledge receipt

On request of the carrier or the performing party that delivers the goods, the consignee shall acknowledge receipt of the goods from the carrier or the performing party in the manner that is customary at the place of delivery. The carrier may refuse delivery if the consignee refuses to acknowledge such receipt.

Article 45

Delivery when no negotiable transport document or negotiable electronic transport record is issued

When neither a negotiable transport document nor a negotiable electronic transport record has been issued:

(a)   The carrier shall deliver the goods to the consignee at the time and location referred to in article 43. The carrier may refuse delivery if the person claiming to be the consignee does not properly identify itself as the consignee on the request of the carrier;

(b)   If the name and address of the consignee are not referred to in the contract particulars, the controlling party shall prior to or upon the arrival of the goods at the place of destination advise the carrier of such name and address;

(c)   Without prejudice to article 48, paragraph 1, if the goods are not deliverable because

(i)   the consignee, after having received a notice of arrival, does not, at the time or within the time period referred to in article 43, claim delivery of the goods from the carrier after their arrival at the place of destination,

(ii)   the carrier refuses delivery because the person claiming to be the consignee does not properly identify itself as the consignee, or

(iii)   the carrier is, after reasonable effort, unable to locate the consignee in order to request delivery instructions, the carrier may so advise the controlling party and request instructions in respect of the delivery of the goods. If, after reasonable effort, the carrier is unable to locate the controlling party, the carrier may so advise the shipper and request instructions in respect of the delivery of the goods. If, after reasonable effort, the carrier is unable to locate the shipper, the carrier may so advise the documentary shipper and request instructions in respect of the delivery of the goods;

(d)   The carrier that delivers the goods upon instruction of the controlling party, the shipper or the documentary shipper pursuant to subparagraph (c) of this article is discharged from its obligations to deliver the goods under the contract of carriage.

Article 46

Delivery when a non-negotiable transport document that requires surrender is issued

When a non-negotiable transport document has been issued that indicates that it shall be surrendered in order to obtain delivery of the goods:

(a)   The carrier shall deliver the goods at the time and location referred to in article 43 to the consignee upon the consignee properly identifying itself on the request of the carrier and surrender of the non-negotiable document. The carrier may refuse delivery if the person claiming to be the consignee fails to properly identify itself on the request of the carrier, and shall refuse delivery if the non-negotiable document is not surrendered. If more than one original of the non-negotiable document has been issued, the surrender of one original will suffice and the other originals cease to have any effect or validity;

(b)   Without prejudice to article 48, paragraph 1, if the goods are not deliverable because

(i)   the consignee, after having received a notice of arrival, does not, at the time or within the time period referred to in article 43, claim delivery of the goods from the carrier after their arrival at the place of destination,

(ii)   the carrier refuses delivery because the person claiming to be the consignee does not properly identify itself as the consignee or does not surrender the document, or

(iii)   the carrier is, after reasonable effort, unable to locate the consignee in order to request delivery instructions, the carrier may so advise the shipper and request instructions in respect of the delivery of the goods. If, after reasonable effort, the carrier is unable to locate the shipper, the carrier may so advise the documentary shipper and request instructions in respect of the delivery of the goods;

(c)   The carrier that delivers the goods upon instruction of the shipper or the documentary shipper pursuant to subparagraph (b) of this article is discharged from its obligation to deliver the goods under the contract of carriage, irrespective of whether the non-negotiable transport document has been surrendered to it.

Article 47

Delivery when a negotiable transport document or negotiable electronic transport record is issued

1. When a negotiable transport document or a negotiable electronic transport record has been issued:

(a) The holder of the negotiable transport document or negotiable electronic transport record is entitled to claim delivery of the goods from the carrier after they have arrived at the place of destination, in which event the carrier shall deliver the goods at the time and location referred to in article 43 to the holder:

(i) Upon surrender of the negotiable transport document and, if the holder is one of the persons referred to in article 1, subparagraph 10 (a) (I), upon the holder properly identifying itself; or

(ii) Upon demonstration by the holder, in accordance with the procedures referred to in article 9, paragraph 1, that it is the holder of the negotiable electronic transport record;

(b) The carrier shall refuse delivery if the requirements of subparagraph (a) (I) or (a) (ii) of this paragraph are not met;

(c) If more than one original of the negotiable transport document has been issued, and the number of originals is stated in that document, the surrender of one original will suffice and the other originals cease to have any effect or validity. When a negotiable electronic transport record has been used, such electronic transport record ceases to have any effect or validity upon delivery to the holder in accordance with the procedures required by article 9, paragraph 1.

2. Without prejudice to article 48, paragraph 1, if the negotiable transport document or the negotiable electronic transport record expressly states that the goods may be delivered without the surrender of the transport document or the electronic transport record, the following rules apply:

(a) If the goods are not deliverable because (I) the holder, after having received a notice of arrival, does not, at the time or within the time period referred to in article 43, claim delivery of the goods from the carrier after their arrival at the place of destination, (ii) the carrier refuses delivery because the person claiming to be a holder does not properly identify itself as one of the persons referred to in article 1, subparagraph 10 (a) (I), or (iii) the carrier is, after reasonable effort, unable to locate the holder in order to request delivery instructions, the carrier may so advise the shipper and request instructions in respect of the delivery of the goods. If, after reasonable effort, the carrier is unable to locate the shipper, the carrier may so advise the documentary shipper and request instructions in respect of the delivery of the goods;

(b) The carrier that delivers the goods upon instruction of the shipper or the documentary shipper in accordance with subparagraph 2 (a) of this article is discharged from its obligation to deliver the goods under the contract of carriage to the holder, irrespective of whether the negotiable transport document has been surrendered to it, or the person claiming delivery under a negotiable electronic transport record has demonstrated, in accordance with the procedures referred to in article 9, paragraph 1, that it is the holder;

(c) The person giving instructions under subparagraph 2 (a) of this article shall indemnify the carrier against loss arising from its being held liable to the holder under subparagraph 2 (e) of this article. The carrier may refuse to follow those instructions if the person fails to provide adequate security as the carrier may reasonably request;

(d) A person that becomes a holder of the negotiable transport document or the negotiable electronic transport record after the carrier has delivered the goods pursuant to subparagraph 2 (b) of this article, but pursuant to contractual or other arrangements made before such delivery acquires rights against the carrier under the contract of carriage, other than the right to claim delivery of the goods;

(e) Notwithstanding subparagraphs 2 (b) and 2 (d) of this article, a holder that becomes a holder after such delivery, and that did not have and could not reasonably have had knowledge of such delivery at the time it became a holder, acquires the rights incorporated in the negotiable transport document or negotiable electronic transport record. When the contract particulars state the expected time of arrival of the goods, or indicate how to obtain information as to whether the goods have been delivered, it is presumed that the holder at the time that it became a holder had or could reasonably have had knowledge of the delivery of the goods.

Article 48

Goods remaining undelivered

1. For the purposes of this article, goods shall be deemed to have remained undelivered only if, after their arrival at the place of destination:

(a) The consignee does not accept delivery of the goods pursuant to this chapter at the time and location referred to in article 43;

(b) The controlling party, the holder, the shipper or the documentary shipper cannot be found or does not give the carrier adequate instructions pursuant to articles 45, 46 and 47;

(c)   The carrier is entitled or required to refuse delivery pursuant to articles 44, 45, 46 and 47;

(d)   The carrier is not allowed to deliver the goods to the consignee pursuant to the law or regulations of the place at which delivery is requested; or

(e)   The goods are otherwise undeliverable by the carrier.

2.   Without prejudice to any other rights that the carrier may have against the shipper, controlling party or consignee, if the goods have remained undelivered, the carrier may, at the risk and expense of the person entitled to the goods, take such action in respect of the goods as circumstances may reasonably require, including:

(a)   To store the goods at any suitable place;

(b)   To unpack the goods if they are packed in containers or vehicles, or to act otherwise in respect of the goods, including by moving them; and

(c)   To cause the goods to be sold or destroyed in accordance with the practices or pursuant to the law or regulations of the place where the goods are located at the time.

3.   The carrier may exercise the rights under paragraph 2 of this article only after it has given reasonable notice of the intended action under paragraph 2 of this article to the person stated in the contract particulars as the person, if any, to be notified of the arrival of the goods at the place of destination, and to one of the following persons in the order indicated, if known to the carrier: the consignee, the controlling party or the shipper.

4.   If the goods are sold pursuant to subparagraph 2 © of this article, the carrier shall hold the proceeds of the sale for the benefit of the person entitled to the goods, subject to the deduction of any costs incurred by the carrier and any other amounts that are due to the carrier in connection with the carriage of those goods.

5.   The carrier shall not be liable for loss of or damage to goods that occurs during the time that they remain undelivered pursuant to this article unless the claimant proves that such loss or damage resulted from the failure by the carrier to take steps that would have been reasonable in the circumstances to preserve the goods and that the carrier knew or ought to have known that the loss or damage to the goods would result from its failure to take such steps.

Article 49

Retention of goods

Nothing in this Convention affects a right of the carrier or a performing party that may exist pursuant to the contract of carriage or the applicable law to retain the goods to secure the payment of sums due.

Chapter 10
Rights of the controlling party

Article 50

Exercise and extent of right of control

1. The right of control may be exercised only by the controlling party and is limited to:

(a) The right to give or modify instructions in respect of the goods that do not constitute a variation of the contract of carriage;

(b) The right to obtain delivery of the goods at a scheduled port of call or, in respect of inland carriage, any place en route; and

(c) The right to replace the consignee by any other person including the controlling party.

2. The right of control exists during the entire period of responsibility of the carrier, as provided in article 12, and ceases when that period expires.

Article 51

Identity of the controlling party and transfer of the right of control

1. Except in the cases referred to in paragraphs 2, 3 and 4 of this article:

(a) The shipper is the controlling party unless the shipper, when the contract of carriage is concluded, designates the consignee, the documentary shipper or another person as the controlling party;

(b) The controlling party is entitled to transfer the right of control to another person. The transfer becomes effective with respect to the carrier upon its notification of the transfer by the transferor, and the transferee becomes the controlling party; and

(c) The controlling party shall properly identify itself when it exercises the right of control.

2. When a non-negotiable transport document has been issued that indicates that it shall be surrendered in order to obtain delivery of the goods:

(a) The shipper is the controlling party and may transfer the right of control to the consignee named in the transport document by transferring the document to that person without endorsement. If more than one original of the document was issued, all originals shall be transferred in order to effect a transfer of the right of control; and

(b) In order to exercise its right of control, the controlling party shall produce the document and properly identify itself. If more than one original of the document was issued, all originals shall be produced, failing which the right of control cannot be exercised.

3.   When a negotiable transport document is issued:

(a)   The holder or, if more than one original of the negotiable transport document is issued, the holder of all originals is the controlling party;

(b)   The holder may transfer the right of control by transferring the negotiable transport document to another person in accordance with article 57. If more than one original of that document was issued, all originals shall be transferred to that person in order to effect a transfer of the right of control; and

(c)   In order to exercise the right of control, the holder shall produce the negotiable transport document to the carrier, and if the holder is one of the persons referred to in article 1, subparagraph 10 (a) (I), the holder shall properly identify itself. If more than one original of the document was issued, all originals shall be produced, failing which the right of control cannot be exercised.

4.   When a negotiable electronic transport record is issued:

(a)   The holder is the controlling party;

(b)   The holder may transfer the right of control to another person by transferring the negotiable electronic transport record in accordance with the procedures referred to in article 9, paragraph 1; and

(c)   In order to exercise the right of control, the holder shall demonstrate, in accordance with the procedures referred to in article 9, paragraph 1, that it is the holder.

Article 52

Carrier's execution of instructions

1.   Subject to paragraphs 2 and 3 of this article, the carrier shall execute the instructions referred to in article 50 if:

(a)   The person giving such instructions is entitled to exercise the right of control;

(b)   The instructions can reasonably be executed according to their terms at the moment that they reach the carrier; and

(c)   The instructions will not interfere with the normal operations of the carrier, including its delivery practices.

2.   In any event, the controlling party shall reimburse the carrier for any reasonable additional expense that the carrier may incur and shall indemnify the carrier against loss or damage that the carrier may suffer as a result of diligently executing any instruction pursuant to this article, including compensation that the carrier may become liable to pay for loss of or damage to other goods being carried.

3.   The carrier is entitled to obtain security from the controlling party for the amount of additional expense, loss or damage that the carrier reasonably expects will arise in connection with the execution of

an instruction pursuant to this article. The carrier may refuse to carry out the instructions if no such security is provided.

4. The carrier's liability for loss of or damage to the goods or for delay in delivery resulting from its failure to comply with the instructions of the controlling party in breach of its obligation pursuant to paragraph 1 of this article shall be subject to articles 17 to 23, and the amount of the compensation payable by the carrier shall be subject to articles 59 to 61.

Article 53

Deemed delivery

Goods that are delivered pursuant to an instruction in accordance with article 52, paragraph 1, are deemed to be delivered at the place of destination, and the provisions of chapter 9 relating to such delivery apply to such goods.

Article 54

Variations to the contract of carriage

1. The controlling party is the only person that may agree with the carrier to variations to the contract of carriage other than those referred to in article 50, subparagraphs 1 (*b*) and (*c*).

2. Variations to the contract of carriage, including those referred to in article 50, subparagraphs 1 (*b*) and (*c*), shall be stated in a negotiable transport document or in a non-negotiable transport document that requires surrender, or incorporated in a negotiable electronic transport record, or, upon the request of the controlling party, shall be stated in a non-negotiable transport document or incorporated in a nonnegotiable electronic transport record. If so stated or incorporated, such variations shall be signed in accordance with article 38.

Article 55

Providing additional information, instructions or documents to carrier

1. The controlling party, on request of the carrier or a performing party, shall provide in a timely manner information, instructions or documents relating to the goods not yet provided by the shipper and not otherwise reasonably available to the carrier that the carrier may reasonably need to perform its obligations under the contract of carriage.

2. If the carrier, after reasonable effort, is unable to locate the controlling party or the controlling party is unable to provide adequate information, instructions or documents to the carrier, the shipper shall provide them. If the carrier, after reasonable effort, is unable to locate the shipper, the documentary shipper shall provide such information, instructions or documents.

Article 56

Variation by agreement

The parties to the contract of carriage may vary the effect of articles 50, subparagraphs 1 (*b*) and (*c*), 50, paragraph 2, and 52. The parties may also restrict or exclude the transferability of the right of control referred to in article 51, subparagraph 1 (*b*).

Chapter 11

Transfer of rights

Article 57

*When a negotiable transport document or negotiable
electronic transport record is issued*

1.   When a negotiable transport document is issued, the holder may transfer the rights incorporated in the document by transferring it to another person:

(a)   Duly endorsed either to such other person or in blank, if an order document; or

(b)   Without endorsement, if:

(i)   a bearer document or a blank endorsed document; or

(ii)   a document made out to the order of a named person and the transfer is between the first holder and the named person.

2.   When a negotiable electronic transport record is issued, its holder may transfer the rights incorporated in it, whether it be made out to order or to the order of a named person, by transferring the electronic transport record in accordance with the procedures referred to in article 9, paragraph 1.

Article 58

Liability of holder

1.   Without prejudice to article 55, a holder that is not the shipper and that does not exercise any right under the contract of carriage does not assume any liability under the contract of carriage solely by reason of being a holder.

2.   A holder that is not the shipper and that exercises any right under the contract of carriage assumes any liabilities imposed on it under the contract of carriage to the extent that such liabilities are incorporated in or ascertainable from the negotiable transport document or the negotiable electronic transport record.

3.   For the purposes of paragraphs 1 and 2 of this article, a holder that is not the shipper does not exercise any right under the contract of carriage solely because:

(a)   It agrees with the carrier, pursuant to article 10, to replace a negotiable transport document by a negotiable electronic transport record or to replace a negotiable electronic transport record by a negotiable transport document; or

(b)   It transfers its rights pursuant to article 57.

Chapter 12

Limits of liability

Article 59

Limits of liability

1.   Subject to articles 60 and 61, paragraph 1, the carrier's liability for breaches of its obligations under this Convention is limited to 875 units of account per package or other shipping unit, or 3 units of account per kilogram of the gross weight of the goods that are the subject of the claim or dispute, whichever amount is the higher, except when the value of the goods has been declared by the shipper and included in the contract particulars, or when a higher amount than the amount of limitation of liability set out in this article has been agreed upon between the carrier and the shipper.

2.   When goods are carried in or on a container, pallet or similar article of transport used to consolidate goods, or in or on a vehicle, the packages or shipping units enumerated in the contract particulars as packed in or on such article of transport or vehicle are deemed packages or shipping units. If not so enumerated, the goods in or on such article of transport or vehicle are deemed one shipping unit.

3.   The unit of account referred to in this article is the Special Drawing Right as defined by the International Monetary Fund. The amounts referred to in this article are to be converted into the national currency of a State according to the value of such currency at the date of judgement or award or the date agreed upon by the parties. The value of a national currency, in terms of the Special Drawing Right, of a Contracting State that is a member of the International Monetary Fund is to be calculated in accordance with the method of valuation applied by the International Monetary Fund in effect at the date in question for its operations and transactions. The value of a national currency, in terms of the Special Drawing Right, of a Contracting State that is not a member of the International Monetary Fund is to be calculated in a manner to be determined by that State.

Article 60

Limits of liability for loss caused by delay

Subject to article 61, paragraph 2, compensation for loss of or damage to the goods due to delay shall be calculated in accordance with article 22 and liability for economic loss due to delay is limited to an amount equivalent to two and one-half times the freight payable on the goods delayed. The total amount payable pursuant to this article and article 59, paragraph 1, may not exceed the limit that would be established pursuant to article 59, paragraph 1, in respect of the total loss of the goods concerned.

Article 61

Loss of the benefit of limitation of liability

1.   Neither the carrier nor any of the persons referred to in article 18 is entitled to the benefit of the limitation of liability as provided in article 59, or as provided in the contract of carriage, if the claimant proves that the loss resulting from the breach of the carrier's obligation under this Convention was attributable to a personal act or omission of the person claiming a right to limit done with the intent to cause such loss or recklessly and with knowledge that such loss would probably result.

2.   Neither the carrier nor any of the persons mentioned in article 18 is entitled to the benefit of the limitation of liability as provided in article 60 if the claimant proves that the delay in delivery resulted from a personal act or omission of the person claiming a right to limit done with the intent to cause the loss due to delay or recklessly and with knowledge that such loss would probably result.

Chapter 13

Time for suit

Article 62

Period of time for suit

1.   No judicial or arbitral proceedings in respect of claims or disputes arising from a breach of an obligation under this Convention may be instituted after the expiration of a period of two years.

2.   The period referred to in paragraph 1 of this article commences on the day on which the carrier has delivered the goods or, in cases in which no goods have been delivered or only part of the goods have been delivered, on the last day on which the goods should have been delivered. The day on which the period commences is not included in the period.

3.   Notwithstanding the expiration of the period set out in paragraph 1 of this article, one party may rely on its claim as a defence or for the purpose of set-off against a claim asserted by the other party.

Article 63

Extension of time for suit

The period provided in article 62 shall not be subject to suspension or interruption, but the person against which a claim is made may at any time during the running of the period extend that period by a declaration to the claimant. This period may be further extended by another declaration or declarations.

Article 64

Action for indemnity

An action for indemnity by a person held liable may be instituted after the expiration of the period provided in article 62 if the indemnity action is instituted within the later of:

(a) The time allowed by the applicable law in the jurisdiction where proceedings are instituted; or

(b) Ninety days commencing from the day when the person instituting the action for indemnity has either settled the claim or been served with process in the action against itself, whichever is earlier.

Article 65

Actions against the person identified as the carrier

An action against the bareboat charterer or the person identified as the carrier pursuant to article 37, paragraph 2, may be instituted after the expiration of the period provided in article 62 if the action is instituted within the later of:

(a) The time allowed by the applicable law in the jurisdiction where proceedings are instituted; or

(b) Ninety days commencing from the day when the carrier has been identified, or the registered owner or bareboat charterer has rebutted the presumption that it is the carrier, pursuant to article 37, paragraph 2.

Chapter 14

Jurisdiction

Article 66

Actions against the carrier

Unless the contract of carriage contains an exclusive choice of court agreement that complies with article 67 or 72, the plaintiff has the right to institute judicial proceedings under this Convention against the carrier:

(a) In a competent court within the jurisdiction of which is situated one of the following places:

(i) The domicile of the carrier;

(ii) The place of receipt agreed in the contract of carriage;

(iii) The place of delivery agreed in the contract of carriage; or

(iv) The port where the goods are initially loaded on a ship or the port where the goods are finally discharged from a ship; or

(b)   In a competent court or courts designated by an agreement between the shipper and the carrier for the purpose of deciding claims against the carrier that may arise under this Convention.

Article 67

Choice of court agreements

1.   The jurisdiction of a court chosen in accordance with article 66, subparagraph b), is exclusive for disputes between the parties to the contract only if the parties so agree and the agreement conferring jurisdiction:

(a)   Is contained in a volume contract that clearly states the names and addresses of the parties and either (I) is individually negotiated or (ii) contains a prominent statement that there is an exclusive choice of court agreement and specifies the sections of the volume contract containing that agreement; and

(b)   Clearly designates the courts of one Contracting State or one or more specific courts of one Contracting State.

2.   A person that is not a party to the volume contract is bound by an exclusive choice of court agreement concluded in accordance with paragraph 1 of this article only if:

(a)   The court is in one of the places designated in article 66, subparagraph (a);

(b)   That agreement is contained in the transport document or electronic transport record;

(c)   That person is given timely and adequate notice of the court where the action shall be brought and that the jurisdiction of that court is exclusive; and

(d)   The law of the court seized recognizes that that person may be bound by the exclusive choice of court agreement.

Article 68

Actions against the maritime performing party

The plaintiff has the right to institute judicial proceedings under this Convention against the maritime performing party in a competent court within the jurisdiction of which is situated one of the following places:

(a)   The domicile of the maritime performing party; or

(b)   The port where the goods are received by the maritime performing party, the port where the goods are delivered by the maritime performing party or the port in which the maritime performing party performs its activities with respect to the goods.

Article 69

No additional bases of jurisdiction

Subject to articles 71 and 72, no judicial proceedings under this Convention against the carrier or a maritime performing party may be instituted in a court not designated pursuant to article 66 or 68.

Article 70

Arrest and provisional or protective measures

Nothing in this Convention affects jurisdiction with regard to provisional or protective measures, including arrest. A court in a State in which a provisional or protective measure was taken does not have jurisdiction to determine the case upon its merits unless:

(a) The requirements of this chapter are fulfilled; or

(b) An international convention that applies in that State so provides.

Article 71

Consolidation and removal of actions

1. Except when there is an exclusive choice of court agreement that is binding pursuant to article 67 or 72, if a single action is brought against both the carrier and the maritime performing party arising out of a single occurrence, the action may be instituted only in a court designated pursuant to both article 66 and article 68. If there is no such court, such action may be instituted in a court designated pursuant to article 68, subparagraph (*b*), if there is such a court.

2. Except when there is an exclusive choice of court agreement that is binding pursuant to article 67 or 72, a carrier or a maritime performing party that institutes an action seeking a declaration of non-liability or any other action that would deprive a person of its right to select the forum pursuant to article 66 or 68 shall, at the request of the defendant, withdraw that action once the defendant has chosen a court designated pursuant to article 66 or 68, whichever is applicable, where the action may be recommenced.

Article 72

Agreement after a dispute has arisen and jurisdiction when the defendant has entered an appearance

1. After a dispute has arisen, the parties to the dispute may agree to resolve it in any competent court.

2. A competent court before which a defendant appears, without contesting jurisdiction in accordance with the rules of that court, has jurisdiction.

Article 73

Recognition and enforcement

1.   A decision made in one Contracting State by a court having jurisdiction under this Convention shall be recognized and enforced in another Contracting State in accordance with the law of such latter Contracting State when both States have made a declaration in accordance with article 74.

2.   A court may refuse recognition and enforcement based on the grounds for the refusal of recognition and enforcement available pursuant to its law.

3.   This chapter shall not affect the application of the rules of a regional economic integration organization that is a party to this Convention, as concerns the recognition or enforcement of judgements as between member States of the regional economic integration organization, whether adopted before or after this Convention.

Article 74

Application of chapter 14

The provisions of this chapter shall bind only Contracting States that declare in accordance with article 91 that they will be bound by them.

Chapter 15

Arbitration

Article 75

Arbitration agreements

1.   Subject to this chapter, parties may agree that any dispute that may arise relating to the carriage of goods under this Convention shall be referred to arbitration.

2.   The arbitration proceedings shall, at the option of the person asserting a claim against the carrier, take place at:

(a) Any place designated for that purpose in the arbitration agreement; or

(b) Any other place situated in a State where any of the following places is located:

(i)   The domicile of the carrier;

(ii)   The place of receipt agreed in the contract of carriage;

(iii) The place of delivery agreed in the contract of carriage; or

(iv) The port where the goods are initially loaded on a ship or the port where the goods are finally discharged from a ship.

3.   The designation of the place of arbitration in the agreement is binding for disputes between the parties to the agreement if the

agreement is contained in a volume contract that clearly states the names and addresses of the parties and either:

(a) Is individually negotiated; or

(b) Contains a prominent statement that there is an arbitration agreement and specifies the sections of the volume contract containing the arbitration agreement.

4. When an arbitration agreement has been concluded in accordance with paragraph 3 of this article, a person that is not a party to the volume contract is bound by the designation of the place of arbitration in that agreement only if:

(a) The place of arbitration designated in the agreement is situated in one of the places referred to in subparagraph 2 (b) of this article;

(b) The agreement is contained in the transport document or electronic transport record;

(c) The person to be bound is given timely and adequate notice of the place of arbitration; and

(d) Applicable law permits that person to be bound by the arbitration agreement.

5. The provisions of paragraphs 1, 2, 3 and 4 of this article are deemed to be part of every arbitration clause or agreement, and any term of such clause or agreement to the extent that it is inconsistent therewith is void.

Article 76

Arbitration agreement in non-liner transportation

1. Nothing in this Convention affects the enforceability of an arbitration agreement in a contract of carriage in non-liner transportation to which this Convention or the provisions of this Convention apply by reason of:

(a) The application of article 7; or

(b) The parties' voluntary incorporation of this Convention in a contract of carriage that would not otherwise be subject to this Convention.

2. Notwithstanding paragraph 1 of this article, an arbitration agreement in a transport document or electronic transport record to which this Convention applies by reason of the application of article 7 is subject to this chapter unless such a transport document or electronic transport record:

(a) Identifies the parties to and the date of the charter party or other contract excluded from the application of this Convention by reason of the application of article 6; and

(b)   Incorporates by specific reference the clause in the charter party or other contract that contains the terms of the arbitration agreement.

Article 77

Agreement to arbitrate after a dispute has arisen

Notwithstanding the provisions of this chapter and chapter 14, after a dispute has arisen the parties to the dispute may agree to resolve it by arbitration in any place.

Article 78

Application of chapter 15

The provisions of this chapter shall bind only Contracting States that declare in accordance with article 91 that they will be bound by them.

Chapter 16
Validity of contractual terms

Article 79

General provisions

1.   Unless otherwise provided in this Convention, any term in a contract of carriage is void to the extent that it:

(a)   Directly or indirectly excludes or limits the obligations of the carrier or a maritime performing party under this Convention;

(b)   Directly or indirectly excludes or limits the liability of the carrier or a maritime performing party for breach of an obligation under this Convention; or

(c)   Assigns a benefit of insurance of the goods in favour of the carrier or a person referred to in article 18.

2.   Unless otherwise provided in this Convention, any term in a contract of carriage is void to the extent that it:

(a)   Directly or indirectly excludes, limits or increases the obligations under this Convention of the shipper, consignee, controlling party, holder or documentary shipper; or

(b)   Directly or indirectly excludes, limits or increases the liability of the shipper, consignee, controlling party, holder or documentary shipper for breach of any of its obligations under this Convention.

Article 80

Special rules for volume contracts

1.   Notwithstanding article 79, as between the carrier and the shipper, a volume contract to which this Convention applies may provide for greater or lesser rights, obligations and liabilities than those imposed by this Convention.

2.   A derogation pursuant to paragraph 1 of this article is binding only when:

(a)   The volume contract contains a prominent statement that it derogates from this Convention;

(b)   The volume contract is (I) individually negotiated or (ii) prominently specifies the sections of the volume contract containing the derogations;

(c)   The shipper is given an opportunity and notice of the opportunity to conclude a contract of carriage on terms and conditions that comply with this Convention without any derogation under this article; and

(d)   The derogation is neither

(i)   incorporated by reference from another document nor

(ii)   included in a contract of adhesion that is not subject to negotiation.

3.   A carrier's public schedule of prices and services, transport document, electronic transport record or similar document is not a volume contract pursuant to paragraph 1 of this article, but a volume contract may incorporate such documents by reference as terms of the contract.

4.   Paragraph 1 of this article does not apply to rights and obligations provided in articles 14, subparagraphs (a) and (b), 29 and 32 or to liability arising from the breach thereof, nor does it apply to any liability arising from an act or omission referred to in article 61.

5.   The terms of the volume contract that derogate from this Convention, if the volume contract satisfies the requirements of paragraph 2 of this article, apply between the carrier and any person other than the shipper provided that:

(a)   Such person received information that prominently states that the volume contract derogates from this Convention and gave its express consent to be bound by such derogations; and

(b)   Such consent is not solely set forth in a carrier's public schedule of prices and services, transport document or electronic transport record.

6.   The party claiming the benefit of the derogation bears the burden of proof that the conditions for derogation have been fulfilled.

Article 81

Special rules for live animals and certain other goods

Notwithstanding article 79 and without prejudice to article 80, the contract of carriage may exclude or limit the obligations or the liability of both the carrier and a maritime performing party if:

(a) The goods are live animals, but any such exclusion or limitation will not be effective if the claimant proves that the loss of or damage to the goods, or delay in delivery, resulted from an act or omission of the carrier or of a person referred to in article 18, done with the intent to cause such loss of or damage to the goods or such loss due to delay or done recklessly and with knowledge that such loss or damage or such loss due to delay would probably result; or

(b) The character or condition of the goods or the circumstances and terms and conditions under which the carriage is to be performed are such as reasonably to justify a special agreement, provided that such contract of carriage is not related to ordinary commercial shipments made in the ordinary course of trade and that no negotiable transport document or negotiable electronic transport record is issued for the carriage of the goods.

Chapter 17

Matters not governed by this convention

Article 82

International conventions governing the carriage of goods by other modes of transport

Nothing in this Convention affects the application of any of the following international conventions in force at the time this Convention enters into force, including any future amendment to such conventions, that regulate the liability of the carrier for loss of or damage to the goods:

(a) Any convention governing the carriage of goods by air to the extent that such convention according to its provisions applies to any part of the contract of carriage;

(b) Any convention governing the carriage of goods by road to the extent that such convention according to its provisions applies to the carriage of goods that remain loaded on a road cargo vehicle carried on board a ship;

(c) Any convention governing the carriage of goods by rail to the extent that such convention according to its provisions applies to carriage of goods by sea as a supplement to the carriage by rail; or

(d) Any convention governing the carriage of goods by inland waterways to the extent that such convention according to its provisions applies to a carriage of goods without trans-shipment both by inland waterways and sea.

Article 83

Global limitation of liability

Nothing in this Convention affects the application of any international convention or national law regulating the global limitation of liability of vessel owners.

Article 84

General average

Nothing in this Convention affects the application of terms in the contract of carriage or provisions of national law regarding the adjustment of general average.

Article 85

Passengers and luggage

This Convention does not apply to a contract of carriage for passengers and their luggage.

Article 86

Damage caused by nuclear incident

No liability arises under this Convention for damage caused by a nuclear incident if the operator of a nuclear installation is liable for such damage:

(a)   Under the Paris Convention on Third Party Liability in the Field of Nuclear Energy of 29 July 1960 as amended by the Additional Protocol of 28 January 1964 and by the Protocols of 16 November 1982 and 12 February 2004, the Vienna Convention on Civil Liability for Nuclear Damage of 21 May 1963 as amended by the Joint Protocol Relating to the Application of the Vienna Convention and the Paris Convention of 21 September 1988 and as amended by the Protocol to Amend the 1963 Vienna Convention on Civil Liability for Nuclear Damage of 12 September 1997, or the Convention on Supplementary Compensation for Nuclear Damage of 12 September 1997, including any amendment to these conventions and any future convention in respect of the liability of the operator of a nuclear installation for damage caused by a nuclear incident; or

(b) Under national law applicable to the liability for such damage, provided that such law is in all respects as favourable to persons that may suffer damage as either the Paris or Vienna Conventions or the Convention on Supplementary Compensation for Nuclear Damage.

Chapter 18

Final clauses

Article 87

Depositary

The Secretary-General of the United Nations is hereby designated as the depositary of this Convention.

Article 88

Signature, ratification, acceptance, approval or accession

1.   This Convention is open for signature by all States at Rotterdam, the Netherlands, on 23 September 2009, and thereafter at the Headquarters of the United Nations in New York.

2.   This Convention is subject to ratification, acceptance or approval by the signatory States.

3.   This Convention is open for accession by all States that are not signatory States as from the date it is open for signature.

4.   Instruments of ratification, acceptance, approval and accession are to be deposited with the Secretary-General of the United Nations.

Article 89

Denunciation of other conventions

1.   A State that ratifies, accepts, approves or accedes to this Convention and is a party to the International Convention for the Unification of certain Rules of Law relating to Bills of Lading signed at Brussels on 25 August 1924, to the Protocol to amend the International Convention for the Unification of certain Rules of Law relating to Bills of Lading, signed at Brussels on 23 February 1968, or to the Protocol to amend the International Convention for the Unification of certain Rules of Law relating to Bills of Lading as Modified by the Amending Protocol of 23 February 1968, signed at Brussels on 21 December 1979, shall at the same time denounce that Convention and the protocol or protocols thereto to which it is a party by notifying the Government of Belgium to that effect, with a declaration that the denunciation is to take effect as from the date when this Convention enters into force in respect of that State.

2.   A State that ratifies, accepts, approves or accedes to this Convention and is a party to the United Nations Convention on the Carriage of Goods by Sea concluded at Hamburg on 31 March 1978 shall at the same time denounce that Convention by notifying the Secretary-General of the United Nations to that effect, with a declaration that the denunciation is to take effect as from the date when this Convention enters into force in respect of that State.

3.   For the purposes of this article, ratifications, acceptances, approvals and accessions in respect of this Convention by States parties to the instruments listed in paragraphs 1 and 2 of this article that are notified to the depositary after this Convention has entered into force are not effective until such denunciations as may be required on the part of those States in respect of these instruments have become effective. The depositary of this Convention shall consult with the Government of Belgium, as the depositary of the instruments referred to in paragraph 1 of this article, so as to ensure necessary coordination in this respect.

Article 90

Reservations

No reservation is permitted to this Convention.

Article 91

Procedure and effect of declarations

1.   The declarations permitted by articles 74 and 78 may be made at any time. The initial declarations permitted by article 92, paragraph 1, and article 93, paragraph 2, shall be made at the time of signature, ratification, acceptance, approval or accession. No other declaration is permitted under this Convention.

2.   Declarations made at the time of signature are subject to confirmation upon ratification, acceptance or approval.

3.   Declarations and their confirmations are to be in writing and to be formally notified to the depositary.

4.   A declaration takes effect simultaneously with the entry into force of this Convention in respect of the State concerned. However, a declaration of which the depositary receives formal notification after such entry into force takes effect on the first day of the month following the expiration of six months after the date of its receipt by the depositary.

5.   Any State that makes a declaration under this Convention may withdraw it at any time by a formal notification in writing addressed to the depositary. The withdrawal of a declaration, or its modification where permitted by this Convention, takes effect on the first day of the month following the expiration of six months after the date of the receipt of the notification by the depositary.

Article 92

Effect in domestic territorial units

1.   If a Contracting State has two or more territorial units in which different systems of law are applicable in relation to the matters dealt with in this Convention, it may, at the time of signature, ratification, acceptance, approval or accession, declare that this Convention is to extend to all its territorial units or only to one or more of them, and may amend its declaration by submitting another declaration at any time.

2.   These declarations are to be notified to the depositary and are to state expressly the territorial units to which the Convention extends.

3.   When a Contracting State has declared pursuant to this article that this Convention extends to one or more but not all of its territorial units, a place located in a territorial unit to which this Convention does not extend is not considered to be in a Contracting State for the purposes of this Convention.

4.   If a Contracting State makes no declaration pursuant to paragraph 1 of this article, the Convention is to extend to all territorial units of that State.

Article 93

Participation by regional economic integration organizations

1. A regional economic integration organization that is constituted by sovereign States and has competence over certain matters governed by this Convention may similarly sign, ratify, accept, approve or accede to this Convention. The regional economic integration organization shall in that case have the rights and obligations of a Contracting State, to the extent that that organization has competence over matters governed by this Convention. When the number of Contracting States is relevant in this Convention, the regional economic integration organization does not count as a Contracting State in addition to its member States which are Contracting States.

2. The regional economic integration organization shall, at the time of signature, ratification, acceptance, approval or accession, make a declaration to the depositary specifying the matters governed by this Convention in respect of which competence has been transferred to that organization by its member States. The regional economic integration organization shall promptly notify the depositary of any changes to the distribution of competence, including new transfers of competence, specified in the declaration pursuant to this paragraph.

3. Any reference to a "Contracting State" or "Contracting States" in this Convention applies equally to a regional economic integration organization when the context so requires.

Article 94

Entry into force

1. This Convention enters into force on the first day of the month following the expiration of one year after the date of deposit of the twentieth instrument of ratification, acceptance, approval or accession.

2. For each State that becomes a Contracting State to this Convention after the date of the deposit of the twentieth instrument of ratification, acceptance, approval or accession, this Convention enters into force on the first day of the month following the expiration of one year after the deposit of the appropriate instrument on behalf of that State.

3. Each Contracting State shall apply this Convention to contracts of carriage concluded on or after the date of the entry into force of this Convention in respect of that State.

Article 95

Revision and amendment

1. At the request of not less than one third of the Contracting States to this Convention, the Secretary-General of the United Nations shall convene a conference of the Contracting States for revising or amending it.

2. Any instrument of ratification, acceptance, approval or accession deposited after the entry into force of an amendment to this Convention is deemed to apply to the Convention as amended.

Article 96

Denunciation of this Convention

1. A Contracting State may denounce this Convention at any time by means of a notification in writing addressed to the depositary.

2. The denunciation takes effect on the first day of the month following the expiration of one year after the notification is received by the depositary. If a longer period is specified in the notification, the denunciation takes effect upon the expiration of such longer period after the notification is received by the depositary.

B. CARRIAGE OF PASSENGERS

CONVENTION RELATING TO THE CARRIAGE OF PASSENGERS AND THEIR LUGGAGE BY SEA

IMCO No. 75.03E
Athens, December 13, 1974

Article 1

Definitions

In this Convention the following expressions have the meaning hereby assigned to them:

1. (a) "carrier" means a person by or on behalf of whom a contract of carriage has been concluded, whether the carriage is actually performed by him or by a performing carrier;

(b) "performing carrier" means a person other than the carrier, being the owner, charterer or operator of a ship, who actually performs the whole or a part of the carriage;

2. "contract of carriage" means a contract made by or on behalf of a carrier for the carriage by sea of a passenger or of a passenger and his luggage, as the case may be;

3. "ship" means only a seagoing vessel, excluding an air-cushion vehicle;

4. "passenger" means any person carried in a ship,

(a) under a contract of carriage, or

(b) who, with the consent of the carrier, is accompanying a vehicle or live animals which are covered by a contract for the carriage of goods not governed by this Convention;

5. "luggage" means any article or vehicle carried by the carrier under a contract of carriage, excluding:

(a)   articles and vehicles carried under a charter party, bill of lading or other contract primarily concerned with the carriage of goods, and

(b)   live animals;

6.   "cabin luggage" means luggage which the passenger has in his cabin or is otherwise in his possession, custody or control. Except for the application of paragraph 8 of this Article and Article 8, cabin luggage includes luggage which the passenger has in or on his vehicle;

7.   "loss of or damage to luggage" includes pecuniary loss resulting from the luggage not having been re-delivered to the passenger within a reasonable time after the arrival of the ship on which the luggage has been or should have been carried, but does not include delays resulting from labour disputes;

8.   "carriage" covers the following periods:

(a)   with regard to the passenger and his cabin luggage, the period during which the passenger and/or his cabin luggage are on board the ship or in the course of embarkation or disembarkation, and the period during which the passenger and his cabin luggage are transported by water from land to the ship or vice-versa, if the cost of such transport is included in the fare or if the vessel used for this purpose of auxiliary transport has been put at the disposal of the passenger by the carrier. However, with regard to the passenger, carriage does not include the period during which he is in a marine terminal or station or on a quay or in or on any other port installation;

(b)   with regard to cabin luggage, also the period during which the passenger is in a marine terminal or station or on a quay or in or on any other port installation if that luggage has been taken over by the carrier or his servant or agent and has not been redelivered to the passenger;

(c)   with regard to other luggage which is not cabin luggage, the period from the time of its taking over by the carrier or his servant or agent on shore or on board until the time of its re-delivery by the carrier or his servant or agent;

9.   "international carriage" means any carriage in which, according to the contract of carriage, the place of departure and the place of destination are situated in two different States, or in a single State if, according to the contract of carriage or the scheduled itinerary, there is an intermediate port of call in another State;

10. "Organization" means the Inter-Governmental Maritime Consultative Organization.

Article 2

Application

1.   This Convention shall apply to any international carriage if:

    (a)   the ship is flying the flag of or is registered in a State Party to this Convention, or

    (b)   the contract of carriage has been made in a State Party to this Convention, or

    (c)   the place of departure or destination, according to the contract of carriage, is in a State Party to this Convention.

2.   Notwithstanding paragraph 1 of this Article, this Convention shall not apply when the carriage is subject, under any other international convention concerning the carriage of passengers or luggage by another mode of transport, to a civil liability regime under the provisions of such convention, in so far as those provisions have mandatory application to carriage by sea.

Article 3

Liability of the carrier

1.   The carrier shall be liable for the damage suffered as a result of the death of or personal injury to a passenger and the loss of or damage to luggage if the incident which caused the damage so suffered occurred in the course of the carriage and was due to the fault or neglect of the carrier or of his servants or agents acting within the scope of their employment.

2.   The burden of proving that the incident which caused the loss or damage occurred in the course of the carriage, and the extent of the loss or damage, shall lie with the claimant.

3.   Fault or neglect of the carrier or of his servants or agents acting within the scope of their employment shall be presumed, unless the contrary is proved, if the death of or personal injury to the passenger or the loss of or damage to cabin luggage arose from or in connection with the shipwreck, collision, stranding, explosion or fire, or defect in the ship. In respect of loss of or damage to other luggage, such fault or neglect shall be presumed, unless the contrary is proved, irrespective of the nature of the incident which caused the loss or damage. In all other cases the burden of proving fault or neglect shall lie with the claimant.

Article 4

Performing carrier

1.   If the performance of the carriage or part thereof has been entrusted to a performing carrier, the carrier shall nevertheless remain liable for the entire carriage according to the provisions of this Convention. In addition, the performing carrier shall be subject and entitled to the provisions of this Convention for the part of the carriage performed by him.

2. The carrier shall, in relation to the carriage performed by the performing carrier, be liable for the acts and omissions of the performing carrier and of his servants and agents acting within the scope of their employment.

3. Any special agreement under which the carrier assumes obligations not imposed by this Convention or any waiver of rights conferred by this Convention shall affect the performing carrier only if agreed by him expressly and in writing.

4. Where and to the extent that both the carrier and the performing carrier are liable, their liability shall be joint and several.

5. Nothing in this Article shall prejudice any right of recourse as between the carrier and the performing carrier.

Article 5

Valuables

The carrier shall not be liable for the loss of or damage to monies, negotiable securities, gold, silverware, jewelry, ornaments, works of art, or other valuables, except where such valuables have been deposited with the carrier for the agreed purpose of safe-keeping in which case the carrier shall be liable up to the limit provided for in paragraph 3 of Article 8 unless a higher limit is agreed upon in accordance with paragraph 1 of Article 10.

Article 6

Contributory fault

If the carrier proves that the death of or personal injury to a passenger or the loss of or damage to his luggage was caused or contributed to by the fault or neglect of the passenger, the court seized of the case may exonerate the carrier wholly or partly from his liability in accordance with the provisions of the law of that court.

Article 7

Limit of liability for personal injury

1. The liability of the carrier for the death of or personal injury to a passenger shall in no case exceed 700,000 francs per carriage. Where in accordance with the law of the court seized of the case damages are awarded in the form of periodical income payments, the equivalent capital value of those payments shall not exceed the said limit.

2. Notwithstanding paragraph 1 of this Article, the national law of any State Party to this Convention may fix, as far as carriers who are nationals of such State are concerned, a higher *per capita* limit of liability.

Article 8

Limit of liability for loss of or damage to luggage

1. The liability of the carrier for the loss of or damage to cabin luggage shall in no case exceed 12,500 francs per passenger, per carriage.

2. The liability of the carrier for the loss of or damage to vehicles including all luggage carried in or on the vehicle shall in no case exceed 50,000 francs per vehicle, per carriage.

3. The liability of the carrier for the loss of or damage to luggage other than that mentioned in paragraphs 1 and 2 of this Article shall in no case exceed 18,000 francs per passenger, per carriage.

4. The carrier and the passenger may agree that the liability of the carrier shall be subject to a deductible not exceeding 1,750 francs in the case of damage to a vehicle and not exceeding 200 francs per passenger in the case of loss of or damage to other luggage, such sum to be deducted from the loss or damage.

Article 9

Monetary unit and conversion

1. The franc mentioned in this Convention shall be deemed to refer to a unit consisting of 65.5 milligrams of gold of millesimal fineness 900.

2. The amounts referred to in Articles 7 and 8 shall be converted into the national currency of the State of the court seized of the case on the basis of the official value of that currency, by reference to the unit defined in paragraph 1 of this Article, on the date of the judgment or the date agreed upon by the parties. If there is no such official value, the competent authority of the State concerned shall determine what shall be considered as the official value for the purpose of this Convention.

Article 10

Supplementary provisions on limits of liability

1. The carrier and the passenger may agree, expressly and in writing, to higher limits of liability than those prescribed in Articles 7 and 8.

2. Interest on damages and legal costs shall not be included in the limits of liability prescribed in Articles 7 and 8.

Article 11

Defences and limits for carriers' servants

If an action is brought against a servant or agent of the carrier or of the performing carrier arising out of damage covered by this Convention, such servant or agent, if he proves that he acted within the scope of his employment, shall be entitled to avail himself of the defences and limits of liability which the carrier or the performing carrier is entitled to invoke under this Convention.

Article 12

Aggregation of claims

1.   Where the limits of liability prescribed in Articles 7 and 8 take effect, they shall apply to the aggregate of the amounts recoverable in all claims arising out of the death of or personal injury to any one passenger or the loss of or damage to his luggage.

2.   In relation to the carriage performed by a performing carrier, the aggregate of the amounts recoverable from the carrier and the performing carrier and from their servants and agents acting within the scope of their employment shall not exceed the highest amount which could be awarded against either the carrier or the performing carrier under this Convention, but none of the persons mentioned shall be liable for a sum in excess of the limit applicable to him.

3.   In any case where a servant or agent of the carrier or of the performing carrier is entitled under Article 11 of this Convention to avail himself of the limits of liability prescribed in Articles 7 and 8, the aggregate of the amounts recoverable from the carrier, or the performing carrier as the case may be, and from that servant or agent, shall not exceed those limits.

Article 13

Loss of right to limit liability

1.   The carrier shall not be entitled to the benefit of the limits of liability prescribed in Articles 7 and 8 and paragraph 1 of Article 10, if it is proved that the damage resulted from an act or omission of the carrier done with the intent to cause such damage, or recklessly and with knowledge that such damage would probably result.

2.   The servant or agent of the carrier or of the performing carrier shall not be entitled to the benefit of those limits if it is proved that the damage resulted from an act or omission of that servant or agent done with the intent to cause such damage, or recklessly and with knowledge that such damage would probably result.

Article 14

Basis for claims

No action for damages for the death of or personal injury to a passenger, or for the loss of or damage to luggage, shall be brought against a carrier or performing carrier otherwise than in accordance with this Convention.

Article 15

Notice of loss or damage to luggage

1.   The passenger shall give written notice to the carrier or his agent:

(a)   in the case of apparent damage to luggage:

171

(i) for cabin luggage, before or at the time of disembarkation of the passenger;

(ii) for all other luggage, before or at the time of its redelivery;

(b) in the case of damage to luggage which is not apparent, or loss of luggage, within fifteen days from the date of disembarkation or redelivery should have taken place.

2. If the passenger fails to comply with this Article, he shall be presumed, unless the contrary is proved, to have received the luggage undamaged.

3. The notice in writing need not be given if the condition of the luggage has at the time of its receipt been the subject of joint survey or inspection.

Article 16

Time-bar for actions

1. Any action for damages arising out of the death of or personal injury to a passenger or for the loss of or damage to luggage shall be time-barred after a period of two years.

2. The limitation period shall be calculated as follows:

(a) in the case of personal injury, from the date of disembarkation of the passenger.

(b) in the case of death occurring during carriage, from the date when the passenger should have disembarked, and in the case of personal injury occurring during carriage and resulting in the death of the passenger after disembarkation, from the date of death, provided that this period shall not exceed three years from the date of disembarkation;

(c) in the case of loss of or damage to luggage, from the date of disembarkation or from the date when disembarkation should have taken place, whichever is later.

3. The law of the court seized of the case shall govern the grounds of suspension and interruption of limitation periods, but in no case shall an action under this Convention be brought after the expiration of a period of three years from the date of disembarkation of the passenger or from the date when disembarkation should have taken place, whichever is later.

4. Notwithstanding paragraphs 1, 2 and 3 of this Article, the period of limitation may be extended by a declaration of the carrier or by agreement of the parties after the cause of action has arisen. The declaration or agreement shall be in writing.

Article 17

Competent jurisdiction

1.   An action arising under this Convention shall, at the option of the claimant, be brought before one of the courts listed below, provided that the court is located in a State Party to this Convention.

(a)   the court of the place of permanent residence or principal place of business of the defendant, or

(b)   the court of the place of departure or that of the destination according to the contract of carriage, or

(c)   a court of the State of the domicile or permanent residence of the claimant, if the defendant has a place of business and is subject to jurisdiction in that State, or

(d)   a court of the State where the contract of carriage was made, if the defendant has a place of business and is subject to jurisdiction in that State.

2.   After the occurrence of the incident which has caused the damage, the parties may agree that the claim for damages shall be submitted to any jurisdiction or to arbitration.

Article 18

Invalidity of contractual provisions

Any contractual provision concluded before the occurrence of the incident which has caused the death of or personal injury to a passenger or the loss of or damage to his luggage, purporting to relieve the carrier of his liability towards the passenger or to prescribe a lower limit of liability than that fixed in this Convention except as provided in paragraph 4 of Article 8, and any such provision purporting to shift the burden of proof which rests on the carrier, or having the effect of restricting the option specified in paragraph 1 of Article 17, shall be null and void, but the nullity of that provision shall not render void the contract of carriage which shall remain subject to the provisions of this Convention.

Article 19

Other conventions on limitation of liability

This Convention shall not modify the rights or duties of the carrier, the performing carrier, and their servants or agents provided for in international conventions relating to the limitation of liability of owners of seagoing ships.

Article 20

Nuclear damage

No liability shall arise under this Convention for damage caused by a nuclear incident:

(a) if the operator of a nuclear installation is liable for such damage under either the Paris Convention of 29 July 1960 on Third Party Liability in the Field of Nuclear Energy as amended by its Additional Protocol of 28 January 1964, or the Vienna Convention of 21 May 1963 on Civil Liability for Nuclear Damage, or

(b) if the operator of a nuclear installation is liable for such damage by virtue of a national law governing the liability for such damage, provided that such law is in all respects as favourable to persons who may suffer damage as either the Paris or the Vienna Conventions.

Article 21

Commercial carriage by public authorities

This Convention shall apply to commercial carriage undertaken by States or Public Authorities under contracts of carriage within the meaning of Article 1.

PROTOCOL TO THE ATHENS CONVENTION RELATING TO THE CARRIAGE OF PASSENGERS AND THEIR LUGGAGE BY SEA OF 13 DECEMBER 1974

International Maritime Organization
London, November 19, 1976

Article I

For the purpose of the present Protocol:

1. "Convention" means the Athens Convention Relating to the Carriage of Passengers and their Luggage by Sea, 1974.

2. "Organization" has the same meaning as in the Convention.

3. "Secretary-General" means the Secretary-General of the Organization.

Article II

(1) Article 7, paragraph 1 of the Convention is replaced by the following text:

1. The liability of the carrier for the death of or personal injury to a passenger shall in no case exceed 46,666 units of account per carriage. Where in accordance with the law of the court seized of the case damages are awarded in the form of periodical income payments, the equivalent capital value of those payments shall not exceed the said limit.

(2) Article 8 of the Convention is replaced by the following text:

1. The liability of the carrier for the loss of or damage to cabin luggage shall in no case exceed 833 units of account per passenger, per carriage.

2. The liability of the carrier for the loss of or damage to vehicles including all luggage carried in or on the vehicle shall in no case exceed 3,333 units of account per vehicle, per carriage.

3. The liability of the carrier for the loss of or damage to luggage other than that mentioned in paragraphs 1 and 2 of this Article shall in no case exceed 1,200 units of account per passenger, per carriage.

4. The carrier and the passenger may agree that the liability of the carrier shall be subject to a deductible not exceeding 117 units of account in the case of damage to a vehicle and not exceeding 13 units of account per passenger in the case of loss of or damage to other luggage, such sum to be deducted from the loss or damage.

(3) Article 9 of the Convention and its title are replaced by the following:

Unit of Account or Monetary Unit and Conversion

1. The Unit of Account mentioned in this Convention is the Special Drawing Right as defined by the International Monetary Fund. The amounts mentioned in Articles 7 and 8 shall be converted into the national currency of the State of the Court seized of the case on the basis of the value of that currency on the date of the judgment or the date agreed upon by the Parties. The value of the national currency, in terms of the Special Drawing Right, of a State which is a member of the International Monetary Fund, shall be calculated in accordance with the method of valuation applied by the International Monetary Fund in effect at the date in question for its operations and transactions. The value of the national currency, in terms of the Special Drawing Right, of a State which is not a member of the International Monetary Fund, shall be calculated in a manner determined by that State.

2. Nevertheless, a State which is not a member of the International Monetary Fund and whose law does not permit the application of the provisions of paragraph 1 of this Article may, at the time of ratification or accession or at any time thereafter, declare that the limits of liability provided for in this Convention to be applied in its territory shall be fixed as follows:

(a) in respect of Article 7, paragraph 1, 700,000 monetary units;

(b) in respect of Article 8, paragraph 1, 12,500 monetary units;

(c) in respect of Article 8, paragraph 2, 50,000 monetary units;

(d) in respect of Article 8, paragraph 3, 18,000 monetary units;

(e)   in respect of Article 8, paragraph 4, the deductible shall not exceed 1,750 monetary units in the case of damage to a vehicle and shall not exceed 200 monetary units per passenger in the case of loss of or damage to other luggage.

The monetary unit referred to in this paragraph corresponds to sixty-five and a half milligrammes of gold of millesimal fineness nine hundred. The conversion of the amounts specified in this paragraph into the national currency shall be made according to the law of the State concerned.

3.   The calculation mentioned in the last sentence of paragraph 1 and the conversion mentioned in paragraph 2 shall be made in such a manner as to express in the national currency of the State as far as possible the same real value for the amounts in Article 7 and 8 as is expressed there in units of account. States shall communicate to the depositary the manner of calculation pursuant to paragraph 1 or the result of the conversion in paragraph 2 as the case may be, when depositing an instrument referred to in Article III and whenever there is a change in either.

PROTOCOL OF 2002 TO THE ATHENS CONVENTION RELATING TO THE CARRIAGE OF PASSENGERS AND THEIR LUGGAGE BY SEA, 1974

International Maritime Organization
London, November 1, 2002

[Preamble omitted]

ARTICLE 1

For the purposes of this Protocol:

1.   "Convention" means the text of the Athens Convention relating to the Carriage of Passengers and their Luggage by Sea, 1974.

2.   "Organization" means the International Maritime Organization. 3 "Secretary-General" means the Secretary-General of the Organization.

ARTICLE 2

Article 1, paragraph 1 of the Convention is replaced by the following text:

1.   (a) "carrier" means a person by or on behalf of whom a contract of carriage has been concluded, whether the carriage is actually performed by that person or by a performing carrier;

(b)   "performing carrier" means a person other than the carrier, being the owner, charterer or operator of a ship, who actually performs the whole or a part of the carriage; and 3

(c) "carrier who actually performs the whole or a part of the carriage" means the performing carrier, or, in so far as the carrier actually performs the carriage, the carrier.

ARTICLE 3

1.   Article 1, paragraph 10 of the Convention is replaced by the following:

10. Organization. means the International Maritime Organization.

2.   The following text is added as Article 1, paragraph 11, of the Convention:

11. "Secretary-General" means the Secretary-General of the Organization.

ARTICLE 4

Liability of the carrier

Article 3 of the Convention is replaced by the following text:

Article 3

1.   For the loss suffered as a result of the death of or personal injury to a passenger caused by a shipping incident, the carrier shall be liable to the extent that such loss in respect of that passenger on each distinct occasion does not exceed 250,000 units of account, unless the carrier proves that the incident:

(a) resulted from an act of war, hostilities, civil war, insurrection or a natural phenomenon of an exceptional, inevitable and irresistible character; or

(b) was wholly caused by an act or omission done with the intent to cause the incident by a third party. If and to the extent that the loss exceeds the above limit, the carrier shall be further liable unless the carrier proves that the incident which caused the loss occurred without the fault or neglect of the carrier.

2.   For the loss suffered as a result of the death of or personal injury to a passenger not caused by a shipping incident, the carrier shall be liable if the incident which caused the loss was due to the fault or neglect of the carrier. The burden of proving fault or neglect shall lie with the claimant.

3.   For the loss suffered as a result of the loss of or damage to cabin luggage, the carrier shall be liable if the incident which caused the loss was due to the fault or neglect of the carrier. The fault or neglect of the carrier shall be presumed for loss caused by a shipping incident.

4.   For the loss suffered as a result of the loss of or damage to luggage other than cabin luggage, the carrier shall be liable unless the carrier proves that the incident which caused the loss occurred without the fault or neglect of the carrier.

5.   For the purposes of this Article:

(a) shipping incident. means shipwreck, capsizing, collision or stranding of the ship, explosion or fire in the ship, or defect in the ship;

(b) fault or neglect of the carrier. includes the fault or neglect of the servants of the carrier, acting within the scope of their employment;

(c) defect in the ship. means any malfunction, failure or non-compliance with applicable safety regulations in respect of any part of the ship or its equipment when used for the escape, evacuation, embarkation and disembarkation of passengers; or when used for the propulsion, steering, safe navigation, mooring, anchoring, arriving at or leaving berth or anchorage, or damage control after flooding; or when used for the launching of life saving appliances; and

(d) loss. shall not include punitive or exemplary damages.

6.   The liability of the carrier under this Article only relates to loss arising from incidents that occurred in the course of the carriage. The burden of proving that the incident which caused the loss occurred in the course of the carriage, and the extent of the loss, shall lie with the claimant.

7.   Nothing in this Convention shall prejudice any right of recourse of the carrier against any third party, or the defence of contributory negligence under Article 6 of this Convention. Nothing in this Article shall prejudice any right of limitation under Articles 7 or 8 of this Convention.

8.   Presumptions of fault or neglect of a party or the allocation of the burden of proof to a party shall not prevent evidence in favour of that party from being considered.

ARTICLE 5

The following text is added as Article 4*bis* of the Convention:

Article 4*bis*

Compulsory insurance

1.   When passengers are carried on board a ship registered in a State Party that is licensed to carry more than twelve passengers, and this Convention applies, any carrier who actually performs the whole or a part of the carriage shall maintain insurance or other financial security, such as the guarantee of a bank or similar financial institution, to cover liability under this Convention in respect of the death of and personal injury to passengers. The limit of the compulsory insurance or other financial security shall not be less than 250,000 units of account per passenger on each distinct occasion.

2.   A certificate attesting that insurance or other financial security is in force in accordance with the provisions of this Convention shall be issued to each ship after the appropriate authority of a State Party has determined that the requirements of paragraph 1 have been complied with. With respect to a ship registered in a State Party, such certificate shall be issued or certified by the appropriate authority of the State of the ship's registry; with respect to a ship not registered in a State Party it may be issued or certified by the appropriate authority of any State Party. This certificate shall be in the form of the model set out in the annex to this Convention and shall contain the following particulars:

(a)   name of ship, distinctive number or letters and port of registry;

(b)   name and principal place of business of the carrier who actually performs the whole or a part of the carriage;

(c)   IMO ship identification number;

(d)   type and duration of security;

(e)   name and principal place of business of insurer or other person providing financial security and, where appropriate, place of business where the insurance or other financial security is established; and

(f)   period of validity of the certificate, which shall not be longer than the period of validity of the insurance or other financial security.

3.   (a) A State Party may authorize an institution or an Organization recognised by it to issue the certificate. Such institution or organization shall inform that State of the issue of each certificate. In all cases, the State Party shall fully guarantee the completeness and accuracy of the certificate so issued, and shall undertake to ensure the necessary arrangements to satisfy this obligation.

(b)   A State Party shall notify the Secretary-General of:

(i)   the specific responsibilities and conditions of the authority delegated to an institution or organization recognised by it;

(ii)   the withdrawal of such authority; and (iii) the date from which such authority or withdrawal of such authority takes effect. An authority delegated shall not take effect prior to three months from the date from which notification to that effect was given to the Secretary-General.

(c)   The institution or organization authorized to issue certificates in accordance with this paragraph shall, as a minimum, be authorized to withdraw these certificates if the conditions under which they have been issued are not complied with. In all cases the institution or organization shall report such withdrawal to the State on whose behalf the certificate was issued.

4. The certificate shall be in the official language or languages of the issuing State. If the language used is not English, French or Spanish, the text shall include a translation into one of these languages, and, where the State so decides, the official language of the State may be omitted.

5. The certificate shall be carried on board the ship, and a copy shall be deposited with the authorities who keep the record of the ship's registry or, if the ship is not registered in a State Party, with the authority of the State issuing or certifying the certificate.

6. An insurance or other financial security shall not satisfy the requirements of this Article if it can cease, for reasons other than the expiry of the period of validity of the insurance or security specified in the certificate, before three months have elapsed from the date on which notice of its termination is given to the authorities referred to in paragraph 5, unless the certificate has been surrendered to these authorities or a new certificate has been issued within the said period. The foregoing provisions shall similarly apply to any modification which results in the insurance or other financial security no longer satisfying the requirements of this Article.

7. The State of the ship's registry shall, subject to the provisions of this Article, determine the conditions of issue and validity of the certificate.

8. Nothing in this Convention shall be construed as preventing a State Party from relying on information obtained from other States or the Organization or other international organizations relating to the financial standing of providers of insurance or other financial security for the purposes of this Convention. In such cases, the State Party relying on such information is not relieved of its responsibility as a State issuing the certificate.

9. Certificates issued or certified under the authority of a State Party shall be accepted by other States Parties for the purposes of this Convention and shall be regarded by other States Parties as having the same force as certificates issued or certified by them, even if issued or certified in respect of a ship not registered in a State Party. A State Party may at any time request consultation with the issuing or certifying State should it believe that the insurer or guarantor named in the insurance certificate is not financially capable of meeting the obligations imposed by this Convention.

10. Any claim for compensation covered by insurance or other financial security pursuant to this Article may be brought directly against the insurer or other person providing financial security. In such case, the amount set out in paragraph 1 applies as the limit of

liability of the insurer or other person providing financial security, even if the carrier or the performing carrier is not entitled to limitation of liability. The defendant may further invoke the defences (other than the bankruptcy or winding up) which the carrier referred to in paragraph 1 would have been entitled to invoke in accordance with this Convention. Furthermore, the defendant may invoke the defence that the damage resulted from the wilful misconduct of the assured, but the defendant shall not invoke any other defence which the defendant might have been entitled to invoke in proceedings brought by the assured against the defendant. The defendant shall in any event have the right to require the carrier and the performing carrier to be joined in the proceedings.

11. Any sums provided by insurance or by other financial security maintained in accordance with paragraph 1 shall be available exclusively for the satisfaction of claims under this Convention, and any payments made of such sums shall discharge any liability arising under this Convention to the extent of the amounts paid.

12. A State Party shall not permit a ship under its flag to which this Article applies to operate at any time unless a certificate has been issued under paragraphs 2 or 15.

13. Subject to the provisions of this Article, each State Party shall ensure, under its national law, that insurance or other financial security, to the extent specified in paragraph 1, is in force in respect of any ship that is licensed to carry more than twelve passengers, wherever registered, entering or leaving a port in its territory in so far as this Convention applies.

14. Notwithstanding the provisions of paragraph 5, a State Party may notify the Secretary-General that, for the purposes of paragraph 13, ships are not required to carry on board or to produce the certificate required by paragraph 2 when entering or leaving ports in its territory, provided that the State Party which issues the certificate has notified the Secretary-General that it maintains records in an electronic format, accessible to all States Parties, attesting the existence of the certificate and enabling States Parties to discharge their obligations under paragraph 13.

15. If insurance or other financial security is not maintained in respect of a ship owned by a State Party, the provisions of this Article relating thereto shall not be applicable to such ship, but the ship shall carry a certificate issued by the appropriate authorities of the State of the ship's registry, stating that the ship is owned by that State and that the liability is covered within the amount prescribed in accordance with paragraph 1. Such a certificate shall follow as closely as possible the model prescribed by paragraph 2.

ARTICLE 6

Limit of liability for death and personal injury

Article 7 of the Convention is replaced by the following text:

Article 7

1.   The liability of the carrier for the death of or personal injury to a passenger under Article 3 shall in no case exceed 400,000 units of account per passenger on each distinct occasion. Where, in accordance with the law of the court seized of the case, damages are awarded in the form of periodical income payments, the equivalent capital value of those payments shall not exceed the said limit.

2.   A State Party may regulate by specific provisions of national law the limit of liability prescribed in paragraph 1, provided that the national limit of liability, if any, is not lower than that prescribed in paragraph 1. A State Party, which makes use of the option provided for in this paragraph, shall inform the Secretary-General of the limit of liability adopted or of the fact that there is none.

ARTICLE 7

Limit of liability for loss of or damage to luggage and vehicles

Article 8 of the Convention is replaced by the following text:

Article 8

1.   The liability of the carrier for the loss of or damage to cabin luggage shall in no case exceed 2,250 units of account per passenger, per carriage.

2.   The liability of the carrier for the loss of or damage to vehicles including all luggage carried in or on the vehicle shall in no case exceed 12,700 units of account per vehicle, per carriage.

3.   The liability of the carrier for the loss of or damage to luggage other than that mentioned in paragraphs 1 and 2 shall in no case exceed 3,375 units of account per passenger, per carriage.

4.   The carrier and the passenger may agree that the liability of the carrier shall be subject to a deductible not exceeding 330 units of account in the case of damage to a vehicle and not exceeding 149 units of account per passenger in the case of loss of or damage to other luggage, such sum to be deducted from the loss or damage.

ARTICLE 8

Unit of Account and conversion

Article 9 of the Convention is replaced by the following text:

Article 9

1.   The Unit of Account mentioned in this Convention is the Special Drawing Right as defined by the International Monetary Fund. The amounts mentioned in Article 3, paragraph 1, Article

4bis, paragraph 1, Article 7, paragraph 1, and Article 8 shall be converted into the national currency of the State of the court seized of the case on the basis of the value of that currency by reference to the Special Drawing Right on the date of the judgment or the date agreed upon by the parties. The value of the national currency, in terms of the Special Drawing Right, of a State Party which is a member of the International Monetary Fund, shall be calculated in accordance with the method of valuation applied by the International Monetary Fund in effect on the date in question for its operations and transactions. The value of the national currency, in terms of the Special Drawing Right, of a State Party which is not a member of the International Monetary Fund, shall be calculated in a manner determined by that State Party.

2.   Nevertheless, a State which is not a member of the International Monetary Fund and whose law does not permit the application of the provisions of paragraph 1 may, at the time of ratification, acceptance, approval of or accession to this Convention or at any time thereafter, declare that the Unit of Account referred to in paragraph 1 shall be equal to 15 gold francs. The gold franc referred to in this paragraph corresponds to sixty-five and a half milligrams of gold of millesimal fineness nine hundred. The conversion of the gold franc into the national currency shall be made according to the law of the State concerned.

3.   The calculation mentioned in the last sentence of paragraph 1, and the conversion mentioned in paragraph 2 shall be made in such a manner as to express in the national currency of the States Parties, as far as possible, the same real value for the amounts in Article 3, paragraph 1, Article 4bis, paragraph 1, Article 7, paragraph 1, and Article 8 as would result from the application of the first three sentences of paragraph 1. States shall communicate to the Secretary-General the manner of calculation pursuant to paragraph 1, or the result of the conversion in paragraph 2, as the case may be, when depositing an instrument of ratification, acceptance, approval of or accession to this Convention and whenever there is a change in either.

ARTICLE 9

Article 16, paragraph 3, of the Convention is replaced by the following text:

3.   The law of the Court seized of the case shall govern the grounds for suspension and interruption of limitation periods, but in no case shall an action under this Convention be brought after the expiration of any one of the following periods of time:

(a) A period of five years beginning with the date of disembarkation of the passenger or from the date when disembarkation should have taken place, whichever is later; or, if earlier

(b) a period of three years beginning with the date when the claimant knew or ought reasonably to have known of the injury, loss or damage caused by the incident.

ARTICLE 10

Competent jurisdiction

Article 17 of the Convention is replaced by the following text:

Article 17

1. An action arising under Articles 3 and 4 of this Convention shall, at the option of the claimant, be brought before one of the courts listed below, provided that the court is located in a State Party to this Convention, and subject to the domestic law of each State Party governing proper venue within those States with multiple possible forums:

(a) the court of the State of permanent residence or principal place of business of the defendant, or

(b) the court of the State of departure or that of the destination according to the contract of carriage, or

(c) the court of the State of the domicile or permanent residence of the claimant, if the defendant has a place of business and is subject to jurisdiction in that State, or

(d) the court of the State where the contract of carriage was made, if the defendant has a place of business and is subject to jurisdiction in that State.

2. Actions under Article 4bis of this Convention shall, at the option of the claimant, be brought before one of the courts where action could be brought against the carrier or performing carrier according to paragraph 1. 3 After the occurrence of the incident which has caused the damage, the parties may agree that the claim for damages shall be submitted to any jurisdiction or to arbitration.

ARTICLE 11

Recognition and enforcement

The following text is added as Article 17*bis* of the Convention:

Article 17*bis*

1. Any judgment given by a court with jurisdiction in accordance with Article 17 which is enforceable in the State of origin where it is no longer subject to ordinary forms of review, shall be recognised in any State Party, except

(a) where the judgment was obtained by fraud; or

(b) where the defendant was not given reasonable notice and a fair opportunity to present the case.

2.   A judgment recognised under paragraph 1 shall be enforceable in each State Party as soon as the formalities required in that State have been complied with. The formalities shall not permit the merits of the case to be re-opened.

3.   A State Party to this Protocol may apply other rules for the recognition and enforcement of judgments, provided that their effect is to ensure that judgments are recognised and enforced at least to the same extent as under paragraphs 1 and 2.

ARTICLE 12

Invalidity of contractual provision

Article 18 of the Convention is replaced by the following text:

Article 18

Any contractual provision concluded before the occurrence of the incident which has caused the death of or personal injury to a passenger or the loss of or damage to the passenger's luggage, purporting to relieve any person liable under this Convention of liability towards the passenger or to prescribe a lower limit of liability than that fixed in this Convention except as provided in Article 8, paragraph 4, and any such provision purporting to shift the burden of proof which rests on the carrier or performing carrier, or having the effect of restricting the options specified in Article 17, paragraphs 1 or 2, shall be null and void, but the nullity of that provision shall not render void the contract of carriage which shall remain subject to the provisions of this Convention.

ARTICLE 13

Nuclear damage

Article 20 of the Convention is replaced by the following text:

Article 20

No liability shall arise under this Convention for damage caused by a nuclear incident:

(a)   if the operator of a nuclear installation is liable for such damage under either the Paris Convention of 29 July 1960 on Third Party Liability in the Field of Nuclear Energy as amended by its Additional Protocol of 28 January 1964, or the Vienna Convention of 21 May 1963 on Civil Liability for Nuclear Damage, or any amendment or Protocol thereto which is in force; or

(b)   if the operator of a nuclear installation is liable for such damage by virtue of a national law governing the liability for such damage, provided that such law is in all respects as favourable to persons who may suffer damage as either the Paris or the Vienna Conventions or any amendment or Protocol thereto which is in force.

ARTICLE 14

Model certificate

1,   The model certificate set out in the annex to this Protocol shall be incorporated as an annex to the Convention.

2.   The following text is added as Article 1bis of the Convention: Article 1bis Annex The annex to this Convention shall constitute an integral part of the Convention.

ARTICLE 15

Interpretation and application

1.   The Convention and this Protocol shall, as between the Parties to this Protocol, be read and interpreted together as one single instrument.

2.   The Convention as revised by this Protocol shall apply only to claims arising out of occurrences which take place after the entry into force for each State of this Protocol.

3.   Articles 1 to 22 of the Convention, as revised by this Protocol, together with Articles 17 to 25 of this Protocol and the annex thereto, shall constitute and be called the Athens Convention relating to the Carriage of Passengers and their Luggage by Sea, 2002.

[Articles 16 through 25 and the Annex are omitted]

C. SALVAGE

CONVENTION FOR THE UNIFICATION OF CERTAIN RULES OF LAW RELATING TO ASSISTANCE AND SALVAGE AT SEA

37 Stat. 1658, TS 576

Brussels, September 23, 1910

[Preamble deleted]

Article 1

Assistance and salvage of sea-going vessels in danger, of any things on board, of freight and passage money, and also services of the same nature rendered by sea-going vessels to vessels of inland navigation or vice-versa, are subject to the following provisions, without any distinction being drawn between these two kinds of service (viz., assistance and salvage), and in whatever waters the services have been rendered.

Article 2

Every act of assistance or salvage of which has had a useful result gives a right to equitable remuneration.

No remuneration is due if the services rendered have no beneficial result.

In no case shall the sum to be paid exceed the value of the property salved.

Article 3

Persons who have taken part in salvage operations notwithstanding the express and reasonable prohibition on the part of the vessel to which the services were rendered, have no right to any remuneration.

Article 4

A tug has no right to remuneration for assistance to or salvage of the vessel she is towing or of the vessel's cargo, except where she has rendered exceptional services which cannot be considered as rendered in fulfilment of the contract of towage.

Article 5

Remuneration is due notwithstanding that the salvage services have been rendered by or to vessels belonging to the same owner.

Article 6

The amount of remuneration is fixed by agreement between the parties, and, failing agreement, by the court.

The proportion in which the remuneration is to be distributed amongst the salvors is fixed in the same manner.

The apportionment of the remuneration amongst the owner, master and other persons in the service of each salving vessel shall be determined by the law of the vessel's flag.

Article 7

Every agreement as to assistance or salvage entered into at the moment and under the influence of danger may, at the request of either party, be annulled, or modified by the court, if it considers that the conditions agreed upon are not equitable.

In all cases, when it is proved that the consent of one of the parties is vitiated by fraud or concealment, or when the remuneration is, in proportion to the services rendered, in an excessive degree too large or too small, the agreement may be annulled or modified by the court at the request of the party affected.

Article 8

The remuneration is fixed by the court according to the circumstances of each case, on the basis of the following considerations: a) firstly, the measure of success obtained, the efforts and deserts of the salvors, the danger run by the salved vessel, by her passengers, crew and cargo, by the salvors, and by the salving vessel, the time expended, the expenses incurred and losses suffered, and the risks of liability and other risks run by the salvors, and also the value of the property exposed to such risks, due regard being had to the special appropriation (if any) of the salvors' vessel for salvages purposes; b) secondly, the value of the property salved.

The same provisions apply for the purpose of fixing the apportionment provided for the second paragraph of Article 6.

The court may deprive the salvors of all remuneration, or may award a reduced remuneration, if it appears that the salvors have by their fault rendered the salvage or assistance necessary or have been guilty of theft, fraudulent concealment, or other acts of fraud.

Article 9

No remuneration is due from the persons whose lives are saved, but nothing in this Article shall affect the provisions of the national laws on this subject.

Salvors of human life, who have taken part in the services rendered on the occasion of the accident giving rise to salvage or assistance, are entitled to a fair share of the remuneration awarded to the salvors of the vessel, her cargo, and accessories.

Article 10

A salvage action is barred after an interval of two years from the day on which the operations of assistance or salvage terminate.

The grounds upon which the said period of limitation may be suspended or interrupted are determined by the law of the court where the case is tried.

The High Contracting Parties reserve to themselves the right to provide, by legislation in their respective countries, that the said period shall be extended in cases where it has not been possible to arrest the vessel assisted or salved in the territorial waters of the State in which the plaintiff has his domicile or principal place of business.

Article 11

Every master is bound, so far as he can do so without serious danger to his vessel, her crew and her passengers, to render assistance to everybody, even though an enemy, found at sea in danger of being lost.

The owner of a vessel incurs no liability by reason of contravention of the above provision.

Article 12

The High Contracting Parties, whose legislation does not forbid infringements of the preceding Article, bind themselves to take or to propose to their respective Legislatures the measures necessary for the prevention of such infringements.

The High Contracting Parties will communicate to one another as soon as possible the laws or regulations which have already been or may be hereafter promulgated in their States for giving effect to the above provision.

Article 13

This Convention does not affect the provisions of national laws or international treaties as regards the organization of services of assistance and salvage by or under the control of public authorities, nor, in particular, does it affect such laws or treaties on the subject of the salvage of fishing gear.

Article 14

This Convention does not apply to ships of war or to Government ships appropriated exclusively to a public service.

Article 15

The provisions of this Convention shall be applied as regards all persons interested when either the assisting or salving vessel or the vessel assisted or salved belongs to a State of the High Contracting Parties, as well as in any other cases for which the national laws provide.

Provided always that:

1.   As regards persons interested who belong to a non-contracting State the application of the above provisions may be made by each of the contracting States conditional upon reciprocity.

2.   Where all the persons interested belong to the same State as the court trying the case, the provisions of the national law and not of the Convention are applicable.

3.   Without prejudice to any wider provisions of any national laws, Article 11 only applies as between vessels belonging to the States of the High Contracting Parties.

INTERNATIONAL CONVENTION ON SALVAGE

IMO, London, April 28, 1989.

[Preamble omitted]

CHAPTER I.   GENERAL PROVISIONS

Article 1

Definitions

For the purpose of this Convention:

(a) *Salvage operation* means any act or activity undertaken to assist a vessel or any other property in danger in navigable waters or in any other waters whatsoever.

(b) *Vessel* means any ship or craft, or any structure capable of navigation.

(c) *Property* means any property not permanently and intentionally attached to the shoreline and includes freight at risk.

(d) *Damage to the environment* means substantial physical damage to human health or to marine life or resources in coastal or

189

inland waters or areas adjacent thereto, caused by pollution, contamination, fire, explosion or similar major incidents.

(e) *Payment* means any reward, remuneration or compensation due under this Convention.

(f) *Organization* means the International Maritime Organization.

(g) *Secretary-General* means the Secretary-General of the Organization.

Article 2

Application of the Convention

This Convention shall apply whenever judicial or arbitral proceedings relating to matters dealt with in this Convention are brought in a State Party.

Article 3

Platforms and Drilling Units

This Convention shall not apply to fixed or floating platforms or to mobile offshore drilling units when such platforms or units are on location engaged in the exploration, exploitation or production of sea-bed mineral resources.

Article 4

State-Owned Vessels

(1) Without prejudice to article 5, this Convention shall not apply to warships or other non-commercial vessels owned or operated by a State and entitled, at the time of salvage operations, to sovereign immunity under generally recognized principles of international law unless that State decides otherwise.

(2) Where a State Party decides to apply the Convention to its warships or other vessels described in paragraph 1, it shall notify the Secretary-General thereof specifying the terms and conditions of such application.

Article 5

Salvage Operations Controlled by Public Authorities

(1) This Convention shall not affect any provisions of national law or any international convention relating to salvage operations by or under the control of public authorities.

(2) Nevertheless, salvors carrying out such salvage operations shall be entitled to avail themselves of the rights and remedies provided for in this Convention in respect of salvage operations.

(3) The extent to which a public authority under a duty to perform salvage operations may avail itself of the rights and remedies provided for in this Convention shall be determined by the law of the State where such authority is situated.

Article 6

Salvage Contracts

(1) This Convention shall apply to any salvage operations save to the extent that a contract otherwise provides expressly or by implication.

(2) The master shall have the authority to conclude contracts for salvage operations on behalf of the owner of the vessel. The master or the owner of the vessel shall have the authority to conclude such contracts on behalf of the owner of the property on board the vessel.

(3) Nothing in this article shall affect the application of article 7 nor duties to prevent or minimize damage to the environment.

Article 7

Annulment and Modification of Contracts

A contract or any terms thereof may be annulled or modified if:

(a) the contract has been entered into under undue influence or the influence of danger and its terms are inequitable; or

(b) the payment under the contract is in an excessive degree too large or too small for the services actually rendered.

CHAPTER II.   PERFORMANCE OF SALVAGE OPERATIONS

Article 8

Duties of the Salvor and of the Owner and Master

(1) The salvor shall owe a duty to the owner of the vessel or other property in danger:

(a) to carry out the salvage operations with due care;

(b) in performing the duty specified in subparagraph (a), to exercise due care to prevent or minimize damage to the environment;

(c) whenever circumstances reasonably require, to seek assistance from other salvors; and

(d) to accept the intervention of other salvors when reasonably requested to do so by the owner or master of the vessel or other property in danger; provided however that the amount of his reward shall not be prejudiced should it be found that such a request was unreasonable.

(2) The owner and master of the vessel or the owner of other property in danger shall owe a duty to the salvor:

(a) to cooperate fully with him during the course of the salvage operations;

(b) in so doing, to exercise due care to prevent or minimize damage to the environment; and

(c) when the vessel or other property has been brought to a place of safety, to accept redelivery when reasonably requested by the salvor to do so.

Article 9

Rights of Coastal States

Nothing in this Convention shall affect the right of the coastal State concerned to take measures in accordance with generally recognized principles of international law to protect its coastline or related interests from pollution or the threat of pollution following upon a maritime casualty or acts relating to such a casualty which may reasonably be expected to result in major harmful consequences, including the right of a coastal State to give directions in relation to salvage operations.

Article 10

Duty To Render Assistance

(1) Every master is bound, so far as he can do so without serious danger to his vessel and persons thereon, to render assistance to any person in danger of being lost at sea.

(2) The States Parties shall adopt the measures necessary to enforce the duty set out in paragraph 1.

(3) The owner of the vessel shall incur no liability for a breach of the duty of the master under paragraph 1.

Article 11

Cooperation

A State Party shall, whenever regulating or deciding upon matters relating to salvage operations such as admittance to ports of vessels in distress or the provision of facilities to salvors, take into account the need for cooperation between salvors, other interested parties and public authorities in order to ensure the efficient and successful performance of salvage operations for the purpose of saving life or property in danger as well as preventing damage to the environment in general.

CHAPTER III.   RIGHTS OF SALVORS

Article 12

Conditions for Reward

(1) Salvage operations which have had a useful result give right to a reward.

(2) Except as otherwise provided, no payment is due under this Convention if the salvage operations have had no useful result.

(3) This chapter shall apply, notwithstanding that the salved vessel and the vessel undertaking the salvage operations belong to the same owner.

Article 13

Criteria for Fixing the Reward

(1)   The reward shall be fixed with a view to encouraging salvage operations, taking into account the following criteria without regard to the order in which they are presented below:

(a)   the salved value of the vessel and other property;

(b)   the skill and efforts of the salvors in preventing or minimizing damage to the environment;

(c)   the measure of success obtained by the salvor;

(d)   the nature and degree of the danger;

(e)   the skill and efforts of the salvors in salving the vessel, other property and life;

(f)   the time used and expenses and losses incurred by the salvors;

(g)   the risk of liability and other risks run by the salvors or their equipment;

(h)   the promptness of the services rendered;

(i)   the availability and use of vessels or other equipment intended for salvage operations;

(j)   the state of readiness and efficiency of the salvor's equipment and the value thereof.

(2)   Payment of a reward fixed according to paragraph 1 shall be made by all of the vessel and other property interests in proportion to their respective salved values. However, a State Party may in its national law provide that the payment of a reward has to be made by one of these interests, subject to a right of recourse of this interest against the other interests for their respective shares. Nothing in this article shall prevent any right of defence.

(3)   The rewards, exclusive of any interest and recoverable legal costs that may be payable thereon, shall not exceed the salved value of the vessel and other property.

Article 14

Special Compensation

(1)   If the salvor has carried out salvage operations in respect of a vessel which by itself or its cargo threatened damage to the environment and has failed to earn a reward under article 13 at least equivalent to the special compensation assessable in accordance with this article, he shall be entitled to special compensation from the owner of that vessel equivalent to his expenses as herein defined.

(2)   If, in the circumstances set out in paragraph 1, the salvor by his salvage operations has prevented or minimized damage to the environment, the special compensation payable by the owner to the

salvor under paragraph 1 may be increased up to a maximum of 30% of the expenses incurred by the salvor. However, the tribunal, if it deems it fair and just to do so and bearing in mind the relevant criteria set out in article 13, paragraph 1, may increase such special compensation further, but in no event shall the total increase be more than 100% of the expenses incurred by the salvor.

(3)   Salvor's expenses for the purpose of paragraphs 1 and 2 means the out-of-pocket expenses reasonably incurred by the salvor in the salvage operation and a fair rate for equipment and personnel actually and reasonably used in the salvage operation, taking into consideration the criteria set out in article 13, paragraph 1(h), (i) and (j).

(4)   The total special compensation under this article shall be paid only if and to the extent that such compensation is greater than any reward recoverable by the salvor under article 13.

(5)   If the salvor has been negligent and has thereby failed to prevent or minimize damage to the environment, he may be deprived of the whole or part of any special compensation due under this article.

(6)   Nothing in this article shall affect any right of recourse on the part of the owner of the vessel.

Article 15

Apportionment Between Salvors

(1)   The apportionment of a reward under article 13 between salvors shall be made on the basis of the criteria contained in that article.

(2)   The apportionment between the owner, master and other persons in the service of each salving vessel shall be determined by the law of the flag of that vessel. If the salvage has not been carried out from a vessel, the apportionment shall be determined by the law governing the contract between the salvor and his servants.

Article 16

Salvage of Persons

(1)   No remuneration is due from persons whose lives are saved, but nothing in this article shall affect the provisions of national law on this subject.

(2)   A salvor of human life, who has taken part in the services rendered on the occasion of the accident giving rise to salvage, is entitled to a fair share of the payment awarded to the salvor for salving the vessel or other property or preventing or minimizing damage to the environment.

Article 17

Services Rendered Under Existing Contracts

No payment is due under the provisions of this Convention unless the services rendered exceed what can be reasonably considered as due performance of a contract entered into before the danger arose.

Article 18

The Effect of Salvor's Misconduct

A salvor may be deprived of the whole or part of the payment due under this Convention to the extent that the salvage operations have become necessary or more difficult because of fault or neglect on his part or if the salvor has been guilty of fraud or other dishonest conduct.

Article 19

Prohibition of Salvage Operations

Services rendered notwithstanding the express and reasonable prohibition of the owner or master of the vessel or the owner of any other property in danger which is not and has not been on board the vessel shall not give rise to payment under this Convention.

CHAPTER IV.   CLAIMS AND ACTIONS

Article 20

Maritime Lien

(1)   Nothing in this Convention shall affect the salvor's maritime lien under any international convention or national law.

(2)   The salvor may not enforce his maritime lien when satisfactory security for his claim, including interest and costs, has been duly tendered or provided.

Article 21

Duty To Provide Security

(1)   Upon the request of the salvor a person liable for a payment due under this Convention shall provide satisfactory security for the claim, including interest and costs of the salvor.

(2)   Without prejudice to paragraph 1, the owner of the salved vessel shall use his best endeavours to ensure that the owners of the cargo provide satisfactory security for the claims against them including interest and costs before the cargo is released.

(3)   The salved vessel and other property shall not, without the consent of the salvor, be removed from the port or place at which they first arrive after the completion of the salvage operations until satisfactory security has been put up for the salvor's claim against the relevant vessel or property.

Article 22

Interim Payment

(1)   The tribunal having jurisdiction over the claim of the salvor may, by interim decision, order that the salvor shall be paid on account such amount as seems fair and just, and on such terms including terms as to security where appropriate, as may be fair and just according to the circumstances of the case.

(2) In the event of an interim payment under this article the security provided under article 21 shall be reduced accordingly.

Article 23

Limitation of Actions

(1) Any action relating to payment under this Convention shall be time-barred if judicial or arbitral proceedings have not been instituted within a period of two years. The limitation period commences on the day on which the salvage operations are terminated.

(2) The person against whom a claim is made may at any time during the running of the limitation period extend that period by a declaration to the claimant. This period may in the like manner be further extended.

(3) An action for indemnity by a person liable may be instituted even after the expiration of the limitation period provided for in the preceding paragraphs, if brought within the time allowed by the law of the State where proceedings are instituted.

Article 24

Interest

The right of the salvor to interest on any payment due under this Convention shall be determined according to the law of the State in which the tribunal seized of the case is situated.

Article 25

State-Owned Cargoes

Unless the State owner consents, no provision of this Convention shall be used as a basis for the seizure, arrest or detention by any legal process of, nor for any proceedings *in rem* against, non-commercial cargoes owned by a State and entitled, at the time of the salvage operations, to sovereign immunity under generally recognized principles of international law.

Article 26

Humanitarian Cargoes

No provision of this Convention shall be used as a basis for the seizure, arrest or detention of humanitarian cargoes donated by a State, if such State has agreed to pay for salvage services rendered in respect of such humanitarian cargoes.

Article 27

Publication of Arbitral Awards

States Parties shall encourage, as far as possible and with the consent of the parties, the publication of arbitral awards made in salvage cases.

[Articles 28 through 34 omitted]

D. GENERAL AVERAGE

YORK-ANTWERP RULES 1994

(Adopted by the Comité Maritime Internationale at Sydney, October 7, 1994 and effective January 1, 1995, superseding York-Antwerp Rules 1974 as amended 1990)

Rule of Interpretation

In the adjustment of general average the following Rules shall apply to the exclusion of any Law and Practice inconsistent therewith.

Except as provided by the Rule Paramount and the numbered Rules, general average shall be adjusted according to the lettered Rules.

Rule Paramount

In no case shall there be any allowance for sacrifice or expenditure unless reasonably made or incurred.

Rule A

There is a general average act when, and only when, any extraordinary sacrifice or expenditure is intentionally and reasonably made or incurred for the common safety for the purpose of preserving from peril the property involved in a common maritime adventure.

General average sacrifices and expenditures shall be borne by the different contributing interests on the basis hereinafter provided.

Rule B

There is a common maritime adventure when one or more vessels are towing or pushing another vessel or vessels, provided that they are all involved in commercial activities and not in a salvage operation.

When measures are taken to preserve the vessels and their cargoes, if any, from a common peril, these Rules shall apply.

A vessel is not in common peril with another vessel or vessels if by simply disconnecting from the other vessel or vessels she is in safety; but if the disconnection is itself a general average act the common maritime adventure continues.

Rule C

Only such losses, damages or expenses which are the direct consequence of the general average act shall be allowed as general average.

In no case shall there be any allowance in general average for losses, damages or expenses incurred in respect of damage to the environment or in consequence of the escape or release of pollutant substances from the property involved in the common maritime adventure.

Demurrage, loss of market, and any loss or damage sustained or expense incurred by reason of delay, whether on the voyage or subsequently, and any indirect loss whatsoever, shall not be admitted as general average.

Rule D

Rights to contribution in general average shall not be affected, though the event which gave rise to the sacrifice or expenditure may have been due to the fault of one of the parties to the adventure; but this shall not prejudice any remedies or defences which may be open against or to that party in respect of such fault.

Rule E

The onus of proof is upon the party claiming in general average to show that the loss or expense claimed is properly allowable as general average.

All parties claiming in general average shall give notice in writing to the average adjuster of the loss or expense in respect of which they claim contribution within 12 months of the date of the termination of the common maritime adventure.

Failing such notification, or if within 12 months of a request for the same any of the parties shall fail to supply evidence in support of a notified claim, or particulars of value in respect of a contributory interest, the average adjuster shall be at liberty to estimate the extent of the allowance or the contributory value on the basis of the information available to him, which estimate may be challenged only on the ground that it is manifestly incorrect.

Rule F

Any additional expense incurred in place of another expense which would have been allowable as general average shall be deemed to be general average and so allowed without regard to the saving, if any, to other interests, but only up to the amount of the general average expense avoided.

Rule G

General average shall be adjusted as regards both loss and contribution upon the basis of values at the time and place when and where the adventure ends.

This rule shall not affect the determination of the place at which the average statement is to be made up.

When a ship is at any port or place in circumstances which would give rise to an allowance in general average under the provisions of Rules X and XI, and the cargo or part thereof is forwarded to destination by other means, rights and liabilities in general average shall, subject to cargo interests being notified if practicable, remain as nearly as possible the same as they would have been in the absence of such forwarding, as if the adventure had continued in the original ship for so long as justifiable under the contract of affreightment and the applicable law.

The proportion attaching to cargo of the allowances made in general average by reason of applying the third paragraph of this Rule shall not exceed the cost which would have been borne by the owners of cargo if the cargo had been forwarded at their expense.

Rule I—Jettison of Cargo

No jettison of cargo shall be made good as general average, unless such cargo is carried in accordance with the recognised custom of the trade.

Rule II—Loss or Damage by Sacrifices for the Common Safety

Loss of or damage to the property involved in the common maritime adventure by or in consequence of a sacrifice made for the common safety, and by water which goes down a ship's hatches opened or other opening made for the purpose of making a jettison for the common safety, shall be made good as general average.

Rule III—Extinguishing Fire on Shipboard

Damage done to a ship and cargo, or either of them, by water or otherwise, including damage by beaching or scuttling a burning ship, in extinguishing a fire on board the ship, shall be made good as general average; except that no compensation shall be made for damage by smoke however caused or by heat of the fire.

Rule IV—Cutting away Wreck

Loss or damage sustained by cutting away wreck or parts of the ship which have previously carried away or are effectively lost by accident shall not be made good as general average.

Rule V—Voluntary Stranding

When a ship is intentionally run on shore for the common safety, whether or not she might have been driven on shore, the consequent loss or damage to the property involved in the common maritime adventure shall be allowed in general average

Rule VI—Salvage Remuneration

(a) Expenditure incurred by the parties to the adventure in the nature of salvage, whether under contract or otherwise, shall be allowed in general average provided that the salvage operations were carried out for the purpose of preserving from peril the property involved in the common maritime adventure.

Expenditure allowed in general average shall include any salvage remuneration in which the skill and efforts of the salvors in preventing or minimising damage to the environment such as is referred to in Art. 13 ¶ 1(b) of the International Convention on Salvage, 1989 have been taken into account.

(b) Special compensation payable to a salvor by the shipowner under Art. 14 of the said Convention to the extent specified in ¶ 4 of that

Article or under any other provision similar in substance shall not be allowed in general average.

Rule VII—Damage to Machinery and Boilers

Damage caused to any machinery and boilers of a ship which is ashore and in a position of peril, in endeavouring to refloat, shall be allowed in general average when shown to have arisen from an actual intention to float the ship for the common safety at the risk of such damage; but where a ship is afloat no loss or damage caused by working the propelling machinery and boilers shall in any circumstances be made good as general average.

Rule VIII—Expenses lightening a Ship when Ashore, and Consequent Damage

When a ship is ashore and cargo and ship's fuel and stores or any of them are discharged as a general average act, the extra cost of lightening, lighter hire and reshipping (if incurred), and any loss or damage to the property involved in the common maritime adventure in consequence thereof, shall be admitted as general average.

Rule IX—Cargo, Ship's Materials and Stores used for Fuel

Cargo, ship's materials and stores, or any of them, necessarily used for fuel for the common safety at a time of peril shall be admitted as general average, but when such an allowance is made for the cost of ship's materials and stores the general average shall be credited with the estimated cost of the fuel which would otherwise have been consumed in prosecuting the intended voyage.

Rule X—Expenses at Port of Refuge, etc.

(a) When a ship shall have entered a port or place of refuge or shall have returned to her port or place of loading in consequence of accident, sacrifice or other extraordinary circumstances which render that necessary for the common safety, the expenses of entering such port or place shall be admitted as general average; and when she shall have sailed thence with her original cargo, or a part of it, the corresponding expenses of leaving such port or place consequent upon such entry or return shall likewise be admitted as general average.

When a ship is at any port or place of refuge and is necessarily removed to another port or place because repairs cannot be carried out in the first port or place, the provisions of this Rule shall be applied to the second port or place as if it were a port or place of refuge and the cost of such removal including temporary repairs and towage shall be admitted as general average. The provisions of Rule XI shall be applied to the prolongation of the voyage occasioned by such removal.

(b) The cost of handling on board or discharging cargo, fuel or stores whether at a port or place of loading, call or refuge, shall be admitted as general average, when the handling or discharge was necessary for the common safety or to enable damage to the ship caused by sacrifice or accident to be repaired, if the repairs were necessary for the safe prosecution of the voyage, except in cases where the damage to the ship is discovered at a port or place of loading or call without any accident or other extraordinary circumstances connected with such damage having taken place during the voyage.

The cost of handling on board or discharging cargo, fuel or stores shall not be admissible as general average when incurred solely for the purpose of restowage due to shifting during the voyage, unless such restowage is necessary for the common safety.

(c) Whenever the cost of handling or discharging cargo, fuel or stores is admissible as general average, the costs of storage, including insurance if reasonably incurred, reloading and stowing of such cargo, fuel or stores shall likewise be admitted as general average. The provisions of Rule XI shall be applied to the extra period of detention occasioned by such reloading or restowing.

But when the ship is condemned or does not proceed on her original voyage, storage expenses shall be admitted as general average only up to the date of the ship's condemnation or of the abandonment of the voyage or up to the date of completion of discharge of cargo if the condemnation or abandonment takes place before that date.

Rule XI—Wages and Maintenance of Crew and other expenses
bearing up for and in a port of refuge, etc.

(a) Wages and maintenance of master, officers and crew reasonably incurred and fuel and stores consumed during the prolongation of the voyage occasioned by a ship entering a port or place of refuge or returning to her port or place of loading shall be admitted as general average when the expenses of entering such port or place are allowable in general average in accordance with Rule X(a).

(b) When a ship shall have entered or been detained in any port or place in consequence of accident, sacrifice or other extraordinary circumstances which render that necessary for the common safety, or to enable damage to the ship caused by sacrifice or accident to be repaired, if the repairs were necessary for the safe prosecution of the voyage, the wages and maintenance of the master, officers and crew reasonably incurred during the extra period of detention in such port or place until the ship shall or should have been made ready to proceed upon her voyage, shall be admitted in general average.

Fuel and stores consumed during the period of detention shall be admitted as general average, except such fuel and stores as are consumed in effecting repairs not allowable in general average.

Port charges incurred during the extra period of detention shall likewise be admitted as general average except such charges as are incurred solely by reason of repairs not allowable in general average.

Provided that when damage to the ship is discovered at a port or place of loading or call without any accident or other extraordinary circumstance connected with such damage having taken place during the voyage, then the wages and maintenance of master, officers and crew and fuel and stores consumed and port charges incurred during the extra detention for repairs to damages so discovered shall not be admissible as general average, even if the repairs are necessary for the safe prosecution of the voyage.

When the ship is condemned or does not proceed on her original voyage, the wages and maintenance of the master, officers and crew and fuel and stores consumed and shall port charges be admitted as general average only up to the date of the ship's condemnation or of the abandonment of the voyage or up to the date of completion of discharge of cargo if the condemnation or abandonment takes place before that date.

(c) For the purpose of this and the other Rules wages shall include all payments made to or for the benefit of the master, officers and crew, whether such payments be imposed by law upon the shipowners or be made under the terms of articles of employment.

(d) The cost of measures undertaken to prevent or minimise damage to the environment shall be allowed in general average when incurred in any or all of the following circumstances:

(i) as part of an operation performed for the common safety which, had it been undertaken by a party outside the common maritime adventure, would have entitled such party to a salvage reward;

(ii) as a condition of entry into or departure from any port or place in the circumstances prescribed in Rule X(a);

(iii) as a condition of remaining at any port or place in the circumstances prescribed in Rule X(a), provided that when there is an actual escape or release of pollutant substances the cost of any additional measures required on that account to prevent or minimise pollution or environmental damage shall not be allowed as general average;

(iv) necessarily in connection with the discharging, storing or reloading of cargo whenever the cost of those operations is admissible as general average.

Rule XII—Damage to Cargo in Discharging, etc.

Damage to or loss of cargo, fuel or stores sustained in consequence of their handling, discharging, storing, reloading and stowing shall be made good as general average, when and only when the cost of those measures respectively is admitted as general average.

Rule XIII—Deduction from Cost of Repairs

Repairs to be allowed in general average shall not be subject to deductions in respect of "new for old" where old material or parts are replaced by new unless the ship is over fifteen years old in which case there shall be a deduction of one third. The deductions shall be regulated by the age of the ship from the 31st December of the year of completion of construction to the date of the general average act, except for insulation, life and similar boats, communications and navigational apparatus and equipment, machinery and boilers for which the deductions shall be regulated by the age of the particular parts to which they apply.

The deductions shall be made only from the cost of the new material or parts when finished and ready to be installed in the ship.

No deduction shall be made in respect of provisions, stores, anchors and chain cables.

Drydock and slipway dues and costs of shifting the ship shall be allowed in full.

The costs of cleaning, painting or coating of bottom shall not be allowed in general average unless the bottom has been painted or coated within the twelve months preceding the date of the general average act in which case one half of such costs shall be allowed.

Rule XIV—Temporary Repairs

Where temporary repairs are effected to a ship at a port of loading, call or refuge, for the common safety, or of damage caused by general average sacrifice, the cost of such repairs shall be admitted as general average.

Where temporary repairs of accidental damage are effected in order to enable the adventure to be completed, the cost of such repairs shall be admitted as general average without regard to the saving, if any, to other interests, but only up to the savings in expense which would have been incurred and allowed in general average if such repairs had not been effected there.

No deductions "new for old" shall be made from the cost of temporary repairs allowable as general average.

Rule XV—Loss of Freight

Loss of freight arising from damage to or loss of cargo shall be made good as general average, either when caused by a general average act, or when the damage to or loss of cargo is so made good.

Deduction shall be made from the amount of gross freight loss, of the charges which the owner thereof would have incurred to earn such freight, but has, in consequence of the sacrifice, not incurred.

Rule XVI—Amount to be made good for Cargo
Lost or Damaged by Sacrifice

The amount to be made good as general average for damage to or loss of cargo sacrificed shall be the loss which has been sustained thereby based on the value at the time of discharge, ascertained from the commercial invoice rendered to the receiver or if there is no such invoice from the shipped value. The value at the time of discharge shall include the cost of insurance and freight except insofar as such freight is at the risk of interests other than the cargo.

When cargo so damaged is sold and the amount of the damage has not been otherwise agreed, the loss to be made good in general average shall be the difference between the net proceeds of sale and the net sound value as computed in the first paragraph of this Rule.

Rule XVII—Contributory Values

The contribution to a general average shall be made upon the actual net values of the property at the termination of the adventure except that the value of cargo shall be the value at the time of discharge, ascertained from the commercial invoice rendered to the receiver or if there is no such invoice from the shipped value. The value of the cargo shall include the cost of insurance and freight unless and insofar as such freight is at the risk of interests other than the cargo, deducting therefrom any loss or damage suffered by the cargo prior to or at the time of discharge. The value of the ship shall be assessed without taking into account the beneficial or detrimental effect of any demise or time charterparty to which the ship may be committed.

To these values shall be added the amount made good as general average for property sacrificed, if not already included, deduction being made from the freight and passage money at risk of such charges and crew's wages as would not have been incurred in earning the freight had the ship and cargo been totally lost at the date of the general average; deduction being also made from the value of the property of all extra charges incurred in respect thereof subsequently to the general average act, except such charges as are allowed in general average or fall upon the ship by virtue of an award for special compensation under Art. 14 of the International Convention on Salvage, 1989 or under any other provision similar in substance.

In the circumstances envisaged in the third paragraph of Rule G, the cargo and other property shall contribute on the basis of its value upon delivery at original destination unless sold or otherwise disposed of short of that destination, and the ship shall contribute upon its actual net value at the time of completion of discharge of cargo.

Where cargo is sold short of destination, however, it shall contribute upon the actual net proceeds of sale, with the addition of any amount made good as general average.

Mails, passengers' luggage, personal effects and accompanied private motor vehicles shall not contribute in general average.

Rule XVII—Damage to Ship

The amount to be allowed as general average for damage or loss to the ship, her machinery and/or gear caused by a general average act shall be as follows;

(a) When repaired or replaced,

The actual reasonable cost of repairing or replacing such damage or loss, subject to deductions in accordance with Rule XIII;

(b) When not repaired or replaced.

The reasonable depreciation arising from such damage or loss, but not exceeding the estimated cost of repairs. But where the ship is an actual total loss or when the cost of repairs of the damage would exceed the value of the ship when repaired, the amount to be allowed as general average shall be the difference between the estimated sound value of the ship after deducting therefrom the estimated cost of repairing damage which is not general average and the value of the ship in her damaged state which may be measured by the net proceeds of sale, if any.

Rule XIX—Undeclared or Wrongfully Declared Cargo

Damage or loss caused to goods loaded without the knowledge of the shipowner or his agent or to goods wilfully misdescribed at time of shipment shall not be allowed as general average, but such goods shall remain liable to contribute, if saved.

Damage or loss caused to goods which have been wrongfully declared on shipment at a value which is lower than their real value shall be contributed for at the declared value, but such goods shall contribute upon their actual value.

Rule XX—Provision of Funds

A commission of 2 per cent on general average disbursements, other than the wages and maintenance of master, officers and crew and fuel and stores not replaced during the voyage, shall be allowed in general average.

The capital loss sustained by the owners of goods sold for the purpose of raising funds to defray general average disbursements shall be allowed in general average.

The cost of insuring general average disbursements shall also be admitted in general average.

Rule XXI—Interest on Losses made good in General Average

Interest shall be allowed on expenditure, sacrifices and allowances in general average at the rate of 7 percent per annum until three months after the date of issue of the general average adjustment, due allowance being made for any payment on account by the contributory interests or from the general average deposit fund.

Rule XXII—Treatment of Cash Deposits

Where cash deposits have been collected in respect of cargo's liability for general average, salvage or special charges, such deposits shall be paid without any delay into a special account in the joint names of a representative nominated on behalf of the shipowner and a representative nominated on behalf of the depositors in a bank to be approved by both. The sum so deposited, together with accrued interest, if any, shall be held as security for payment to the parties entitled thereto of the general average, salvage or special charges payable by cargo in respect to which the deposits have been collected. Payments on account or refunds of deposits may be made if certified to in writing by the average adjuster. Such deposits and payments or refunds shall be without prejudice to the ultimate liability of the parties.

STATEMENT OF THE DELEGATION OF THE MARITIME LAW ASSOCIATION OF THE UNITED STATES OF AMERICA

The delegation of the United States of America understands that the proposed York-Antwerp Rules 1994 exclude allowances in General Average in respect of liability in consequence of the escape or release of pollutant substances from the property involved in the common maritime adventure.

YORK-ANTWERP RULES 2016

(Adopted by the Comité Maritime International at it conference in New York in May 2016.)

Rule of Interpretation

In the adjustment of general average the following Rules shall apply to the exclusion of any law and practice inconsistent therewith.

Except as provided by the Rule Paramount and the numbered Rules, general average shall be adjusted according to the lettered Rules.

Rule Paramount

In no case shall there be any allowance for sacrifice or expenditure unless reasonably made or incurred.

Rule A

1. There is a general average act when, and only when, any extraordinary sacrifice or expenditure is intentionally and reasonably made or incurred for the common safety for the purpose of preserving from peril the property involved in a common maritime adventure.

2. General average sacrifices and expenditures shall be borne by the different contributing interests on the basis hereinafter provided.

Rule B

1.   There is a common maritime adventure when one or more vessels are towing or pushing another vessel or vessels, provided that they are all involved in commercial activities and not in a salvage operation.

When measures are taken to preserve the vessels and their cargoes, if any, from a common peril, these Rules shall apply.

2.   If the vessels are in common peril and one is disconnected either to increase the disconnecting vessel's safety alone, or the safety of all vessels in the common maritime adventure, the disconnection will be a general average act.

3.   Where vessels involved in a common maritime adventure resort to a port or place of refuge, allowances under these Rules may be made in relation to each of the vessels. Subject to the provisions of paragraphs 3 and 4 of Rule G, allowances in general average shall cease at the time that the common maritime adventure comes to an end.

Rule C

1.   Only such losses, damages or expenses which are the direct consequence of the general average act shall be allowed as general average.

2.   In no case shall there be any allowance in general average for losses, damages or expenses incurred in respect of damage to the environment or in consequence of the escape or release of pollutant substances from the property involved in the common maritime adventure.

3.   Demurrage, loss of market, and any loss or damage sustained or expense incurred by reason of delay, whether on the voyage or subsequently, and any indirect loss whatsoever, shall not be allowed as general average.

Rule D

Rights to contribution in general average shall not be affected, though the event which gave rise to the sacrifice or expenditure may have been due to the fault of one of the parties to the common maritime adventure, but this shall not prejudice any remedies or defenses which may be open against or to that party in respect of such fault.

Rule E

1.   The onus of proof is upon the party claiming in general average to show that the loss or expense claimed is properly allowable as general average.

2.   All parties to the common maritime adventure shall, as soon as possible, supply particulars of value in respect of their contributory interest and, if claiming in general average, shall give notice in writing

to the average adjuster of the loss or expense in respect of which they claim contribution, and supply evidence in support thereof.

3.   Failing notification, or if any party does not supply particulars in support of a notified claim, within 12 months of the termination of the common maritime adventure or payment of the expense, the average adjuster shall be at liberty to estimate the extent of the allowance on the basis of the information available to the adjuster. Particulars of value shall be provided within 12 months of the termination of the common maritime adventure, failing which the average adjuster shall be at liberty to estimate the contributory value on the same basis. Such estimates shall be communicated to the party in question in writing. Estimates may only be challenged within two months of receipt of the communication and only on the grounds that they are manifestly incorrect.

4.   Any party to the common maritime adventure pursuing a recovery from a third party in respect of sacrifice or expenditure claimed in general average, shall so advise the average adjuster and, in the event that a recovery is achieved, shall supply to the average adjuster full particulars of the recovery within two months of receipt of the recovery.

Rule F

Any additional expense incurred in place of another expense which would have been allowable as general average shall be deemed to be general average and so allowed without regard to the saving, if any, to other interests, but only up to the amount of the general average expense avoided.

Rule G

1.   General average shall be adjusted as regards both loss and contribution upon the basis of values at the time and place when and where the common maritime adventure ends.

2.   This rule shall not affect the determination of the place at which the average adjustment is to be prepared.

3.   When a ship is at any port or place in circumstances which would give rise to an allowance in general average under the provisions of Rules X and XI, and the cargo or part thereof is forwarded to destination by other means, rights and liabilities in general average shall, subject to cargo interests being notified if practicable, remain as nearly as possible the same as they would have been in the absence of such forwarding, as if the common maritime adventure had continued in the original ship for so long as justifiable under the contract of carriage and the applicable law.

4.   The proportion attaching to cargo of the allowances made in general average by reason of applying the third paragraph of this Rule shall be limited to the cost which would have been borne by the owners

of cargo if the cargo had been forwarded at their expense. This limit shall not apply to any allowances made under Rule F.

Rule I—Jettison of Cargo

No jettison of cargo shall be allowed as general average, unless such cargo is carried in accordance with the recognised custom of the trade.

Rule II—Loss or Damage by Sacrifices for the Common Safety

Loss of or damage to the property involved in the common maritime adventure by or in consequence of a sacrifice made for the common safety, and by water which goes down a ship's hatches opened or other opening made for the purpose of making a jettison for the common safety, shall be allowed as general average.

Rule III—Extinguishing Fire on Shipboard

Damage done to a ship and cargo, or either of them, by water or otherwise, including damage by beaching or scuttling a burning ship, in extinguishing a fire on board the ship, shall be allowed as general average; except that no allowance shall be made for damage by smoke however caused or by heat of the fire.

Rule IV—Cutting Away Wreck

Loss or damage sustained by cutting away wreck or parts of the ship which have been previously carried away or are effectively lost by accident shall not be allowed as general average.

Rule V—Voluntary Stranding

When a ship is intentionally run on shore for the common safety, whether or not she might have been driven on shore, the consequent loss or damage to the property involved in the common maritime adventure shall be allowed in general average.

Rule VI—Salvage Remuneration

(a) Expenditure incurred by the parties to the common maritime adventure in the nature of salvage, whether under contract or otherwise, shall be allowed in general average provided that the salvage operations were carried out for the purpose of preserving from peril the property involved in the common maritime adventure and subject to the provisions of paragraphs (b), (c) and (d)

(b) Notwithstanding (a) above, where the parties to the common maritime adventure have separate contractual or legal liability to salvors, salvage shall only be allowed should any of the following arise:

(i) there is a subsequent accident or other circumstances resulting in loss or damage to property during the voyage that results in significant differences between salved and contributory values,

(ii) there are significant general average sacrifices,

(iii) salved values are manifestly incorrect and there is a significantly incorrect apportionment of salvage expenses,

(iv) any of the parties to the salvage has paid a significant proportion of salvage due from another party,

(v) a significant proportion of the parties have satisfied the salvage claim on substantially different terms, no regard being had to interest, currency correction or legal costs of either the salvor or the contributing interest.

(c) Salvage expenditures referred to in paragraph (a) above shall include any salvage remuneration in which the skill and efforts of the salvors in preventing or minimising damage to the environment such as is referred to in Article 13 paragraph 1(b) of the International Convention on Salvage, 1989 have been taken into account.

(d) Special compensation payable to a salvor by the shipowner under Article 14 of the International Convention on Salvage, 1989 to the extent specified in paragraph 4 of that Article or under any other provision similar in substance (such as SCOPIC) shall not be allowed in general average and shall not be considered a salvage expenditure as referred to in paragraph (a) of this Rule.

Rule VII—Damage to Machinery and Boilers

Damage caused to any machinery and boilers of a ship which is ashore and in a position of peril, in endeavouring to refloat, shall be allowed in general average when shown to have arisen from an actual intention to float the ship for the common safety at the risk of such damage; but where a ship is afloat no loss or damage caused by working the propelling machinery and boilers shall in any circumstances be allowed as general average.

Rule VIII—Expenses Lightening a Ship when Ashore, and Consequent Damage

When a ship is ashore and cargo and ship's fuel and stores or any of them are discharged as a general average act, the extra cost of lightening, lighter hire and reshipping (if incurred), and any loss or damage to the property involved in the common maritime adventure in consequence thereof, shall be allowed as general average.

Rule IX—Cargo, Ship's Materials and Stores Used for Fuel

Cargo, ship's materials and stores, or any of them, necessarily used for fuel for the common safety at a time of peril shall be allowed as general average, but when such an allowance is made for the cost of ship's materials and stores the general average shall be credited with the estimated cost of the fuel which would otherwise have been consumed in prosecuting the intended voyage.

Rule X—Expenses at Port of Refuge, etc.

1.   (i)   When a ship shall have entered a port or place of refuge or shall have returned to her port or place of loading in consequence of accident, sacrifice or other extraordinary circumstances which render that necessary for the common safety, the expenses of entering such port or place shall be allowed as general average; and when she shall have sailed thence with her original cargo, or a part of it, the corresponding expenses of leaving such port or place consequent upon such entry or return shall likewise be allowed as general average.

(ii)   When a ship is at any port or place of refuge and is necessarily removed to another port or place because repairs cannot be carried out in the first port or place, the provisions of this Rule shall be applied to the second port or place as if it were a port or place of refuge and the cost of such removal including temporary repairs and towage shall be allowed as general average. The provisions of Rule XI shall be applied to the prolongation of the voyage occasioned by such removal.

2.   (i)   The cost of handling on board or discharging cargo, fuel or stores, whether at a port or place of loading, call or refuge, shall be allowed as general average when the handling or discharge was necessary for the common safety or to enable damage to the ship caused by sacrifice or accident to be repaired, if the repairs were necessary for the safe prosecution of the voyage, except in cases where the damage to the ship is discovered at a port or place of loading or call without any accident or other extraordinary circumstances connected with such damage having taken place during the voyage.

(ii)   The cost of handling on board or discharging cargo, fuel or stores shall not be allowable as general average when incurred solely for the purpose of restowage due to shifting during the voyage, unless such restowage is necessary for the common safety.

(c)   Whenever the cost of handling or discharging cargo, fuel or stores is allowable as general average, the costs of storage, including insurance if reasonably incurred, reloading and stowing of such cargo, fuel or stores shall likewise be allowed as general average. The provisions of Rule XI shall apply to the extra period of detention occasioned by such reloading or restowing.

(d)   When the ship is condemned or does not proceed on her original voyage, storage expenses shall be allowed as general average only up to the date of the ship's condemnation or of the abandonment of the voyage or up to the date of completion of discharge of cargo if the condemnation or abandonment takes place before that date.

Rule XI—Wages and Maintenance of Crew and Other
Expenses Putting in to and at a Port of Refuge, etc.

(a)   Wages and maintenance of master, officers and crew reasonably incurred and fuel and stores consumed during the prolongation of the voyage occasioned by a ship entering a port or place of refuge or returning to her port or place of loading shall be allowed as general average when the expenses of entering such port or place are allowable in general average in accordance with Rule X(a).

(b)(i)   When a ship shall have entered or been detained in any port or place in consequence of accident, sacrifice or other extra-ordinary circumstances which render that entry or detention necessary for the common safety, or to enable damage to the ship caused by sacrifice or accident to be repaired, if the repairs were necessary for the safe prosecution of the voyage, the wages and maintenance of the master, officers and crew reasonably incurred during the extra period of detention in such port or place until the ship shall or should have been made ready to proceed upon her voyage, shall be allowed in general average.

(ii) Fuel and stores consumed during the extra period of detention shall be allowed as general average, except such fuel and stores as are consumed in effecting repairs not allowable in general average.

(iii) Port charges incurred during the extra period of detention shall likewise be allowed as general average except such charges as are incurred solely by reason of repairs not allowable in general average.

(iv) Provided that when damage to the ship is discovered at a port or place of loading or call without any accident or other extraordinary circumstance connected with such damage having taken place during the voyage, then the wages and maintenance of master, officers and crew and fuel and stores consumed and port charges incurred during the extra detention for repairs to damages so discovered shall not be allowable as general average, even if the repairs are necessary for the safe prosecution of the voyage.

(v) When the ship is condemned or does not proceed on her original voyage, the wages and maintenance of the master, officers and crew and fuel and stores consumed and port charges shall be allowed as general average only up to the date of the ship's condemnation or of the abandonment of the voyage or up to the date of completion of discharge of cargo if the condemnation or abandonment takes place before that date.

(c) (i) For the purpose of these Rules wages shall include all payments made to or for the benefit of the master, officers and crew, whether such payments be imposed by law upon the shipowners or be made under the terms of articles of employment.

(ii) For the purpose of these Rules, port charges shall include all customary or additional expenses incurred for the common safety or to enable a vessel to enter or remain at a port of refuge or call in the circumstances outlined in Rule XI(b)(i).

(d) The cost of measures undertaken to prevent or minimise damage to the environment shall be allowed in general average when incurred in any or all of the following circumstances:

(i)   as part of an operation performed for the common safety which, had it been undertaken by a party outside the common maritime adventure, would have entitled such party to a salvage reward;

(ii) as a condition of entry into or departure from any port or place in the circumstances prescribed in Rule X(a);

(iii) as a condition of remaining at any port or place in the circumstances prescribed in Rule XI(b), provided that when there is an actual escape or release of pollutant substances, the cost of any additional measures required on that account to prevent or minimise pollution or environmental damage shall not be allowed as general average;

(iv) necessarily in connection with the handling on board, discharging, storing or reloading of cargo, fuel or stores whenever the cost of those operations is allowable as general average.

Rule XII—Damage to Cargo in Discharging, etc.

Damage to or loss of cargo, fuel or stores sustained in consequence of their handling, discharging, storing, reloading and stowing shall be allowed as general average, when and only when the cost of those measures respectively is allowed as general average.

Rule XIII—Deductions from Cost of Repairs

(a) Repairs to be allowed in general average shall not be subject to deductions in respect of "new for old" where old material or parts are replaced by new unless the ship is over fifteen years old in which case there shall be a deduction of one third. The deductions shall be regulated by the age of the ship from the 31st December of the year of completion of construction to the date of the general average act, except for insulation, life and similar boats, communications and navigational apparatus and equipment, machinery and boilers for which the deductions shall be regulated by the age of the particular parts to which they apply.

(b) The deductions shall be made only from the cost of the new material or parts when finished and ready to be installed in the ship. No deduction shall be made in respect of provisions, stores, anchors and chain cables. Drydock and slipway dues and costs of shifting the ship shall be allowed in full.

(c) The costs of cleaning, painting or coating of bottom shall not be allowed in general average unless the bottom has been painted or coated within the 24 months preceding the date of the general average act in which case one half of such costs shall be allowed.

Rule XIV—Temporary Repairs

(a) Where temporary repairs are effected to a ship at a port of loading, call or refuge, for the common safety, or of damage caused by general average sacrifice, the cost of such repairs shall be allowed as general average.

(b) Where temporary repairs of accidental damage are effected in order to enable the common maritime adventure to be completed, the cost of such repairs shall be allowed as general average without regard to the saving, if any, to other interests, but only up to the saving in expense which would have been incurred and allowed in general average if such repairs had not been effected there.

(c) No deductions "new for old" shall be made from the cost of temporary repairs allowable as general average.

Rule XV—Loss of Freight

Loss of freight arising from damage to or loss of cargo shall be allowed as general average, either when caused by a general average act, or when the damage to or loss of cargo is so allowed.

Deduction shall be made from the amount of gross freight lost, of the charges which the owner thereof would have incurred to earn such freight, but has, in consequence of the sacrifice, not incurred.

Rule XVI—Amount to be Allowed for Cargo
Lost or Damaged by Sacrifice

(a) (i) The amount to be allowed as general average for damage to or loss of cargo sacrificed shall be the loss which has been sustained thereby based on the value at the time of discharge, ascertained from the commercial invoice rendered to the receiver or if there is no such invoice from the shipped value. Such commercial invoice may be deemed by the average adjuster to reflect the value at the time of discharge irrespective of the place of final delivery under the contract of carriage.

(ii) The value at the time of discharge shall include the cost of insurance and freight except insofar as such freight is at the risk of interests other than the cargo.

(b) When cargo so damaged is sold and the amount of the damage has not been otherwise agreed, the loss to be allowed in general average shall be the difference between the net proceeds of sale and the net sound value as computed in the first paragraph of this Rule.

Rule XVII—Contributory Values

(a) (i) The contribution to a general average shall be made upon the actual net values of the property at the termination of the common maritime adventure except that the value of cargo shall be the value at the time of discharge, ascertained from the commercial invoice rendered to the receiver or if there is no such invoice from the shipped value. Such commercial invoice may be deemed by the average adjuster to reflect the value at the time of discharge irrespective of the place of final delivery under the contract of carriage.

(ii) The value of the cargo shall include the cost of insurance and freight unless and insofar as such freight is at the risk of interests other than the cargo, deducting therefrom any loss or damage suffered by the cargo prior to or at the time of discharge. Any cargo may be excluded from contributing to general average should the average adjuster consider that the cost of including it in the adjustment would be likely to be disproportionate to its eventual contribution.

(iii) The value of the ship shall be assessed without taking into account the beneficial or detrimental effect of any demise or time charterparty to which the ship may be committed.

(b) To these values shall be added the amount allowed as general average for property sacrificed, if not already included, deduction being made from the freight and passage money at risk of such charges and crew's wages as would not have been incurred in earning the freight had the ship and cargo been totally lost at the date of the general average act and have not been allowed as general average; deduction being also made from the value of the property of all extra charges incurred in respect thereof subsequently to the general average act, except such charges as are allowed in general average or fall upon the ship by virtue of an award for special compensation under Article 14 of the international Convention on Salvage, 1989 or under any other provision similar in substance. Where payment for salvage services has not been allowed as general average by reason of paragraph (b) of Rule VI, deductions in respect of payment for salvage services shall be limited to the amount paid to the salvors including interest and salvors' costs.

(c) In the circumstances envisaged in the third paragraph of Rule G, the cargo and other property shall contribute on the basis of its value upon delivery at original destination unless sold or otherwise disposed of short of that destination, and the ship shall contribute upon its actual net value at the time of completion of discharge of cargo.

(d) Where cargo is sold short of destination, however, it shall contribute upon the actual net proceeds of sale, with the addition of any amount allowed as general average.

(e) Mails, passengers' luggage and accompanied personal effects and accompanied private motor vehicles shall not contribute to general average.

Rule XVIII—Damage to Ship

The amount to be allowed as general average for damage or loss to the ship, her machinery and/or gear caused by a general average act shall be as follows:

(a) When repaired or replaced,

215

The actual reasonable cost of repairing or replacing such damage or loss, subject to deductions in accordance with Rule XIII;

(b)   When not repaired or replaced,

The reasonable depreciation arising from such damage or loss, but not exceeding the estimated cost of repairs. But where the ship is an actual total loss or when the cost of repairs of the damage would exceed the value of the ship when repaired, the amount to be allowed as general average shall be the difference between the estimated sound value of the ship after deducting therefrom the estimated cost of repairing damage which is not general average and the value of the ship in her damaged state which may be measured by the net proceeds of sale, if any.

Rule XIX—Undeclared or Wrongfully Declared Cargo

(a)   Damage or loss caused to goods loaded without the knowledge of the shipowner or his agent or to goods wilfully misdescribed at the time of shipment shall not be allowed as general average, but such goods shall remain liable to contribute, if saved.

(b)   Where goods have been wrongfully declared at the time of shipment at a value which is lower than their real value, any general average loss or damage shall be allowed on the basis of their declared value, but such goods shall contribute on the basis of their actual value.

Rule XX—Provision of Funds

(a)   The capital loss sustained by the owners of goods sold for the purpose of raising funds to defray general average disbursements shall be allowed in general average.

(b)   The cost of insuring general average disbursements shall be allowed in general average.

Rule XXI—Interest on Losses Allowed in General Average

(c)   Interest shall be allowed on expenditure, sacrifices and allowances in general average until three months after the date of issue of the general average adjustment, due allowance being made for any payment on account by the contributory interests or from the general average deposit fund.

(d)   The rate for calculating interest accruing during each calendar year shall be the 12-month ICE LIBOR for the currency in which the adjustment is prepared, as announced on the first banking day of that calendar year, increased by four percentage points. If the adjustment is prepared in a currency for which no ICE LIBOR is announced, the rate shall be the 12-month US Dollar ICE LIBOR, increased by four percentage points.

Rule XXII—Treatment of Cash Deposits

(a)   Where cash deposits have been collected in respect of general average, salvage or special charges, such sums shall be remitted forthwith to the average adjuster who shall deposit the sums into a special account, earning interest where possible, in the name of the average adjuster.

(b)   The special account shall be constituted in accordance with the law regarding client or third party funds applicable in the domicile of the average adjuster. The account shall be held separately from the average adjuster's own funds, in trust or in compliance with similar rules of law providing for the administration of the funds of third parties.

(c)   The sums so deposited, together with accrued interest, if any, shall be held as security for payment to the parties entitled thereto, of the general average, salvage or special charges in respect of which the deposits have been collected. Payments on account or refunds of deposits may only be made when such payments are certified in writing by the average adjuster and notified to the depositor requesting their approval. Upon the receipt of the depositor's approval, or in the absence of such approval within a period of 90 days, the average adjuster may deduct the amount of the payment on account or the final contribution from the deposit.

(d)   All deposits and payments or refunds shall be without prejudice to the ultimate liability of the parties.

Rule XXIII—Time Bar for Contributing to General Average

(a)   Subject always to any mandatory rule on time limitation contained in any applicable law:

(i)   Any rights to general average contribution including any rights to claim under general average bonds and guarantees, shall be extinguished unless an action is brought by the party claiming such contribution within a period of one year after the date upon which the general average adjustment is issued. However, in no case shall such an action be brought after six years from the date of termination of the common maritime adventure.

(ii)   These periods may be extended if the parties so agree after the termination of the common maritime adventure.

(b)   This rule shall not apply as between the parties to the general average and their respective insurers.

E. COLLISIONS

INTERNATIONAL CONVENTION FOR THE UNIFICATION OF CERTAIN RULES RELATING TO COLLISIONS BETWEEN VESSELS

Signed at Brussels September 23, 1910.

Art. 1. Where a collision occurs between seagoing vessels or between seagoing vessels and vessels of inland navigation the compensation due for damages caused to the vessels, or to any things or persons on board thereof, shall be settled in accordance with the following provisions, in whatever waters the collision takes place.

Art. 2. If the collision is accidental, if it is caused by *force majeure,* or if the causes of the collision are in doubt, the damages shall be borne by those who have suffered them.

This provision shall be applicable notwithstanding the fact that the vessels, or any one of them, may be at anchor (or otherwise made fast) at the time of the casualty.

Art. 3. If the collision is caused by the fault of one of the vessels, liability to make good the damages shall attach to the one which has committed the fault.

Art. 4. If two or more vessels are in fault the liability of each vessel shall be in proportion to the degree of the faults respectively committed. Provided that if, having regard to the circumstances, it is not possible to establish the degree of the respective faults, or if it appears that the faults are equal, the liability shall be apportioned equally.

The damages caused either to the vessels, or to their cargoes, or to the effects or other property of the crews, passengers, or other persons on board, shall be borne by the vessels in fault in the above proportion without joint and several liability toward third parties.

In respect of damages caused by death or personal injury, the vessels in fault shall be jointly as well as severally liable to third parties, without prejudice to the right of recourse of the vessel which has paid a larger part than that which in accordance with the provisions of the first paragraph of this article she ought ultimately to bear.

It is left to the law of each country to determine, as regards such recourse, the scope and effect of any legal or contractual provisions which limit the liability of the owners of a vessel toward persons on board.

Art. 5. The liability imposed by the preceding articles shall attach, in cases where the collision is caused by the fault of a pilot, even when the carrying of the pilot is obligatory.

Art. 6. The right of action for the recovery of damages resulting from a collision shall not be conditional upon the entering of a protest or the fulfillment of any other special formality.

There shall be no legal presumptions of fault in regard to liability for collision.

Art. 7. Actions for the recovery of damages shall be barred after an interval of two years from the date of the casualty.

The period within which the action to enforce the right of recourse allowed by paragraph 3 of Article 4 must be instituted shall be one year. This limitation shall run only from the date of payment.

The grounds upon which the said periods of limitation may be suspended or interrupted shall be determined by the law of the court where the case is tried.

The High Contracting Parties reserve to themselves the right to admit into their legislations, as ground for extending the periods fixed above, the fact that it has not been possible to arrest the defendant vessel in the territorial waters of the state in which the plaintiff has his domicile or his principal place of business.

Art. 8. After a collision, the master of each of the vessels in collision shall be bound, so far as he can do so without serious danger to his vessel, her crew, and her passengers, to render assistance to the other vessel, her crew, and her passengers.

He shall likewise be bound, so far as possible, to make known to the other vessel the name of his vessel and the port to which she belongs, and also the names of the ports from which she comes and to which she is bound.

A breach of the above provisions shall not of itself impose any liability on the owner of a vessel.

Art. 9. The High Contracting Parties whose legislation does not forbid infringements of the preceding article bind themselves to take or to propose to their respective legislatures the measures necessary for the prevention of such infringements.

The High Contracting Parties will communicate to one another, as soon as possible, the laws or regulations which have already been or may be hereafter promulgated in their states for giving effect to the above undertaking.

Art. 10. Without prejudice to any conventions which may hereafter be made, the provisions of this Convention shall not affect in any way the rules in force in each country with regard to the limitation of shipowners' liability, nor shall they affect the obligations arising from contracts of carriage or from any other contracts.

Art. 11. This Convention shall not apply to ships of war or to Government ships appropriated exclusively to a public service.

Art. 12. The provisions of this Convention shall be applied as regards all persons interested when all the vessels concerned in any action are subject to the jurisdiction of the Governments of the High

Contracting Parties and in any other cases for which the national laws provide.

Provided always that:

1. As regards persons interested who belong to a Noncontracting State, the application of the above provisions may be made by each of the Contracting States conditional upon reciprocity.

2. Where all the persons interested belong to the same state as the court trying the case, the provisions of the national law and not of the Convention shall be applicable.

Art. 13. This Convention shall extend to the making good of damages which a vessel has caused to another vessel or to persons or things on board either vessel, either by the execution or nonexecution of a manoeuvre or by the nonobservance of the regulations, even if no collision has actually taken place.

Additional Article

* * * (I)t is understood that the provisions of Article 5, establishing liability in cases where the collision is caused by the fault of a compulsory pilot, shall not come into full force until the High Contracting Parties shall have arrived at an agreement regarding the limitation of liability of shipowners.

In witness whereof, the Plenipotentiaries of the respective High Contracting Parties have signed this Convention and have affixed their seals thereto.

Done at Brussels, in a single copy, September 23rd, 1910.

INTERNATIONAL CONVENTION ON CERTAIN RULES CONCERNING CIVIL JURISDICTION IN MATTERS OF COLLISION

Brussels, May 10, 1952
439 UNTS 217

[Preamble deleted]

Article 1

Courts Having Jurisdiction

(1) An action for collision occurring between seagoing vessels, or between seagoing vessels and inland navigation craft, can only be introduced:

(a) either before the Court where the defendant has his habitual residence or a place of business;

(b) or before the Court of the place where arrest has been effected of the defendant ship or of any other ship belonging to the defendant which can be lawfully arrested, or where arrest could have been effected and bail or other security has been furnished;

(c)   or before the Court of the place of collision when the collision has occurred within the limits of a port or in inland waters.

(2)   It shall be for the plaintiff to decide in which of the Courts referred to in sec. 1 of this article the action shall be instituted.

(3)   A claimant shall not be allowed to bring a further action against the same defendant on the same facts in another jurisdiction, without discontinuing an action already instituted.

Article 2

Agreement or Arbitration

The provisions of article 1 shall not in any way prejudice the right of the parties to bring an action in respect of a collision before a Court they have chosen by agreement or to refer it to arbitration.

Article 3

Counter Claims

(1)   Counterclaims arising out of the same collision can be brought before the Court having jurisdiction over the principal action in accordance with the provisions of article 1.

(2)   In the event of there being several claimants any claimant may bring his action before the Court previously seized of an action against the same party arising out of the same collision.

(3)   In the case of collision or collisions in which two or more vessels are involved, nothing in this Convention shall prevent any Court seized of an action by reason of the provisions of this Convention from exercising jurisdiction under its national laws in further actions arising out of the same incident.

Article 4

Damage Without Contact

This Convention shall also apply to an action of damage caused by one ship to another or to the property or person on board such ships through the carrying out of or the omission to carry out a manoeuvre or through non-compliance with regulations even when there has been no actual collision.

Article 5

State Vessels

Nothing contained in this Convention shall modify the rules of law now or hereafter in force in the various Contracting States in regard to collisions involving warships or vessels owned by or in the service of a State.

Article 6

Contracts of Carriage

This Convention does not affect claims arising from contracts of carriage or from any other contracts.

Article 7

Rhine Navigation

This Convention shall not apply in the case of any collision which is within the provisions of the revised Rhine Navigation Convention of October 17, 1868.

Article 8

Application

The provisions of this Convention shall be applied as regards all persons interested when all the vessels concerned in any action belong to States of High Contracting Parties.

Provided always that:

(1) As regards persons interested who belong to a Noncontracting State the application of the above provisions may be made by each of the Contracting States conditional upon reciprocity;

(2) Where all the persons interested belong to the same State as the court trying the case, the provisions of the national law and not of the convention are applicable.

[Articles 9 through 15 deleted]

Signatories: Belgium, Brazil, Denmark, Egypt, France, Federal Republic of Germany, Greece, Italy, Lebanon, Monaco, Nicaragua, Portugal, Spain, United Kingdom, Vatican City, Yugoslavia.

DRAFT RULES FOR THE ASSESSMENT OF DAMAGES IN MARITIME COLLISIONS

("Lisbon Rules")

Comité Maritime Internationale

February 29, 1988

DEFINITIONS

In these Rules, the following words are used with the meaning set out below:

"Vessel" means any ship, craft, machine, rig or platform whether capable of navigation or not, which is involved in a collision.

"Collision" means any accident involving two or more vessels which causes loss or damage even if no actual contact has taken place.

"Claimant" means any person, corporate body or legal entity to whom damages are due in respect of loss or damage (excluding death and personal injury) as a result of a collision.

"Damages" means the financial compensation payable to the Claimant.

"Total Loss" means an actual total loss of the vessel or such damage to the vessel that the cost of saving and repairing her would exceed her market value at the time of the collision

"Property" means cargo, goods and other things on board a vessel.

"Freight" means the remuneration payable for the carriage by the vessel of property or passengers or for the use of the vessel.

"Detention" means the period of time during which the Claimant is deprived of the use of the vessel.

RULE A

These Rules are available for adoption in cases where damages are claimed following a collision. Their adoption does not imply an admission of liability.

RULE B

When a vessel is involved in a collision, these Rules shall apply to the assessment of the damages. These Rules shall not extend to the determination of liability or affect rights of limitation of liability.

RULE C

Subject to the application of the numbered rules the Claimant shall be entitled to recover only such damages as may reasonably be considered to be the direct and immediate consequence of the collision.

RULE D

Subject to the application of Rule C and of the numbered Rules, damages shall place the Claimant in the same financial position as he would have occupied had the collision not occurred.

RULE E

The burden of proving the loss or damage sustained in accordance with these Rules shall be upon the Claimant. Damages shall not be recoverable to the extent that the person against whom the claim is made is able to show that the Claimant could have avoided or mitigated the loss or damage by the exercise of reasonable diligence.

RULE I

Total Loss

1.   In the event of a vessel being a total loss, the Claimant shall be entitled to damages equal to the cost of purchasing a similar vessel in the market at the date of the collision, less the residual or net salvage value of the vessel after the collision. Where no similar vessel is available, the Claimant shall be entitled to recover as damages the value of the vessel

at the date of the collision calculated by reference to the type, age, condition, nature of operation of the vessel and any other relevant factors, less the residual or net salvage value of the vessel after the collision.

2. Damages recoverable in the event of a total loss shall also include:

(a) Reimbursement of salvage, general average and other charges and expenses reasonably incurred as a result of the collision.

RULE II
DAMAGE TO VESSEL

1. In the event of the vessel being damaged but not being a total loss as defined in these Rules, the claimant shall be entitled to recover as damages:

(a) The cost of temporary repairs reasonably effected, and the reasonable cost of permanent repairs.

The cost of those repairs shall include but not be limited to the cost of any necessary drydocking, gasfreeing or tank cleaning, port charges, supervision and classification surveys, together with drydock dues and/or wharfage, for the time occupied in carrying out such repairs.

However, when the collision damage repairs are carried out in conjunction with Owners' work which is essential to the seaworthiness of the vessel or with essential repair work arising out of another incident or are deferred to and carried out at a routine docking, the damages shall include but not be limited to drydock dues, wharfage and/or other time-based charges only to the extent that the period to which such charges relate has been extended by reason of the collision damage repairs.

(b) Reimbursement of salvage, general average and other charges and expenses reasonably incurred as a result of the collision.

(c) Reimbursement of sums, for which the claimant has become legally liable and has paid to third parties in respect of such liability, arising out of the collision by reason of contractual, statutory or other legal obligations.

(d) Reimbursement for the net freight lost and the cost of replacing bunkers and vessel's gear lost as a result of the collision and not included in the cost of repairs under Rule II 1 (a).

2. Damages recoverable shall also include:

(a) Subject to reimbursement for any claim for loss of freight under Rule II 1 (d), compensation for the net loss of earnings arising from the collision. This compensation shall be assessed by establishing the gross earnings of the vessel lost during detention, calculated by reference to the vessel's earnings or by reference to the earnings of comparable vessels in the same trade and then deducting from the gross earnings the operating costs which would normally have been incurred in order to achieve the gross earnings, such as hire payable, crew and bunker costs, port disbursements and insurance.

(b) Operating costs and expenses actually incurred during detention, other than those included under Rule II 1.

3.   In the interpretation of Rule II 2., the following particular provisions will also apply:

(a) When detention occurs during the performance of a voyage charterparty and such detention does not entail cancellation of the charterparty, compensation shall be calculated by applying the average net earnings on the two voyages prior to and the two voyages subsequent to the detention.

When no reference to two prior and two subsequent voyages is possible, the net earnings on other relevant voyages or if there are no other relevant voyages on the voyage during which the collision took place shall form the basis of compensation.

If in consequence of such detention the charterparty is cancelled, and freight remains unearned compensation shall include the net freight lost.

(b) When detention occurs while the vessel is being operated on a liner service, compensation for detention shall be assessed as follows:

i.   when detention occurs during the voyage which the vessel is performing at the time of the collision by applying to the detention the net daily earnings for that voyage, computed for the time the voyage would have taken had the collision not occurred,

ii.   when detention occurs other than during the voyage which the vessel is performing at the time of the collision, by applying to the detention the average net earnings on the two voyages prior to and the two voyages subsequent to the detention. When reference to two prior and two subsequent voyages is not possible, the basis of the computation will be the net earnings on other relevant voyages. If there are no other relevant voyages the compensation will be assessed by reference to the net earnings of a similar vessel operating in a similar trade.

(c) When detention occurs while the vessel is performing under a time charter, compensation shall include the net loss of hire during the detention. If in consequence of such detention the charterparty is cancelled, compensation shall include the net hire which would have been paid during the unperformed portion of the charter, allowance being made for any actual net earnings during that portion.

4.   When collision damage repairs are carried out in conjunction with Owners' work which is essential to the seaworthiness of the vessel or with essential repair work arising out of another incident or are deferred to and carried out at a routine docking, damages shall include compensation for detention only to the extent that the period under repair is extended by reason of the collision damage repairs.

RULE III

Property on Board

1.   The Claimant shall be entitled to recover damages when property has been lost or damaged in consequence of the collision.

2.   In the case of property having a commercial value such damages shall be calculated as follows:

(a)   If such property is lost, the claimant shall be entitled to reimbursement of the market value at the port of destination at the time when it should have arrived, less any expenses saved.

When such market value cannot be determined, the value of the property shall be the shipped value plus freight and the cost of insurance if incurred by the Claimant, plus a margin for profit assessed at no more than 10% of the value of the property calculated as above.

(b)   If such property is damaged, the Claimant shall be entitled to damages equal to the difference between the value of the property in sound condition at destination and its value in damaged condition.

Where physical damage to such property arises from the prolongation of the voyage following the collision, the compensation shall be fixed on the same basis. However, where the loss arises from a fall in the market during such prolongation there shall be no right to damages.

3.   In the case of any other property the claimant shall be entitled to recover:

(a)   Where the property has been lost or is irreparable: its value or the reasonable cost of its replacement;

(b)   Where the property is damaged and can be repaired: the reasonable cost of repairs, but not exceeding its value or the reasonable cost of its replacement.

RULE IV

Interest

1.   Interest on damages is recoverable in addition to the principal sum.

2.   For claims under Rule I 1, interest shall run from the date of the collision to the date of payment.

For all other claims, interest shall run from the date the loss was sustained or the expense was incurred to the date of payment.

3.   Where under Rule V damages are to be calculated in Special Drawing Rights (SDR), the rate of interest shall be the average London rate for three months SDR linked deposits in the period that interest runs; otherwise the rate of interest shall be ten per cent per annum.

RULE V

Currency

Unless the parties have agreed to apply a specific currency in the calculation of their damages the following procedure shall be adopted:

—losses or expenses shall be converted from the currency in which they are incurred into Special Drawing Rights (SDR) at the rate of exchange prevailing on the day the losses or expenses were incurred.

—the final amounts due shall be calculated in SDR and the balance due shall be paid to the Claimant in the currency of his choice at the rate of exchange prevailing on the date of payment.

—where no official SDR exchange rate is quoted for the currency, conversions to and from SDR shall be made by reference to U.S. dollars.

INTERNATIONAL REGULATIONS FOR PREVENTING COLLISIONS AT SEA, 1972

International Maritime Organization
Revised 1981, 1987, 1989, 1993, 2001

PART A—GENERAL

Rule 1

Application

(a)   These Rules shall apply to all vessels upon the high seas and in all waters connected therewith navigable by seagoing vessels.

(b)   Nothing in these Rules shall interfere with the operation of special rules made by an appropriate authority for roadsteads, harbours, rivers, lakes or inland waterways connected with the high seas and navigable by seagoing vessels. Such special rules shall conform as closely as possible to these Rules.

(c)   Nothing in these Rules shall interfere with the operation of any special rules made by the Government of any State with respect to additional station or signal lights or whistle signals for ships of war and vessels proceeding under convoy, or with respect to additional station or signal lights for fishing vessels engaged in fishing as a fleet. These additional station or signal lights or whistle signals shall, so far as possible, be such that they cannot be mistaken for any light or signal authorized elsewhere under these Rules.

(d) Traffic separation schemes may be adopted by the Organization for the purpose of these Rules.

(e) Whenever the Government concerned shall have determined that a vessel of special construction or purpose cannot comply fully with the provisions of any of these Rules with respect to the number, position, range or arc of visibility of lights or shapes, as well as to the disposition and characteristics of sound-signalling appliances, such vessel shall comply with such other provisions in regard to the number, position, range or arc of visibility of lights or shapes, as well as to the disposition and characteristics of sound-signalling appliances, as her Government shall have determined to be the closest possible compliance with these Rules in respect of that vessel.

Rule 2

Responsibility

(a) Nothing in these Rules shall exonerate any vessel, or the owner, master or crew thereof, from the consequences of any neglect to comply with these Rules or of the neglect of any precaution which may be required by the ordinary practice of seamen, or by the special circumstances of the case.

(b) In construing and complying with these Rules due regard shall be had to all dangers of navigation and collision and to any special circumstances, including the limitations of the vessels involved, which may make a departure from these Rules necessary to avoid immediate danger.

Rule 3

General Definitions

For the purpose of these Rules, except where the context otherwise requires:

(a) The word "vessel" includes every description of water craft, including non-displacement craft and seaplanes, used or capable of being used as a means of transportation on water.

(b) The term "power-driven vessel" means any vessel propelled by machinery.

(c) The term "sailing vessel" means any vessel under sail provided that propelling machinery, if fitted, is not being used.

(d) The term "vessel engaged in fishing" means any vessel fishing with nets, lines, trawls or other fishing apparatus which restrict manoeuvrability, but does not include a vessel fishing with trolling lines or other fishing apparatus which do not restrict manoeuvrability.

(e) The word "seaplane" includes any aircraft designed to manoeuvre on the water.

(f) The term "vessel not under command" means a vessel which through some exceptional circumstance is unable to manoeuvre as required by these Rules and is therefore unable to keep out of the way of another vessel.

(g) The term "vessel restricted in her ability to manoeuvre" means a vessel which from the nature of her work is restricted in her ability to manoeuvre as required by these Rules and is therefore unable to keep out of the way of another vessel.

The term "vessels restricted in their ability to manoeuvre" shall include but not be limited to:

(i)   a vessel engaged in laying, servicing or picking up a navigation mark, submarine cable or pipeline;

(ii)   a vessel engaged in dredging, surveying or underwater operations;

(iii) a vessel engaged in replenishment or transferring persons, provisions or cargo while underway;

(iv) a vessel engaged in the launching or recovery of aircraft;

(v)   a vessel engaged in mineclearance operations;

(vi) a vessel engaged in a towing operation such as severely restricts the towing vessel and her tow in their ability to deviate from their course.

(h) The term "vessel constrained by her draught" means a power-driven vessel which, because of her draught in relation to the available depth and width of navigable water, is severely restricted in her ability to deviate from the course she is following.

(i) The word "underway" means that a vessel is not at anchor, or made fast to the shore, or aground.

(j) he words "length" and "breadth" of a vessel mean her length overall and greatest breadth.

(k) Vessels shall be deemed to be in sight of one another only when one can be observed visually from the other.

(l) The term "restricted visibility" means any condition in which visibility is restricted by fog, mist, falling snow, heavy rainstorms, sandstorms, or any other similar causes.

(m) The term "Wing-In-Ground (WIG) craft" means a multimodal craft which, in its main operational mode, flies in close proximity to the surface by utilizing surface-effect action.

PART B—STEERING AND SAILING RULES

SECTION I—CONDUCT OF VESSELS IN
ANY CONDITION OF VISIBILITY

Rule 4

Application

Rules in this Section apply in any condition of visibility.

Rule 5

Look-out

Every vessel shall at all times maintain a proper look-out by sight and hearing as well as by all available means appropriate in the prevailing circumstances and conditions so as to make a full appraisal of the situation and of the risk of collision.

Rule 6

Safe Speed

Every vessel shall at all times proceed at a safe speed so that she can take proper and effective action to avoid collision and be stopped within a distance appropriate to the prevailing circumstances and conditions.

In determining a safe speed the following factors shall be among those taken into account:

(a) By all vessels:

(i) the state of visibility;

(ii) the traffic density including concentrations of fishing vessels or any other vessels;

(iii) the manoeuvrability of the vessel with special reference to stopping distance and turning ability in the prevailing conditions;

(iv) at night the presence of background light such as from shore lights or from back scatter of her own lights;

(v) the state of wind, sea and current, and the proximity of navigational hazards;

(vi) the draught in relation to the available depth of water.

(b) Additionally, by vessels with operational radar:

(i) the characteristics, efficiency and limitations of the radar equipment;

(ii) any constraints imposed by the radar range scale in use;

(iii) the effect on radar detection of the sea state, weather and other sources of interference;

(iv) the possibility that small vessels, ice and other floating objects may not be detected by radar at an adequate range;

(v)   the number, location and movement of vessels detected by radar;

(vi) the more exact assessment of the visibility that may be possible when radar is used to determine the range of vessels or other objects in the vicinity.

Rule 7

Risk of Collision

(a) Every vessel shall use all available means appropriate to the prevailing circumstances and conditions to determine if risk of collision exists. If there is any doubt such risk shall be deemed to exist.

(b) Proper use shall be made of radar equipment if fitted and operational, including long-range scanning to obtain early warning of risk of collision and radar plotting or equivalent systematic observation of detected objects.

(c) Assumptions shall not be made on the basis of scanty information, especially scanty radar information.

(d) In determining if risk of collision exists the following considerations shall be among those taken into account:

(i)   such risk shall be deemed to exist if the compass bearing of an approaching vessel does not appreciably change;

(ii) such risk may sometimes exist even when an appreciable bearing change is evident, particularly when approaching a very large vessel or a tow or when approaching a vessel at close range.

Rule 8

Action to Avoid Collision

(a) Any action to avoid collision shall be taken in accordance with the Rules of this Part and shall, if the circumstances of the case admit, be positive, made in ample time and with due regard to the observance of good seamanship

(b) Any alteration of course and/or speed to avoid collision shall, if the circumstances of the case admit, be large enough to be readily apparent to another vessel observing visually or by radar; a succession of small alterations of course and/or speed should be avoided.

(c) If there is sufficient sea room, alteration of course alone may be the most effective action to avoid a close-quarters situation provided that it is made in good time, is substantial and does not result in another close-quarters situation.

(d) Action taken to avoid collision with another vessel shall be such as to result in passing at a safe distance. The effectiveness of the action shall be carefully checked until the other vessel is finally past and clear.

(e) If necessary to avoid collision or allow more time to assess the situation, a vessel shall slacken her speed or take all way off by stopping or reversing her means of propulsion.

(f)(i) A vessel which, by any of these Rules, is required not to impede the passage or safe passage of another vessel shall, when required by the circumstances of the case, take early action to allow sufficient sea room for the safe passage of the other vessel.

(ii) A vessel required not to impede the passage or safe passage of another vessel is not relieved of this obligation if approaching the other vessel so as to involve risk of collision and shall, when taking action, have full regard to the action which may be required by the Rules of this Part.

(iii) A vessel the passage of which is not to be impeded remains fully obliged to comply with the Rules of this Part when the two vessels are approaching one another so as to involve risk of collision.

Rule 9

Narrow Channels

(a) A vessel proceeding along the course of a narrow channel or fairway shall keep as near to the outer limit of the channel or fairway which lies on her starboard side as is safe and practicable.

(b) A vessel of less than 20 metres in length or a sailing vessel shall not impede the passage of a vessel which can safely navigate only within a narrow channel or fairway.

(c) A vessel engaged in fishing shall not impede the passage of any other vessel navigating within a narrow channel or fairway.

(d) A vessel shall not cross a narrow channel or fairway if such crossing impedes the passage of a vessel which can safely navigate only within such channel or fairway. The latter vessel may use the sound signal prescribed in Rule 34(d) if in doubt as to the intention of the crossing vessel.

(e)(i) In a narrow channel or fairway when overtaking can take place only if the vessel to be overtaken has to take action to permit safe passing, the vessel intending to overtake shall indicate her intention by sounding the appropriate signal prescribed in Rule 34(c)(i). The vessel to be overtaken shall, if in agreement, sound the appropriate signal prescribed in Rule 34(c)(ii) and take steps to permit safe passing. If in doubt she may sound the signals prescribed in Rule 34(d).

(ii) This Rule does not relieve the overtaking vessel of her obligation under Rule 13.

(f) A vessel nearing a bend or an area of a narrow channel or fairway where other vessels may be obscured by an intervening obstruction shall navigate with particular alertness and caution and shall sound the appropriate signal prescribed in Rule 34(e).

(g)   Any vessel shall, if the circumstances of the case admit, avoid anchoring in a narrow channel.

Rule 10

Traffic Separation Schemes

(a)   This Rule applies to traffic separation schemes adopted by the Organization and does not relieve any vessel of her obligation under any other Rule.

(b)   A vessel using a traffic separation scheme shall:

(i)   proceed in the appropriate traffic lane in the general direction of traffic flow for that lane;

(ii)   so far as practicable keep clear of a traffic separation line or separation zone;

(iii)   normally join or leave a traffic lane at the termination of the lane, but when joining or leaving from the side shall do so at as small an angle to the general direction of traffic flow as practicable.

(c)   A vessel shall, so far as practicable, avoid crossing traffic lanes but if obliged to do so shall cross on a heading as nearly as practicable at right angles to the general direction of traffic flow.

(d)(i)   A vessel shall not use an inshore traffic zone when she can safely use the appropriate traffic lane within the adjacent traffic separation scheme. However, vessels of less than 20 metres in length, sailing vessels and vessels engaged in fishing may use the inshore traffic zone.

(ii)   Notwithstanding subparagraph (d)(i), a vessel may use an inshore traffic zone when en route to or from a port, offshore installation, or structure, pilot station or any other place situated within the inshore traffic zone, or to avoid immediate danger.

(e)   A vessel, other than a crossing vessel, shall not normally enter a separation zone or cross a separation line except:

(i)   in cases of emergency to avoid immediate danger;

(ii)   to engage in fishing within a separation zone.

(f)   A vessel navigating in areas near the terminations of traffic separation schemes shall do so with particular caution.

(g)   A vessel shall so far as practicable avoid anchoring in a traffic separation scheme or in areas near its terminations.

(h)   A vessel not using a traffic separation scheme shall avoid it by as wide a margin as is practicable.

(i)   A vessel engaged in fishing shall not impede the passage of any vessel following a traffic lane.

(j)   A vessel of less than 20 metres in length or a sailing vessel shall not impede the safe passage of a power-driven vessel following a traffic lane.

(k) A vessel restricted in her ability to manoeuvre when engaged in an operation for the maintenance of safety of navigation in a traffic separation scheme is exempted from complying with this Rule to the extent necessary to carry out the operation.

(*l*) A vessel restricted in her ability to manoeuvre when engaged in an operation for the laying, servicing or picking up of a submarine cable, within a traffic separation scheme, is exempted from complying with this Rule to the extent necessary to carry out the operation.

SECTION II—CONDUCT OF VESSELS IN SIGHT OF ONE ANOTHER

Rule 11

Application

Rules in this Section apply to vessels in sight of one another.

Rule 12

Sailing Vessels

(a) When two sailing vessels are approaching one another, so as to involve risk of collision, one of them shall keep out of the way of the other as follows:

(i) when each has the wind on a different side, the vessel which has the wind on the port side shall keep out of the way of the other;

(ii) when both have the wind on the same side, the vessel which is to windward shall keep out of the way of the vessel which is to leeward;

(iii) if a vessel with the wind on the port side sees a vessel to windward and cannot determine with certainty whether the other vessel has the wind on the port or on the starboard side, she shall keep out of the way of the other.

(b) For the purposes of this Rule the windward side shall be deemed to be the side opposite to that on which the mainsail is carried or, in the case of a square-rigged vessel, the side opposite to that on which the largest fore-and-aft sail is carried.

Rule 13

Overtaking

(a) Notwithstanding anything contained in the Rules of Part B, Sections I and II, any vessel overtaking any other shall keep out of the way of the vessel being overtaken.

(b) A vessel shall be deemed to be overtaking when coming up with another vessel from a direction more than 22.5 degrees abaft her beam, that is, in such a position with reference to the vessel she is overtaking, that at night she would be able to see only the sternlight of that vessel but neither of her sidelights.

(c)   When a vessel is in any doubt as to whether she is overtaking another, she shall assume that this is the case and act accordingly.

(d)   Any subsequent alteration of the bearing between the two vessels shall not make the overtaking vessel a crossing vessel within the meaning of these Rules or relieve her of the duty of keeping clear of the overtaken vessel until she is finally past and clear.

Rule 14

Head-on Situation

(a)   When two power-driven vessels are meeting on reciprocal or nearly reciprocal courses so as to involve risk of collision each shall alter her course to starboard so that each shall pass on the port side of the other.

(b)   Such a situation shall be deemed to exist when a vessel sees the other ahead or nearly ahead and by night she could see the masthead lights of the other in a line or nearly in a line and/or both sidelights and by day she observes the corresponding aspect of the other vessel.

(c)   When a vessel is in any doubt as to whether such a situation exists she shall assume that it does exist and act accordingly.

Rule 15

Crossing Situation

When two power-driven vessels are crossing so as to involve risk of collision, the vessel which has the other on her own starboard side shall keep out of the way and shall, if the circumstances of the case admit, avoid crossing ahead of the other vessel.

Rule 16

Action by Give-way Vessel

Every vessel which is directed by these Rules to keep out of the way of another vessel shall, so far as possible, take early and substantial action to keep well clear.

Rule 17

Action by Stand-on Vessel

(a)(i)   Where by any of these Rules one of two vessels is to keep out of the way the other shall keep her course and speed.

(ii)   The latter vessel may however take action to avoid collision by her manoeuvre alone, as soon as it becomes apparent to her that the vessel required to keep out of the way is not taking appropriate action in compliance with these Rules.

(b)   When, from any cause, the vessel required to keep her course and speed finds herself so close that collision cannot be avoided by the action of the give-way vessel alone, she shall take such action as will best aid to avoid collision.

(c) A power-driven vessel which takes action in a crossing situation in accordance with sub-paragraph (a)(ii) of this Rule to avoid collision with another power-driven vessel shall, if the circumstances of the case admit, not alter course to port for a vessel on her own port side.

(d) This Rule does not relieve the give-way vessel of her obligation to keep out of the way.

Rule 18

Responsibilities between Vessels

Except where Rules 9, 10 and 13 otherwise require:

(a) A power-driven vessel underway shall keep out of the way of:

    (i)   a vessel not under command;

    (ii)   a vessel restricted in her ability to manoeuvre;

    (iii) a vessel engaged in fishing;

    (iv) a sailing vessel.

(b) A sailing vessel underway shall keep out of the way of:

    (i)   a vessel not under command;

    (ii)   a vessel restricted in her ability to manoeuvre;

    (iii) a vessel engaged in fishing.

(c) A vessel engaged in fishing when underway shall, so far as possible, keep out of the way of:

    (i)   a vessel not under command;

    (ii)   a vessel restricted in her ability to manoeuvre.

(d)(i)   A vessel other than a vessel not under command or a vessel restricted in her ability to manoeuvre shall, if the circumstances of the case admit, avoid impeding the safe passage of a vessel constrained by her draught, exhibiting the signals in Rule 28.

    (ii) A vessel constrained by her draught shall navigate with particular caution having full regard to her special condition.

(e) A seaplane on the water shall, in general, keep well clear of all vessels and avoid impeding their navigation. In circumstances, however, where risk of collision exists, she shall comply with the Rules of this Part.

(f)(i) A WIG craft shall, when taking off, landing and in flight near the surface, keep well clear of all other vessels and avoid impeding their navigation;

    (ii) a WIG craft operating on the water surface shall comply with the Rules of this Part as a power-driven vessel.

SECTION III—CONDUCT OF VESSELS IN RESTRICTED VISIBILITY

Rule 19

Conduct of Vessels in Restricted Visibility

(a)   This Rule applies to vessels not in sight of one another when navigating in or near an area of restricted visibility.

(b)   Every vessel shall proceed at a safe speed adapted to the prevailing circumstances and conditions of restricted visibility. A power-driven vessel shall have her engines ready for immediate manoeuvre.

(c)   Every vessel shall have due regard to the prevailing circumstances and conditions of restricted visibility when complying with the Rules of Section 1 of this Part.

(d)   A vessel which detects by radar alone the presence of another vessel shall determine if a close-quarters situation is developing and/or risk of collision exists. If so, she shall take avoiding action in ample time, provided that when such action consists of an alteration of course, so far as possible the following shall be avoided:

(i)   an alteration of course to port for a vessel forward of the beam, other than for a vessel being overtaken;

(ii)   an alteration of course towards a vessel abeam or abaft the beam.

(e)   Except where it has been determined that a risk of collision does not exist, every vessel which hears apparently forward of her beam the fog signal of another vessel, or which cannot avoid a close-quarters situation with another vessel forward of her beam, shall reduce her speed to the minimum at which she can be kept on her course. She shall if necessary take all her way off and in any event navigate with extreme caution until danger of collision is over.

PART C—LIGHTS AND SHAPES

Rule 20

Application

(a)   Rules in this Part shall be complied with in all weathers.

(b)   The Rules concerning lights shall be complied with from sunset to sunrise, and during such times no other lights shall be exhibited, except such lights as cannot be mistaken for the lights specified in these Rules or do not impair their visibility or distinctive character, or interfere with the keeping of a proper look-out.

(c)   The lights, prescribed by these Rules shall, if carried, also be exhibited from sunrise to sunset in restricted visibility and may be exhibited in all other circumstances when it is deemed necessary.

(d)   The Rules concerning shapes shall be complied with by day.

(e)   The lights and shapes specified in these Rules shall comply with the provisions of Annex I to these Regulations.

Rule 21

Definitions

(a)   "Masthead light" means a white light placed over the fore and aft centreline of the vessel showing an unbroken light over an arc of the horizon of 225 degrees and so fixed as to show the light from right ahead to 22.5 degrees abaft the beam on either side of the vessel.

(b)   "Sidelights" means a green light on the starboard side and a red light on the port side each showing an unbroken light over an arc of the horizon of 112.5 degrees and so fixed as to show the light from right ahead to 22.5 degrees abaft the beam on its respective side. In a vessel of less than 20 metres in length the sidelights may be combined in one lantern carried on the fore and aft centreline of the vessel.

(c)   "Sternlight" means a white light placed as nearly as practicable at the stern showing an unbroken light over an arc of the horizon of 135 degrees and so fixed as to show the light 67.5 degrees from right aft on each side of the vessel.

(d)   "Towing light" means a yellow light having the same characteristics as the "sternlight" defined in paragraph (c) of this Rule.

(e)   "All-round light" means a light showing an unbroken light over an arc of the horizon of 360 degrees.

(f)   "Flashing light" means a light flashing at regular intervals at a frequency of 120 flashes or more per minute.

Rule 22

Visibility of Lights

The lights prescribed in these Rules shall have an intensity as specified in Section 8 of Annex I to these Regulations so as to be visible at the following minimum ranges:

(a)   In vessels of 50 metres or more in length: A masthead light, 6 miles; A sidelight, 3 miles; A sternlight, 3 miles; A towing light, 3 miles; and A white, red, green or yellow all-round light, 3 miles.

(b)   In vessels of 12 metres or more in length but less than 50 metres in length:

1.   a masthead light, 5 miles; except that where the length of the vessel is less than 20 metres, 3 miles;

2.   a sidelight, 2 miles;

3.   a sternlight, 2 miles;

4.   a towing light, 2 miles; and

5.   a white, red, green or yellow all-round light, 2 miles.

(c)   In vessels of less than 12 metres in length:

1.   a masthead light, 2 miles;

2.   a sidelight, 1 mile;

3.   a sternlight, 2 miles;

4.   a towing light, 2 miles; and

5.   a white, red, green or yellow all-round light, 2 miles.

Rule 23

Power-driven Vessels Underway

(a)   A power-driven vessel underway shall exhibit:

(i)   a masthead light forward;

(ii)   a second masthead light abaft of and higher than the forward one; except that a vessel of less than 50 metres in length shall not be obliged to exhibit such light but may do so;

(iii)   sidelights;

(iv)   a sternlight.

(b)   An air-cushion vessel when operating in the non-displacement mode shall, in addition to the lights prescribed in paragraph (a) of this Rule, exhibit an all-round flashing yellow light.

(c)   A WIG craft only when taking off, landing and in flight near the surface shall, in addition to the lights prescribed in paragraph (a) of this Rule, exhibit a high intensity all-round flashing red light.

(i)   A power-driven vessel of less than 12 metres in length may in lieu of the lights prescribed in paragraph (a) of this Rule exhibit an all-round white light and sidelights;

(ii)   A power-driven vessel of less than 7 metres in length whose maximum speed does not exceed 7 knots may in lieu of the lights prescribed in paragraph (a) of this Rule exhibit an all-round white light and shall, if practicable, also exhibit sidelights;

(iii)   The masthead light or all-round white light on a power-driven vessel of less than 12 metres in length may be displaced from the fore and aft centreline of the vessel if centreline fitting is not practicable, provided that the sidelights are combined in one lantern which shall be carried on the fore and aft centreline of the vessel or located as nearly as practicable in the same fore and aft line as the masthead light or the all-round white light.

Rule 24

Towing and Pushing

(a)   A power-driven vessel when towing shall exhibit:

(i)   Instead of the light prescribed in Rule 23(a)(i), two masthead lights forward in a vertical line; when the length of the tow measuring from the stern of the towing vessel to the after end of the tow exceeds 200 metres, three such lights in a vertical line;

(ii) Sidelights;

(iii) A sternlight;

(iv) A towing light in a vertical line above the sternlight; and

(v) When the length of the tow exceeds 200 metres, a diamond shape where it can best be seen.

(b) When a pushing vessel and a vessel being pushed ahead are rigidly connected in a composite unit they shall be regarded as a power-driven vessel and exhibit the lights prescribed in Rule 23.

(c) A power-driven vessel when pushing ahead or towing alongside, except in the case of a composite unit, shall exhibit:

(i) Instead of the light prescribed in Rule 23(a)(i) or (a)(ii), two masthead lights in a vertical line;

(ii) Sidelights; and

(iii) A sternlight.

(d) A power-driven vessel to which paragraphs (a) or (c) of this Rule apply shall also comply with Rule 23(a)(ii).

(e) A vessel or object being towed, other than those mentioned in paragraph (g) of this Rule, shall exhibit:

(i) Sidelights;

(ii) A sternlight;

(iii) When the length of the tow exceeds 200 metres, a diamond shape where it can best be seen.

(f) Provided that any number of vessels being towed alongside or pushed in a group shall be lighted as one vessel, (i) A vessel being pushed ahead, not being part of a composite unit, shall exhibit at the forward end, sidelights; (ii) A vessel being towed alongside shall exhibit a sternlight and at the forward end, sidelights.

(g) An inconspicuous, partly submerged vessel or object, or combination of such vessels or objects being towed, shall exhibit:

(i) If it is less than 25 metres in breadth, one all-round white light at or near the forward end and one at or near the after end except that dracones need not exhibit a light at or near the forward end;

(ii) If it is 25 metres or more in breadth, two additional all-round white lights at or near the extremities of its breadth;

(iii) If it exceeds 100 metres in length, additional all-round white lights between the lights prescribed in sub-paragraphs (i) and (ii) so that the distance between the lights shall not exceed 100 metres;

(iv) A diamond shape at or near the aftermost extremity of the last vessel or object being towed and if the length of the tow exceeds 200 metres an additional diamond shape where it can best be seen and located as far forward as is practicable.

(h) Where from any sufficient cause it is impracticable for a vessel or object being towed to exhibit the lights or shapes prescribed in paragraph (e) or (g) of this Rule, all possible measures shall be taken to light the vessel or object towed or at least to indicate the presence of such vessel or object.

(i)   Where from any sufficient cause it is impracticable for a vessel not normally engaged in towing operations to display the lights prescribed in paragraph (a) or (c) of this Rule, such vessel shall not be required to exhibit those lights when engaged in towing another vessel in distress or otherwise in need of assistance. All possible measures shall be taken to indicate the nature of the relationship between the towing vessel and the vessel being towed as authorized by Rule 36, in particular by illuminating the towline.

Rule 25

Sailing Vessels Underway and Vessels Under Oars

(a)   A sailing vessel underway shall exhibit:

(i)   Sidelights;

(ii) A sternlight.

(b) In a sailing vessel of less than 20 metres in length the lights prescribed in paragraph (a) of this Rule may be combined in one lantern carried at or near the top of the mast where it can best be seen.

(c)   A sailing vessel underway may, in addition to the lights prescribed in paragraph (a) of this Rule, exhibit at or near the top of the mast, where they can best be seen, two all-round lights in a vertical line, the upper being red and the lower green, but these lights shall not be exhibited in conjunction with the combined lantern permitted by paragraph (b) of this Rule.

(d)(i)   A sailing vessel of less than 7 metres in length shall, if practicable, exhibit the lights prescribed in paragraph (a) or (b) of this Rule, but if she does not, she shall have ready at hand an electric torch or lighted lantern showing a white light which shall be exhibited in sufficient time to prevent collision.

(ii) A vessel under oars may exhibit the lights prescribed in this Rule for sailing vessels, but if she does not, she shall have ready at hand an electric torch or lighted lantern showing a white light which shall be exhibited in sufficient time to prevent collision.

(e) A vessel proceeding under sail when also being propelled by machinery shall exhibit forward where it can best be seen a conical shape, apex downwards.

Rule 26

Fishing Vessels

(a) A vessel engaged in fishing, whether underway or at anchor, shall exhibit only the lights and shapes prescribed in this Rule.

(b) A vessel when engaged in trawling, by which is meant the dragging through the water of a dredge net or other apparatus used as a fishing appliance, shall exhibit:

(i) Two all-round lights in a vertical line, the upper being green and the lower white, or a shape consisting of two cones with their apexes together in a vertical line one above the other; a vessel of less than 20 metres in length may instead of this shape exhibit a basket;

(ii) A masthead light abaft of and higher than the all-round green light; a vessel of less than 50 metres in length shall not be obliged to exhibit such a light but may do so;

(iii) When making way through the water, in addition to the lights prescribed in this paragraph, sidelights and a sternlight.

(c) A vessel engaged in fishing, other than trawling, shall exhibit:

(i) Two all-round lights in a vertical line, the upper being red and the lower white, or a shape consisting of two cones with apexes together in a vertical line one above the other; a vessel of less than 20 metres in length may instead of this shape exhibit a basket;

(ii) When there is outlying gear extending more than 150 metres horizontally from the vessel, an all-round white light or a cone apex upwards in the direction of the gear;

(iii) When making way through the water, in addition to the lights prescribed in this paragraph, sidelights and a sternlight.

(d) A vessel engaged in fishing in close proximity to other vessels engaged in fishing may exhibit the additional signals described in Annex II to these Regulations.

(e) A vessel when not engaged in fishing shall not exhibit the lights or shapes prescribed in this Rule, but only those prescribed for a vessel of her length.

Rule 27

Vessels not Under Command or Restricted in Their Ability to Manoeuvre

(a) A vessel not under command shall exhibit:

(i) Two all-round red lights in a vertical line where they can best be seen;

(ii) Two balls or similar shapes in a vertical line where they can best be seen;

(iii) When making way through the water, in addition to the lights prescribed in this paragraph, sidelights and a sternlight.

(b) A vessel restricted in her ability to manoeuvre, except a vessel engaged in mineclearance operations, shall exhibit:

(i) Three all-round lights in a vertical line where they can best be seen. The highest and lowest of these lights shall be red and the middle light shall be white;

(ii) Three shapes in a vertical line where they can best be seen. The highest and lowest of these shapes shall be balls and the middle one a diamond;

(iii) When making way through the water, a masthead light or lights, sidelights and a sternlight, in addition to the lights prescribed in subparagraph (i);

(iv) When at anchor, in addition to the lights or shapes prescribed in subparagraphs (i) and (ii), the light, lights or shape prescribed in Rule 30.

(c) A power-driven vessel engaged in a towing operation such as severely restricts the towing vessel and her tow in their ability to deviate from their course shall, in addition to the lights or shapes prescribed in Rule 24(a), exhibit the lights or shapes prescribed in subparagraphs (b)(i) and (ii) of this Rule.

(d) A vessel engaged in dredging or underwater operations, when restricted in her ability to manoeuvre, shall exhibit the lights and shapes prescribed in subparagraphs (b)(i), (ii) and (iii) of this Rule and shall in addition, when an obstruction exists, exhibit:

(i) Two all-round red lights or two balls in a vertical line to indicate the side on which the obstruction exists;

(ii) Two all-round green lights or two diamonds in a vertical line to indicate the side on which another vessel may pass;

(iii) When at anchor, the lights or shapes prescribed in this paragraph instead of the lights or shape prescribed in Rule 30.

(e) Whenever the size of a vessel engaged in diving operations makes it impracticable to exhibit all lights and shapes prescribed in paragraph (d) of this Rule, the following shall be exhibited:

(i) Three all-round lights in a vertical line where they can best be seen. The highest and lowest of these lights shall be red and the middle light shall be white;

(ii) A rigid replica of the International Code flag "A" not less than 1 metre in height. Measures shall be taken to ensure its all-round visibility.

(f) A vessel engaged in mineclearance operations shall in addition to the lights prescribed for a power-driven vessel in Rule 23 or to the lights or shape prescribed for a vessel at anchor in Rule 30 as appropriate, exhibit three all-round green lights or three balls. One of these lights or shapes shall be exhibited near the foremast head and one at each end of the fore yard. These lights or shapes indicate that it is dangerous for another vessel to approach within 1000 metres of the mineclearance vessel.

(g) Vessels of less than 12 metres in length, except those engaged in diving operations, shall not be required to exhibit the lights and shapes prescribed in this Rule.

(h) The signals prescribed in this Rule are not signals of vessels in distress and requiring assistance. Such signals are contained in Annex IV to these Regulations.

Rule 28

Vessels Constrained by Their Draught

A vessel constrained by her draught may, in addition to the lights prescribed for power-driven vessels in Rule 23, exhibit where they can best be seen three all-round red lights in a vertical line, or a cylinder.

Rule 29

Pilot Vessels

(a) A vessel engaged on pilotage duty shall exhibit:

(i) At or near the masthead, two all-round lights in a vertical line, the upper being white and the lower red,

(ii) When underway, in addition, sidelights and a sternlight;

(iii) When at anchor, in addition to the lights prescribed in sub-paragraph (i), the light, lights or shape prescribed in Rule 30 for vessels at anchor.

Rule 30

Anchored Vessels and Vessels Aground

(a) A vessel at anchor shall exhibit where it can best be seen:

(i) In the fore part, an all-round white light or one ball;

(ii) At or near the stern and at a lower level than the light prescribed in sub-paragraph (i), an all-round white light.

(b) A vessel of less than 50 metres in length may exhibit an all-round white light where it can best be seen instead of the lights prescribed in paragraph (a) of this Rule.

(c) A vessel at anchor may, and a vessel of 100 metres and more in length shall, also use the available working or equivalent lights to illuminate her decks.

(d) A vessel aground shall exhibit the lights prescribed in paragraph (a) or (b) of this Rule and in addition, where they can best be seen:

(i) two all-round red lights in a vertical line;

(ii)   three balls in a vertical line.

(e)   A vessel of less than 7 metres in length, when at anchor, not in or near a narrow channel, fairway or anchorage, or where other vessels normally navigate, shall not be required to exhibit the lights or shape prescribed in paragraphs (a) and (b) of this Rule.

(f)   A vessel of less than 12 metres in length, when aground, shall not be required to exhibit the lights or shapes prescribed in subparagraphs (d)(i) and (ii) of this Rule.

Rule 31

Seaplanes

Where it is impracticable for a seaplane or a WIG craft to exhibit lights and shapes of the characteristics or in the positions prescribed in the Rules of this Part she shall exhibit lights and shapes as closely similar in characteristics and position as is possible.

PART D—SOUND AND LIGHT SIGNALS

Rule 32

Definitions

(a)   The word "whistle" means any sound signalling appliance capable of producing the prescribed blasts and which complies with the specifications in Annex III to these Regulations.

(b)   The term "short blast" means a blast of about one second's duration.

(c)   The term "prolonged blast" means a blast of from four to six seconds' duration.

Rule 33

Equipment for Sound Signals

(a)   A vessel of 12 metres or more in length shall be provided with a whistle, a vessel of 20 metres or more in length shall be provided with a bell in addition to a whistle, and a vessel of 100 metres or more in length shall, in addition be provided with a gong, the tone and sound of which cannot be confused with that of the bell. The whistle, bell and gong shall comply with the specifications in Annex III to these Regulations. The bell or gong or both may be replaced by other equipment having the same respective sound characteristics, provided that manual sounding of the required signals shall always be possible.

(b)   A vessel of less than 12 metres in length shall not be obliged to carry the sound signalling appliances prescribed in paragraph (a) of this Rule but if she does not, she shall be provided with some other means of making an efficient sound signal.

Rule 34

Manoeuvring and Warning Signals

(a) When vessels are in sight of one another, a power-driven vessel underway, when manoeuvring as authorized or required by these Rules, shall indicate that manoeuvre by the following signals on her whistle:

> 1. one short blast to mean "I am altering my course to starboard";
>
> 2. two short blasts to mean "I am altering my course to port";
>
> 3. three short blasts to mean "I am operating astern propulsion".

(b) Any vessel may supplement the whistle signals prescribed in paragraph (a) of this Rule by light signals, repeated as appropriate, whilst the manoeuvre is being carried out:

> (i) These light signals shall have the following significance:
>
> 1. one flash to mean "I am altering my course to starboard";
>
> 2. two flashes to mean "I am altering my course to port";
>
> 3. three flashes to mean "I am operating astern propulsion";

(ii) The duration of each flash shall be about one second, the interval between flashes shall be about one second, and the interval between successive signals shall be not less than ten seconds;

(iii) The light used for this signal shall, if fitted, be an all-round white light, visible at a minimum range of 5 miles, and shall comply with the provisions of Annex I to these Regulations.

(c) When in sight of one another in a narrow channel or fairway:

> (i) A vessel intending to overtake another shall in compliance with Rule 9(e)(i) indicate her intention by the following signals on her whistle:
>
> 1. two prolonged blasts followed by one short blast to mean "I intend to overtake you on your starboard side";
>
> 2. two prolonged blasts followed by two short blasts to mean "I intend to overtake you on your port side";

(ii) The vessel about to be overtaken when acting in accordance with Rule 9(e)(i) shall indicate her agreement by the following signal on her whistle:

> 1. one prolonged, one short, one prolonged and one short blast, in that order.

(d)   When vessels in sight of one another are approaching each other and from any cause either vessel fails to understand the intentions or actions of the other, or is in doubt whether sufficient action is being taken by the other to avoid collision, the vessel in doubt shall immediately indicate such doubt by giving at least five short and rapid blasts on the whistle. Such signal may be supplemented by a light signal of at least five short and rapid flashes.

(e)   A vessel nearing a bend or an area of a channel or fairway where other vessels may be obscured by an intervening obstruction shall sound one prolonged blast. Such signal shall be answered with a prolonged blast by any approaching vessel that may be within hearing around the bend or behind the intervening obstruction.

(f)   If whistles are fitted on a vessel at a distance apart of more than 100 metres, one whistle only shall be used for giving manoeuvring and warning signals.

Rule 35

Sound Signals in Restricted Visibility

In or near an area of restricted visibility, whether by day or night, the signals prescribed in this Rule shall be used as follows:

(a)   A power-driven vessel making way through the water shall sound at intervals of not more than 2 minutes one prolonged blast.

(b)   A power-driven vessel underway but stopped and making no way through the water shall sound at intervals of not more than 2 minutes two prolonged blasts in succession with an interval of about 2 seconds between them.

(c)   A vessel not under command, a vessel restricted in her ability to manoeuvre, a vessel constrained by her draught, a sailing vessel, a vessel engaged in fishing and a vessel engaged in towing or pushing another vessel shall, instead of the signals prescribed in paragraphs (a) or (b) of this Rule, sound at intervals of not more than 2 minutes three blasts in succession, namely one prolonged followed by two short blasts.

(d)   A vessel engaged in fishing, when at anchor, and a vessel restricted in her ability to manoeuvre when carrying out her work at anchor, shall instead of the signals prescribed in paragraph (g) of this Rule sound the signal prescribed in paragraph (c) of this Rule.

(e)   A vessel towed or if more than one vessel is towed the last vessel of the tow, if manned, shall at intervals of not more than 2 minutes sound four blasts in succession, namely one prolonged followed by three short blasts. When practicable, this signal shall be made immediately after the signal made by the towing vessel.

(f)   When a pushing vessel and a vessel being pushed ahead are rigidly connected in a composite unit they shall be regarded as a power-driven vessel and shall give the signals prescribed in paragraphs (a) or (b) of this Rule.

(g) A vessel at anchor shall at intervals of not more than one minute ring the bell rapidly for about 5 seconds. In a vessel of 100 metres or more in length the bell shall be sounded in the forepart of the vessel and immediately after the ringing of the bell the gong shall be sounded rapidly for about 5 seconds in the after part of the vessel. A vessel at anchor may in addition sound three blasts in succession, namely one short, one prolonged and one short blast, to give warning of her position and of the possibility of collision to an approaching vessel.

(h) A vessel aground shall give the bell signal and if required the gong signal prescribed in paragraph (g) of this Rule and shall, in addition, give three separate and distinct strokes on the bell immediately before and after the rapid ringing of the bell. A vessel aground may in addition sound an appropriate whistle signal.

(i) A vessel of 12 metres or more but less than 20 metres in length shall not be obliged to give the bell signals prescribed in paragraphs (g) and (h) of this Rule. However, if she does not, she shall make some other efficient sound signal at intervals of not more than 2 minutes.

(j) A vessel of less than 12 metres in length shall not be obliged to give the above-mentioned signals but, if she does not, shall make some other efficient sound signal at intervals of not more than 2 minutes.

(k) A pilot vessel when engaged on pilotage duty may in addition to the signals prescribed in paragraphs (a), (b) or (g) of this Rule sound an identity signal consisting of four short blasts.

Rule 36

Signals to attract attention

If necessary to attract the attention of another vessel any vessel may make light or sound signals that cannot be mistaken for any signal authorized elsewhere in these Rules, or may direct the beam of her searchlight in the direction of the danger, in such a way as not to embarrass any vessel. Any light to attract the attention of another vessel shall be such that it cannot be mistaken for any aid to navigation. For the purpose of this Rule the use of high intensity intermittent or revolving lights, such as strobe lights, shall be avoided.

Rule 37

Distress signals

When a vessel is in distress and requires assistance she shall use or exhibit the signals prescribed in Annex IV to these Regulations.

PART E—EXEMPTIONS

Rule 38

Exemptions

Any vessel (or class of vessels) provided that she complies with the requirements of the International Regulations for Preventing Collisions at Sea, 1960, the keel of which is laid or which is at a corresponding stage of construction before the entry into force of these Regulations may be exempted from compliance therewith as follows:

(a)   The installation of lights with ranges prescribed in Rule 22, until four years after the date of entry into force of these Regulations.

(b)   The installation of lights with colour specifications as prescribed in Section 7 of Annex I to these Regulations, until four years after the date of entry into force of these Regulations.

(c)   The repositioning of lights as a result of conversion from Imperial to metric units and rounding off measurement figures, permanent exemption.

(d)(i)   The repositioning of masthead lights on vessels of less than 150 metres in length, resulting from the prescriptions of Section 3(a) of Annex I, permanent exemption.

(ii) The repositioning of masthead lights on vessels of 150 metres or more in length, resulting from the prescriptions of Section 3(a) of Annex I to these Regulations, until nine years after the date of entry into force of these Regulations.

(e)   The repositioning of masthead lights resulting from the prescriptions of Section 2(b) of Annex I, until nine years after the date of entry into force of these Regulations.

(f)   The repositioning of sidelights resulting from the prescriptions of Sections 2(g) and 3(b) of Annex I, until nine years after the date of entry into force of these Regulations.

(g)   The requirements for sound signal appliances prescribed in Annex III, until nine years after the date of entry into force of these Regulations.

F. LIMITATION OF LIABILITY

INTERNATIONAL CONVENTION ON LIMITATION OF LIABILITY FOR MARITIME CLAIMS

IMCO No. 77.04.E
London, November 19, 1976

[Preamble deleted]

CHAPTER I. THE RIGHT OF LIMITATION

Article 1

Persons entitled to limit liability

1.   Shipowners and salvors, as hereinafter defined, may limit their liability in accordance with the rules of this Convention for claims set out in Article 2.

2.   The term "shipowner" shall mean the owner, charterer, manager and operator of a seagoing ship.

3.   Salvor shall mean any person rendering services in direct connexion with salvage operations. Salvage operations shall also include operations referred to in Article 2, paragraph 1(d), (e) and (f).

4.   If any claims set out in Article 2 are made against any person for whose act, neglect or default the shipowner or salvor is responsible, such person shall be entitled to avail himself of the limitation of liability provided for in this Convention.

5.   In this Convention the liability of a shipowner shall include liability in an action brought against the vessel herself.

6.   An insurer of liability for claims subject to limitation in accordance with the rules of this Convention shall be entitled to the benefits of this Convention to the same extent as the assured himself.

7.   The act of invoking limitation of liability shall not constitute an admission of liability.

Article 2

Claims subject to limitation

1.   Subject to Articles 3 and 4 the following claims, whatever the basis of liability may be, shall be subject to limitation of liability:

(a)   claims in respect of loss of life or personal injury or loss of or damage to property (including damage to harbour works, basins and waterways and aids to navigation), occurring on board or in direct connexion with the operation of the ship or with salvage operations, and consequential loss resulting therefrom;

(b)   claims in respect of loss resulting from delay in the carriage by sea of cargo, passengers or their luggage;

(c)   claims in respect of other loss resulting from infringement of rights other than contractual rights, occurring in direct connexion with the operation of the ship or salvage operations;

(d)   claims in respect of the raising, removal, destruction or the rendering harmless of a ship which is sunk, wrecked or abandoned, including anything that is or has been on board such ship;

(e)   claims in respect of the removal, destruction or the rendering harmless of the cargo of the ship;

(f)   claims of a person other than liable in respect of measures taken in order to avert or minimize loss for which the person liable may limit his liability in accordance with this Convention, and further loss caused by such measures.

2.   Claims set out in paragraph 1 shall be subject to limitation of liability even if brought by way of recourse or for indemnity under a contract or otherwise. However, claims set out under paragraph 1(d), (e) and (f) shall not be subject to limitation of liability to the extent that they relate to remuneration under a contract with the person liable.

Article 3

Claims excepted from limitation

The rules of this Convention shall not apply to:

(a)   claims for salvage or contribution in general average;

(b)   claims for oil pollution damage within the meaning of the International Convention on Civil Liability for Oil Pollution Damage, dated 29 November 1969 or of any amendment or Protocol thereto which is in force;

(c)   claims subject to any international convention or national legislation governing or prohibiting limitation of liability for nuclear damage;

(d)   claims against the shipowner of a nuclear ship for nuclear damage;

(e)   claims by servants of the shipowner or salvor whose duties are connected with the ship or the salvage operations, including claims of their heirs, dependants or other persons entitled to make such claims, if under the law governing the contract of service between the shipowner or salvor and such servants the shipowner or salvor is not entitled to limit his liability in respect of such claims, or if he is by such law only permitted to limit his liability to an amount greater than that provided for in Article 6.

Article 4

Conduct barring limitation

A person shall not be entitled to limit his liability if it is proved that the loss resulted from his personal act or omission, committed with the intent to cause such loss, or recklessly and with knowledge that such loss would probably result.

Article 5

Counterclaims

Where a person entitled to limitation of liability under the rules of this Convention has a claim against the claimant arising out of the same occurrence, their respective claims shall be set off against each other and the provisions of this Convention shall only apply to the balance, if any.

CHAPTER II.   LIMITS OF LIABILITY

Article 6

The general limits

1.   The limits of liability for claims other than those mentioned in Article 7, arising on any distinct occasion, shall be calculated as follows:

(a)   in respect of claims for loss of life or personal injury,

(i)   333,000 Units of Account for a ship with a tonnage not exceeding 500 tons,

(ii) for a ship with a tonnage in excess thereof, the following amount in addition to that mentioned in (i):

for each ton from 501 to 3,000 tons, 500 Units of Account;

for each ton from 3,001 to 30,000 tons, 333 Units of Account;

for each ton from 30,001 to 70,000 tons, 250 Units of Account; and

for each ton in excess of 70,000 tons, 167 Units of Account,

(b) in respect of any other claims,

(i) 167,000 Units of Account for a ship with a tonnage not exceeding 500 tons,

(ii) for a ship with a tonnage in excess thereof the following amount in addition to that mentioned in (i):

for each ton from 501 to 30,000 tons, 167 Units of Account;

for each ton from 30,001 to 70,000 tons, 125 Units of Account; and

for each ton in excess of 70,000 tons, 83 Units of Account.

2. Where the amount calculated in accordance with paragraph 1(a) is insufficient to pay the claims mentioned therein in full, the amount calculated in accordance with paragraph 1(b) shall be available for payment of the unpaid balance of claims under paragraph 1(a) and such unpaid balance shall rank rateably with claims mentioned under paragraph 1(b).

3. However, without prejudice to the right of claims for loss of life or personal injury according to paragraph 2, a State Party may provide in its national law that claims in respect of damage to harbour works, basins and waterways and aids to navigation shall have such priority over other claims under paragraph 1(b) as is provided by that law.

4. The limits of liability for any salvor not operating from any ship or for any salvor operating solely on the ship to, or in respect of which he is rendering salvage services, shall be calculated according to a tonnage of 1,500 tons.

5. For the purpose of this Convention the ship's tonnage shall be the gross tonnage calculated in accordance with the tonnage measurement rules contained in Annex 1 of the International Convention on Tonnage Measurement of Ships, 1969.

Article 7

The limit for passenger claims

1.   In respect of claims arising on any distinct occasion for loss of life or personal injury to passengers of a ship, the limit of liability of the shipowner thereof shall be an amount of 46,666 Units of Account multiplied by the number of passengers which the ship is authorized to carry according to the ship's certificate, but not exceeding 25 million Units of Account.

2.   For the purpose of this Article "claims for loss of life or personal injury to passengers of a ship" shall mean any such claims brought by or on behalf of any person carried in that ship:

(a)   under a contract of passenger carriage, or

(b)   who, with the consent of the carrier, is accompanying a vehicle or live animals which are covered by a contract for the carriage of goods.

Article 8

Unit of Account

1.   The Unit of Account referred to in Articles 6 and 7 is the Special Drawing Right as defined by the International Monetary Fund. The amounts mentioned in Articles 6 and 7 shall be converted into the national currency of the State in which limitation is sought, according to the value of that currency at the date the limitation fund shall have been constituted, payment is made, or security is given which under the law of that State is equivalent to such payment. The value of a national currency in terms of the Special Drawing Right, of a State Party which is a member of the International Monetary Fund, shall be calculated in accordance with the method of valuation applied by the International Monetary Fund in effect at the date in question for its operations and transactions. The value of a national currency in terms of the Special Drawing Right, of a State Party which is not a member of the International Monetary Fund, shall be calculated in a manner determined by that State Party.

2.   Nevertheless, those States which are not members of the International Monetary Fund and whose law does not permit the application of the provisions of paragraph 1 may, at the time of signature without reservation as to ratification, acceptance or approval or at the time of ratification, acceptance, approval or accession or at any time thereafter, declare that the limits of liability provided for in this Convention to be applied in their territories shall be fixed as follows:

(a)   in respect of Article 6, paragraph 1(a) at an amount of:

(i)   5 million monetary units for a ship with a tonnage not exceeding 500 tons;

(ii) for a ship with a tonnage in excess thereof, the following amount in addition to that mentioned in (i):

for each ton from 501 to 3,000 tons, 7,500 monetary units;

for each ton from 3,001 to 30,000 tons, 5,000 monetary units;

for each ton from 30,001 to 70,000 tons, 3,750 monetary units; and

for each ton in excess of 70,000 tons, 2,500 monetary units; and

(b)   in respect of Article 6, paragraph 1(b), at an amount of:

(i)   2.5 million monetary units for a ship with a tonnage not exceeding 500 tons;

(ii)   or a ship with a tonnage in excess thereof, the following amount in addition to that mentioned in (i):

for each ton from 501 to 30,000 tons, 2,500 monetary units;

for each ton from 30,001 to 70,000 tons, 1,850 monetary units; and

for each ton in excess of 70,000 tons, 1,250 monetary units; and

(c)   in respect of Article 7, paragraph 1, at an amount of 700,000 monetary units multiplied by the number of passengers which the ship is authorized to carry according to its certificate, but not exceeding 375 million monetary units.

Paragraphs 2 and 3 of Article 6 apply correspondingly to subparagraphs (a) and (b) of this paragraph.

3.   The monetary unit referred to in paragraph 2 corresponds to sixty-five and a half milligrammes of gold of millesimal fineness nine hundred. The conversion of the amounts referred to in paragraph 2 into the national currency shall be made according to the law of the State concerned.

4.   The calculation mentioned in the last sentence of paragraph 1 and the conversion mentioned in paragraph 3 shall be made in such a manner as to express in the national currency of the State Party as far as possible the same real value for the amounts in Articles 6 and 7 as is expressed there in units of account. States Parties shall communicate to the depositary the manner of calculation pursuant to paragraph 1, or the result of the conversion in paragraph 3, as the case may be, at the time of the signature without reservation as to ratification, acceptance or approval, or when depositing an instrument referred to in Article 16 and whenever there is a change in either.

Article 9

Aggregation of claims

1.   The limits of liability determined in accordance with Article 6 shall apply to the aggregate of all claims which arise on any distinct occasion:

(a)   against the person or persons mentioned in paragraph 2 of Article 1 and any person for whose act, neglect or default he or they are responsible; or

(b)   against the shipowner of a ship rendering salvage services from that ship and the salvor or salvors operating from such ship and any person for whose act, neglect or default he or they are responsible; or

(c)   against the salvor or salvors who are not operating from a ship or who are operating solely on the ship to, or in respect of which, the salvage services are rendered and any person for whose act, neglect or default he or they are responsible.

2.   The limits of liability determined in accordance with Article 7 shall apply to the aggregate of all claims subject thereto which may arise on any distinct occasion against the person or persons mentioned in paragraph 2 of Article 1 in respect of the ship referred to in Article 7 and any person for whose act, neglect or default he or they are responsible.

Article 10

Limitation of liability without constitution of a limitation fund

1.   Limitation of liability may be invoked notwithstanding that a limitation fund as mentioned in Article 11 has not been constituted. However, a State Party may provide in its national law that, where an action is brought in its Courts to enforce a claim subject to limitation, a person liable may only invoke the right to limit if a limitation fund has been constituted in accordance with the provisions of this Convention or is constituted when the right to limit liability is invoked.

2.   If limitation of liability is invoked without the constitution of a limitation fund, the provisions of Article 12 shall apply correspondingly.

3.   Questions of procedure arising under the rules of this Article shall be decided in accordance with the national law of the State Party in which action is brought.

CHAPTER III.   THE LIMITATION FUND

Article 11

Constitution of the fund

1.   Any person alleged to be liable may constitute a fund with the Court or other competent authority in any State Party in which legal proceedings are instituted in respect of claims subject to limitation. The fund shall be constituted in the sum of such of the amounts set out in Articles 6 and 7 as are applicable to claims for which that person may be

liable, together with interest thereon from the date of the occurrence giving rise to the liability until the date of the constitution of the fund. Any fund thus constituted shall be available only for the payment of claims in respect of which limitation of liability can be invoked.

2.   A fund may be constituted, either by depositing the sum, or by producing a guarantee acceptable under the legislation of the State Party where the fund is constituted and considered to be adequate by the Court or other competent authority.

3.   A fund constituted by one of the persons mentioned in paragraph 1(a), (b) or (c) or paragraph 2 of Article 9 or his insurer shall be deemed constituted by all persons mentioned in paragraph 1(a), (b) or (c) or paragraph 2, respectively.

Article 12

Distribution of the fund

1.   Subject to the provisions of paragraphs 1, 2 and 3 of Article 6 and of Article 7, the fund shall be distributed among the claimants in proportion to their established claims against the fund.

2.   If, before the fund is distributed, the person liable, or his insurer, has settled a claim against the fund such person shall, up to the amount he has paid, acquire by subrogation the rights which the person so compensated would have enjoyed under this Convention.

3.   The right of subrogation provided for in paragraph 2 may also be exercised by persons other than those therein mentioned in respect of any amount of compensation which they may have paid, but only to the extent that such subrogation is permitted under the applicable national law.

4.   Where the person liable or any other person establishes that he may be compelled to pay, at a later date, in whole or in part any such amount of compensation with regard to which such person would have enjoyed a right of subrogation pursuant to paragraphs 2 and 3 had the compensation been paid before the fund was distributed, the Court or other competent authority of the State where the fund has been constituted may order that a sufficient sum shall be provisionally set aside to enable such person at such later date to enforce his claim against the fund.

Article 13

Bar to other actions

1.   Where a limitation fund has been constituted in accordance with Article 11, any person having made a claim against the fund shall be barred from exercising any right in respect of such claim against any other assets of a person by or on behalf of whom the fund has been constituted.

2.   After a limitation fund has been constituted in accordance with Article 11, any ship or other property, belonging to a person on behalf of whom the fund has been constituted, which has been arrested or attached within the jurisdiction of a State Party for a claim which may be raised against the fund, or any security given, may be released by order of the Court or other competent authority of such State. However, such release shall always be ordered if the limitation fund has been constituted:

(a)   at the port where the occurrence took place, or, if it took place out of port, at the first port of call thereafter; or

(b)   at the port of disembarkation in respect of claims for loss of life or personal injury; or

(c)   at the port of discharge in respect of damage to cargo; or

(d)   in the State where the arrest is made.

3.   The rules of paragraphs 1 and 2 shall apply only if the claimant may bring a claim against the limitation fund before the Court administering that fund and the fund is actually available and freely transferable in respect of that claim.

Article 14

Governing law

Subject to the provisions of this Chapter the rules relating to the constitution and distribution of a limitation fund, and all rules of procedure in connection therewith, shall be governed by the law of the State Party in which the fund is constituted.

CHAPTER IV.   SCOPE OF APPLICATION

Article 15

1.   This Convention shall apply whenever any person referred to in Article 1 seeks to limit his liability before the Court of a State Party or seeks to procure the release of a ship or other property or the discharge of any security given within the jurisdiction of any such State. Nevertheless, each State Party may exclude wholly or partially from the application of this Convention any person referred to in Article 1 who at the time when the rules of this Convention are invoked before the Courts of that State does not have his habitual residence in a State Party or does not have his principal place of business in a State Party or any ship in relation to which the right of limitation is invoked or whose release is sought and which does not at the time specified above fly the flag of a State Party.

2.   A State Party may regulate by specific provisions of national law the system of limitation of liability to be applied to vessels which are:

(a)   according to the law of that State, ships intended for navigation on inland waterways;

(b)   ships of less than 300 tons.

A State Party which makes use of the option provided for in this paragraph shall inform the depositary of the limits of liability adopted in its national legislation or of the fact that there are none.

3. A State Party may regulate by specific provisions of national law the system of limitation of liability to be applied to claims arising in cases in which interests of persons who are nationals of other States Parties are in no way involved.

4. The Courts of a State Party shall not apply this Convention to ships constructed for, or adapted to, and engaged in, drilling:

(a) when that State has established under its national legislation a higher limit of liability than that otherwise provided for in Article 6; or

(b) when that State has become party to an international convention regulating the system of liability in respect of such ships.

In a case to which sub-paragraph (a) applies that State Party shall inform the depositary accordingly.

5. This Convention shall not apply to:

(a) air-cushion vehicles;

(b) floating platforms constructed for the purpose of exploring or exploiting the natural resources of the sea-bed or the subsoil thereof.

[Chapter V—Final Clauses and Articles 16 through 23 omitted.]

IV. HISTORICAL MATERIALS

A. ENGLISH STATUTES

13 RICH. II, C. 5

* * * that the admirals and their deputies shall not meddle henceforth of any thing done within the realm, but only of a thing done upon the sea, according as it hath been duly used in the time of the noble King Edward [III], grandfather of our lord the king that now is.

15 RICH. II, C. 3 ("ADMIRALTY ACT OF 1391")

* * * that of all manner of contracts, pleas and quereles and of all other things done or arising within the bodies of counties, as well by land as by water; and also of wreck of the sea, the admiral's court shall have no manner of cognizance, power nor jurisdiction; but all such manner of contracts, pleas and quereles, and all other things rising within the bodies of counties, as well by land as by water, as afore, and also wreck of the sea, shall be tried, determined, discussed and remedied, by the laws of the land, and not before or by the admiral, nor his lieutenant, in any wise. Nevertheless the death of a man, and of a maihem done in great ships, being hovering in the mainstream of great rivers, only, beneath the bridges of the same rivers nigh to the sea, and in none other places of the same rivers, the admiral shall have cognizance; and also to arrest ships in the great flotes for the great voyages of the king and of the realm; saving always to the king all manner of forfeitures and profits thereof coming; and he shall have jurisdiction upon the said flotes during the said voyages, only saving always to the lords, cities and boroughs, their liberties and franchises.

2 HEN. IV, C. 11

* * * that the statute of 13 Rich. II be firmly holden and kept, and put in due execution; and that, as touching a pain to be set upon the admiral or his lieutenant, that the statute and the common law be holden against them; and that he, that feeleth himself grieved against the form of the said statute, shall have his action grounded upon the case against him that doth so pursue in the admiral's court, and recover his double damages against the pursuant, and the same pursuant shall incure the pain of £ 10 to the king for the pursuit so made, if he be attained.

3 & 4 VICTORIA C. 65 ("ADMIRALTY COURT ACT OF 1840")

Whereas the Jurisdiction of the High Court of Admiralty of *England* may be in certain respects advantageously extended, and the Practice thereof improved: Be it therefore enacted by the Queen's most Excellent

Majesty, by and with the Advice and Consent of the Lords Spiritual and Temporal, and Commons, in this present Parliament assembled, and by the Authority of the same, That it shall be lawful for the Dean of the Arches for the Time being to be Assistant to and to exercise all the Power, Authority, and Jurisdiction, and to have all the Privileges and Protections of the Judge of the said High Court of Admiralty with respect to all Suits and Proceedings in the said Court, and that all such Suits and Proceedings, and all Things relating thereto, brought or taking place before the Dean of the Arches, whether the Judge of the said High Court of Admiralty be or be not at the same Time sitting or transacting the Business of the same Court, and also during any Vacancy of the Office of Judge of the said Court, shall be of the same Force and Effect in all respects as if the same had been brought or had been taken place before the Judge himself, and all such Suits and Proceedings shall be entered and registered as having been brought and as having taken place before the Dean of the Arches sitting for the Judge of the High Court of Admiralty.

II.   And be it declared and enacted, That all Persons who now are or at any Time hereafter may be entitled to practise as Advocates in the Court of Arches are and shall be entitled to practise as Advocates in the said High Court of Admiralty; and that all Persons who now are or hereafter may be entitled to act as Surrogates or Proctors in the Court of Arches shall be entitled respectively to practise and act, or to be admitted to practise and act, as the Case may be, as Surrogates and Proctors in the said High Court of Admiralty, according to the Rules and Practice now prevailing and observed or hereafter to be made in and by the said High Court of Admiralty touching the Admission and practising of Advocates, Surrogates, and Proctors in the said Court respectively.

III.   And be it enacted, That after the passing of this Act, whenever any Ship or Vessel shall be under Arrest by Process issuing from the said High Court of Admiralty, or the Proceeds of any Ship or Vessel having been so arrested shall have been brought into and be in the Registry of the said Court, in either such Case the said Court shall have full Jurisdiction to take cognizance of all Claims and Causes of Action of any Person in respect of any Mortgage of such Ship or Vessel, and to decide any Suit instituted by any such Person in respect of any such Claims or Causes of Action respectively.

IV.   And be it enacted, That the said Court of Admiralty shall have Jurisdiction to decide all Questions as to the Title to or Ownership of any Ship or Vessel, or the Proceeds thereof remaining in the Registry, arising in any Cause of Possession, Salvage, Damage, Wages, or Bottomry, which shall be instituted in the said Court after the passing of this Act.

V.   And be it enacted, That whenever any Award shall have been made by any Justices of the Peace, or by any Person nominated by them, or within the Jurisdiction of the Cinque Ports by any Commissioners, respecting the Amount of Salvage to be paid, or respecting any Claims and Demands for Services or Compensation, which such Justices and Commissioners within their several Jurisdictions are empowered to decide under the Provisions of Two Acts passed in the Second Year of the Reign of King *George* the Fourth, for remedying certain Defects relative to the Adjustment of Salvage, or whenever any Sum shall have been voluntarily paid on any such Account of Salvage, Services, or Compensation, it shall be lawful for any Person interested in the Distribution of the Amount awarded or paid to require Distribution to be forthwith made thereof, and the Person or Persons by whom such Amount shall be awarded, or in the Case of voluntary Payment the Person by whom the same shall have been received, shall forthwith proceed to the Distribution thereof among the several Persons entitled thereunto, to be certified in the Case of an Award under the Hand of the Person or Persons by whom such Amount shall be awarded, and an Account of every such Distribution shall be annexed to the Award; and if any Person interested in the Distribution shall think himself aggrieved on account of its not being made according to the Award, or otherwise, it shall be lawful for him, within Fourteen Days after the making of the Award, or Payment of the Money, but not afterwards, to take out a Monition from the said High Court of Admiralty, requiring any Person being in Possession of any Part of the Amount awarded or voluntarily paid to bring in the same, to abide the Judgment of the Court concerning the Distribution thereof; and in the Case of an Award the Person or Persons by whom the Award shall have been made shall, upon Monition, send without Delay to the said High Court of Admiralty a Copy of the Proceedings before him and them, and of the Award, on unstamped Paper, certified under his or their Hand; and the same shall be admitted by the Court as Evidence, and the Amount awarded or voluntarily paid shall be distributed according to the Judgment of the Court.

VI. And be it enacted, That the High Court of Admiralty shall have Jurisdiction to decide all Claims and Demands whatsoever in the Nature of Salvage for Services rendered to or Damage received by any Ship or Sea-going Vessel, or in the Nature of Towage, or for Necessaries supplied to any Foreign Ship or Sea-going Vessel, and to enforce the Payment thereof, whether such Ship or Vessel may have been within the Body of a County, or upon the High Seas, at the Time when the Services were rendered or Damage received, or Necessaries furnished, in respect of which such Claim is made.

VII. And be it enacted, That in any Suit depending in the said High Court of Admiralty the Court (if it shall think fit) may summon before it and examine or cause to be examined Witnesses by Word of Mouth, and either before or after Examination by Deposition, or before a Commissioner, as herein-after mentioned; and Notes of such Evidence shall be taken down in Writing by the Judge or Registrar, or by such other Person or Persons, and in such Manner as the Judge of the said Court shall direct.

VIII. And be it enacted, That the said Court may, if it shall think fit, in any such Suit issue One or more Special Commissions to some Person, being an Advocate of the said High Court of Admiralty of not less than Seven Years standing, or a Barrister at Law of not less than Seven Years standing, to take Evidence by Word of Mouth, upon Oath, which every such Commissioner is hereby empowered to administer, at such Time or Times, Place or Places, and as to such Fact or Facts, and in such Manner, Order, and Course, and under such Limitations and Restrictions, and to transmit the same to the Registry of the said Court, in such Form and Manner as in and by the Commission shall be directed; and that such Commissioner shall be attended, and the Witnesses shall be examined, cross-examined, and re-examined by the Parties, their Counsel, Proctors, or Agents, if such Parties, or either of them, shall think fit so to do; and such Commission shall, if need be, make a Special Report to the Court touching such Examination, and the Conduct or Absence of any Witness or other Person thereon or relating thereto; and the said High Court of Admiralty is hereby authorized to institute such Proceedings, and make such Order or Orders, upon such Report, as Justice may require, and as may be instituted or made in any Case of Contempt of the said Court.

IX. And be it enacted, That it shall be lawful in any Suit depending in the said Court of Admiralty for the Judge of the said Court, or for any such Commissioner appointed in pursuance of this Act, to require the Attendance of any Witnesses, and the Production of any Deeds, Evidences, Books, or Writings, by Writ, to be issued by such Judge or Commissioner, in such and the same Form, or as nearly as may be, as that in which a Writ of Subpoena ad testificandum, or of Subpoena duces tecum, is now issued by Her Majesty's Court of Queen's Bench at *Westminster;* and that every Person disobeying any such Writ so to be issued by the said Judge or Commissioner shall be considered as in Contempt of the said High Court of Admiralty, and may be punished for such Contempt in the said Court.

X. And be it enacted, That all the Provisions of an Act passed in the Fourth Year of the Reign of His late Majesty, intituled *An Act for the further Amendment of the Law, and better Administration of Justice,* with respect to the Admissibility of the Evidence of Witnesses interested on account of the Verdict or Judgment shall extend to the Admissibility of Evidence in any Suit pending in the said Court of Admiralty, and the Entry directed by the said Act to be made on the Record of Judgment shall be made upon the Document containing the final Sentence of the said Court, and shall have the like Effect as the Entry of such Record.

XI. And be it enacted, That in any contested Suit depending in the said Court of Admiralty the said Court shall have Power, if it shall think fit so to do, to direct a Trial by Jury of any Issue or Issues on any Question or Questions of Fact arising in any such Suit, and that the Substance and Form of such Issue or Issues shall be specified by the Judge of the said Court at the Time of directing the same; and if the Parties differ in drawing such Issue or Issues, it shall be referred to the Judge of the said Court to settle the same; and such Trial shall be had before some Judge of Her Majesty's Superior Courts of Common Law at *Westminster,* at the Sittings at Nisi Prius in *London* or *Middlesex,* or before some Judge of Assize at Nisi Prius, as to the said Court shall seem fit.

XII. And be it enacted, That the Costs of such Issues, or of such Commission as aforesaid, as the Judge of the said High Court of Admiralty shall under this Act direct, shall be paid by such Party or Parties, Person or Persons, and be taxed by the Registrar of the said High Court of Admiralty, in such Manner as the said Judge shall direct, and that Payment of such Costs shall be enforced in the same Manner as Costs between Party and Party may be enforced in other Proceedings in the said Court.

XIII. And be it enacted, That the said Court of Admiralty, upon Application to be made within Three Calendar Months after the Trial of any such Issue by any Party concerned, may grant and direct One or more new Trials of any such Issue, and may order such new Trial to take place in the Manner herein-before directed with regard to the first Trial of such Issue, and may by Order of the same Court direct such Costs to be paid as to the said Court shall seem fit upon any Application for a new Trial, or upon any new Trial, or second or other new Trial, and may direct by whom and to whom and at what Times and in what Manner such Costs shall be paid.

XIV. And be it enacted, That the granting or refusing to grant an Issue, or a new Trial of any such Issue, may be Matter of Appeal to Her Majesty in Council.

XV. And be it enacted, That at the Trial of any Issue directed by the said High Court of Admiralty, either Party shall have all the like Powers, Rights, and Remedies with respect to Bills of Exceptions as Parties impleaded before Justices may have, by virtue of the Statute made in that Behalf in the Thirteenth Year of the Reign of King *Edward* the First, with respect to Exceptions alleged by them before such Justices, or by any other Statute made in the like Behalf; and every such Bill of Exceptions, sealed with the Seal of the Judge or Judges to whom such Exceptions shall have been made, shall be annexed to the Record of the Trial of the said Issue.

XVI. And be it enacted, That the Record of the said Issue, and of the Verdict therein, shall be transmitted by the Associate or other proper Officer to the Registrar of the said Court of Admiralty; and the Verdict of the Jury upon any such Issue (unless the same shall be set aside) shall be conclusive upon the said Court, and upon all such Persons; and in all further Proceedings in the Cause in which such Fact is found the said Court shall assume such Fact to be as found by the Jury.

XVII.   And be it enacted, That every Person who, if this Act had not been passed, might have appealed and made Suit to Her Majesty in

Council against any Proceeding, Decree, or Sentence of the said High Court of Admiralty under or by virtue of an Act passed in the Third Year of the Reign of His late Majesty, intituled *An Act for transferring the Powers of the High Court of Delegates, both in Ecclesiastical and Maritime Causes, to His Majesty in Council,* may in like Manner appeal and make Suits to Her Majesty in Council against the Proceedings, Decrees, and Sentences of the said Court in all Suits instituted and Proceedings had in the same by virtue of the Provisions of this Act, and that all the Provisions of the said last-mentioned Act shall apply to all Appeals and Suits against the Proceedings, Decrees, and Sentences of the said Court in Suits instituted and Proceedings had by virtue of the Provisions of this Act; and such Appeals and Suits shall be proceeded in the Manner and Form provided by an Act passed in the Fourth Year of the Reign of His late Majesty, intituled *An Act for the better Administration of Justice in His Majesty's Privy Council;* and all the Provisions of the said last-mentioned Act relating to Appeals and Suits from the High Court of Admiralty shall be applied to Appeals and Suits from the said Court in Suits instituted and Proceedings had by virtue of the Provisions of this Act: Provided always, that in any such Appeal the Notes of Evidence taken as herein-before provided by or under the Direction of the Judge of the said High Court of Admiralty shall be certified by the said Judge to Her Majesty in Council, and shall be admitted to prove the oral Evidence given in the said Court of Admiralty, and that no Evidence shall be admitted on such Appeal to contradict the Notes of Evidence so taken and certified as aforesaid, but this Proviso shall not enure to prevent the Judicial Committee of the Privy Council from directing Witnesses to be examined and re-examined upon such Facts as to the Committee shall seem fit, in the Manner directed by the last-recited Act.

XVIII.   And be it enacted, That it shall be lawful for the Judge of the said High Court of Admiralty from Time to Time to make such Rules, Orders, and Regulations respecting the Practice and Mode of Proceeding of the said Court, and the Conduct and Duties of the Officers and Practitioners therein, as to him shall seem fit, and from Time to Time to repeal or alter such Rules, Orders, or Regulations: Provided always, that no such Rules, Orders, or Regulations shall be of any Force or Effect until the same shall have been approved by Her Majesty in Council.

XIX.   And be it declared and enacted, That no Action shall lie against the Judge of the said High Court of Admiralty for Error in Judgment, and that the said Judge shall be entitled to and have all Privileges and Protections in the Exercise of his Jurisdiction as Judge of the said Court which by Law appertain to the Judges of Her Majesty's Superior Courts of Common Law in the Exercise of their several Jurisdictions.

XX. And be it enacted, That the Keeper for the Time being of every Common Gaol or Prison shall be bound to receive and take into his

Custody all Persons who shall be committed thereunto by the said Court of Admiralty, or who shall be committed thereunto by any Coroner appointed by the Judge of the said Court of Admiralty, upon any Inquest taken within or upon the High Seas adjacent to the County or other Jurisdiction to which such Gaol or Prison belongs; and every Keeper of any Gaol or Prison who shall refuse to receive into his Custody any Person so committed, or wilfully or carelessly suffer such Person to escape and go at large without lawful Warrant, shall be liable to the like Penalties and Consequences as if such Person had been committed to his Custody by any other lawful Authority.

XXI.   And be it enacted, That it shall be lawful for the Judge of the said High Court of Admiralty to order the Discharge of any Person who shall be in Custody for Contempt of the said Court, for any Cause other than for Nonpayment of Money, on such Conditions as to the Judge shall seem just: Provided always, that the Order for such Discharge shall not be deemed to have purged the original Contempt in case the Conditions on which such Order shall be made be not fulfilled.

XXII.   And be it enacted, That the said High Court of Admiralty shall have Jurisdiction to decide all Matters and Questions concerning Booty of War, or the Distribution thereof, which it shall please Her Majesty, Her Heirs and Successors, by the Advice of Her and Their Privy Council, to refer to the Judgment of the said Court; and in all Matters so referred the Court shall proceed as in Cases of Prize of War, and the Judgment of the Court therein shall be binding upon all Parties concerned.

XXIII. Provided always, and be it enacted, That nothing herein contained shall be deemed to preclude any of Her Majesty's Courts of Law or Equity now having Jurisdiction over the several Subject Matters and Causes of Action herein-before mentioned from continuing to exercise such Jurisdiction as fully as if this Act had not been passed.

XXIV.   And be it enacted, That this Act may be repealed or amended by any Act to be passed in this Session of Parliament.

B. AMERICAN STATUTES

Judiciary Act of 1789, 1 Stat. 73, § 9

Sec. 9.   *And be it further enacted,* That the district courts shall have, exclusively of the courts of the several States, cognizance of all crimes and offences that shall be cognizable under the authority of the United States, committed within their respective districts, or upon the high seas; where no other punishment than whipping, not exceeding thirty stripes, a fine not exceeding one hundred dollars, or a term of imprisonment not exceeding six months, is to be inflicted; and shall also have exclusive original cognizance of all civil causes of admiralty and maritime jurisdiction, including all seizures under laws of impost, navigation or trade of the United States, where the seizures are made, on waters which are navigable from the sea by vessels of ten or more tons burthen, within their respective districts as well as upon the high seas; saving to suitors, in all cases, the right of a common law remedy, where the common law is competent to give it; and shall also have exclusive original cognizance of all seizures on land, or other waters than as aforesaid, made, and of all suits for penalties and forfeitures incurred, under the laws of the United States. And shall also have cognizance, concurrent with the courts of the several States, or the circuit courts, as the case may be, of all causes where an alien sues for a tort only in violation of the law of nations or a treaty of the United States. And shall also have cognizance, concurrent as last mentioned, of all suits at common law where the United States sue, and the matter in dispute amounts, exclusive of costs, to the sum or value of one hundred dollars. And shall also have jurisdiction exclusively of the courts of the several States, of all suits against consuls, or vice-consuls, except for offences above the description aforesaid. And the trial of issues in fact, in the district courts, in all causes except civil causes of admiralty and maritime jurisdiction, shall be by jury.

Great Lakes Act of 1845
Act of Feb. 26, 1845, Ch. 20, 5 Stat. 726–727

"That the district courts of the United States shall have, possess, and exercise, the same jurisdiction in matters of contract and tort, arising in, upon, or concerning, steamboats and other vessels of twenty tons burden and upwards, enrolled and licensed for the coastal trade, and at the time employed in business of commerce and navigation between ports and places in different States and Territories upon the lakes and navigable waters connecting said lakes, as is now possessed and exercised by the said courts in cases of the like steamboats and other vessels employed in navigation and commerce upon the high seas, or tide waters, within the admiralty and maritime jurisdiction of the United States; and in all suits brought in such courts in all such matters of contract or tort, the remedies, and the forms of process, and the modes of proceeding, shall be the same as are or may be used by such courts in cases of admiralty and maritime jurisdiction; and the maritime law of the United States, so far as the same is or may be applicable thereto, shall constitute the rule of decision in such suits, in the same manner, and to the same extent, and with the same equities, as it now does in cases of admiralty and maritime jurisdiction; saving, however, to the parties the right of trial by jury of all facts put in issue in such suits, where either party shall require it; and saving also to the parties the right of a concurrent remedy at the common law, where it is competent to give it, and any concurrent remedy which may be given by the State laws, where such steamer or other vessel is employed in such business of commerce and navigation."

C. THE LAWS OF OLERON

Article I

When several joint owners make a man master of a ship or vessel, and the ship or vessel departing from her own port, arrives at *Bordeaux, Rouen,* or any other such place, and is there freighted to sail for *Scotland,* or some other foreign country; the master in such case may not sell or dispose of that ship or vessel, without a special procuration from the owners: but in case he wants money for the victualling, or other necessary provisions of the said vessel, he may for that end, with the advice of his mariners, pawn or pledge part of the tackle or furniture of a ship.

Article II

If a ship or other vessel be in a port, waiting for weather, and a wind to depart, the master ought when that comes, before his departure to consult his company, and say to them, *Gentlemen, What think you of this wind?* If any of them see that it is not settled, and advise him to stay until it is, and others, on the contrary, would have him make use of it as fair, he ought to follow the advice of the major part: If he does otherwise, and the vessel happens to miscarry, he shall be obliged to make good the same, according to the value upon a just appraisement.

Article III

If any vessel, through misfortune, happens to be cast away, in whatsoever place it be, the mariners shall be obliged to use their best endeavours for saving as much of the ship and lading as possibly they can: and if they preserve part thereof, the master shall allow them a reasonable consideration to carry them home to their own country. And in case they save enough to enable the master to do this, he may lawfully pledge to some honest persons such part thereof as may be sufficient for that occasion. But if they have not endeavoured to save as aforesaid, then the master shall not be bound to provide for them in any thing, but ought to keep them in safe custody, until he knows the pleasure of the owners, in which he may act as becomes a prudent master; for if he does otherwise, he shall be obliged to make satisfaction.

Article IV

If a vessel departing with her lading from *Bordeaux,* or any other place, happens in the course of her voyage, to be rendered unfit to proceed therein, and the mariners save as much of the lading as possibly they can; if the merchants require their goods of the master, he may deliver them if he pleases, they paying the freight in proportion to the part of the voyage that is performed, and the costs of the salvage. But if the master can readily repair his vessel, he may do it; or if he pleases, he may freight another ship to perform his voyage. And if he has promised the people who helped him to save the ship the third, or the half part of the goods saved for the danger they ran, the judicatures of the country should consider the pains and trouble they have been at, and reward them

267

accordingly, without any regard to the promises made them by the parties concerned in the time of their distress.

Article V

If a vessel departing from one port, laden or empty, arrives at another, the mariners shall not leave the ship without the master's consent: if they do, and by that means she happens to be lost or damnified, they shall be answerable for the damage; but if the vessel be moored, and lying at anchor, with a sufficient number of men aboard to keep the decks and lading, they may go without the master's consent, if they come back in good time; otherwise they shall be liable to make satisfaction, if they have wherewithal.

Article VI

If any of the mariners hired by the master of any vessel, go out of the ship without his leave, and get themselves drunk, and thereby there happens contempt to their master, debates, or fighting and quarrelling among themselves, whereby some happen to be wounded: in this case the master shall not be obliged to get them cured, or in any thing to provide for them, but may turn them and their accomplices out of the ship; and if they make words of it, they are bound to pay the master besides: but if by the master's orders and commands any of the ship's company be in the service of the ship, and thereby happen to be wounded or otherwise hurt, in that case they shall be cured and provided for at the costs and charges of the said ship.

Article VII

If it happens that sickness seizes on any one of the mariners, while in the service of the ship, the master ought to set him ashore, to provide lodging and candlelight for him, and also to spare him one of the shipboys, or hire a woman to attend him, and likewise to afford him such diet as is usual in the ship; that is to say, so much as he had on shipboard in his health, and nothing more, unless it please the master to allow it him; and if he will have better diet, the master shall not be bound to provide it for him, unless it be at the mariner's own cost and charges; and if the vessel be ready for her departure, she ought not to stay for the said sick party—but if he recover, he ought to have his full wages, deducting only such charges as the master has been at for him. And if he dies, his wife or next kin shall have it.

Article VIII

If a vessel be laden to sail from Bordeaux to Caen, or any other place, and it happens that a storm overtakes her at sea, so violent, that she cannot escape without casting some of the cargo overboard for lightening the vessel, and preserving the rest of the lading, as well as the vessel itself; then the master ought to say, *Gentlemen, We must throw part of the goods overboard;* and, if there are no merchants to answer him, or if those that are there approve of what he says by their silence, then the master may do as he thinks fit; and if the merchants are not pleased with his throwing over any part of the merchandize, and forbid him, yet the master ought not to forbear casting out so many of the goods as he shall see to be for the common good and safety; he and the third part of his mariners making oath on the Holy Evangelists, when they arrive at their port of discharge, that he did it only for the preservation of the vessel, and the rest of the lading that remains yet in her. And the wines, or other goods, that were cast overboard, ought to be valued or prized according to the just value of the other goods that arrive in safety. And when these shall be sold, the price or value thereof ought to be divided livre a livre among the merchants. The master may compute the damage his vessel has sustained, or reckon the freight of the goods thrown overboard at his own choice. If the master does not make it appear that he and his men did the part of able seamen, then neither he nor they shall have any thing. The mariners also ought to have one tun free, and another divided by cast of the dice, according as it shall happen, and the merchants in this case may lawfully put the master to his oath.

Article IX

If it happen, that by reason of much foul weather the master is like to be constrained to cut his masts, he ought first to call the merchants, if there be any aboard the ship, and such as have goods and merchandize in the vessel, and to consult them, saying, *Sirs, it is requisite to cut down the mast to save the ship and lading, it being in this case my duty.* And frequently they also cut their mooring cables, leaving behind them their cables and anchors to save the ship and her lading; all which things are reckoned and computed *livre* by *livre,* as the goods are that were cast overboard. And when the vessel arrives in safety at her port of discharge, the merchants ought to pay the master their shares or proportions without delay, or sell or pawn the goods and employ the money he raises to satisfy by it the same, before the said goods be unladen out of the said ship: but if he lets them go, and there happens controversies and debates touching the premises if the master observes collusion therein, he ought not to suffer, but is to have his complete freight, as well for what goods were thrown overboard, as for what he brought home.

Article X

The master of a ship, when he lets her out to freight to the merchants, ought to shew them his cordage, ropes and slings, with which the goods are to be hoisted aboard or ashore; and if they find they need mending, he ought to mend them; for if a pipe, hogshead or other vessel, should happen by default of such cordage or slings to be spoiled or lost, the master and mariners ought to make satisfaction for the same to the merchants. So also if the ropes or slings break, the master not shewing them before hand to the merchants, he is obliged to make good the damage. But if the merchants say the cordage, ropes or slings are good and sufficient, and notwithstanding it happens that they break, in that case they ought to divide the damage between them; that is to say, the merchant to whom such goods belong, and the said master with his mariners.

Article XI

If a vessel being laden at *Bordeaux* with wines, or other goods, hoists sail to carry them to some other port, and the master does not do his duty as he ought, nor the mariners handle their sails, and it happens that ill weather overtakes them at sea; so that the main yard shakes or strikes out the head of one of the pipes or hogsheads of wine; this vessel being safely arrived at her port of discharge, if the merchant alleges, that by reason of the main yard his wine was lost; and the master denies it: In this case the master and his mariners ought to make oath (whether it be four or six of them, such as the merchant hath no exception against) that the wine perished not by the main yard, nor through any default of theirs, as the merchants charge them, they ought then to be acquitted thereof; but if they refuse to make oath to the effect aforesaid, they shall be obliged to make satisfaction for the same, because they ought to have ordered their sails aright before they departed from the port, where they took in their lading.

Article XII

A master, having hired his mariners, ought to keep the peace betwixt them, and to be as their judge at sea; so that if there be any of them that gives another the lie, whilst they have wine and bread on the table, he ought to pay four deniers; and if the master himself give any the lie, he ought to pay eight deniers; and if any of the mariners impudently contradict the master, he also ought to pay eight deniers; and if the master strike any of the mariners, he ought to bear with the first stroke, be it with the fist or open hand; but if the master strikes him more than one blow, the mariner may defend himself: but if the said mariner doth first assault the master, he ought to pay five sols, or lose his hand.

Article XIII

If a difference happens between the master of a ship, and one of his mariners, the master ought to deny him his mess thrice, ere he turn him out of the ship, or discharge him thereof: but if the said mariner offer, in the presence of the rest of the mariners, to make the master satisfaction, and the master be resolved to accept of no satisfaction from him, but to put him out of the ship; in such case the said mariner may follow the said vessel to her port of discharge, and ought to have as good hire or wages, as if he had come in the ship, or as if he had made satisfaction for his fault in the sight and presence of the ship's company; and if the master take not another mariner into the ship in his stead, as able as the other, and the ship or lading happens thereby to be, through any misfortune, damnified, the master shall be obliged to make good the same, if he hath wherewithal.

Article XIV

If a vessel, being moored, lying at anchor, be struck or grappled with another vessel under sail, that is not very well steered, whereby the vessel at anchor is prejudiced, as also wines, or other merchandize in each of the said ships damnified. In this case the whole damage shall be in common, and be equally divided and appraised half by half; and the master and mariners of the vessel that struck or grappled with the other, shall be bound to swear on the Holy Evangelists, that they did it not willingly or wilfully. The reason why this judgment was first given, being, that an old decayed vessel might not purposely be put in the way of a better, which will the rather be prevented when they know that the damage must be divided.

Article XV

Suppose two or more vessels in a harbour, where there is but little water, so that the anchor of one of the vessels lie dry; the master of the other vessel ought, in that case, to say unto him whose anchor lies dry; *Master, take up your anchor, for it is too nigh us, and may do us a prejudice:* if neither the said master nor his mariners will take up the said anchor accordingly, then may that other master and his mariners (who might be otherwise thereby damnified) take up the said anchor, and let it down at a farther distance from them; and if the others oppose or withstand the taking up of their anchor, and there afterwards happens damage thereby, they shall be bound to give full satisfaction for the same: but if they put out a buoy or anchor-mark, and the anchor does any damage, the master and mariners to whom it belongs are not bound to make it good; if they do not, they are; for all masters and mariners ought to fasten such buoys or anchor-marks, and such cables to their anchors, as may plainly appear and be seen at full sea.

Article XVI

When a ship arrives with her lading at *Bordeaux,* or elsewhere, the master is bound to say to his company, when she is ready to load again, *Gentlemen, will you freight your own share yourselves, or be allowed for it in proportion with the ship's general freight?* the mariners are bound to answer one or the other. If they take as the freight of the ship shall happen, they shall have proportionably as the ship hath; and if they will freight by themselves, they ought to freight so as the ship be not impeded or hindered thereby. And if it so happen, that they cannot let out their freight, or get goods themselves, when he has tendered them their share or stowage, the master is blameless; and if they will there lade a tun of water instead of so much wine, they may: and in case there should happen at sea, an ejection or a casting of goods overboard, the case shall be the same for a tun of water, as for a tun of wine, or other goods, livre by livre. If they let out their proportion of freight to merchants, what freedom and immunity the said mariners have, the said merchants shall also have.

Article XVII

The mariners of *Britany* ought to have but one meal a day from the kitchen, because they have beverage going and coming. But those of *Normandy* are to have two meals a day, because they have only water at the ship's allowance; and when the ship arrives in a wine country, there the master shall procure them wine to drink.

Article XVIII

When a vessel is unladen, and the mariners demand their freight, some of them having neither bed, chest, nor trunk aboard, the master may lawfully retain part of their wages, till they have brought back the ship to the port from whence she came; unless they give good security to serve out the whole voyage.

Article XIX

If the master hire the mariners in the town to which the vessel belongs, either for so much a day, week or month, or for such a share of the freight; and it happens that the ship cannot procure freight in those parts where she is arrived, but must sail further to obtain it: in such case, those that were hired for a share of the freight, ought to follow the master, and such as are at wages ought to have their wages advanced course by course, that is, in proportion to the length of the voyage, in what it was longer than they agreed for, because he hired them to one certain place. And if they go not so far as that place for which the contract was made, yet they ought to have the whole promised hire, as if they had gone thither; but they ought likewise to bring back the vessel to the place from whence she at first departed.

Article XX

When a vessel arrives at *Bordeaux,* or any other place, two of the mariners at a time may go ashore, and take with them one meal of such victuals as are in the ship, therein cut and provided; as also bread proportionably as much as they eat at once, but no drink: and they ought very speedily, and in season, to return to their vessel, that thereby the master may not lose his tide; for if so, and damage come thereby, they are bound to make satisfaction; or if any of their company be hurt for want of their help, they are to be at such charge for his recovery, as one of his fellow mariners, or the master, with those of his table shall judge convenient.

Article XXI

If a master freight his ship to a merchant, and set him a certain time within which he shall lade his vessel, that she may be ready to depart at the time appointed, and he lade it not within the time, but keep the master and mariners by the space of eight days, or a fortnight, or more, beyond the time agreed on, whereby the master loses the opportunity of a fair wind to depart; the said merchant in this case shall be obliged to make the master satisfaction for such delay, the fourth part whereof is to go among the mariners, and the other three-fourths to the master, because he finds them their provisions.

Article XXII

When a merchant freights a vessel at his own charge, and sets her to sea, and the said vessel enters into an harbour, where she is wind-bound, so that she stays till her monies be all spent, the master in that case ought speedily to write home to his own country for money; but ought not to lose his voyage on that account; for if so happen, he shall be obliged to make good to the merchant all damages that shall ensue. But the master may take part of the wines or other merchant goods, and dispose thereof for his present necessities; and when the said vessel shall be arrived at her port of discharge, the said wines that the master hath so disposed of, ought to be valued and appraised at the same rate as the other wines shall be commonly sold for, and accordingly be accounted for to the merchant. And the master ought to have the freight of such wines, as he hath so taken and disposed of, for the use and reason aforesaid.

Article XXIII

If a pilot undertakes the conduct of a vessel, to bring her to *St. Malo*, or any other port, and fail of his duty therein, so as the vessel miscarry by reason of his ignorance in what he undertook, and the merchants sustain damage thereby, he shall be obliged to make full satisfaction for the same, if he hath wherewithal; and if not, lose his head.

Article XXIV

And if the master, or any one of his mariners, or any one of the merchants, cut off his head, they shall not be bound to answer for it; but before they do it, they must be sure he had not wherewith to make satisfaction.

Article XXV

If a ship or other vessel arriving at any place, and making in towards a port or harbour, set out her flag, or give any other sign to have a pilot come aboard, or a boat to tow her into the harbour, the wind or tide being contrary, and a contract be made for piloting the said vessel into the said harbour accordingly; but by reason of an unreasonable and accursed custom, in some places, that the third or fourth part of the ships that are lost, shall accrue to the lord of the place where such sad casualties happen, as also the like proportion to the salvors, and only the remainder to the master, merchant and mariners: the persons contracting for the pilotage of the said vessel, to ingratiate themselves with their lords, and to gain to themselves a part of the ship and lading, do like faithless and treacherous villains, sometimes even willingly, and out of design to ruin ship and goods, guide and bring her upon the rocks, and then feigning to aid, help and assist, the now distressed mariners, are the first in dismembering and pulling the ship to pieces; purloining and carrying away the lading thereof contrary to all reason and good conscience: and afterwards that they may be the more welcome to their lord, do with all speed post to his house with the sad narrative of this unhappy disaster; whereupon the said lord, with his retinue appearing at the places, takes his share; the salvors theirs; and what remains the merchant and mariners may have. But seeing this is contrary to the law of God, our edict and determination is, that notwithstanding any law or custom to the contrary, it is said and ordained, the said lord of that place, salvors, and all others that take away any of the said goods, shall be accursed and excommunicated, and punished as robbers and thieves, as formerly hath been declared. But all false and treacherous pilots shall be condemned to suffer a most rigorous and unmerciful death; and high gibbets shall be erected for them in the same place, or as high as conveniently may be, where they so guided and brought any ship or vessel to ruin as aforesaid, and thereon these accursed pilots are with ignominy and much shame to end their days; which said gibbets are to abide and remain to succeeding ages on that place, as a visible caution to other ships that shall afterwards sail thereby.

Article XXVI

If the lord of any place be so barbarous, as not only to permit such inhuman people, but also to maintain and assist them in such villanies, that he may have a share in such wrecks, the said lord shall be apprehended, and all his goods confiscated and sold, in order to make restitution to such as of right it appertaineth; and himself to be fastened to a post or stake in the midst of his own mansion house, which being fired at the four corners, all shall be burnt together, the walls thereof shall be demolished, the stones pulled down, and the place converted into a market place for the sale only of hogs and swine to all posterity.

Article XXVII

A vessel being arrived at her port of discharge, and hauled up there into dry ground, so as the mariners deeming her to be in good safety, do take down her sails, and so fit the vessel aloof and aft, the master then ought to consider an increase of their wages kenning by kenning; and if in hoisting up wines, it happens that they leave open any of the pipes or other vessels, or that they fasten not the ropes well at the ends of the vessel, by reason whereof it slips, and falls, and so is lost, and falling on another, both are lost; in these cases the master and mariners shall be bound to make them good to the merchants, and the merchants must pay the freight of the said damnified or lost wines, because they are to receive for them from the master and mariners, according to the value that the rest of the wines are sold; and the owners of the ship ought not to suffer hereby, because the damage happened by default of the master and mariners, in not making fast the said vessels or pipes of wine.

Article XXVIII

If two vessels go on a fishing-design in partnership, as for mackarel, herrings, or the like, and do set their nets or lay their lines at *Olonne, St. Gilles, Survie,* or elsewhere; the one of the vessels ought to employ as many fishing engines as the other, and so shall go in equal shares, as to the gain, according to the agreement betwixt them made. And if it happens that one of the said vessels, with her fishing-instruments, engines and crew, perish, and the other escaping, arrives in safety; if the surviving friends of those that perished, require of the other to have their part of the gain, as also of their fish, fishing-instruments, and boat, they are to have, upon the oaths of those that escape, their part of the fish, and fishing-instruments; but they shall not have any part or share in the vessel itself.

Article XXIX

If any ship or other vessel sailing to and fro, and coasting the seas, as well in the way of merchandizing, as upon the fishing account, happen by some misfortune through the violence of the weather to strike herself against the rocks, whereby she becomes so bruised and broken, that there she perishes, upon what coasts, country or dominion soever; and the master, mariners, merchant or merchants, or any one of these escape and come safe to land; in this case the lord of that place or country, where such misfortune shall happen, ought not to let, hinder, or oppose such as have so escaped, or such to whom the said ship or vessel, and her lading belong, in using their utmost endeavours for the preservation of as much thereof as may possibly be saved. But on the contrary, the lord of that place or country, by his own interest, and by those under his power and jurisdiction, ought to be aiding and assisting to the said distressed merchants or mariners, in saving their shipwrecked goods, and that without the least embezzlement, or taking any part thereof from the right owners; but, however, there may be a remuneration or consideration for salvage to such as take pains therein, according to right reason, a good conscience, and as justice shall appoint; notwithstanding what promises may in that case have been made to the salvors by such distressed merchants and mariners, as is declared in the fourth article of these laws; and in case any shall act contrary hereunto, or take any part of the said goods from the said poor, distressed, ruined, undone, shipwrecked persons, against their wills, and without their consent, they shall be declared to be excommunicated by the church, and ought to receive the punishment of thieves; except speedy restitution be made by them: nor is there any custom or statute whatsoever, that can protect them against the aforesaid penalties, as is said in the 26th article of these laws.

Article XXX

If a ship or other vessel entering into harbour, happens by misfortune to be broken and perish, and the master, mariners and merchants, which were on board her, be all drowned; and if the goods thereof be driven ashore, or remain floating on the sea, without being sought after by those to whom they belong, they being ignorant of this said disaster, and knowing nothing thereof; in this most lamentable case, the lord of that place or country ought to send persons to save the said goods, which he ought to secure and to put into safe custody; and give the relations of the deceased persons who were drowned, notice of it, and to satisfy for the salvage thereof, not out of his own purse, but of the goods saved, according to the hazards run, and the pains taken therein; and what remains must be kept in safe custody for one year or more; and if in that time they to whom the said goods appertain, do not appear and claim the same, and the said year be fully expired, he may publicly sell and dispose thereof to such as will give most, and with the monies proceeding of the sale thereof, he ought to give among the poor, and for portions to poor maids, and other charitable uses, according to reason and good conscience. But if he assumes the said goods either in whole or in part unto himself, he shall incur the curse and malediction of our mother the holy church, with the aforesaid pains and penalties, without ever obtaining remission, unless he make satisfaction.

Article XXXI

If a ship or other vessel happens to be lost by striking on some shore, and the mariners thinking to save their lives, reach the shore, in hope of help, and instead thereof it happens, as it often does, that in many places they meet with people more barbarous, cruel, and inhuman than mad dogs, who to gain their monies, apparel, and other goods, do sometimes murder and destroy these poor distressed seamen; in this case, the lord of that country ought to execute justice on such wretches, to punish them as well corporally as pecuniarily, to plunge them in the sea till they be half dead, and then to have them drawn forth out of the sea, and stoned to death.

Article XXXII

If by reason of tempestuous weather, it be thought expedient, for the lightening of any ship or vessel at sea, or riding at anchor in any road, to cast part of the lading overboard, and it be done accordingly for the common safety, though the said goods so ejected, and cast overboard, do become his that can first possess himself thereof, and carry them away: nevertheless, it is here to be further understood, that this holds true only in such cases, as when the master, merchant, and mariners have so ejected or cast out the said goods, as that they give over all hope or desire of ever recovering them again, and so leave them as things utterly lost and given over by them, without ever making any enquiry or pursuit after them: in which case only the first occupant becomes the lawful proprietor thereof.

Article XXXIII

If a ship, or any other vessel, hath cast overboard several goods or merchandizes, which are in chests well locked and made fast; or books well clasped and shut close, that they may not be damnified by salt water; in such cases it is to be presumed, that they who did cast such goods overboard, do still retain an intention, hope, and desire of recovering the same: for which reason, such as shall happen to find such things, are obliged to make restitution thereof to him who shall make a due enquiry after them; or put them to pious uses, according to his conscience and the advice of some prudent neighbour.

Article XXXIV

If any man happens to find any thing in the sea, or in the sand on the shore, in floods or in rivers, if it be precious stones, fishes, or any treasure of the sea, which never belonged to any man in point of property, it belongs to the first finder.

Article XXXV

If any searches the sea-coasts to fish, or find gold or silver, and he finds it, he ought to restore it all without any diminution.

Article XXXVI

If any going along the sea-shore to fish, or otherwise, happens to find gold or silver, he shall be bound to make restitution thereof, deducting for his own pains; or if he be poor he may keep it to himself; that is, if he knows not to whom to restore it; yet he shall give notice of the place where he found it, to the neighbourhood and parts next adjacent, and advise with his superiors, who ought to weigh and take into consideration the property of the finder, and then to give him such advice as is consonant to good conscience.

Article XXXVII

Touching great fishes that are taken or found dead on the sea shore, regard must be had to the custom of that country where such great fishes are taken or found. For by the custom, the lord of that country ought to have his share, and with good reason, since the subject owes obedience and tribute to his sovereign.

Article XXXVIII

The lord ought to have his share of oil fish, and of no other, according to the laudable custom of the country where they are found; and he that finds them is no farther obliged than to save them, by bringing them without the reach of the sea, and presently to make it known to the said lord of the place, that he may come and demand what is his right.

Article XXXIX

If the lord of the place pleases, and if it be the custom of the country where the fish is found, he may cause the same to be brought by him that found it, to the public and open market place, but no where else; and there the said fish shall be appraised by the said lord, or his deputy according to custom. And the price being set, the other party that made not the price, shall have his choice, either to take or leave it at that price; and if either of them, whether *per fas* or *nefas* be an occasion of loss or damage to the other, though but to the value of a denier, he shall be obliged to make him restitution.

Article XL

If the costs and charges of carrying the said fish to the said market place would amount to a greater sum than the fish itself may be worth, then the said lord shall be bound to take his share at the place where such fish was found.

Article XLI

The said lord ought likewise to pay his part of the aforesaid costs and charges, because he ought not by another's damage to enrich himself.

Article XLII

If by some chance or misfortune the said fish happens to be stolen away, or otherwise lost from the place where it was found, after or before the said lord has visited it; in this case he that first found it shall not any ways be obliged to make it good, *Casus fortuiti in quibus est agressura latronum anemine praestantur l. quae fortuitis. C. pignoratitia actione.*

Article XLIII

In all other things found by the sea side, which have formerly been in the possession of some one or other, as wines, oil, and other merchandize, although they have been cast overboard, and left by the merchants, and so ought to appertain to him that first finds the same; yet herein also the custom of the country is to be observed as well as in the case of fish. But if there be a presumption that these were the goods of some ship that perished, then neither the said lord, nor finder thereof, shall take any, to convert any part of it to their own use; but as has been said, distribute the money it produces amongst the poor and needy.

Article XLIV

If any ship or other vessel at sea, happens to find an oil fish, it shall be wholly theirs that found it, in case no due pursuit be made after it; and no lord of any place ought to demand any part thereof though they bring it to his ground.

Article XLV

If a vessel by stress of weather be constrained to cut her cables or ropes by the end, and so to quit and leave behind her both cables and anchors and put to sea at the mercy of the wind and weather; in this case the said cables and anchors ought not to be lost to the said vessel, if there were any buoy at them; and such as fish for them, shall be bound to restore them, if they know to whom they belong; but they ought to be paid for their pains, according to justice. And if they know not to whom to restore them, the lords of the place shall have their shares, as well as the salvors; but for preventing further inconveniences, every master of a ship shall cause to be engraven, or set upon the buoys thereof, his own name, or the name of his ship, or of the port or haven to which she belongs: and such as detain them from him shall be reputed thieves and robbers.

Article XLVI

If any ship, or other vessel, by any casualty or misfortune happens to be wrecked and perish, in that case, the pieces of the hulk of the vessel, as well as the lading thereof, ought to be reserved and kept in safety for them to whom it belonged before such disaster happened, notwithstanding any custom to the contrary. And all takers, partakers, or consenters of, or to the said wreck, if they be bishops, prelates or clerks, they shall be deposed and deprived of their benefices respectively; and if they be laymen they shall incur the penalties aforesaid. *De his autem quos diripuisse probatum sit, praesides ut de latronibus, gravem sententiam dicere convenit. l. ne quid. l. quo Naufrag. D. Incendio, ruina, & naufragio. l. navigia, C. furtis.* The penalties aforesaid are in the 25th, 26th and 29th articles.

Article XLVII

This is to be understood only when the said ship or vessel so wrecked, did not exercise the trade of pillaging, and when the mariners thereof were not pirates, sea-rovers, or enemies to our holy *Catholic* faith; but if they are found to be either the one or the other, every man may then deal with such as with rogues, and despoil them of their goods without any punishment for so doing.

V. SELECTED FEDERAL RULES OF CIVIL PROCEDURE

(With the Advisory Committee Notes for those rules amended in connection with the merger of the civil and admiralty rules in 1966.)

Rule 1. Scope of Rules

These rules govern the procedure in all civil actions and proceedings in the United States district courts, except as stated in Rule 81. They should be construed and administered to secure the just, speedy, and inexpensive determination of every action and proceeding.

Rule 2. One Form of Action

There is one form of action—the civil action.

Rule 4. Process

* * *

(k) Territorial Limits of Effective Service.

(1) *In general.* Serving a summons or filing a waiver of service establishes personal jurisdiction over a defendant:

(A) who is subject to the jurisdiction of a court of general jurisdiction in the state where the district court is located;

(B) who is a party joined under Rule 14 or Rule 19 and is served within a judicial district of the United States and not more than 100 miles from where the summons was issued; or

(C) when authorized by a federal statute.

(2) *Federal claims outside state-court jurisdiction.* For a claim that arises under federal law, serving a summons or filing a waiver of service establishes personal jurisdiction over a defendant if:

(A) the defendant is not subject to jurisdiction in any state's courts of general jurisdiction; and

(B) exercising jurisdiction is consistent with the United States Constitution and laws.

Rule 9. Pleading Special Matters

* * *

(h) Admiralty or Maritime Claim.

(1) *How Designated.* If a claim for relief is within the admiralty or maritime jurisdiction and also within the court's subject-matter jurisdiction on some other ground, the pleading may designate the claim as an admiralty or maritime claim for purposes of Rules 14(c), 38(e), and 82 and the Supplemental Rules for Admiralty or Maritime Claims and Asset Forfeiture Actions. A claim cognizable only in the admiralty or maritime jurisdiction is an admiralty or maritime claim for those purposes, whether or not so designated.

(2) *Designation for Appeal.* A case that includes an admiralty or maritime claim within this subdivision (h) is an admiralty case within 28 U.S.C. § 1292(a)(3).

1966 Advisory Committee Note

Certain distinctive features of the admiralty practice must be preserved for what are now suits in admiralty. This raises the question: After unification, when a single form of action is established, how will the counterpart of the present suit in admiralty be identifiable? In part the question is easily answered. Some claims for relief can only be suits in admiralty, either because the admiralty jurisdiction is exclusive or because no nonmaritime ground of federal jurisdiction exists. Many claims, however, are cognizable by the district courts whether asserted in admiralty or in a civil action, assuming the existence of a nonmaritime ground of jurisdiction. Thus at present the pleader has power to determine procedural consequences by the way in which he exercises the classic privilege given by the saving-to-suitors clause (28 U.S.C. § 1333) or by equivalent statutory provisions. For example, a longshoreman's claim for personal injuries suffered by reason of the unseaworthiness of a vessel may be asserted in a suit in admiralty or, if diversity of citizenship exists, in a civil action. One of the important procedural consequences is that in the civil action either party may demand a jury trial, while in the suit in admiralty there is no right to jury trial except as provided by statute.

It is no part of the purpose of unification to inject a right to jury trial into those admiralty cases in which that right is not provided by statute. Similarly, as will be more specifically noted below, there is no disposition to change the present law as to interlocutory appeals in admiralty, or as to the venue of suits in admiralty; and, of course, there is no disposition to inject into the civil practice as it now is the distinctively maritime remedies (maritime attachment and garnishment, actions in rem, possessory, petitory, and partition actions and limitation of liability). The unified rules must therefore provide some device for preserving the present power of the pleader to determine whether these historically maritime procedures shall be applicable to his claim or not; the pleader must be afforded some means of designating his claim as the counterpart of the present suit in admiralty, where its character as such is not clear.

The problem is different from the similar one concerning the identification of claims that were formerly suits in equity. While that problem is not free from complexities, it is broadly true that the modern counterpart of the suit in equity is distinguishable from the former action at law by the character of the relief sought. This mode of identification is possible in only a limited category of admiralty cases. In large numbers of cases the relief sought in admiralty is simple money damages, indistinguishable from the remedy afforded by the common law. This is true, for example, in the case of the longshoreman's action for personal injuries stated above. After unification has abolished the distinction between civil actions and suits in admiralty, the complaint in such an action would be almost completely ambiguous as to the pleader's intentions regarding the procedure invoked. The allegation of diversity of citizenship might be regarded as a clue indicating an intention to proceed as at present under the saving-to-suitors clause; but this, too, would be ambiguous if there were also reference to the admiralty jurisdiction, and the pleader ought not to be required to forego mention of all available jurisdictional grounds.

Other methods of solving the problem were carefully explored, but the Advisory Committee concluded that the preferable solution is to allow the pleader who now has power to determine procedural consequences by filing a suit in admiralty to exercise that power under unification, for the limited instances in which procedural differences will remain, by a simple statement in his pleading to the effect that the claim is an admiralty or maritime claim.

The choice made by the pleader in identifying or in failing to identify his claim as an admiralty or maritime claim is not an irrevocable election. The rule provides that the amendment of a pleading to add or withdraw an identifying statement is subject to the principles of Rule 15.

1997 ADVISORY COMMITTEE NOTE

Section 1292(a)(3) of the Judicial Code provides for appeal from "[i]nterlocutory decrees of * * * district courts * * * determining the rights and liabilities of the parties to admiralty cases in which appeals from final decrees are allowed."

Rule 9(h) was added in 1966 with the unification of civil and admiralty procedure. Civil Rule 73(h) was amended at the same time to provide that the § 1292(a)(3) reference "to admiralty cases shall be construed to mean admiralty and maritime claims within the meaning of Rule 9(h)." This provision was transferred to Rule 9(h) when the Appellate Rules were adopted.

A single case can include both admiralty or maritime claims and nonadmiralty claims or parties. This combination reveals an ambiguity in the statement in present Rule 9(h) that an admiralty "claim" is an admiralty "case." An order "determining the rights and liabilities of the parties" within the meaning of § 1292(a)(3) may resolve only a nonadmiralty claim, or may simultaneously resolve interdependent admiralty and nonadmiralty claims. Can appeal be taken as to the nonadmiralty matter, because it is part of a case that includes an admiralty claim, or is appeal limited to the admiralty claim?

The courts of appeals have not achieved full uniformity in applying the § 1292(a)(3) requirement that an order "determin[e] the rights and liabilities of the parties." It is common to assert that the statute should be construed narrowly, under the general policy that exceptions to the final judgment rule should be construed narrowly. This policy would suggest that the ambiguity should be resolved by limiting the interlocutory appeal right to orders that determine the rights and liabilities of the parties to an admiralty claim.

A broader view is chosen by this amendment for two reasons. The statute applies to admiralty "cases," and may itself provide for appeal from an order that disposes of a nonadmiralty claim that is joined in a single case with an admiralty claim. Although a rule of court may help to clarify and implement a statutory grant of jurisdiction, the line is not always clear between permissible implementation and impermissible withdrawal of jurisdiction. In addition, so long as an order truly disposes of the rights and liabilities of the parties within the meaning of § 1292(a)(3), it may prove important to permit appeal as to the nonadmiralty claim. Disposition of the nonadmiralty claim, for example, may make it unnecessary to consider the admiralty claim and have the same effect on the case and parties as disposition of the admiralty claim. Or the admiralty and nonadmiralty claims may be interdependent. An illustration is provided by Roco Carriers, Ltd. v. M/V Nurnberg Express, 899 F.2d 1292 (2d Cir.1990). Claims for losses of ocean shipments were made against two defendants, one subject to admiralty jurisdiction and the other not. Summary judgment was granted in favor of the admiralty defendant and against the nonadmiralty defendant. The nonadmiralty defendant's appeal was accepted, with the explanation that the determination of its liability was "integrally linked with the determination of non-liability" of the admiralty defendant, and that "section 1292(a)(3) is not limited to admiralty claims; instead, it refers to admiralty cases." 899 F.2d at 1297. The advantages of permitting appeal by the nonadmiralty defendant would be particularly clear if the plaintiff had appealed the summary judgment in favor of the admiralty defendant.

It must be emphasized that this amendment does not rest on any particular assumptions as to the meaning of the § 1292(a)(3) provision that limits interlocutory appeal to orders that determine the rights and liabilities of the parties. It simply reflects the conclusion that so long as the case involves an admiralty claim and an order otherwise meets statutory requirements, the opportunity to appeal should not turn on the circumstance that the order does—or does not—dispose of an admiralty claim. No attempt is made to invoke the authority conferred by 28 U.S.C. § 1292(e) to provide by rule for appeal of an interlocutory decision that is not otherwise provided for by other subsections of § 1292.

Rule 14.   Third-Party Practice

* * *

(c) Admiralty or Maritime Claim.

(1) *Scope of Impleader*. If a plaintiff asserts an admiralty or maritime claim under Rule 9(h), the defendant or a person who asserts a right under Supplemental Rule C(6)(a)(i) may, as a third-party plaintiff, bring in a third-party defendant who may be wholly

or partly liable—either to the plaintiff or to the third-party plaintiff—for remedy over, contribution, or otherwise on account of the same transaction, occurrence, or series of transactions or occurrences.

(2) *Defending Against a Demand for Judgment for the Plaintiff.* The third-party plaintiff may demand judgment in the plaintiff's favor against the third-party defendant. In that event, the third-party defendant must defend under Rule 12 against the plaintiff's claim as well as the third-party plaintiff's claim; and the action proceeds as if the plaintiff had sued both the third-party defendant and the third-party plaintiff.

1966 ADVISORY COMMITTEE NOTE

Rule 14 was modeled on Admiralty Rule 56. An important feature of Admiralty Rule 56 was that it allowed impleader not only of a person who might be liable to the defendant by way of remedy over, but also of any person who might be liable to the plaintiff. The importance of this provision was that the defendant was entitled to insist that the plaintiff proceed to judgment against the third-party defendant. In certain cases this was a valuable implementation of a substantive right. For example, in a case of ship collision where a finding of mutual fault is possible, one shipowner, if sued alone, faces the prospect of an absolute judgment for the full amount of the damage suffered by an innocent third party; but if he can implead the owner of the other vessel, and if mutual fault is found, the judgment against the original defendant will be in the first instance only for a moiety of the damages; liability for the remainder will be conditioned on the plaintiff's inability to collect from the third-party defendant.

This feature was originally incorporated in Rule 14, but was eliminated by the amendment of 1946, so that under the amended rule a third party could not be impleaded on the basis that he might be liable to the plaintiff. One of the reasons for the amendment was that the Civil Rule, unlike the Admiralty Rule, did not require the plaintiff to go to judgment against the third-party defendant. Another reason was that where jurisdiction depended on diversity of citizenship the impleader of an adversary having the same citizenship as the plaintiff was not considered possible.

Retention of the admiralty practice in those cases that will be counterparts of a suit in admiralty is clearly desirable.

Rule 18.   Joinder of Claims and Remedies

(a) In General. A party asserting a claim, counterclaim, crossclaim, or third-party claim may join, as independent or alternative claims, as many claims as it has against an opposing party.

(b) Joinder of Contingent Claims. A party may join two claims even though one of them is contingent on the disposition of the other; but the court may grant relief only in accordance with the parties' relative substantive rights. In particular, a plaintiff may state a claim for money and a claim to set aside a conveyance that is fraudulent as to that plaintiff, without first obtaining a judgment for the money.

Rule 20.   Permissive Joinder of Parties

(a) Persons Who May Join or Be Joined.

(1) *Plaintiffs.* Persons may join in one action as plaintiffs if:

(A) they assert any right to relief jointly, severally, or in the alternative with respect to or arising out of the same transaction, occurrence, or series of transactions or occurrences; and

(B) any question of law or fact common to all plaintiffs will arise in the action.

(2) *Defendants.* Persons—as well as a vessel, cargo, or other property subject to admiralty process in rem—may be joined in one action as defendants if:

(A) any right to relief is asserted against them jointly, severally, or in the alternative with respect to or arising out of the same transaction, occurrence, or series of transactions or occurrences; and

(B) any question of law or fact common to all defendants will arise in the action.

(3) *Extent of Relief.* Neither a plaintiff nor a defendant need be interested in obtaining or defending against all the relief demanded. The court may grant judgment to one or more plaintiffs according to their rights, and against one or more defendants according to their liabilities.

(b) Protective Measures. The court may issue orders—including an order for separate trials—to protect a party against embarrassment, delay, expense, or other prejudice that arises from including a person against whom the party asserts no claim and who asserts no claim against the party.

Rule 38.   Right to a Jury Trial; Demand

(a) Right Preserved. The right of trial by jury as declared by the Seventh Amendment to the Constitution—or as provided by a federal statute—is preserved to the parties inviolate.

(b) Demand. On any issue triable of right by a jury, a party may demand a jury trial by:

(1) serving the other parties with a written demand—which may be included in a pleading—no later than 14 days after the last pleading directed to the issue is served; and

(2) filing the demand in accordance with Rule 5(d).

(c) Specific Issues. In its demand a party may specify the issues that it wishes to have tried by a jury; otherwise, it is considered to have demanded a jury trial on all the issues so triable. If the party has demanded a jury trial on only some issues, any other party may—within 14 days after being served with the demand or within a shorter time ordered by the court—serve a demand for a jury trial on any other or all factual issues triable by jury.

(d) Waiver; Withdrawal. A party waives a jury trial unless its demand is properly served and filed. A proper demand may be withdrawn only if the parties consent.

(e) Admiralty and Maritime Claims. These rules do not create a right to a jury trial on issues in a claim that is an admiralty or maritime claim under Rule 9(h).

Rule 39. Trial by Jury or by the Court

(a) When a Demand Is Made. When jury trial has been demanded under Rule 38, the action must be designated on the docket as a jury action. The trial on all issues so demanded must be by jury unless:

(1) the parties or their attorneys file a stipulation to a nonjury trial or so stipulate on the record; or

(2) the court, on motion or on its own, finds that on some or all of those issues there is no federal right to a jury trial.

(b) When No Demand Is Made. Issues on which a jury trial is not properly demanded are to be tried by the court. But the court may, on motion, order a jury trial on any issue for which a jury might have been demanded.

(c) Advisory Jury; Jury Trial by Consent. In an action not triable of right by a jury, the court, on motion or on its own:

(1) may try any issue with an advisory jury; or

(2) may, with the parties' consent, try any issue by a jury whose verdict has the same effect as if a jury trial had been a matter of right, unless the action is against the United States and a federal statute provides for a nonjury trial.

VI. SUPPLEMENTAL RULES FOR CERTAIN ADMIRALTY AND MARITIME CLAIMS AND ASSET FORFEITURE ACTION

Adopted February 28, 1966, effective July 1, 1966

(The former Rules of Practice in Admiralty and Maritime Cases, promulgated by the Supreme Court on December 6, 1920, effective March 7, 1921, as revised, amended and supplemented, were rescinded, effective July 1, 1966. The text includes amendments effective through December 1, 2009.)

(WITH THE ADVISORY COMMITTEE NOTES)

Rule A. Scope of Rules

(1) These Supplementary Rules apply to:

(A) the procedure in admiralty and maritime claims within the meaning of Rule 9(h) with respect to the following remedies:

    (i) maritime attachments and garnishments,

    (ii) actions in rem,

    (iii) possessory, petitory, and partition actions, and

    (iv) actions for exoneration from or limitation of liability;

(B) forfeiture actions in rem arising from a federal statute; and

(C) procedure in statutory condemnation proceedings analogous to maritime actions in rem, whether within the admiralty and maritime jurisdiction or not. Except as otherwise provided, references in these Supplemental Rules to actions in rem include such analogous statutory condemnation proceedings.

(2) The Federal Rules of Civil Procedure apply also to the foregoing proceedings except to the extent that they are inconsistent with these Supplemental Rules.

ADVISORY COMMITTEE NOTES

1966 ADOPTION

Certain distinctively maritime remedies must be preserved in unified rules. The commencement of an action by attachment or garnishment has heretofore been practically unknown in federal jurisprudence except in admiralty, although the amendment of Rule 4(e) effective July 1, 1963, makes available that procedure in accordance with state law. The maritime proceeding in rem is unique, except as it has been emulated by statute, and is closely related to the substantive maritime law relating to liens. Arrest of the vessel or other maritime property is an historic remedy in controversies over title or right to possession, and in disputes among co-owners over the vessel's employment. The statutory right to limit liability is limited to owners of vessels, and has its own complexities. While the unified federal rules are generally applicable to these distinctive proceedings, certain special rules dealing with them are needed.

Arrest of the person and imprisonment for debt are not included because these remedies are not peculiarly maritime. The practice is not uniform but conforms to state law. See 2 Benedict § 286; 28 U.S.C.A. § 2007; FRCP 64, 69. The relevant provisions of Admiralty Rules 2, 3, and 4 are unnecessary or obsolete.

No attempt is here made to compile a complete and self-contained code governing these distinctively maritime remedies. The more limited objective is to carry forward the relevant provisions of the former Rules of Practice for Admiralty and Maritime Cases, modernized and revised to some extent but still in the context of history and precedent. Accordingly, these Rules are not to be construed as limiting or impairing the traditional power of a district court, exercising the admiralty and maritime jurisdiction, to adapt its procedures and its remedies in the individual case, consistently with these rules, to secure the just, speedy, and inexpensive determination of every action. (See Swift & Co. Packers v. Compania Colombiana Del Caribe, S.A., 339 U.S. 684 (1950); Rule 1). In addition, of course, the district courts retain the power to make local rules not inconsistent with these rules. See Rule 83; cf. Admiralty Rule 44.

Rule B. In Personam Actions: Attachment and Garnishment

(1) When Available; Complaint, Affidavit, Judicial Authorization and Process. In an in personam action:

(a) If a defendant is not found within the district when a verified complaint praying for attachment and the affidavit required by Rule B(1)(b) are filed, a verified complaint may contain a prayer for process to attach the defendant's tangible or intangible property—up to the amount sued for—in the hands of garnishees named in the process.

(b) The plaintiff or the plaintiff's attorney must sign and file with the complaint an affidavit stating that, to the affiant's knowledge, or on information and belief, the defendant cannot be found within the district. The court must review the complaint and affidavit and, if the conditions of this Rule B appear to exist, enter an order so stating and authorizing process of attachment and garnishment. The clerk may issue supplemental process enforcing the court's order upon application without further court order.

(c) If the plaintiff or the plaintiff's attorney certifies that exigent circumstances make court review impracticable, the clerk must issue the summons and process of attachment and garnishment. The plaintiff has the burden in any post-attachment hearing under Rule E(4)(f) to show that exigent circumstances existed.

(d)(i)   If the property is a vessel or tangible property on board a vessel, the summons, process, and any supplemental process must be delivered to the marshal for service.

(ii) If the property is other tangible or intangible property, the summons, process, and other supplemental process must be delivered to a person or organization authorized to serve it, who may be (A) a marshal; (B) someone under contract with the United States; (C) someone specially appointed by the court for that purpose; or, (D) in an action brought by the United States, any officer or employee of the United States.

(e)   The plaintiff may invoke state-law remedies under Rule 64 for seizure of person or property for the purpose of securing satisfaction of the judgment.

(2) Notice to Defendant. No default judgment may be entered except upon proof—which may be by affidavit—that:

(a) the complaint, summons, and process of attachment or garnishment have been served on the defendant in a manner authorized by Rule 4;

(b) the plaintiff or the garnishee has mailed to the defendant the complaint, summons, and process of attachment or garnishment, using any form of mail requiring a return receipt; or

(c) the plaintiff or the garnishee has tried diligently to give notice of the action to the defendant but could not do so.

(3) Answer.

(a) By Garnishee. The garnishee shall serve an answer, together with answers to any interrogatories served with the complaint, within 21 days after service of process upon the garnishee. Interrogatories to the garnishee may be served with the complaint without leave of court. If the garnishee refuses or neglects to answer on oath as to the debts, credits, or effects of the defendant in the garnishee's hands, or any interrogatories concerning such debts, credits, and effects that may be propounded by the plaintiff, the court may award compulsory process against the garnishee. If the garnishee admits any debts, credits, or effects, they shall be held in the garnishee's hands or paid into the registry of the court, and shall be held in either case subject to the further order of the court.

(b) By Defendant. The defendant shall serve an answer within 30 days after process has been executed, whether by attachment of property or service on the garnishee.

ADVISORY COMMITTEE NOTES
1966 Adoption

Subdivision (1)

This preserves the traditional maritime remedy of attachment and garnishment, and carries forward the relevant substance of Admiralty Rule 2. In addition, or in the alternative, provision is made for the use of similar state remedies made available by the amendment of Rule 4(e) effective July 1, 1963. On the effect of appearance to defend against attachment see Rule E(8).

The rule follows closely the language of Admiralty Rule 2. No change is made with respect to the property subject to attachment. No change is made in the condition that makes the remedy available. The rules have never defined the clause, "if the defendant shall not be found within the district," and no definition is attempted here. The subject seems one best left for the time being to development on a case-by-case basis. The proposal does shift from the marshal (on whom it now rests in theory) to the plaintiff the burden of establishing that the defendant cannot be found in the district.

A change in the context of the practice is brought about by Rule 4(f), which will enable summons to be served throughout the state instead of, as heretofore, only within the district. The Advisory Committee considered whether the rule on attachment and garnishment should be correspondingly changed to permit those remedies only when the defendant cannot be found within the state and concluded that the remedy should not be so limited.

The effect is to enlarge the class of cases in which the plaintiff may proceed by attachment or garnishment although jurisdiction of the person of the defendant may be independently obtained. This is possible at the present time where, for example, a corporate defendant has appointed an agent within the district to accept service of process but is not carrying on activities there sufficient to subject it to jurisdiction. (Seawind Compania, S.A. v. Crescent Line, Inc., 320 F.2d 580 (2d Cir.1963)), or where, though the foreign corporation's activities in the district are sufficient to subject it personally to the jurisdiction, there is in the district no officer on whom process can be served (United States v. Cia. Naviera Continental, S.A., 178 F.Supp. 561 (S.D.N.Y.1959)).

Process of attachment or garnishment will be limited to the district. See Rule E(3)(a).

Subdivision (2)

The former Admiralty Rules did not provide for notice to the defendant in attachment and garnishment proceedings. None is required by the principles of due process, since it is assumed that the garnishee or custodian of the property attached will either notify the defendant or be deprived of the right to plead the judgment as a defense in an action against him by the defendant. Harris v. Balk, 198 U.S. 215 (1905); Pennoyer v. Neff, 95 U.S. 714 (1877). Modern conceptions of fairness, however, dictate that actual notice be given to persons known to claim an interest in the property that is the subject of the action where that is reasonably practicable. In attachment and garnishment proceedings the persons whose interests will be affected by the judgment are identified by the complaint. No substantial burden is imposed on the plaintiff by a simple requirement that he notify the defendant of the action by mail.

In the usual case the defendant is notified of the pendency of the proceedings by the garnishee or otherwise, and appears to claim the property and to make his answer. Hence notice by mail is not routinely required in all cases, but only in those in which the defendant has not appeared prior to the time when a default judgment is demanded. The rule therefore provides only that no default judgment shall be entered except upon proof of notice, or of inability to give notice despite diligent efforts to do so. Thus the burden of giving notice is further minimized.

In some cases the plaintiff may prefer to give notice by serving process in the usual way instead of simply by mail. (Rule 4(d).) In particular, if the defendant is in a foreign country the plaintiff may wish to utilize the modes of notice recently provided to facilitate compliance with foreign laws and procedure (Rule 4(i)). The rule provides for these alternatives.

The rule does not provide for notice by publication because there is no problem concerning unknown claimants, and publication has little utility in proportion to its expense where the identity of the defendant is known.

Subdivision (3)

Subdivision (a) incorporates the substance of Admiralty Rule 36.

The Admiralty Rules were silent as to when the garnishee and the defendant were to answer. See also 2 Benedict ch. XXIV.

The rule proceeds on the assumption that uniform and definite periods of time for responsive pleadings should be substituted for return days (see the discussion under Rule C(6), below). Twenty days seem sufficient time for the garnishee to answer (cf. FRCP 12(a)), and an additional 10 days should suffice for the defendant. When allowance is made for the time required for notice to reach the defendant this gives the defendant in attachment and garnishment approximately the same time that defendants have to answer when personally served.

1985 AMENDMENT

Since their promulgation in 1966, the Supplemental Rules for Certain Admiralty and Maritime Claims have preserved the special procedures of arrest and attachment unique to admiralty law. In recent years, however, these Rules have been challenged as violating the principles of procedural due process enunciated in the United States

Supreme Court's decision in Sniadach v. Family Finance Corp., 395 U.S. 337 (1969), and later developed in Fuentes v. Shevin, 407 U.S. 67 (1972), Mitchell v. W.T. Grant Co., 416 U.S. 600 (1974), and North Georgia Finishing, Inc. v. Di-Chem, Inc., 419 U.S. 601 (1975). These Supreme Court decisions provide five basic criteria for a constitutional seizure of property: (1) effective notice to persons having interests in the property seized, (2) judicial review prior to attachment, (3) avoidance of conclusory allegations in the complaint, (4) security posted by the plaintiff to protect the owner of the property under attachment, and (5) a meaningful and timely hearing after attachment.

Several commentators have found the Supplemental Rules lacking on some or all five grounds, E.g., Batiza & Partridge, The Constitutional Challenge to Maritime Seizures, 26 Loyola L.Rev. 203 (1980); Morse, The Conflict Between the Supreme Court Admiralty Rules and Sniadach-Fuentes: A Collision Course?, 3 Fla.St.L.Rev. 1 (1975). The federal courts have varied in their disposition of challenges to the Supplemental Rules. The Fourth and Fifth Circuits have both affirmed the constitutionality of Rule C. Amstar Corp. v. S/S Alexandros T., 664 F.2d 904 (4th Cir.1981); Merchants National Bank v. The Dredge General G.L. Gillespie, 663 F.2d 1338 (5th Cir.1981), cert. dismissed, 456 U.S. 966 (1982). However, a district court in the Ninth Circuit found Rule C unconstitutional. Alyeska Pipeline Service Co. v. The Vessel Bay Ridge, 509 F.Supp. 1115 (D.Alaska 1981), appeal dismissed, 703 F.2d 381 (9th Cir.1983). Rule B has received similar inconsistent treatment in the district courts. Two district courts have found Rule B constitutionally deficient. Schiffahartsgesellschaft Leonhardt & Co. v. A. Bottacchi S.A. De Navegacion, 552 F.Supp. 771 (S.D.Ga.1982); Grand Bahama Petroleum Co. v. Canadian Transportation Agencies, Ltd., 450 F.Supp. 447 (W.D.Wash.1978). The constitutionality of both rules was questioned in Techem Chemical Co. v. M/T Choyo Maru, 416 F.Supp. 960 (D.Md.1976). Thus, there is uncertainty as to whether the current rules prescribe constitutionally sound procedures for guidance of courts and counsel. See generally Note, Due Process in Admiralty Arrest and Attachment, 56 Texas L.Rev. 1091 (1978).

Due to the controversy and uncertainty that have surrounded the Supplemental Rules, local admiralty bars and the Maritime Law Association of the United States have sought to strengthen the constitutionality of maritime arrest and attachment by encouraging promulgation of local admiralty rules providing for prompt post-seizure hearings. Some districts also adopted rules calling for judicial scrutiny of applications for arrest or attachment. Nonetheless, the result has been a lack of uniformity and continued concern over the constitutionality of the existing practice. The amendments that follow are intended to provide rules that meet the requirements prescribed by the Supreme Court and to develop uniformity in the admiralty practice.

1985 AMENDMENT

Rule B(1) has been amended to provide for judicial scrutiny before the issuance of any attachment or garnishment process. Its purpose is to eliminate doubts as to whether the rule is consistent with the principles of procedural due process enunciated by the Supreme Court in Sniadach v. Family Finance Corp., 395 U.S. 337 (1969), and later developed in Fuentes v. Shevin, 407 U.S. 67 (1972), Mitchell v. W.T. Grant Co., 416 U.S. 600 (1974), and North Georgia Finishing, Inc. v. Di-Chem, Inc., 419 U.S. 601 (1975). Such doubts were raised in Grand Bahama Petroleum Co. v. Canadian Transportation Agencies, Ltd., 450 F.Supp. 447 (W.D.Wash.1978), and Schiffahartsgesellschaft Leonhardt & Co. v. A. Bottacchi S.A. De Navegacion, 552 F.Supp. 771 (S.D.Ga.1982). But compare Polar Shipping Ltd. v. Oriental Shipping Corp., 680 F.2d 627 (9th Cir.1982), in which a majority of the panel upheld the constitutionality of Rule B because of the unique commercial context in which it is invoked. The practice described in Rule B(1) has been adopted in some districts by local rule. E.g., N.D.Calif.Local Rule 603–3; W.D.Wash. Local Admiralty Rule 115(d).

The rule envisions that the order will issue when the plaintiff makes a prima facie showing that he has a maritime claim against the defendant in the amount sued for and the defendant is not present in the district. A simple order with conclusory findings is contemplated. The reference to review by the "court" is broad enough to embrace review by a magistrate as well as by a district judge.

The new provision recognizes that in some situations, such as when the judge is unavailable and the ship is about to depart from the jurisdiction, it will be impracticable, if not impossible, to secure the judicial review contemplated by Rule B(1). When "exigent circumstances" exist, the rule enables the plaintiff to secure the issuance of the summons and process of attachment and garnishment, subject to a later showing that the necessary circumstances actually existed. This provision is intended to provide a safety value without undermining the requirement of preattachment scrutiny. Thus, every effort to secure judicial review, including conducting a hearing by telephone, should be pursued before resorting to the exigent circumstances procedure.

2000 AMENDMENT

Rule B(1) is amended in two ways, and style changes have been made.

The service provisions of Rule C(3) are adopted in paragraph (d), providing alternatives to service by a marshal if the property to be seized is not a vessel or tangible property on board a vessel.

The provision that allows the plaintiff to invoke state attachment and garnishment remedies is amended to reflect the 1993 amendments of Civil Rule 4. Former Civil Rule 4(e), incorporated in Rule B(1), allowed general use of state quasi-in-rem jurisdiction if the defendant was not an inhabitant of, or found within, the state. Rule 4(e) was replaced in 1993 by Rule 4(n)(2) which permits use of state law to seize a defendant's assets only if personal jurisdiction over the defendant cannot be obtained in the district where the action is brought. Little purpose would be served by incorporating Rule 4(n)(2) in Rule B, since maritime attachment and garnishment are available whenever the defendant is not found within the district, a concept that allows attachment or garnishment even in some circumstances in which personal jurisdiction also can be asserted. In order to protect against any possibility that elimination of the reference state quasi-in-rem jurisdiction remedies might seem to defeat continued use of state security devices, paragraph (e) expressly incorporates Civil Rule 64. Because Rule 64 looks only to security, not jurisdiction, the former reference to Rule E(8) is deleted as no longer relevant.

Rule B(2)(a) is amended to reflect the 1993 redistribution of the service provisions once found in Civil Rule 4(d) and (i). These provisions, are now found in many different subdivisions of Rule 4. The new reference simply incorporates Rule 4, without designating the new subdivisions, because the function of Rule B(2) is simply to describe the methods of notice that suffice to support a default judgment. Style changes also have been made.

2005 AMENDMENT

Rule B(1) is amended to incorporate the decisions in Heidmar, Inc. v. Anomina Ravennate Di Armamento Sp.A. of Ravenna, 132 F.3d 264, 267–268 (5th Cir. 1998), and Navieros InterAmericanos, S.A. v. M/V Vasilia Express, 120 F.3d 304, 314–315 (1st Cir. 1997). The time for determining whether a defendant is "found" in the district is set at the time of filing the verified complaint that prays for attachment and the affidavit required by Rule B(1)(b). As provided by Rule B(1)(b), the affidavit must be filed with the complaint. A defendant cannot defeat the security purpose of attachment by appointing an agent for service of process after the complaint and affidavit are filed. The complaint praying for attachment need not be the initial complaint. So long as the defendant is not found in the district, the prayer for attachment may be made in an amended complaint; the affidavit that the defendant cannot be found must be filed with the amended complaint.

Rule C. Actions in Rem: Special Provisions

(1)　When Available. An action in rem may be brought:

(a)　To enforce any maritime lien;

(b)　Whenever a statute of the United States provides for a maritime action in rem or a proceeding analogous thereto.

Except as otherwise provided by law a party who may proceed in rem may also, or in the alternative, proceed in personam against any person who may be liable.

Statutory provisions exempting vessels or other property owned or possessed by or operated by or for the United States from arrest or seizure are not affected by this rule. When a statute so provides, an action against the United States or an instrumentality thereof may proceed on in rem principles.

(2) Complaint. In an action in rem the complaint must:

(a) be verified;

(b) describe with reasonable particularity the property that is the subject of the action; and

(c) state that the property is within the district or will be within the district while the action is pending;.

(3) Judicial Authorization and Process.

(a) Arrest Warrant.

(i) The court must review the complaint and any supporting papers. If the conditions for an in rem action appear to exist, the court must issue an order directing the clerk to issue a warrant for the arrest of the vessel or other property that is the subject of the action.

(ii) If the plaintiff or the plaintiff's attorney certifies that exigent circumstances make court review impracticable, the clerk must promptly issue a summons and a warrant for the arrest of the vessel or other property that is the subject of the action. The plaintiff has the burden in any post-arrest hearing under Rule E(4)(f) to show that exigent circumstances existed.

(b) Service.

(i) If the property that is the subject of the action is a vessel or tangible property on board a vessel, the warrant and any supplemental process must be delivered to the marshal for service.

(ii) If the property that is the subject of the action is other property, tangible or intangible, the warrant and any supplemental process must be delivered to a person or organization authorized to enforce it, who may be (A) a marshal; (B) someone under contract with the United States; someone specially appointed by the court for that purpose; or, (D) in an action brought by the United States, any officer or employee of the United States.

(c) Deposit in Court. If the property that is the subject of the action consists in whole or in part of freight, the proceeds of property sold, or other intangible property, the clerk must issue—in addition to the warrant—a summons directing any person controlling the property to show cause why it should not be deposited in court to abide the judgment.

(d) Supplemental Process. The clerk may upon application issue supplemental process to enforce the court's order without further court order.

(4) Notice. No notice other than execution of process is required when the property that is the subject of the action has been released under Rule E(5). If the property is not released within 14 days after execution, the plaintiff must promptly—or within the time that the court allows—give public notice of the action and arrest in a newspaper designated by court order and having general circulation in the district, but publication may be terminated if the property is released before publication is completed. The notice must specify the time under Rule C(6) to file a statement of interest in or right against the seized property and to answer. This rule does not affect the notice requirements in an action to foreclose a preferred ship mortgage under 46 U.S.C. §§ 31301 et seq., as amended.

(5) Ancillary Process. In any action in rem in which process has been served as provided by this rule, if any part of the property that is the subject of the action has not been brought within the control of the court because it has been removed or sold, or because it is intangible property in the hands of a person who has not been served with process, the court may, on motion, order any person having possession or control of such property or its proceeds to show cause why it should not be delivered into the custody of the marshal or other person or organization having a warrant for the arrest of the property or paid into court to abide the judgment; and, after hearing, the court may enter such judgment as law and justice may require.

(6) Responsive Pleading; Interrogatories.

(a) Statement of Interest; Answer. In an action in rem:

(i) A person who asserts a right of possession or any ownership interest in the property that is the subject of the action must file a verified statement of right or interest:

(A) within 14 days after the execution of process, or

(B) within the time that the court allows;

(ii) the statement of right or interest must describe the interest in the property that supports the person's demand for its restitution or right to defend the action;

(iii) an agent, bailee, or attorney must state the authority to file a statement of right or interest on behalf of another; and

(iv) a person who asserts a right of possession or any ownership interest must serve an answer within 21 days after filing the statement of interest or right.

(b) Interrogatories. Interrogatories may be served with the complaint in an in rem action without leave of court. Answers to the interrogatories must be served with the answer to the complaint.

ADVISORY COMMITTEE NOTE
1966 Adoption

Subdivision (1)

This rule is designed not only to preserve the proceeding in rem as it now exists in admiralty cases, but to preserve the substance of Admiralty Rules 13–18. The general reference to enforcement of any maritime lien is believed to state the existing law, and is an improvement over the enumeration in the former Admiralty Rules, which is repetitious and incomplete (e.g., there was no reference to general average). The reference to any maritime lien is intended to include liens created by state law which are enforceable in admiralty.

The main concern of Admiralty Rules 13–18 was with the question whether certain actions might be brought in rem or also, or in the alternative, in personam. Essentially, therefore, these rules deal with questions of substantive law, for in general an action in rem may be brought to enforce any maritime lien, and no action in personam may be brought when the substantive law imposes no personal liability.

These rules may be summarized as follows:

1.   Cases in which the plaintiff may proceed in rem and/or in personam:

     a.   Suits for seamen's wages;

     b.   Suits by materialmen for supplies, repairs, etc.;

     c.   Suits for pilotage;

     d.   Suits for collision damages;

     e.   Suits founded on mere maritime hypothecation;

     f.   Suits for salvage.

2.   Cases in which the plaintiff may proceed only in personam:

     a.   Suits or assault and beating.

3.   Cases in which the plaintiff may proceed only in rem:

     a.   Suits on bottomry bonds.

The coverage is incomplete, since the rules omit mention of many cases in which the plaintiff may proceed in rem or in personam. This revision proceeds on the principle that it is preferable to make a general statement as to the availability of the remedies, leaving out conclusions on matters of substantive law. Clearly it is not necessary to enumerate the cases listed under Item 1, above, nor to try to complete the list.

The rule eliminates the provision of Admiralty Rule 15 that actions for assault and beating may be brought only in personam. A preliminary study fails to disclose any reason for the rule. It is subject to so many exceptions that it is calculated to deceive rather than to inform. A seaman may sue in rem when he has been beaten by a fellow member of the crew so vicious as to render the vessel unseaworthy, The Rolph, 293 Fed. 269 (D.Cal.1923), aff'd 299 Fed. 52 (9th Cir.1924), or where the theory of the action is that a beating by the master is a breach of the obligation under the shipping articles to treat the seaman with proper kindness, The David Evans, 187 Fed. 775 (9th Cir.1911); and a passenger may sue in rem on the theory that the assault is a breach of the contract of passage, The Western States, 159 Fed. 354 (2d Cir.1908). To say that an action for money damages may be brought only in personam seems equivalent to saying that a maritime lien shall not exist; and that, in turn, seems equivalent to announcing a rule of substantive law rather than a rule of procedure. Dropping the rule will leave it to the courts to determine whether a lien exists as a matter of substantive law.

The specific reference to bottomry bonds is omitted because, as a matter of hornbook substantive law, there is no personal liability on such bonds.

Subdivision (2)

This incorporates the substance of Admiralty Rules 21 and 22.

Subdivision (3)

Derived from Admiralty Rules 10 and 37. The provision that the warrant is to be issued by the clerk is new, but is assumed to state existing law.

There is remarkably little authority bearing on Rule 37, although the subject would seem to be an important one. The rule appears on its face to have provided for a sort of ancillary process, and this may well be the case when tangible property, such as a vessel, is arrested, and intangible property such as freight is incidentally involved. It can easily happen, however, that the only property against which the action may be brought is intangible, as where the owner of a vessel under charter has a lien on subfreights. See 2 Benedict § 299 and cases cited. In such cases it would seem that the order to the person holding the fund is equivalent to original process, taking the place of the warrant for arrest. That being so, it would also seem that (1) there should be some provision for notice, comparable to that given when tangible property is arrested and (2) it should not be necessary, as Rule 37 provided, to petition the court for issuance of the process, but that it should issue as of course. Accordingly the substance of Rule 37 is included in the rule covering ordinary process, and notice will be required by Rule C(4). Presumably the rules omit any requirement of notice in these cases because the holder of the funds (e.g., the cargo owner) would be required on general principles (cf. Harris v. Balk, 198 U.S. 215 (1905)) to notify his obligee (e.g., the charterer); but in actions in rem such notice seems plainly inadequate because there may be adverse claims to the fund (e.g., there may be liens against the subfreights for seamen's wages, etc.). Compare Admiralty Rule 9.

Subdivision (4)

This carries forward the notice provision of Admiralty Rule 10, with one modification. Notice by publication is too expensive and ineffective a formality to be routinely required. When, as usually happens, the vessel or other property is released on bond or otherwise there is no point in publishing notice; the vessel is freed from the claim of the plaintiff and no other interest in the vessel can be affected by the proceedings. If, however, the vessel is not released, general notice is required in order that all persons, including unknown claimants, may appear and be heard, and in order that the judgment in rem shall be binding on all the world.

Subdivision (5)

This incorporates the substance of Admiralty Rule 9.

There are remarkably few cases dealing directly with the rule. In The George Prescott, 10 Fed.Cas. 222 (No. 5,339) (E.D.N.Y.1865), the master and crew of a vessel libeled her for wages, and other lienors also filed libels. One of the lienors suggested to the court that prior to the arrest of the vessel the master had removed the sails, and asked that he be ordered to produce them. He admitted removing the sails and selling them, justifying on the ground that he held a mortgage on the vessel. He was ordered to pay the proceeds into court. Cf. United States v. The Zarco, 187 F.Supp. 371 (S.D.Cal.1960), where an armature belonging to a vessel subject to a preferred ship mortgage was in possession of a repairman claiming a lien.

It is evident that, though the rule has had a limited career in the reported cases, it is a potentially important one. It is also evident that the rule is framed in terms narrower than the principle that supports it. There is no apparent reason for limiting it to ships and their appurtenances (2 Benedict § 299). Also, the reference to "third parties" in the existing rule seems unfortunate. In The George Prescott, the person who removed and sold the sails was a plaintiff in the action, and relief against him was just as necessary as if he had been a stranger.

Another situation in which process of this kind would seem to be useful is that in which the principal property that is the subject of the action is a vessel, but her pending freight is incidentally involved. The warrant of arrest, and notice of its service, should be all that is required by way of original process and notice; ancillary process without notice should suffice as to the incidental intangibles.

The distinction between Admiralty Rules 9 and 37 is not at once apparent, but seems to be this: Where the action was against property that could not be seized by the marshal because it was intangible, the original process was required to be similar to that issued against a garnishee, and general notice was required (though not provided for by the present rule; cf. Advisory Committee's Note to Rule C(3)). Under Admiralty Rule 9 property had been arrested and general notice had been given, but some of the property had been removed or for some other reason could not be arrested. Here no further notice was necessary.

The rule also makes provision for this kind of situation: The proceeding is against a vessel's pending freight only; summons has been served on the person supposedly holding the funds, and general notice has been given; it develops that another person holds all or part of the funds. Ancillary process should be available here without further notice.

Subdivision (6)

Adherence to the practice of return days seems unsatisfactory. The practice varies significantly from district to district. A uniform rule should be provided so that any claimant or defendant can readily determine when he is required to file or serve a claim or answer.

A virtue of the return-day practice is that it requires claimants to come forward and identify themselves at an early stage of the proceedings—before they could fairly be required to answer. The draft is designed to preserve this feature of the present practice by requiring early filing of the claim. The time schedule contemplated in the draft is closely comparable to the present practice in the Southern District of New York, where the claimant has a minimum of 8 days to claim and three weeks thereafter to answer.

This rule also incorporates the substance of Admiralty Rule 25. The present rule's emphasis on "the true and bona fide owner" is omitted, since anyone having the right to possession can claim (2 Benedict § 324).

1985 AMENDMENT

Rule C(3) has been amended to provide for judicial scrutiny before the issuance of any warrant of arrest. Its purpose is to eliminate any doubt as to the rule's constitutionality under the Sniadach line of cases. Sniadach v. Family Finance Corp., 395 U.S. 337 (1969), Fuentes v. Shevin, 407 U.S. 67 (1972), Mitchell v. W.T. Grant Co., 416 U.S. 600 (1974), and North Georgia Finishing, Inc. v. Di-Chem, Inc., 419 U.S. 601 (1975). This was thought desirable even though both the Fourth and the Fifth Circuits have upheld the existing rule. Amstar Corp. v. S/S Alexandros T., 664 F.2d 904 (4th Cir.1981); Merchants National Bank v. The Dredge General G.L. Gillespie, 663 F.2d 1338 (5th Cir.1981), cert. dismissed, 456 U.S. 966 (1982). A contrary view was taken by Judge Tate in the Merchants National Bank case and by the district court in Alyeska Pipeline Service Co. v. The Vessel Bay Ridge, 509 F.Supp. 1115 (D.Alaska 1981), appeal dismissed, 703 F.2d 381 (9th Cir.1983).

The rule envisions that the order will issue upon the plaintiff's making a prima facie case showing that he has an action in rem against the defendant in the amount sued for and that the property is within the district. A simple order with conclusory findings is contemplated. The reference to review by the "court" is broad enough to embrace review by a magistrate as well as by a district judge.

The new provision recognizes that in some situations, such as when the judge is unavailable and the ship is about to depart from the jurisdiction, it will be impracticable, if not impossible to secure the judicial review contemplated by Rule C(3). When "exigent circumstances" exist, the rule enables the plaintiff to secure the issuance of the summons and warrant of arrest, subject to a later showing that the necessary circumstances actually existed. This provision is intended to provide a safety valve without undermining the requirement of prearrest scrutiny. Thus, every effort to secure judicial review, including conducting a hearing by telephone, should be pursued before invoking the exigent circumstances procedure.

1991 AMENDMENT

These amendments are designed to conform the rule to Fed.R.Civ.P. 4, as amended. As with recent amendments to Rule 4, it is intended to relieve the Marshals Service of the burden of using its limited personnel and facilities for execution of process in routine circumstances. Doing so may involve a contractual arrangement with a person or organization retained by the government to perform these services, or the use of other government officers and employees, or the special appointment by the court of persons available to perform suitably.

The seizure of a vessel, with or without cargo, remains a task assigned to the Marshal. Successful arrest of a vessel frequently requires the enforcement presence of an armed government official and the cooperation of the United States Coast Guard and other governmental authorities. If the marshal is called upon to seize the vessel, it is expected that the same officer will also be responsible for the seizure of any property on board the vessel at the time of seizure that is to be the object of arrest or attachment.

2000 AMENDMENT

Style changes have been made throughout the revised portions of Rule C. Several changes of meaning have been made as well.

Subdivision 2. In rem jurisdiction originally extended only to property within the judicial district. Since 1986, Congress has enacted a number of jurisdictional and venue statutes for forfeiture and criminal matters that in some circumstances permit a court to exercise authority over property outside the district. 28 U.S.C. § 1355(b)(1) allows a forfeiture action in the district where an act or omission giving rise to forfeiture occurred, or in any other district where venue is established by § 1395 or by any other statute. Section 1355(b)(2) allows an action to be brought as provided in (b)(1) or in the United States District Court for the District of Columbia when the forfeiture property is located in a foreign country or has been seized by authority of a foreign government. Section 1355(d) allows a court with jurisdiction under § 1355(b) to cause service in any other district of process required to bring the forfeiture property before the court. Section 1395 establishes venue of a civil proceeding for forfeiture in the district where the forfeiture accrues or the defendant is found; in any district where the property is found; in any district into which the property is brought, if the property initially is outside any judicial district; or in any district where the vessel is arrested if the proceeding is an admiralty proceeding to forfeit a vessel. Section 1395(e) deals with a vessel or cargo entering a port of entry closed by the President and transportation to or from a state or section declared to be in insurrection. 18 U.S.C. § 981(h) creates expanded jurisdiction and venue over property located elsewhere that is related to a criminal prosecution pending in the district. These amendments, and related amendments of Rule E(3), bring these Rules into step with the new statutes. No change is made as to admiralty and maritime proceedings that do not involve a forfeiture governed by one of the new statutes.

Subdivision (2) has been separated into lettered paragraphs to facilitate understanding.

Subdivision (3). Subdivision (3) has been rearranged and divided into lettered paragraphs to facilitate understanding.

Paragraph (b)(i) is amended to make it clear that any supplemental process addressed to a vessel or tangible property on board a vessel, as well as the original warrant, is to be served by the marshal.

Subdivision (4). Subdivision (4) has required that public notice state the time for filing an answer, but has not required that the notice set out the earlier time for filing a statement of interest or claim. The amendment requires that both times be stated.

A new provision is added, allowing termination of publication if the property is released more than 10 days after execution but before publication is completed. Termination will save money, and also will reduce the risk of confusion as to the status of the property.

Subdivision (6). Subdivision (6) has applied a single set of undifferentiated provisions to civil forfeiture proceedings and to in rem admiralty proceedings. Because some differences in procedure are desirable, these proceedings are separated by adopting a new paragraph (a) for civil forfeiture proceedings and recasting the present rule as paragraph (b) for in rem admiralty proceedings. The provision for interrogatories and answers is carried forward as paragraph (e). Although this established procedure for serving interrogatories with the complaint departs from the general provisions of Civil Rule 26(d), the special needs of expedition that often arise in admiralty justify continuing the practice.

Both paragraphs (a) and (b) require a statement of interest or right rather than the "claim" formerly required. The new wording permits parallel drafting, and facilitates cross-references in other rules. The substantive nature of the statement remains the same as the former claim. The requirements of (a) and (b) are, however, different in some respects.

In a forfeiture proceeding governed by paragraph (a), a statement must be filed by a person who asserts an interest in or a right against the property involved. This category includes every right against the property, such as a lien, whether or not it establishes ownership or a right to possession. In determining who has an interest in or a right against property, courts may continue to rely on precedents that have developed the meaning of "claims" or "claimants" for the purpose of civil forfeiture proceedings.

In an admiralty and maritime proceeding governed by paragraph (b), a statement is filed only by a person claiming a right of possession or ownership. Other claims against the property are advanced by intervention under Civil Rule 24, as it may be supplemented by local admiralty rules. The reference to ownership includes every interest that qualifies as ownership under domestic or foreign law. If an ownership interest is asserted, it makes no difference whether its character is legal, equitable, or something else.

Paragraph (a) provides more time than paragraph (b) for filing a statement. Admiralty and maritime in rem proceedings often present special needs for prompt action that do not commonly arise in forfeiture proceedings.

Paragraphs (a) and (b) do not limit the right to make a restricted appearance under Rule E(8).

Rule D. Possessory, Petitory, and Partition Actions

In all actions for possession, partition, and to try title maintainable according to the course of the admiralty practice with respect to a vessel, in all actions so maintainable with respect to the possession of cargo or other maritime property, and in all actions by one or more part owners against the others to obtain security for the return of the vessel from any voyage undertaken without their consent, or by one or more part owners against the others to obtain possession of the vessel for any voyage on giving security for its safe return, the process shall be by a warrant of arrest of the vessel, cargo, or other property, and by notice in the manner provided by Rule B(2) to the adverse party or parties.

ADVISORY COMMITTEE NOTES

1966 Adoption

This carries forward the substance of Admiralty Rule 19.

Rule 19 provided the remedy of arrest in controversies involving title and possession in general. See The Tilton, 23 Fed.Cas. 1277 (No. 14,054) (C.C.D.Mass.1830). In addition it provided that remedy in controversies between co-owners respecting the employment of a vessel. It did not deal comprehensively with controversies between co-owners, omitting the remedy of partition. Presumably the omission is traceable to the fact that, when the rules were originally promulgated, concepts of substantive law (sometimes stated as concepts of jurisdiction) denied the remedy of partition except where the parties in disagreement were the owners of equal shares. See The Steamboat Orleans, 36 U.S. (11 Pet.) 175 (1837). The Supreme Court has now removed any doubt as to the jurisdiction of the district courts to partition a vessel, and has held in addition that no fixed principle of federal admiralty law limits the remedy to the case of equal shares. Madruga v. Superior Court, 346 U.S. 556 (1954). It is therefore appropriate to include a reference to partition in the rule.

Rule E. Actions in Rem and Quasi in Rem: General Provisions

(1) Applicability. Except as otherwise provided, this rule applies to actions in personam with process of maritime attachment and garnishment, actions in rem, and petitory, possessory, and partition actions, supplementing Rules B, C, and D.

(2) Complaint; Security.

 (a) Complaint. In actions to which this rule is applicable the complaint shall state the circumstances from which the claim arises with such particularity that the defendant or claimant will be able without moving for a more definite statement, to commence an investigation of the facts and to frame a responsive pleading.

 (b) Security for Costs. Subject to the provisions of Rule 54(d) and of relevant statutes, the court may, on the filing of the complaint or on the appearance of any defendant, claimant, or any other party, or at any later time, require the plaintiff, defendant, claimant, or other party to give security, or additional security, in such sum as the court shall direct to pay all costs and expenses that shall be awarded against the party by any interlocutory order or by the final judgment, or on appeal by any appellate court.

(3) Process.

 (a) In admiralty and maritime proceedings process in rem or of maritime attachment and garnishment may be served only within the district.

 (b) Issuance and Delivery. Issuance and delivery of process in rem, or of maritime attachment and garnishment, shall be held in abeyance if the plaintiff so requests.

(4) Execution Of Process; Marshal's Return; Custody Of Property; Procedures For Release.

 (a) In General. Upon issuance and delivery of the process or, in the case of summons with process of attachment and garnishment, when it appears that the defendant cannot be found within the district, the marshal or other person or organization having a warrant shall forthwith execute the process in accordance with this subdivision (4), making due and prompt return.

 (b) Tangible Property. If tangible property is to be attached or arrested, the marshal shall take it into the marshal's possession for safe custody. If the character or situation of the property is such that the taking of actual possession is impracticable, the marshal or other person executing the process shall affix a copy thereof to the property in a conspicuous place and leave a copy of the complaint and process with the person having possession or the person's agent. In furtherance of the marshal's custody of any vessel the marshal is authorized to make a written request to the collector of customs not to grant clearance to such vessel until notified by the marshal or a deputy marshal or by the clerk that the vessel has been released in accordance with these rules.

(c) Intangible Property. If intangible property is to be attached or arrested the marshal or other person or organization having the warrant shall execute the process by leaving with the garnishee or other obligor a copy of the complaint and process requiring the garnishee or other obligor to answer as provided in Rules B(3)(a) and C(6); or the marshal may accept for payment into the registry of the court the amount owed to the extent of the amount claimed by the plaintiff with interest and costs, in which event the garnishee or other obligor shall not be required to answer unless alias process shall be served.

(d) Directions with Respect to Property in Custody. The marshal or other person or organization having the warrant may at any time apply to the court for directions with respect to property that has been attached or arrested, and shall give notice of such application to any or all of the parties as the court may direct.

(f) Procedure for Release from Arrest or Attachment. Whenever property is arrested or attached, any person claiming an interest in it shall be entitled to a prompt hearing at which the plaintiff shall be required to show why the arrest or attachment should not be vacated or other relief granted consistent with these rules. This subdivision shall have no application to suits for seamen's wages when process is issued upon a certification of sufficient cause filed pursuant to Title 46, U.S.C. §§ 603 and 604 or to actions by the United States for forfeitures for violation of any statute of the United States.

(5) Release of Property.

(a) Special Bond. Whenever process of maritime attachment and garnishment or process in rem is issued the execution of such process shall be stayed, or the property released, on the giving of security, to be approved by the court or clerk, or by stipulation of the parties, conditioned to answer the judgment of the court or of any appellate court. The parties may stipulate the amount and nature of such security. In the event of the inability or refusal of the parties so to stipulate the court shall fix the principal sum of the bond or stipulation at an amount sufficient to cover the amount of the plaintiff's claim fairly stated with accrued interest and costs; but the principal sum shall in no event exceed (i) twice the amount of the plaintiff's claim or (ii) the value of the property on due appraisement, whichever is smaller. The bond or stipulation shall be conditioned for the payment of the principal sum and interest thereon at 6 per cent per annum.

(b)   General Bond. The owner of any vessel may file a general bond or stipulation, with sufficient surety, to be approved by the court, conditioned to answer the judgment of such court in all or any actions that may be brought thereafter in such court in which the vessel is attached or arrested. Thereupon the execution of all such process against such vessel shall be stayed so long as the amount secured by such bond or stipulation is at least double the aggregate amount claimed by plaintiffs in all actions begun and pending in which such vessel has been attached or arrested. Judgments and remedies may be had on such bond or stipulation as if a special bond or stipulation had been filed in each of such actions. The district court may make necessary orders to carry this rule into effect, particularly as to the giving of proper notice of any action against or attachment of a vessel for which a general bond has been filed. Such bond or stipulation shall be indorsed by the clerk with a minute of the actions wherein process is so stayed. Further security may be required by the court at any time.

If a special bond or stipulation is given in a particular case, the liability on the general bond or stipulation shall cease as to that case.

(c)   Release by Consent or Stipulation; Order of Court or Clerk; Costs. Any vessel, cargo, or other property in the custody of the marshal or other person or organization having the warrant may be released forthwith upon the marshal's acceptance and approval of a stipulation, bond, or other security, signed by the party on whose behalf the property is detained or the party's attorney and expressly authorizing such release, if all costs and charges of the court and its officers shall have first been paid. Otherwise no property in the custody of the marshal, other person or organization having the warrant, or other officer of the court shall be released without an order of the court; but such order may be entered as of course by the clerk, upon the giving of approved security as provided by law and these rules, or upon the dismissal or discontinuance of the action; but the marshal or other person or organization having the warrant shall not deliver any property so released until the costs and charges of the officers of the court shall first have been paid.

(d)   Possessory, Petitory, and Partition Actions. The foregoing provisions of this subdivision (5) do not apply to petitory, possessory, and partition actions. In such cases the property arrested shall be released only by order of the court, on such terms and conditions and on the giving of such security as the court may require.

(6) Reduction or Impairment of Security. Whenever security is taken the court may, on motion and hearing, for good cause shown, reduce the amount of security given; and if the surety shall be or become insufficient, new or additional sureties may be required on motion and hearing.

(7) Security on Counterclaim.

(a) When a person who has given security for damages in the original action asserts a counterclaim that arises from the transaction or occurrence that is the subject of the original action, a plaintiff for whose benefit the security has been given must give security for damages demanded in the counterclaim unless the court for cause shown, directs otherwise. Proceedings on the original claim must be stayed until this security is given unless the court directs otherwise.

(b) The plaintiff is required to give security under Rule E(7)(a) when the United States or its corporate instrumentality counterclaims and would have been required to give security to respond in damages if a private party but is relieved by law from giving security.

(8) Restricted Appearance. An appearance to defend against an admiralty and maritime claim with respect to which there has issued process in rem, or process of attachment and garnishment, may be expressly restricted to the defense of such claim, and in that event is not an appearance for the purposes of any other claim with respect to which such process is not available or has not been served.

(9) Disposition of Property; Sales.

(a) Interlocutory Sales; Delivery.

(i) On application of a party, the marshal, or other person having custody of the property, the court may order all or part of the property sold—with the sales proceeds, or as much of them as will satisfy the judgment, paid into court to await further orders of the court—if:

(A) the attached or arrested property is perishable, or liable to deterioration, decay, or injury by being detained in custody pending the action;

(B) the expense of keeping the property is excessive or disproportionate; or

(C) there is an unreasonable delay in securing release of the property.

(ii) In the circumstances described in Rule E(9)(b)(i), the court, on motion by a defendant or a person filing a statement of interest or right under Rule C(6), may order that the property, rather than being sold, be delivered to the movant upon giving security under these rules.

(b) Sales; Proceeds. All sales of property shall be made by the marshal or a deputy marshal, or by any other person or organization having the warrant, or by any other person assigned by the court where the marshal or other person or organization having the warrant is a party in interest; and the proceeds of sale shall be forthwith paid into the registry of the court to be disposed of according to law.

(10) Preservation of Property. When the owner or another person remains in possession of property attached or arrested under the provisions of Rule E(4)(b) that permit execution of process without taking actual possession, the court, on a party's motion or on its own, may enter any order necessary to preserve the property and to prevent its removal.

ADVISORY COMMITTEE NOTE

1966 Adoption

Subdivisions (1), (2)

Adapted from Admiralty Rule 24. The rule is based on the assumption that there is no more need for security for costs in maritime personal actions than in civil cases generally, but that there is reason to retain the requirement for actions in which property is seized. As to proceedings for limitation of liability see Rule F(1).

Subdivision (3)

The Advisory Committee has concluded for practical reasons that process requiring seizure of property should continue to be served only within the geographical limits of the district. Compare Rule B(1), continuing the condition that process of attachment and garnishment may be served only if the defendant is not found within the district.

The provisions of Admiralty Rule 1 concerning the persons by whom process is to be served will be superseded by FRCP 4(c).

Subdivision (4)

This rule is intended to preserve the provisions of Admiralty Rules 10 and 36 relating to execution of process, custody of property seized by the marshal, and the marshal's return. It is also designed to make express provision for matters not heretofore covered.

The provision relating to clearance in subdivision (b) is suggested by Admiralty Rule 44 of the District of Maryland.

Subdivision (d) is suggested by English Rule 12, Order 75.

28 U.S.C. § 1921 as amended in 1962 contains detailed provisions relating to the expenses of seizing and preserving property attached or arrested.

Subdivision (5)

In addition to Admiralty Rule 11 (see Rule E(9)), the release of property seized on process of attachment or in rem was dealt with by Admiralty Rules 5, 6, 12, and 57, and 28 U.S.C. § 2464 (formerly

Rev.Stat. § 941). The rule consolidates these provisions and makes them uniformly applicable to attachment and garnishment and actions in rem.

The rule restates the substance of Admiralty Rule 5. Admiralty Rule 12 dealt only with ships arrested on in rem process. Since the same ground appears to be covered more generally by 28 U.S.C. § 2464, the subject matter of Rule 12 is omitted. The substance of Admiralty Rule 57 is retained. 28 U.S.C. § 2464 is incorporated with changes of terminology, and with a substantial change as to the amount of the bond. See 2 Benedict 395 n. 1a; The Lotosland, 2 F.Supp. 42 (S.D.N.Y.1933). The provision for general bond is enlarged to include the contingency of attachment as well as arrest of the vessel.

Subdivision (6)

Adapted from Admiralty Rule 8.

Subdivision (7)

Derived from Admiralty Rule 50.

Title 46, U.S.C. § 783 extends the principle of Rule 50 to the Government when sued under the Public Vessels Act, presumably on the theory that the credit of the Government is the equivalent of the best security. The rule adopts this principle and extends it to all cases in which the Government is defendant although the Suits in Admiralty Act contains no parallel provisions.

Subdivision (8)

Under the liberal joinder provisions of unified rules the plaintiff will be enabled to join with maritime actions in rem, or maritime actions in personam with process of attachment and garnishment, claims with respect to which such process is not available, including nonmaritime claims. Unification should not, however, have the result that, in order to defend against an admiralty and maritime claim with respect to which process in rem or quasi in rem has been served, the claimant or defendant must subject himself personally to the jurisdiction of the court with reference to other claims with respect to which such process is not available or has not been served, especially when such other claims are nonmaritime. So far as attachment and garnishment are concerned this principle holds true whether process is issued according to admiralty tradition and the Supplemental Rules or according to Rule 4(e) as incorporated by Rule B(1).

A similar problem may arise with respect to civil actions other than admiralty and maritime claims within the meaning of Rule 9(h). That is to say, in an ordinary civil action, whether maritime or not, there may be joined in one action claims with respect to which process of attachment and garnishment is available under state law and Rule 4(e) and claims with respect to which such process is not available or has not been served. The general Rules of Civil Procedure do not specify whether an appearance in such cases to defend the claim with respect to which process of attachment and garnishment has issued is an appearance for the purposes of the other claims. In that context the question has been considered best left to case-by-case development. Where admiralty and maritime claims within the meaning of Rule 9(h) are concerned, however, it seems important to include a specific provision to avoid an unfortunate and unintended effect of unification. No inferences whatever as to the effect of such an appearance in an ordinary civil action should be drawn from the specific provision here and the absence of such a provision in the general Rules.

Subdivision (9)

Adapted from Admiralty Rules 11, 12, and 40. Subdivision (a) is necessary because of various provisions as to disposition of property in forfeiture proceedings. In addition to particular statutes, note the provisions of 28 U.S.C. §§ 2461–65.

The provision of Admiralty Rule 12 relating to unreasonable delay was limited to ships but should have broader application. See 2 Benedict 404. Similarly, both Rules 11 and 12 were limited to actions in rem, but should equally apply to attached property.

1985 AMENDMENT

Rule E(4)(f) makes available the type of prompt post-seizure hearing in proceedings under Supplemental Rules B and C that the Supreme Court has called for in a number of cases arising in other contexts. See North Georgia Finishing, Inc. v. Di-Chem, Inc., 419 U.S. 601 (1975); Mitchell v. W.T. Grant Co., 416 U.S. 600 (1974). Although post-attachment and post-arrest hearings always have been available on motion, an explicit statement emphasizing promptness and elaborating the procedure has been lacking in the Supplemental Rules. Rule E(4)(f) is designed to satisfy the constitutional requirement of due process by guaranteeing to the shipowner a prompt post-seizure hearing at which he can attack the complaint, the arrest, the security demanded, or any other alleged deficiency in the proceedings up to that point. The amendment also is intended to eliminate the previously disparate treatment under local rules of defendants whose property has been seized pursuant to Supplemental Rules B and C.

The new Rule E(4)(f) is based on a proposal by the Maritime Law Association of the United States and on local admiralty rules in the Eastern and Southern Districts of New York. E.D.N.Y. Local Rule 13; S.D.N.Y. Local Rule 12. Similar provisions have been adopted by other maritime districts. E.g., N.D.Calif. Local Rule 603–4; W.D.La. Local Admiralty Rule 21. Rule E(4)(f) will provide uniformity in practice and reduce constitutional uncertainties.

Rule E(4)(f) is triggered by the defendant or any other person with an interest in the property seized. Upon an oral or written application similar to that used in seeking a temporary restraining order, see Rule 65(b), the court is required to hold a hearing as promptly as possible to determine whether to allow the arrest or attachment to stand. The plaintiff has the burden of showing why the seizure should not be vacated. The hearing also may determine the amount of security to be granted or the propriety of imposing counter-security to protect a defendant from an improper seizure.

2000 AMENDMENT

Style changes have been made throughout the revised portions of Rule E. Several changes of meaning have been made as well.

Subdivision (3). Subdivision (3) is amended to reflect the distinction drawn in Rule C(2)(e) and (d). Service in an admiralty or maritime proceeding still must be made within the district, as reflected in Rule C(2)(e), while service in forfeiture proceedings may be made outside the district when authorized by statute, as reflected in Rule C(2)(d).

Subdivision (7). Subdivision (7)(a) is amended to make it clear that a plaintiff need give security to meet a counterclaim only when the counterclaim is asserted by a person who has given security to respond in damages in the original action.

Subdivision (8). Subdivision (8) is amended to reflect the change in Rule B(1*l*)(e) that deletes the former provision incorporating state quasi-in-rem jurisdiction. A restricted appearance is not appropriate when state law is invoked only for security under Civil Rule 64, not as a basis of quasi-in-rem jurisdiction. But if state law allows a special, limited, or restricted appearance as an incident of the remedy adopted from state law, the state practice applies through Rule 64 "in the manner provided by" state law.

Subdivision (9). Subdivision 9(b)(ii) is amended to reflect the change in Rule C(6) that substitutes a statement of interest or right for a claim.

Subdivision (10). Subdivision 10 is new. It makes clear the authority of the court to preserve and to prevent removal of attached or arrested property that remains in the possession of the owner or other person under Rule E(4)(b).

Rule F. Limitation of Liability

(1) Time for Filing Complaint; Security. Not later than six months after receipt of a claim in writing, any vessel owner may file a complaint in the appropriate district court, as provided in subdivision (9) of this rule, for limitation of liability pursuant to statute. The owner (a) shall deposit with the court, for the benefit of claimants, a sum equal to the amount or value of the owner's interest in the vessel and pending freight, or approved security therefor, and in addition such sums, or approved security therefor, as the court may from time to time fix as necessary to carry out the provisions of the statutes as amended; or (b) at the owner's option shall transfer to a trustee to be appointed by the court, for the benefit of claimants, the owner's interest in the vessel and pending freight, together with such sums, or approved security therefor, as the

court may from time to time fix as necessary to carry out the provisions of the statutes as amended. The plaintiff shall also give security for costs and, if the plaintiff elects to give security, for interest at the rate of 6 percent per annum from the date of the security.

(2) Complaint. The complaint shall set forth the facts on the basis of which the right to limit liability is asserted, and all facts necessary to enable the court to determine the amount to which the owner's liability shall be limited. The complaint may demand exoneration from as well as limitation of liability. It shall state the voyage, if any, on which the demands sought to be limited arose, with the date and place of its termination; the amount of all demands including all unsatisfied liens or claims of lien, in contract or in tort or otherwise, arising on that voyage, so far as known to the plaintiff, and what actions and proceedings, if any, are pending thereon; whether the vessel was damaged, lost, or abandoned, and, if so, when and where; the value of the vessel at the close of the voyage or, in case of wreck, the value of her wreckage, strippings, or proceeds, if any, and where and in whose possession they are; and the amount of any pending freight recovered or recoverable. If the plaintiff elects to transfer the plaintiff's interest in the vessel to a trustee, the complaint must further show any prior paramount liens thereon, and what voyages or trips, if any, she has made since the voyage or trip on which the claims sought to be limited arose, and any existing liens arising upon any such subsequent voyage or trip, with the amounts and causes thereof, and the names and addresses of the lienors, so far as known; and whether the vessel sustained any injury upon or by reason of such subsequent voyage or trip.

(3) Claims Against Owner; Injunction. Upon compliance by the owner with the requirements of subdivision (1) of this rule all claims and proceedings against the owner or the owner's property with respect to the matter in question shall cease. On application of the plaintiff the court shall enjoin the further prosecution of any action or proceeding against the plaintiff or the plaintiff's property with respect to any claim subject to limitation in the action.

(4) Notice to Claimants. Upon the owner's compliance with subdivision (1) of this rule the court shall issue a notice to all persons asserting claims with respect to which the complaint seeks limitation, admonishing them to file their respective claims with the clerk of the court and to serve on the attorneys for the plaintiff a copy thereof on or before a date to be named in the notice. The date so fixed shall not be less than 30 days after issuance of the notice. For cause shown, the court may enlarge the time within which claims may be filed. The notice shall be published in such newspaper or newspapers as the court may direct once a week for four successive weeks prior to the date fixed for the filing of claims. The plaintiff not later than the day of second publication shall also mail a copy of the notice to every person known to have made any claim against the vessel or the plaintiff arising out the voyage or trip on

which the claims sought to be limited arose. In cases involving death a copy of such notice shall be mailed to the decedent at the decedent's last known address, and also to any person who shall be known to have made any claim on account of such death.

(5) Claims and Answer. Claims shall be filed and served on or before the date specified in the notice provided for in subdivision (4) of this rule. Each claim shall specify the facts upon which the claimant relies in support of the claim, the items thereof, and the dates on which the same accrued. If a claimant desires to contest either the right to exoneration from or the right to limitation of liability the claimant shall file and serve an answer to the complaint unless the claim has included an answer.

(6) Information to Be Given Claimants. Within 30 days after the date specified in the notice for filing claims, or within such time as the court thereafter may allow, the plaintiff shall mail to the attorney for each claimant (or if the claimant has no attorney to the claimant) a list setting forth (a) the name of each claimant, (b) the name and address of the claimant's attorney (if the claimant is known to have one), (c) the nature of the claim, i.e., whether property loss, property damage, death, personal injury, etc., and (d) the amount thereof.

(7) Insufficiency of Fund or Security. Any claimant may by motion demand that the funds deposited in court or the security given by the plaintiff be increased on the ground that they are less than the value of the plaintiff's interest in the vessel and pending freight. Thereupon the court shall cause due appraisement to be made of the value of the plaintiff's interest in the vessel and pending freight; and if the court finds that the deposit or security is either insufficient or excessive it shall order its increase or reduction. In like manner any claimant may demand that the deposit or security be increased on the ground that it is insufficient to carry out the provisions of the statutes relating to claims in respect of loss of life or bodily injury; and, after notice and hearing, the court may similarly order that the deposit or security be increased or reduced.

(8) Objections to Claims: Distribution of Fund. Any interested party may question or controvert any claim without filing an objection thereto. Upon determination of liability the fund deposited or secured, or the proceeds of the vessel and pending freight, shall be divided pro rata, subject to all relevant provisions of law, among the several claimants in proportion to the amounts of their respective claims, duly proved, saving, however, to all parties any priority to which they may be legally entitled.

(9) Venue; Transfer. The complaint shall be filed in any district in which the vessel has been attached or arrested to answer for any claim with respect to which the plaintiff seeks to limit liability; or, if the vessel has not been attached or arrested, then in any district in which the owner has been sued with respect to any such claim. When the vessel has not been attached or arrested to answer the matters aforesaid, and suit has not been commenced against the owner, the proceedings may be had in

the district in which the vessel may be, but if the vessel is not within any district and no suit has been commenced in any district, then the complaint may be filed in any district. For the convenience of parties and witnesses, in the interest of justice, the court may transfer the action to any district; if venue is wrongly laid the court shall dismiss or, if it be in the interest of justice, transfer the action to any district in which it could have been brought. If the vessel shall have been sold, the proceeds shall represent the vessel for the purposes of these rules.

ADVISORY COMMITTEE NOTE

1966 Adoption

Subdivision (1)

The amendments of 1936 to the Limitation Act superseded to some extent the provisions of Admiralty Rule 51, especially with respect to the time of filing the complaint and with respect to security. The rule here incorporates in substance the 1936 amendment of the Act (46 U.S.C. § 185) with a slight modification to make it clear that the complaint may be filed at any time not later than six months after a claim has been lodged with the owner.

Subdivision (2)

Derived from Admiralty Rules 51 and 53.

Subdivision (3)

This is derived from the last sentence of 46 U.S.C. § 185 and the last paragraph of Admiralty Rule 51.

Subdivision (4)

Derived from Admiralty Rule 51.

Subdivision (5)

Derived from Admiralty Rules 52 and 53.

Subdivision (6)

Derived from Admiralty Rule 52.

Subdivision (7)

Derived from Admiralty Rule 52 and 46 U.S.C. § 185.

Subdivision (8)

Derived from Admiralty Rule 52.

Subdivision (9)

Derived from Admiralty Rule 54. The provision for transfer is revised to conform closely to the language of 28 U.S.C. §§ 1404(a) and 1406(a), though it retains the existing rule's provision for transfer to any district for convenience. The revision also makes clear what has been doubted: that the court may transfer if venue is wrongly laid.

VII. SPECIMEN DOCUMENTS

A. BILLS OF LADING

1. General Bill of Lading

BIMCO

CONGENBILL 2016

BILL OF LADING
To be used with charter parties

PAGE 1

Shipper	Bill of Lading No.	Reference No.
Type here	Type here	Type here
Consignee	Vessel	
Type here	Type here	
Notify address	Port of loading Type here	
Type here	Port of discharge Type here	
Shipper's description of goods		Gross weight
Type here		Type here
	(of which Type here on deck at shipper's risk; the Carrier not being responsible for loss or damage howsoever arising)	

Freight payable as per CHARTER PARTY dated:	SHIPPED at the Port of Loading in apparent good order and condition on the Vessel for carriage to the Port of Discharge or so near thereto as the Vessel may safely get the goods specified above.
Type here	Weight, measure, quality, quantity, condition, contents and value unknown.
FREIGHT ADVANCE Received on account of freight:	IN WITNESS whereof the Master or Owner or Charterer or Agent of the said vessel has signed the number of Bills of Lading indicated below all of this tenor and date, any one of which being accomplished the others shall be void.
Type here	FOR CONDITIONS OF CARRIAGE SEE PAGE 2

Date shipped on board	Place and date of issue	Number of original Bills of Lading
Type here	Type here	Type here

Signature:...(Master*/Agent*/Owner*/Charterer*)

*Delete as appropriate

If signed by an Agent indicate with a tick ☒ whether for and on behalf of:

☐ Master; or

☐ Owner ....(insert name); or

☐ Charterer ....(insert name)

Agent ....(insert name)

CONGENBILL 2016
BILL OF LADING
To be used with charter parties
Page 2

Conditions of Carriage

(1) All terms and conditions, liberties and exceptions of the Charter Party, dated as overleaf, including the Law and Arbitration Clause/Dispute Resolution Clause, are herewith incorporated.

(2) **General Paramount Clause**

The International Convention for the Unification of Certain Rules of Law relating to Bills of Lading signed at Brussels on 25 August 1924 ("the Hague Rules") as amended by the Protocol signed at Brussels on 23 February 1968 ("the Hague-Visby Rules") and as enacted in the country of shipment shall apply to this Contract. When the Hague-Visby Rules are not enacted in the country of shipment, the corresponding legislation of the country of destination shall apply, irrespective of whether such legislation may only regulate outbound shipments.

When there is no enactment of the Hague-Visby Rules in either the country of shipment or in the country of destination, the Hague-Visby Rules shall apply to this Contract save where the Hague Rules as enacted in the country of shipment or if no such enactment is in place, the Hague Rules as enacted in the country of destination apply compulsorily to this Contract.

The Protocol signed at Brussels on 21 December 1979 ("the SDR Protocol 1979") shall apply where the Hague-Visby Rules apply, whether mandatorily or by this Contract.

The Carrier shall in no case be responsible for loss of or damage to cargo arising prior to loading, after discharging, or while the cargo is in the charge of another carrier, or with respect to deck cargo and live animals.

(3) **General Average**

General Average shall be adjusted, stated and settled according to York-Antwerp Rules 2016 in London unless another place is agreed in the Charter Party.

Cargo's contribution to General Average shall be paid to the Carrier even when such average is the result of a fault, neglect or error of the Master, Pilot or Crew.

(4) **New Jason Clause**

In the event of accident, danger, damage or disaster before or after the commencement of the voyage, resulting from any cause whatsoever, whether due to negligence or not, for which, or for the consequence of which, the Carrier is not responsible, by statute, contract or otherwise, the cargo, shippers, consignees or the owners of the cargo shall contribute with the Carrier in General Average to the payment of any sacrifices, losses or expenses of a General Average nature that may be made or incurred and shall pay salvage and special charges incurred in respect of the cargo. If a salving vessel is owned or operated by the Carrier, salvage shall be paid for as fully as if the said salving vessel or vessels belonged to strangers. Such deposit as the Carrier, or its agents, may deem sufficient to cover the estimated contribution of the goods and any salvage and special charges thereon shall, if required, be made by the cargo, shippers, consignees or owners of the goods to the Carrier before delivery.

(5) **Both-to-Blame Collision Clause**

If the Vessel comes into collision with another vessel as a result of the negligence of the other vessel and any act, neglect or default of the Master, Mariner, Pilot or the servants of the Carrier in the navigation or in the management of the Vessel, the owners of the cargo carried hereunder will indemnify the Carrier against all loss or liability to the other or non-carrying vessel or her owners in so far as such loss or liability represents loss of, or damage to, or any claim whatsoever of the owners of said cargo, paid or payable by the other or non-carrying vessel or her owners to the owners of said cargo and set-off, recouped or recovered by the other or non-carrying vessel or her owners as part of their claim against the carrying Vessel or the Carrier.

The foregoing provisions shall also apply where the owners, operators or those in charge of any vessel or vessels or objects other than, or in addition to, the colliding vessels or objects are at fault in respect of a collision or contact.

(6) International Group of P&I Clubs/BIMCO Himalaya Clause for bills of lading and other contracts 2014

(a) For the purposes of this contract, the term "Servant" shall include the owners, managers, and operators of vessels (other than the Carrier); underlying carriers; stevedores and terminal operators; and any direct or indirect servant, agent, or subcontractor (including their own subcontractors), or any other party employed by or on behalf of the Carrier, or whose services or equipment have been used to perform this contract whether in direct contractual privity with the Carrier or not.

(b) It is hereby expressly agreed that no Servant shall in any circumstances whatsoever be under any liability whatsoever to the shipper, consignee, receiver, holder, or other party to this contract (hereinafter termed "Merchant") for any loss, damage or delay of whatsoever kind arising or resulting directly or indirectly from any act, neglect or default on the Servant's part while acting in the course of or in connection with the performance of this contract.

(c) Without prejudice to the generality of the foregoing provisions in this clause, every exemption, limitation, condition and liberty contained herein (other than Art III Rule 8 of the Hague/Hague-Visby Rules if incorporated herein) and every right, exemption from liability, defence and immunity of whatsoever nature applicable to the carrier or to which the carrier is entitled hereunder including the right to enforce any jurisdiction or arbitration provision contained herein shall also be available and shall extend to every such Servant of the carrier, who shall be entitled to enforce the same against the Merchant.

(d)

  (i) The Merchant undertakes that no claim or allegation whether arising in contract, bailment, tort or otherwise shall be made against any Servant of the carrier which imposes or attempts to impose upon any of them or any vessel owned or chartered by any of them any liability whatsoever in connection with this contract whether or not arising out of negligence on the part of such Servant. The Servant shall also be entitled to enforce the foregoing covenant against the Merchant; and

  (ii) The Merchant undertakes that if any such claim or allegation should nevertheless be made, it will indemnify the carrier against all consequences thereof.

(e) For the purpose of sub paragraphs (a)-(d) of this clause the Carrier is or shall be deemed to be acting as agent or trustee on behalf of and for the benefit of all persons mentioned in sub-clause (a) above who are its Servant and all such persons shall to this extent be or be deemed to be parties to this contract.

For particulars of cargo, freight, destination, etc., see Page 1

2. Multimodal Transport Bill of Lading

BIMCO

MULTIDOC 2016

NEGOTIABLE MULTIMODAL TRANSPORT BILL OF LADING
Subject to the UNCTAD/ICC Rules for Multimodal Transport Documents,
(ICC Publication No. 481) **PAGE 1**

Consignor Type here	MT Doc. No. Type here	Reference No. Type here

Consigned to order of Type here	Notify address Type here	Vessel Type here

Place of receipt Type here	Port of loading Type here

Place of delivery Type here	Port of discharge Type here

Marks and Nos. Type here	Quantity and description of goods Type here	Gross weight, kg Type here	Measurement, m³ Type here

Particulars above declared by Consignor

Freight and charges Type here	RECEIVED the goods in apparent good order and condition and, as far as ascertained by reasonable means of checking, as specified above unless otherwise stated.
Freight payable at Type here	The MTO, in accordance with and to the extent of the provisions contained in this MT Bill of Lading, and with liberty to sub-contract, undertakes to perform and/or in its own name to procure performance of the multimodal transport and the delivery of the goods, including all services related thereto, from the place and time of taking the goods in charge to the place and time of delivery and accepts responsibility for such transport and such services.
Consignor's declared value of Type here subject to payment of above extra charge.	One of the MT Bills of Lading must be surrendered duly endorsed in exchange for the goods or delivery order. IN WITNESS whereof MT Bill(s) of Lading has/have been signed in the number indicated below, one of which being accomplished the other(s) to be void.
Note: The Merchant's attention is called to the fact that according to Clauses 10-12 and 26 of this MT Bill of Lading, the liability of the MTO is, in most cases, limited in respect of loss of or damage to the goods.	Place and date of issue Type here	Number of original MT Bills of Lading Type here

MTO as Carrier:..(insert name)

Signature:...(MTO as Carrier*/Master*/Agent*)
*Delete as appropriate

If signed by an Agent indicate with a tick ☒ whether for and on behalf of:

☐ Master; or

☐ MTO as Carrier

Agent...(insert name)

319

MULTIDOC 2016
NEGOTIABLE MULTIMODAL TRANSPORT BILL OF LADING
Page 2

I. GENERAL PROVISIONS

1. Applicability
The provisions of this Contract shall apply irrespective of whether there is a unimodal or a Multimodal Transport Contract involving one or several modes of transport.

2. Definitions
"Multimodal Transport Contract" means a single Contract for the carriage of Goods by at least two different modes of transport. "Multimodal Transport Bill of Lading" (MT Bill of Lading) means this document evidencing a Multimodal Transport Contract and which can be replaced by electronic data interchange messages insofar as permitted by applicable law and is issued in a negotiable form.
"Multimodal Transport Operator" (MTO) means the person named on the face hereof who concludes a Multimodal Transport Contract and assumes responsibility for the performance thereof as a Carrier.
"Carrier" means the person who actually performs or undertakes to perform the carriage, or part thereof, whether it is identical with the Multimodal Transport Operator or not.
"Merchant" includes the Shipper, the Receiver, the Consignor, the Consignee, the holder of this MT Bill of Lading and the owner of the Goods.
"Consignor" means the person who concludes the Multimodal Transport Contract with the Multimodal Transport Operator.
"Consignee" means the person entitled to receive the Goods from the Multimodal Transport Operator.
"Taken in charge" means that the Goods have been handed over to and accepted for carriage by the MTO.
"Delivery" means
(i) the handing over of the Goods to the Consignee; or
(ii) the placing of the Goods at the disposal of the Consignee in accordance with the Multimodal Transport Contract or with the law or usage of the particular trade applicable at the place of delivery; or
(iii) the handing over of the Goods to an authority or other third party to whom, pursuant to the law or regulations applicable at the place of delivery, the Goods must be handed over.
"Special Drawing Rights" (SDR) means the unit of account as defined by the International Monetary Fund.
"Goods" means any property including live animals as well as containers, pallets or similar articles of transport or packaging not supplied by the MTO, irrespective of whether such property is to be or is carried on or under deck.

3. MTO's Tariff
The terms of the MTO's applicable tariff at the date of shipment are incorporated herein. Copies of the relevant provisions of the applicable tariff are available from the MTO upon request. In the case of inconsistency between this MT Bill of Lading and the applicable tariff, this MT Bill of Lading shall prevail.

4. Time Bar
The MTO shall, unless otherwise expressly agreed, be discharged of all liability under this MT Bill of Lading unless suit is brought within nine months after:
(i) the Delivery of the Goods; or
(ii) the date when the Goods should have been delivered; or
(iii) the date when, in accordance with sub-clause 10 (e) failure to deliver the Goods would give the Consignee the right to treat the Goods as lost.

5. Law and Jurisdiction
Disputes arising under this MT Bill of Lading shall be determined by the courts and in accordance with the law at the place where the MTO has its principal place of business.

II. PERFORMANCE OF THE CONTRACT

6. Methods and Routes of Transportation
(a) The MTO is entitled to perform the transport in any reasonable manner and by any reasonable means, methods and routes.
(b) In accordance herewith, for instance, in the event of carriage by sea, vessels may sail with or without pilots, undergo repairs, adjust equipment, drydock and tow vessels in all situations.

7. Optional Stowage
(a) Goods may be stowed by the MTO by means of containers, trailers, transportable tanks, flats, pallets, or similar articles of transport used to consolidate Goods.
(b) Containers, trailers, transportable tanks and covered flats, whether stowed by the MTO or received by him in a stowed condition, may be carried on or under deck without notice to the Merchant.

8. Delivery of the Goods to the Consignee
The MTO undertakes to perform or to procure the performance of all acts necessary to ensure Delivery of the Goods:
(i) when the MT Bill of Lading has been issued in a negotiable form "to bearer", to the person surrendering one original of the document; or
(ii) when the MT Bill of Lading has been issued in a negotiable form "to order", to the person surrendering one original of the document duly endorsed; or
(iii) when the MT Bill of Lading has been issued in a negotiable form to a named person, to that person upon proof of its identity and surrender of one original document; if such document has been transferred "to order" or in blank, the provisions of (ii) above apply.

9. Hindrances, etc. Affecting Performance
(a) The MTO shall use reasonable endeavours to complete the transport and to deliver the Goods at the place designated for Delivery.
(b) If at any time the performance of the Contract as evidenced by this MT Bill of Lading is or will be affected by any hindrance, risk, delay, difficulty or disadvantage of whatsoever kind and if by virtue of sub-clause 9 (a) the MTO has no duty to complete the performance of the Contract, the MTO (whether or not the transport is commenced) may elect to
(i) treat the performance of this Contract as terminated and place the Goods at the Merchant's disposal at any place which the MTO shall deem safe and convenient; or
(ii) deliver the Goods at the place designated for Delivery.
(c) If the Goods are not taken Delivery of by the Merchant within a reasonable time after the MTO has called upon him to take Delivery, the MTO shall be at liberty to put the Goods in safe custody on behalf of the Merchant at the latter's risk and expense.
(d) In any event the MTO shall be entitled to full freight for Goods received for transportation and additional compensation for extra costs resulting from the circumstances referred to above.

III. LIABILITY OF THE MTO

10. Basis of Liability
(a) The responsibility of the MTO for the Goods under this Contract covers the period from the time the MTO has taken the Goods into its charge to the time of their Delivery.
(b) Subject to the defences set forth in Clauses 11 and 12, the MTO shall be liable for loss of or damage to the Goods as well as for delay in Delivery, if the occurrence which caused the loss, damage or delay in Delivery took place while the Goods were in its charge as defined in sub-clause 10 (a), unless the MTO proves that no fault or neglect of its own, its servants or agents or any other person referred to in sub-clause 10 (c) has caused or contributed to the loss, damage or delay in Delivery.
However, the MTO shall only be liable for loss following from delay in Delivery if the Consignor has made a written declaration of interest in timely Delivery which has been accepted in writing by the MTO.
(c) The MTO shall be responsible for the acts and omissions of its servants or agents, when any such servant or agent is acting within the scope of its employment, or of any other person of whose services it makes use for the performance of the Contract, as if such acts and omissions were its own.
(d) Delay in Delivery occurs when the Goods have not been delivered within the time expressly agreed upon or, in the absence of such agreement, within the time which it would be reasonable to require of a diligent MTO, having regard to the circumstances of the case.
(e) If the Goods have not been delivered within ninety (90) consecutive days following the date of Delivery determined according to Clause 10 (d) above, the claimant may, in the absence of evidence to the contrary, treat the Goods as lost.

11. Defences for Carriage by Sea or Inland Waterways
Notwithstanding the provisions of Clause 10 (b), the MTO shall not be responsible for loss, damage or delay in Delivery with respect to Goods carried by sea or inland waterways when such loss, damage or delay during such carriage results from:
(i) act, neglect or default of the master, mariner, pilot or the servants of the Carrier in the navigation or in the management of the vessel;
(ii) fire, unless caused by the actual fault or privity of the Carrier;
(iii) the causes listed in the Hague-Visby Rules article 4.2 (c) to (p);
however, always provided that whenever loss or damage has resulted from unseaworthiness of the vessel, the MTO can prove that due diligence has been exercised to make the vessel seaworthy at the commencement of the voyage.

12. Limitation of Liability
(a) Unless the nature and value of the Goods have been declared by the Consignor before the Goods have been taken in charge by the MTO and inserted in the MT Bill of Lading, the MTO shall in no event be or become liable for any loss of or damage to the Goods in an amount exceeding:
(i) when the Carriage of Goods by Sea Act of the United States of America, 1936 (US COGSA) applies USD 500 per package or customary freight unit; or
(ii) when any other law applies, the equivalent of 666.67 SDR per package or unit or two SDR per kilogramme of gross weight of the Goods lost or damaged, whichever is the higher.
(b) Where a container, pallet or similar article of transport is loaded with more than one package or unit, the packages or other shipping units enumerated in the MT Bill of Lading as packed in such article of transport are deemed packages or shipping units. Except as aforesaid, such article of transport shall be considered the package or unit.
(c) Notwithstanding the above-mentioned provisions, if the Multimodal Transport does not, according to the Contract, include carriage of Goods by sea or by inland waterways, the liability of the MTO shall be limited to an amount not exceeding 8.33 SDR per kilogramme of gross weight of the Goods lost or damaged.
(d) In any case, when the loss of or damage to the Goods occurred during one particular stage of the Multimodal Transport, in respect of which an applicable international convention or mandatory national law would have provided another limit of liability if a separate contract of carriage had been made for that particular stage of transport, then the limit of the MTO's liability for such loss or damage shall be determined by reference to the provisions of such convention or mandatory national law.
(e) If the MTO is liable in respect of loss following from delay in Delivery, or consequential loss or damage other than loss of or damage to the Goods, the liability of the MTO shall be limited to an amount not exceeding the equivalent of the freight under the Multimodal Transport Contract for the Multimodal Transport.
(f) The aggregate liability of the MTO shall not exceed the limits of liability for total loss of the Goods.
(g) The MTO is not entitled to the benefit of the limitation of liability if it is proved that the loss, damage or delay in Delivery resulted from a personal act or omission of the MTO done with the intent to cause such loss, damage or delay, or recklessly and with knowledge that such loss, damage or delay would probably result.

13. Assessment of Compensation
(a) Assessment of compensation for loss of or damage to the Goods shall be made by reference to the value of such Goods at the place and time they are delivered to the Consignee or at the place and time when, in accordance with the Multimodal Transport Contract, they should have been so delivered.
(b) The value of the Goods shall be determined according to the current commodity exchange price or, if there is no such price, according to the current market price or, if there is no commodity exchange price or current market price, by reference to the normal value of Goods of the same kind and quality.

14. Notice of loss of or Damage to the Goods
(a) Unless notice of loss of or damage to the Goods, specifying the general nature of such loss or damage, is given in writing by the Consignee to the MTO when the Goods are handed over to the Consignee, such handing over is prima facie evidence of the Delivery by the MTO of the Goods as described in the MT Bill of Lading.
(b) Where the loss or damage is not apparent, the same prima facie effect shall apply if notice in writing is not given within six consecutive days after the day when the Goods were handed over to the Consignee.

15. Defences and Limits for the MTO, Servants, etc.
The provisions of this Contract apply to all claims against the MTO relating to the performance of the Multimodal Transport Contract, whether the claim be founded in contract or in tort.

16. International Group of P&I Clubs/BIMCO Himalaya Clause for bills of lading and other contracts 2014
(a) For the purposes of this contract, the term "Servant" shall include the owners, managers, and operators of vessels (other than the Carrier); underlying carriers; stevedores and terminal operators; and any direct or indirect servant, agent, or subcontractor (including their own subcontractors), or any other party employed by or on behalf of the Carrier, or whose services or equipment have been used to perform this contract whether in direct contractual privity with the Carrier or not.
(b) It is hereby expressly agreed that no Servant shall in any circumstances whatsoever be under any liability whatsoever to the Merchant or other party to this contract (hereinafter termed "Merchant") for any loss, damage or delay of whatsoever kind arising or resulting directly or indirectly from any act, neglect or default on the Servant's part while acting in the course of or in connection with the performance of this contract.
(c) Without prejudice to the generality of the foregoing provisions in this clause, every exemption, limitation, condition and liberty contained herein (other than Art III Rule 8 of the Hague/Hague-Visby Rules if incorporated herein) and every right, exemption from liability, defence and immunity of whatsoever nature applicable to the carrier or to which the carrier is entitled hereunder including the right to enforce any jurisdiction or arbitration provision contained herein shall also be available and shall extend to every such Servant of the carrier, who shall be entitled to enforce the same against the Merchant.
(d) (i) The Merchant undertakes that no claim or allegation whether arising in contract, bailment, tort or otherwise shall be made against any Servant of the carrier which imposes or attempts to impose upon any of them or any vessel owned or chartered by any of them any liability whatsoever in connection with this contract whether or not arising out of negligence on the part of such Servant. The Servant shall also be entitled to enforce the foregoing covenant against the Merchant; and
(ii) The Merchant undertakes that if any such claim or allegation should nevertheless be made, it will indemnify the carrier against all consequences thereof.
(e) For the purpose of sub-paragraphs (a)-(d) of this clause the Carrier is or shall be deemed to be acting as agent or trustee on behalf of and for the benefit of all persons mentioned in sub-clause (a) above who are its Servant and all such persons shall to this extent be or be deemed to be parties to this contract.

IV. DESCRIPTION OF GOODS

17. MTO's Responsibility
The information in the MT Bill of Lading shall be prima facie evidence of the taking in charge by the MTO of the Goods as described by such information unless a contrary indication, such as "shipper's weight, load and count", "shipper-packed container" or similar expressions, have been made in the printed text or superimposed on the document. Proof to the contrary shall not be admissible when the MT Bill of Lading has been transferred, or the equivalent electronic data interchange message has been transmitted to and acknowledged by the Consignee who in good faith has relied and acted thereon.

18. Consignor's Responsibility
(a) The Consignor shall be deemed to have guaranteed to the MTO the accuracy, at the time the Goods were taken in charge by the MTO, of all particulars relating to the general nature of the Goods, their marks, number, weight, volume and quantity and, if applicable, to the dangerous character of the Goods as furnished by it or on its behalf for insertion in the MT Bill of Lading.
(b) The Consignor shall indemnify the MTO for any loss or expense caused by inaccuracies in or inadequacies of the particulars referred to above.
(c) The right of the MTO to such indemnity shall in no way limit his liability under the Multimodal Transport Contract to any person other than the Consignor.
(d) The Consignor shall remain liable even if the MT Bill of Lading has been transferred by him.

19. Return of Containers
(a) Containers, pallets or similar articles of transport supplied by or on behalf of the MTO shall be returned to the MTO in the same order and condition as when handed over to the Merchant, normal wear and tear excepted, with interiors clean and within the time prescribed in the MTO's tariff or elsewhere.
(b) (i) The Consignor shall be liable for any loss of, damage to, or delay, including demurrage, of such articles, incurred during the period between handing over to the Consignor and return to the MTO for carriage.
(ii) The Consignor and the Consignee shall be jointly and severally liable for any loss of, damage to, or delay, including demurrage, of such articles, incurred during the period between handing over to the Consignee and return to the MTO.

20. Dangerous Goods
(a) The Consignor shall comply with all internationally recognised requirements and all rules which apply according to national law or by reason of international convention, relating to the carriage of Goods of a dangerous nature, and shall in any event inform the MTO in writing of the exact nature of the danger before Goods of a dangerous nature are taken in charge by the MTO and indicate to him, if need be, the precautions to be taken.
(b) If the Consignor fails to provide such information and the MTO is unaware of the dangerous nature of the Goods and the necessary precautions to be taken and if, at any time, they are deemed to be a hazard to life or property, they may at any place be unloaded, destroyed or rendered harmless, as circumstances may require, without compensation and the Consignor shall be liable for all loss, damage, delay or expenses arising out of their being taken in charge, or their carriage, or of any service incidental thereto.
The burden of proving that the MTO knew the exact nature of the danger constituted by the carriage of the said Goods shall rest upon the person entitled to the Goods.
(c) If any Goods shipped with the knowledge of the MTO as to their dangerous nature shall become a danger to the vessel or cargo, they may in like manner be landed at any place or destroyed or rendered innocuous by the MTO without liability on the part of the MTO except to General Average, if any.

21. Consignor-packed Containers, etc.
(a) If a container has not been filled, packed or stowed by the MTO, the MTO shall not be liable for any loss of or damage to its contents and the Consignor shall indemnify any loss or expense incurred by the MTO if such loss, damage or expense has been caused by:
(i) negligent filling, packing or stowing of the container;
(ii) the contents being unsuitable for carriage in container; or
(iii) the unsuitability or defective condition of the container unless the container has been supplied by the MTO and the unsuitability or defective condition would not have been apparent upon reasonable inspection at or prior to the time when the container was filled, packed or stowed.
(b) The provisions of sub-clause (a) of this Clause also apply with respect to trailers, transportable tanks, flats and pallets which have not been filled, packed or stowed by the MTO.
(c) The MTO does not accept liability for damage due to the unsuitability or defective condition of reefer equipment or trailers supplied by the Merchant.

V. FREIGHT AND LIEN

22. Freight
(a) Freight shall be deemed earned when the Goods have been taken into charge by the MTO and shall be paid in any event.
(b) The Merchant's attention is drawn to the stipulations concerning currency in which the freight and charges are to be paid, rate of exchange, devaluation and other contingencies relative to freight and charges in the relevant tariff conditions. If no such stipulation as to devaluation exists or is applicable the following provision shall apply:
If the currency in which freight and charges are quoted is devalued or revalued between the date of the freight agreement and the date when the freight and charges are paid, then all freight and charges shall be automatically and immediately changed in proportion to the extent of the devaluation or revaluation of the said currency. When the MTO has consented to payment in other currency than the above mentioned currency, then all freight and charges shall - subject to the preceding paragraph - be paid at the highest selling rate of exchange for banker's sight draft current on the day when such freight and charges are paid. If the banks are closed on the day when the freight is paid the rate to be used will be the one in force on the last day the banks were open.
(c) For the purpose of verifying the freight basis the MTO reserves the right to have the contents of containers, trailers or similar articles of transport inspected in order to ascertain the weight, measurement, value, or nature of the Goods. If on such inspection it is found that the declaration is not correct, it is agreed that a sum equal either to five times the difference between the correct freight and the freight charged or to double the correct freight less the freight charged, whichever sum is the smaller, shall be payable as liquidated damages to the MTO notwithstanding any other sum having been stated on this MT Bill of Lading as the freight payable.
(d) All dues, taxes and charges levied on the Goods and other expenses in connection therewith shall be paid by the Merchant.

23. Lien
The MTO shall have a lien on the Goods for any amount due under this Contract and for the costs of recovering the same, and may enforce such lien in any reasonable manner, including sale or disposal of the Goods.

VI. MISCELLANEOUS PROVISIONS

24. General Average
(a) General Average shall be adjusted at any port or place at the MTO's option, and to be settled according to the York-Antwerp Rules 2016, this covering all Goods, whether carried on or under deck. The New Jason Clause as approved by BIMCO to be considered as incorporated herein.
(b) Such security including a cash deposit as the MTO may deem sufficient to cover the estimated contribution of the Goods and any salvage and special charges thereon, shall, if required, be submitted to the MTO prior to Delivery of the Goods.

25. Both-to-Blame Collision Clause
The Both-to-Blame Collision Clause as adopted by BIMCO shall be considered incorporated herein.

26. U.S. Trade
In case the Contract evidenced by this MT Bill of Lading is subject to U.S. COGSA, then the Provisions stated in said Act shall govern before loading and after discharge and throughout the entire time the Goods are in the Carrier's custody.

First published 1995.
v. 1.1. Dated 30 May 2016. Clause 24 (General Average) updated to refer to York-Antwerp Rules 2016.

B. CHARTERS

1.   Uniform General Charter

BIMCO

GENCON 1994

UNIFORM GENERAL CHARTER   PART I

1. Shipbroker Type here Type here	2. Place and Date Type here
3. Owners/Place of business (Cl. 1) Type here Type here	4. Charterers/Place of business (Cl. 1) Type here Type here
5. Vessel's name (Cl. 1) Type here	6. GT/NT (Cl. 1) Type here/ Type here
7. DWT all told on summer load line in metric tons (abt.) (Cl. 1) Type here	8. Present position (Cl. 1) Type here
9. Expected ready to load (abt.) (Cl. 1) Type here	
10. Loading port or place (Cl. 1) Type here	11. Discharging port or place (Cl. 1) Type here
12. Cargo (also state quantity and margin in Owners' option, if agreed; if full and complete cargo not agreed state "part cargo") (Cl. 1) Type here	
13. Freight rate (also state whether freight prepaid or payable on delivery) (Cl. 4) Type here	14. Freight payment (state currency and method of payment; also beneficiary and bank account) (Cl. 4) Type here
15. State if vessel's cargo handling gear shall not be used (Cl. 5) Type here	16. Laytime (if separate laytime for load. and disch. is agreed, fill in a) and b). If total laytime for load. and disch., fill in c) only) (Cl. 6) (a) Laytime for loading Type here
17. Shippers/Place of business (Cl. 6) Type here	(b) Laytime for discharging Type here
18. Agents (loading) (Cl. 6) Type here	(c) Total laytime for loading and discharging Type here
19. Agents (discharging) (Cl. 6) Type here	
20. Demurrage rate and manner payable (loading and discharging) (Cl. 7) Type here	21. Cancelling date (Cl. 9) Type here
	22. General Average to be adjusted at (Cl. 12) Type here
23. Freight Tax (state if for the Owners' account (Cl. 13 (c)) Type here	24. Brokerage commission and to whom payable (Cl. 15) Type here
25. Law and Arbitration (state 19 (a), 19 (b) or 19 (c) of Cl. 19; if 19 (c) agreed also state Place of Arbitration) (if not filled in 19 (a) shall apply) (Cl. 19) Choose an item. Type here (a) State maximum amount for small claims/shortened arbitration (Cl. 19)	26. Additional clauses covering special provisions, if agreed Type here

Type here	

It is mutually agreed that this Contract shall be performed subject to the conditions contained in this Charter Party which shall include Part I as well as Part II. In the event of a conflict of conditions, the provisions of Part I shall prevail over those of Part II to the extent of such conflict.

Signature (Owners)	Signature (Charterers)
Type here	Type here

PART II
GENCON 1994 Uniform General Charter

1. It is agreed between the party mentioned in Box 3 as the Owners of the Vessel named in Box 5, of the GT/NT indicated in Box 6 and carrying about the number of metric tons of deadweight capacity all told on summer loadline stated in Box 7, now in position as stated in Box 8 and expected ready to load under this Charter Party about the date indicated in Box 9, and the party mentioned as the Charterers in Box 4 that: The said Vessel shall, as soon as her prior commitments have been completed, proceed to the loading port(s) or place(s) stated in Box 10 or so near thereto as she may safely get and lie always afloat, and there load a full and complete cargo (if shipment of deck cargo agreed same to be at the Charterers' risk and responsibility) as stated in Box 12, which the Charterers bind themselves to ship, and being so loaded the Vessel shall proceed to the discharging port(s) or place(s) stated in Box 11 as ordered on signing Bills of Lading, or so near thereto as she may safely get and lie always afloat, and there deliver the cargo.

2. **Owners' Responsibility Clause**

    The Owners are to be responsible for loss of or damage to the goods or for delay in delivery of the goods only in case the loss, damage or delay has been caused by personal want of due diligence on the part of the Owners or their Manager to make the Vessel in all respects seaworthy and to secure that she is properly manned, equipped and supplied, or by the personal act or default of the Owners or their Manager. And the Owners are not responsible for loss, damage or delay arising from any other cause whatsoever, even from the neglect or default of the Master or crew or some other person employed by the Owners on board or ashore for whose acts they would, but for this Clause, be responsible, or from unseaworthiness of the Vessel on loading or commencement of the voyage or at any time whatsoever.

3. **Deviation Clause**

    The Vessel has liberty to call at any port or ports in any order, for any purpose, to sail without pilots, to tow and/or assist Vessels in all situations, and also to deviate for the purpose of saving life and/or property.

4. **Payment of Freight**

(a) The freight at the rate stated in Box 13 shall be paid in cash calculated on the intaken quantity of cargo.

(b) Prepaid. If according to Box 13 freight is to be paid on shipment, it shall be deemed earned and non-returnable, Vessel and/or cargo lost or not lost. Neither the Owners nor their agents shall be required to sign or endorse bills of lading showing freight prepaid unless the freight due to the Owners has actually been paid.

(c) On delivery. If according to Box 13 freight, or part thereof, is payable at destination it shall not be deemed earned until the cargo is thus delivered. Notwithstanding the provisions under (a), if freight or part thereof is payable on delivery of the cargo the Charterers shall have the option of paying the freight on delivered weight/quantity provided such option is declared before breaking bulk and the weight/quantity can be ascertained by official weighing machine, joint draft survey or tally. Cash for Vessel's ordinary disbursements at the port of loading to be advanced by the Charterers, if required, at highest current rate of exchange, subject to two (2) per cent to cover insurance and other expenses.

5. **Loading/Discharging**

(a) Costs/Risks

    The cargo shall be brought into the holds, loaded, stowed and/or trimmed, tallied, lashed and/or secured and taken from the holds and discharged by the Charterers, free of any risk, liability and expense whatsoever to the Owners. The Charterers shall provide and lay all dunnage material as required for the proper stowage and protection of the cargo on board, the Owners allowing the use of all dunnage available on board. The Charterers shall be responsible for and pay the cost of removing their dunnage after discharge of the cargo under this Charter Party and time to count until dunnage has been removed.

PART II
GENCON 1994 Uniform General Charter

(b)   Cargo Handling Gear

Unless the Vessel is gearless or unless it has been agreed between the parties that the Vessel's gear shall not be used and stated as such in Box 15, the Owners shall throughout the duration of loading/discharging give free use of the Vessel's cargo handling gear and of sufficient motive power to operate all such cargo handling gear. All such equipment to be in good working order. Unless caused by negligence of the stevedores, time lost by breakdown of the Vessel's cargo handling gear or motive power - pro rata the total number of cranes/winches required at that time for the loading/discharging of cargo under this Charter Party - shall not count as laytime or time on demurrage. On request the Owners shall provide free of charge cranemen/winchmen from the crew to operate the Vessel's cargo handling gear, unless local regulations prohibit this, in which latter event shore labourers shall be for the account of the Charterers. Cranemen/winchmen shall be under the Charterers' risk and responsibility and as stevedores to be deemed as their servants but shall always work under the supervision of the Master.

(c)   Stevedore Damage

The Charterers shall be responsible for damage (beyond ordinary wear and tear) to any part of the Vessel caused by Stevedores. Such damage shall be notified as soon as reasonably possible by the Master to the Charterers or their agents and to their Stevedores, failing which the Charterers shall not be held responsible. The Master shall endeavour to obtain the Stevedores' written acknowledgement of liability. The Charterers are obliged to repair any stevedore damage prior to completion of the voyage, but must repair stevedore damage affecting the Vessel's seaworthiness or class before the Vessel sails from the port where such damage was caused or found. All additional expenses incurred shall be for the account of the Charterers and any time lost shall be for the account of and shall be paid to the Owners by the Charterers at the demurrage rate.

6.   Laytime

(a)*   Separate laytime for loading and discharging

The cargo shall be loaded within the number of running days/hours as indicated in Box 16, weather permitting, Sundays and holidays excepted, unless used, in which event time used shall count. The cargo shall be discharged within the number of running days/hours as indicated in Box 16, weather permitting, Sundays and holidays excepted, unless used, in which event time used shall count.

(b)*   Total laytime for loading and discharging

The cargo shall be loaded and discharged within the number of total running days/hours as indicated in Box 16, weather permitting, Sundays and holidays excepted, unless used, in which event time used shall count.

(c)   Commencement of laytime (loading and discharging)

Laytime for loading and discharging shall commence at 13.00 hours, if notice of readiness is given up to and including 12.00 hours, and at 06.00 hours next working day if notice given during office hours after 12.00 hours. Notice of readiness at loading port to be given to the Shippers named in Box 17 or if not named, to the Charterers or their agents named in Box 18. Notice of readiness at the discharging port to be given to the Receivers or, if not known, to the Charterers or their agents named in Box 19.

If the loading/discharging berth is not available on the Vessel's arrival at or off the port of loading/discharging, the Vessel shall be entitled to give notice of readiness within ordinary office hours on arrival there, whether in free pratique or not, whether customs cleared or not. Laytime or time on demurrage shall then count as if she were in berth and in all respects ready for loading/discharging provided that the Master warrants that she is in fact ready in all respects. Time used in moving from the place of waiting to the loading/ discharging berth shall not count as laytime. If, after inspection, the Vessel is found not to be ready in all respects to load/discharge time lost after the discovery thereof until the Vessel is again ready to load/discharge shall not count as laytime. Time used before commencement of laytime shall count.

PART II
GENCON 1994 Uniform General Charter

*Indicate alternative (a) or (b) as agreed, in Box 16.

7. **Demurrage**

Demurrage at the loading and discharging port is payable by the Charterers at the rate stated in Box 20 in the manner stated in Box 20 per day or pro rata for any part of a day. Demurrage shall fall due day by day and shall be payable upon receipt of the Owners' invoice. In the event the demurrage is not paid in accordance with the above, the Owners shall give the Charterers 96 running hours written notice to rectify the failure. If the demurrage is not paid at the expiration of this time limit and if the vessel is in or at the loading port, the Owners are entitled at any time to terminate the Charter Party and claim damages for any losses caused thereby.

8. **Lien Clause**

The Owners shall have a lien on the cargo and on all sub-freights payable in respect of the cargo, for freight, deadfreight, demurrage, claims for damages and for all other amounts due under this Charter Party including costs of recovering same.

9. **Cancelling Clause**

(a) Should the Vessel not be ready to load (whether in berth or not) on the cancelling date indicated in Box 21, the Charterers shall have the option of cancelling this Charter Party.

(b) Should the Owners anticipate that, despite the exercise of due diligence, the Vessel will not be ready to load by the cancelling date, they shall notify the Charterers thereof without delay stating the expected date of the Vessel's readiness to load and asking whether the Charterers will exercise their option of cancelling the Charter Party, or agree to a new cancelling date. Such option must be declared by the Charterers within 48 running hours after the receipt of the Owners' notice. If the Charterers do not exercise their option of cancelling, then this Charter Party shall be deemed to be amended such that the seventh day after the new readiness date stated in the Owners' notification to the Charterers shall be the new cancelling date. The provisions of sub-clause (b) of this Clause shall operate only once, and in case of the Vessel's further delay, the Charterers shall have the option of cancelling the Charter Party as per sub-clause (a) of this Clause.

10. **Bills of Lading**

Bills of Lading shall be presented and signed by the Master as per the "Congenbill" Bill of Lading form, Edition 1994, without prejudice to this Charter Party, or by the Owners' agents provided written authority has been given by Owners to the agents, a copy of which is to be furnished to the Charterers. The Charterers shall indemnify the Owners against all consequences or liabilities that may arise from the signing of bills of lading as presented to the extent that the terms or contents of such bills of lading impose or result in the imposition of more onerous liabilities upon the Owners than those assumed by the Owners under this Charter Party.

11. **Both-to-Blame Collision Clause**

If the Vessel comes into collision with another vessel as a result of the negligence of the other vessel and any act, neglect or default of the Master, Mariner, Pilot or the servants of the Owners in the navigation or in the management of the Vessel, the owners of the cargo carried hereunder will indemnify the Owners against all loss or liability to the other or non-carrying vessel or her owners in so far as such loss or liability represents loss of, or damage to, or any claim whatsoever of the owners of said cargo, paid or payable by the other or non-carrying vessel or her owners to the owners of said cargo and set-off, recouped or recovered by the other or non-carrying vessel or her owners as part of their claim against the carrying Vessel or the Owners. The foregoing provisions shall also apply where the owners, operators or those in charge of any vessel or vessels or objects other than, or in addition to, the colliding vessels or objects are at fault in respect of a collision or contact.

PART II
GENCON 1994 Uniform General Charter

12.   General Average and New Jason Clause

General Average shall be adjusted in London unless otherwise agreed in Box 22 according to York-Antwerp Rules 1994 and any subsequent modification thereof. Proprietors of cargo to pay the cargo's share in the general expenses even if same have been necessitated through neglect or default of the Owners' servants (see Clause 2). If General Average is to be adjusted in accordance with the law and practice of the United States of America, the following Clause shall apply: "In the event of accident, danger, damage or disaster before or after the commencement of the voyage, resulting from any cause whatsoever, whether due to negligence or not, for which, or for the consequence of which, the Owners are not responsible, by statute, contract or otherwise, the cargo shippers, consignees or the owners of the cargo shall contribute with the Owners in General Average to the payment of any sacrifices, losses or expenses of a General Average nature that may be made or incurred and shall pay salvage and special charges incurred in respect of the cargo. If a salving vessel is owned or operated by the Owners, salvage shall be paid for as fully as if the said salving vessel or vessels belonged to strangers. Such deposit as the Owners, or their agents, may deem sufficient to cover the estimated contribution of the goods and any salvage and special charges thereon shall, if required, be made by the cargo, shippers, consignees or owners of the goods to the Owners before delivery."

13.   Taxes and Dues Clause

(a)   On Vessel - The Owners shall pay all dues, charges and taxes customarily levied on the Vessel, howsoever the amount thereof may be assessed.

(b)   On cargo - The Charterers shall pay all dues, charges, duties and taxes customarily levied on the cargo, howsoever the amount thereof may be assessed.

(c)   On freight - Unless otherwise agreed in Box 23, taxes levied on the freight shall be for the Charterers' account.

14.   Agency

In every case the Owners shall appoint their own Agent both at the port of loading and the port of discharge.

15.   Brokerage

A brokerage commission at the rate stated in Box 24 on the freight, dead-freight and demurrage earned is due to the party mentioned in Box 24. In case of non-execution 1/3 of the brokerage on the estimated amount of freight to be paid by the party responsible for such non-execution to the Brokers as indemnity for the latter's expenses and work. In case of more voyages the amount of indemnity to be agreed.

16.   General Strike Clause

(a)   If there is a strike or lock-out affecting or preventing the actual loading of the cargo, or any part of it, when the Vessel is ready to proceed from her last port or at any time during the voyage to the port or ports of loading or after her arrival there, the Master or the Owners may ask the Charterers to declare, that they agree to reckon the laydays as if there were no strike or lock-out. Unless the Charterers have given such declaration in writing (by telegram, if necessary) within 24 hours, the Owners shall have the option of cancelling this Charter Party. If part cargo has already been loaded, the Owners must proceed with same, (freight payable on loaded quantity only) having liberty to complete with other cargo on the way for their own account.

(b)   If there is a strike or lock-out affecting or preventing the actual discharging of the cargo on or after the Vessel's arrival at or off port of discharge and same has not been settled within 48 hours, the Charterers shall have the option of keeping the Vessel waiting until such strike or lock-out is at an end against paying half demurrage after expiration of the time provided for discharging until the strike or lock-out terminates and thereafter full demurrage shall be payable until the completion of discharging, or of ordering the Vessel to a safe port where she can safely discharge without risk of being detained by strike or lock-out. Such orders to be given within 48 hours after the Master or the Owners have given notice to the Charterers of the strike or lock-out affecting the

PART II
GENCON 1994 Uniform General Charter

discharge. On delivery of the cargo at such port, all conditions of this Charter Party and of the Bill of Lading shall apply and the Vessel shall receive the same freight as if she had discharged at the original port of destination, except that if the distance to the substituted port exceeds 100 nautical miles, the freight on the cargo delivered at the substituted port to be increased in proportion.

(c)   Except for the obligations described above, neither the Charterers nor the Owners shall be responsible for the consequences of any strikes or lock-outs preventing or affecting the actual loading or discharging of the cargo.

17.   War Risks ("Voywar 1993")

(a)   For the purpose of this Clause, the words:

(i) The "Owners" shall include the shipowners, bareboat charterers, disponent owners, managers or other operators who are charged with the management of the Vessel, and the Master; and

(ii) "War Risks" shall include any war (whether actual or threatened), act of war, civil war, hostilities, revolution, rebellion, civil commotion, warlike operations, the laying of mines (whether actual or reported), acts of piracy, acts of terrorists, acts of hostility or malicious damage, blockades (whether imposed against all Vessels or imposed selectively against Vessels of certain flags or ownership, or against certain cargoes or crews or otherwise howsoever), by any person, body, terrorist or political group, or the Government of any state whatsoever, which, in the reasonable judgement of the Master and/or the Owners, may be dangerous or are likely to be or to become dangerous to the Vessel, her cargo, crew or other persons on board the Vessel.

(b)   If at any time before the Vessel commences loading, it appears that, in the reasonable judgement of the Master and/or the Owners, performance of the Contract of Carriage, or any part of it, may expose, or is likely to expose,the Vessel, her cargo, crew or other persons on board the Vessel to War Risks, the Owners may give notice to the Charterers cancelling this Contract of Carriage, or may refuse to perform such part of it as may expose, or may be likely to expose, the Vessel, her cargo, crew or other persons on board the Vessel to War Risks; provided always that if this Contract of Carriage provides that loading or discharging is to take place within a range of ports, and at the port or ports nominated by the Charterers the Vessel, her cargo, crew, or other persons onboard the Vessel may be exposed, or may be likely to be exposed, to War Risks, the Owners shall first require the Charterers to nominate any other safe port which lies within the range for loading or discharging, and may only cancel this Contract of Carriage if the Charterers shall not have nominated such safe port or ports within 48 hours of receipt of notice of such requirement.

(c)   The Owners shall not be required to continue to load cargo for any voyage, or to sign Bills of Lading for any port or place, or to proceed or continue on any voyage, or on any part thereof, or to proceed through any canal or waterway, or to proceed to or remain at any port or place whatsoever, where it appears, either after the loading of the cargo commences, or at any stage of the voyage thereafter before the discharge of the cargo is completed, that, in the reasonable judgement of the Master and/or the Owners, the Vessel, her cargo (or any part thereof), crew or other persons on board the Vessel (or any one or more of them) may be, or are likely to be, exposed to War Risks. If it should so appear, the Owners may by notice request the Charterers to nominate a safe port for the discharge of the cargo or any part thereof, and if within 48 hours of the receipt of such notice, the Charterers shall not have nominated such a port, the Owners may discharge the cargo at any safe port of their choice (including the port of loading) in complete fulfilment of the Contract of Carriage. The Owners shall be entitled to recover from the Charterers the extra expenses of such discharge and, if the discharge takes place at any port other than the loading port, to receive the full freight as though the cargo had been carried to the discharging port and if the extra distance exceeds 100 miles, to additional freight which shall be the same percentage of the freight contracted for as the percentage which the extra distance represents to the distance of the normal and customary route, the Owners having a lien on the cargo for such expenses and freight.

(d)   If at any stage of the voyage after the loading of the cargo commences, it appears that, in the reasonable judgement of the Master and/or the Owners, the Vessel, her cargo, crew or other persons on board the Vessel may be, or are likely to be, exposed to War Risks on any part of the route (including any canal or waterway) which is normally and customarily used in a voyage of the nature contracted for, and there is another longer route to the discharging port, the Owners shall give notice to the Charterers that this route will be taken. In this event the

327

PART II
GENCON 1994 Uniform General Charter

Owners shall be entitled, if the total extra distance exceeds 100 miles, to additional freight which shall be the same percentage of the freight contracted for as the percentage which the extra distance represents to the distance of the normal and customary route.

(e)   The Vessel shall have liberty:-

(i) to comply with all orders, directions, recommendations or advice as to departure, arrival, routes, sailing in convoy, ports of call, stoppages, destinations, discharge of cargo, delivery or in any way whatsoever which are given by the Government of the Nation under whose flag the Vessel sails, or other Government to whose laws the Owners are subject, or any other Government which so requires, or any body or group acting with the power to compel compliance with their orders or directions;

(ii) to comply with the orders, directions or recommendations of any war risks underwriters who have the authority to give the same under the terms of the war risks insurance;

(iii) to comply with the terms of any resolution of the Security Council of the United Nations, any directives of the European Community, the effective orders of any other Supranational body which has the right to issue and give the same, and with national laws aimed at enforcing the same to which the Owners are subject, and to obey the orders and directions of those who are charged with their enforcement;

(iv) to discharge at any other port any cargo or part thereof which may render the Vessel liable to confiscation as a contraband carrier;

(v) to call at any other port to change the crew or any part thereof or other persons on board the Vessel when there is reason to believe that they may be subject to internment, imprisonment or other sanctions;

(vi) where cargo has not been loaded or has been discharged by the Owners under any provisions of this Clause, to load other cargo for the Owners' own benefit and carry it to any other port or ports whatsoever, whether backwards or forwards or in a contrary direction to the ordinary or customary route.

(f)   If in compliance with any of the provisions of sub-clauses (2) to (5) of this Clause anything is done or not done, such shall not be deemed to be a deviation, but shall be considered as due fulfilment of the Contract of Carriage.

18.   General Ice Clause

Port of loading

(a)   In the event of the loading port being inaccessible by reason of ice when the Vessel is ready to proceed from her last port or at any time during the voyage or on the Vessel's arrival or in case frost sets in after the Vessel's arrival, the Master for fear of being frozen in is at liberty to leave without cargo, and this Charter Party shall be null and void.

(b)   If during loading the Master, for fear of the Vessel being frozen in, deems it advisable to leave, he has liberty to do so with what cargo he has on board and to proceed to any other port or ports with option of completing cargo for the Owners' benefit for any port or ports including port of discharge. Any part cargo thus loaded under this Charter Party to be forwarded to destination at the Vessel's expense but against payment of freight, provided that no extra expenses be thereby caused to the Charterers, freight being paid on quantity delivered (in proportion if lumpsum), all other conditions as per this Charter Party.

(c)   In case of more than one loading port, and if one or more of the ports are closed by ice, the Master or the Owners to be at liberty either to load the part cargo at the open port and fill up elsewhere for their own account as under section (b) or to declare the Charter Party null and void unless the Charterers agree to load full cargo at the open port.

PART II
GENCON 1994 Uniform General Charter

Port of discharge

(a) Should ice prevent the Vessel from reaching port of discharge the Charterers shall have the option of keeping the Vessel waiting until the re-opening of navigation and paying demurrage or of ordering the Vessel to a safe and immediately accessible port where she can safely discharge without risk of detention by ice. Such orders to be given within 48 hours after the Master or the Owners have given notice to the Charterers of the impossibility of reaching port of destination.

(b) If during discharging the Master for fear of the Vessel being frozen in deems it advisable to leave, he has liberty to do so with what cargo he has on board and to proceed to the nearest accessible port where she can safely discharge.

(c) On delivery of the cargo at such port, all conditions of the Bill of Lading shall apply and the Vessel shall receive the same freight as if she had discharged at the original port of destination, except that if the distance of the substituted port exceeds 100 nautical miles, the freight on the cargo delivered at the substituted port to be increased in proportion.

19.   Law and Arbitration

(a)* This Charter Party shall be governed by and construed in accordance with English law and any dispute arising out of this Charter Party shall be referred to arbitration in London in accordance with the Arbitration Acts 1950 and 1979 or any statutory modification or re-enactment thereof for the time being in force. Unless the parties agree upon a sole arbitrator, one arbitrator shall be appointed by each party and the arbitrators so appointed shall appoint a third arbitrator, the decision of the three-man tribunal thus constituted or any two of them, shall be final. On the receipt by one party of the nomination in writing of the other party's arbitrator, that party shall appoint their arbitrator within fourteen days, failing which the decision of the single arbitrator appointed shall be final. For disputes where the total amount claimed by either party does not exceed the amount stated in Box 25** the arbitration shall be conducted in accordance with the Small Claims Procedure of the London Maritime Arbitrators Association.

(b)* This Charter Party shall be governed by and construed in accordance with Title 9 of the United States Code and the Maritime Law of the United States and should any dispute arise out of this Charter Party, the matter in dispute shall be referred to three persons at New York, one to be appointed by each of the parties hereto, and the third by the two so chosen; their decision or that of any two of them shall be final, and for purpose of enforcing any award, this agreement may be made a rule of the Court. The proceedings shall be conducted in accordance with the rules of the Society of Maritime Arbitrators, Inc. For disputes where the total amount claimed by either party does not exceed the amount stated in Box 25** the arbitration shall be conducted in accordance with the Shortened Arbitration Procedure of the Society of Maritime Arbitrators, Inc.

(c)* Any dispute arising out of this Charter Party shall be referred to arbitration at the place indicated in Box 25, subject to the procedures applicable there. The laws of the place indicated in Box 25 shall govern this Charter Party.

(d) If Box 25 in Part I is not filled in, sub-clause (a) of this Clause shall apply.

* (a), (b) and (c) are alternatives; indicate alternative agreed in Box 25.

** Where no figure is supplied in Box 25 in Part I, this provision only shall be void but the other provisions of this Clause shall have full force and remain in effect.

2. Standard Bareboat Charter Party

BIMCO

BARECON 2017

STANDARD BAREBOAT CHARTER PARTY   PART I

1.	Place and date Type here Type here		
2.	Owners (Cl. 1) (i) Name: Type here (ii) Place of registered office: Type here (iii) Law of registry: Type here	3.	Charterers (Cl. 1) (i) Name: Type here (ii) Place of registered office: Type here (iii) Law of registry: Type here
4.	Vessel (Cl. 1 and 3) (i) Name: Type here (ii) IMO number: Type here (iii) Flag State: Type here (iv) Type: Type here		(v) GT/NT: Type here / Type here (vi) Summer DWT: Type here (vii) When/where built: Type here / Type here (viii) Classification Society: Type here
5.	Date of last special survey by the Vessel's Classification Society Type here	6.	Validity of class certificates (state number of months to apply) (i) Delivery (Cl. 3): Type here (ii) Redelivery (Cl. 10): Type here
7.	Latent Defects (state number of months to apply) (Cl. 1, 3) Type here	8.	Port or place of delivery (Cl. 3) Type here
9.	Delivery notices (Cl. 4) Type here days' approximate notices and Type here days' definite notices	10.	Time for delivery (Cl. 4) Type here
11.	Cancelling date (Cl. 4, 5) Type here	12.	Port or place of redelivery (Cl. 10) Type here
13.	Redelivery notices (Cl. 10) Type here days' approximate notices and Type here definite notices	14.	Trading limits (Cl. 11) Type here
15.	Bunker fuels, unused oils and greases (optional, state if (a) (actual net price), or (b) (current net market price) to apply) (Cl. 9) Type here	16.	Charter period (Cl. 2) Type here
17.	Charter hire (state currency and amount) (Cl. 2, 10 and 15) (i) Charter hire: Type here (ii) Charter hire for optional period: Type here	18.	Optional period and notice (Cl. 2) (i) State extension period in months: Type here (ii) State when declarable: Type here
19.	Rate of interest payable (Cl. 15(g)) Type here	20.	Owners' bank details (state beneficiary and bank account) (Cl. 15) Type here
21.	New class and other regulatory requirements (Cl. 13(b)) (i) State if 13(b)(i) or (ii) to apply: Type here (ii) Threshold amount (AMT): Type here (iii) Vessel's expected remaining life in years on the date of delivery: Type here		
22.	Mortgage(s), if any (state if 16(a) or (b) to apply; if 16(b) applies state date of Financial instrument and name of Mortgagee(s)/Place of business) (Cl. 1, 16) Type here		
23.	Insured Total Loss value (Cl. 17) Type here	24.	Insuring party (state if Cl. 17(b) (Charterers to insure) or Cl. 17(c) (Owners to insure) to apply) Type here

25. Performance guarantee (state amount and entity) (Cl. 27) (optional) Type here	
26. Dispute Resolution (state 33(a), 33(b), 33(c) or 33(d); if 33(c) is agreed, state Singapore or English law; if 33(d) is agreed, state governing law and place of arbitration) (Cl. 33) Choose an item. Type here	
27. Newbuilding Vessel (indicate with "yes" or "no" whether PART III applies and if "yes", complete details below) (optional) Choose an item. (i) Name of Builders: Type here (ii) Hull number: Type here (iii) Date of newbuilding contract: Type here (iv) Liquidated damages for physical defects or deficiencies (state party): Type here (v) Liquidated damages for delay in delivery (state party): Type here	
28. Purchase Option (indicate with "yes" or "no" whether PART IV applies) (optional) Choose an item.	29. Bareboat Charter Registry (indicate with "yes" or "no" whether PART V applies and if "yes", complete details below) (optional) Choose an item. (i) Underlying Registry: Type here (ii) Bareboat Charter Registry: Type here
30. Notices to Owners (state full style details for serving notices) (Cl. 34) Type here	31. Notices to Charterers (state full style details for serving notices) (Cl. 34) Type here

It is mutually agreed that this Charter Party shall be performed subject to the conditions contained in this Charter Party which shall include PART I and PART II. In the event of a conflict of conditions, the provisions of PART I shall prevail over those of PART II to the extent of such conflict but no further. It is further mutually agreed that PART III and/or PART IV and/or PART V shall only apply and only form part of this Charter Party if expressly agreed and stated in Box 27, 28 and 29. If PART III and/or PART IV and/or PART V applies, it is further agreed that in the event of a conflict of conditions, the provisions of PART I and PART II shall prevail over those of PART III and/or PART IV and/or PART V to the extent of such conflict but no further.

Signature (Owners) Type here	Signature (Charterers) Type here

PART II
BARECON 2017 Standard Bareboat Charter Party

1. **Definitions**

    In this Charter Party:

    "Banking Day" means a day on which banks are open in the places stated in Boxes 2, 3, 30 and 31, and, for payments in US dollars, in New York.

    "Charterers" means the party identified in Box 3.

    "Crew" means the Master, officers and ratings and any other personnel employed on board the Vessel.

    "Financial Instrument" means the mortgage, deed of covenant or other such financial security instrument as identified in Box 22.

    "Flag State" means the flag state in Box 4 or such other flag state to which the Charterers may have re-registered the Vessel with the Owners' consent during the Charter Period.

    "Latent Defect" means a defect which could not be discovered on such an examination as a reasonably careful skilled person would make.

    "Owners" means the party identified in Box 2.

    "Total Loss" means an actual, constructive, compromised or agreed total loss of the Vessel under the insurances.

    "Vessel" means the vessel described in Box 4 including its equipment, machinery, boilers, fixtures and fittings.

2. **Charter Period**

    The Owners have agreed to let and the Charterers have agreed to hire the Vessel for the period stated in Box 16 ("Charter Period").

    The Charterers shall have the option to extend the Charter Period by the period stated in Box 18(i) at the rate stated in Box 17(ii), which option shall be exercised by written notice to the Owners latest as stated in Box 18(ii).

    Subject to the terms and conditions herein provided, during the Charter Period the Vessel shall be in the full possession and at the absolute disposal for all purposes of the Charterers and under their complete control in every respect.

3. **Delivery**

    (not applicable when Part III applies, as stated in Box 27).

    (a) The Owners shall deliver the Vessel in a seaworthy condition and in every respect ready for service under this Charter Party and in accordance with the particulars stated in Boxes 4 to 6.

    If the Charterers have inspected the Vessel prior to delivery, the Vessel shall be delivered by the Owners in the same condition as at the time of inspection, fair wear and tear excepted.

    The Vessel shall be delivered by the Owners and taken over by the Charterers at the port or place stated in Box 8 at such readily accessible safe berth or mooring as the Charterers may direct.

    (b) The Vessel shall be properly documented on delivery in accordance with the laws and regulations of the Flag State and the requirements of the Classification Society stated in Box 4. The Vessel upon delivery shall have its

PART II
BARECON 2017 Standard Bareboat Charter Party

survey cycles up to date and class certificates valid and unextended for at least the number of months stated in Box 6(i) free of any conditions or recommendations. If Box 6(i) is not filled in, then six (6) months shall apply.

(c)   The delivery of the Vessel by the Owners and the taking over of the Vessel by the Charterers shall constitute a full performance by the Owners of all the Owners' obligations under this Clause, and thereafter the Charterers shall not be entitled to make or assert any claim against the Owners on account of any conditions, representations or warranties expressed or implied with respect to the Vessel but the Owners shall be liable for the cost of but not the time for repairs or renewals arising out of Latent Defects in the Vessel existing at the time of delivery under this Charter Party, provided such Latent Defects manifest themselves within the number of months after delivery stated in Box 7. If Box 7 is not filled in, then twelve (12) months shall apply.

4.   Time for Delivery

(not applicable when Part III applies, as stated in Box 27)

The Vessel shall not be delivered before the date stated in Box 10 without the Charterers' consent and the Owners shall exercise due diligence to deliver the Vessel not later than the date stated in Box 11.

The Owners shall keep the Charterers informed of the Vessel's itinerary for the voyage leading up to delivery and shall serve the Charterers with the number of days approximate/definite notices of the Vessel's delivery stated in Box 9. Following the tender of any such notices the Owners shall give or allow to be given to the Vessel only such further employment orders as are reasonably expected when given to allow delivery to occur by the date notified.

5.   Cancelling

(not applicable when Part III applies, as stated in Box 27)

(a)   Should the Vessel not be delivered by the cancelling date stated in Box 11, the Charterers shall have the option of cancelling this Charter Party.

(b)   If it appears that the Vessel will be delayed beyond the cancelling date, the Owners may, as soon as they are in a position to state with reasonable certainty the day on which the Vessel should be ready, give notice thereof to the Charterers asking whether they will exercise their option of cancelling, and the option must then be declared within three (3) Banking Days of the receipt by the Charterers of such notice. If the Charterers do not then exercise their option of cancelling, the readiness date stated in the Owners' notice shall be substituted for the cancelling date stated in Box 11 for the purpose of this Clause 5 (Cancelling).

(c)   Cancellation under this Clause 5 (Cancelling) shall be without prejudice to any claim the Charterers may otherwise have against the Owners under this Charter Party.

6.   Familiarisation

(a)   The Charterers shall have the right to place a maximum of two (2) representatives on board the Vessel at their sole risk and expense for a reasonable period prior to the delivery of the Vessel.

The Charterers and the Charterers' representatives shall sign the Owners' usual letter of indemnity prior to embarkation.

(b)   The Owners shall have the right to place a maximum of two (2) representatives on board the Vessel at their sole risk and expense for a reasonable period prior to the redelivery of the Vessel.

The Owners and the Owners' representatives shall sign the Charterers' usual letter of indemnity prior to embarkation.

PART II
BARECON 2017 Standard Bareboat Charter Party

(c)   Such representatives shall be on board for the purpose of familiarisation and in the capacity of observers only, and they shall not interfere in any respect with the operation of the Vessel.

7.   Surveys on Delivery and Redelivery

(a)   The Owners and Charterers shall each appoint and pay for their respective surveyors for the purpose of determining and agreeing in writing the condition of the Vessel at the time of delivery and redelivery hereunder. The Owners shall bear all the Vessel's expenses related to the on-hire survey including loss of time, if any. The Charterers shall bear all the Vessel's expenses related to the off-hire survey including loss of time, if any.

(b)   Divers inspection on delivery/re-delivery

The Charterers shall have the option at delivery and the Owners shall have the option at redelivery, at their respective time, cost and expense, to arrange for an underwater inspection by a diver approved by the Classification Society, in the presence of a Classification Society surveyor, to determine the condition of the rudder, propeller, bottom and other underwater parts of the Vessel.

8.   Inventories

A complete inventory of the Vessel's equipment, outfit, spare parts and consumable stores on board the Vessel shall be made by the parties on delivery and redelivery of the Vessel.

9.   Bunker fuels, oils and greases

The Charterers and the Owners, respectively, shall at the time of delivery and redelivery take over and pay for all bunker fuels and unused lubricating and hydraulic oils and greases in storage tanks and unopened drums at:

(a)*   The actual price paid (excluding barging expenses) as evidenced by invoices or vouchers.

(b)*   The current market price (excluding barging expenses) at the port and date of delivery/redelivery of the Vessel or, if unavailable, at the nearest bunkering port.

*Subclauses (a) and (b) are alternatives; state alternative agreed in Box 15. If Box 15 is not filled in, then subclause (a) shall apply.

10.   Redelivery

At the expiration of the Charter Period the Vessel shall be redelivered by the Charterers and taken over by the Owners at the port or place stated in Box 12 at such readily accessible safe berth or mooring as the Owners may direct.

The Charterers shall keep the Owners informed of the Vessel's itinerary for the voyage leading up to redelivery and shall serve the Owners with the number of days approximate/definite notices of the Vessel's redelivery stated in Box 13.

The Charterers warrant that they will not permit the Vessel to commence a voyage (including any preceding ballast voyage) which cannot reasonably be expected to be completed in time to allow redelivery of the Vessel within the Charter Period and in accordance with the notices given. Notwithstanding the above, should the Charterers fail to redeliver the Vessel within the Charter Period, the Charterers shall pay the daily equivalent to the rate of hire stated in Box 17(i) applicable at the time plus ten (10) per cent or the market rate, whichever is the higher, for the number of days by which the Charter Period is exceeded. Such payment of the enhanced hire rate shall be without prejudice to any claims the Owners may have against the Charterers in this respect. All other terms, conditions and provisions of this Charter Party shall continue to apply.

PART II
BARECON 2017 Standard Bareboat Charter Party

Subject to the provisions of Clause 13 (Maintenance and Operation), the Vessel shall be redelivered to the Owners in the same condition and class as that in which it was delivered, fair wear and tear not affecting class excepted.

The Vessel upon redelivery shall have her survey cycles up to date and class certificates valid and unextended for at least the number of months agreed in Box 6(ii) free of any conditions or recommendations. If Box 6(i) is not filled in, then six (6) months shall apply.

All plans, drawings and manuals (excluding ISM/ISPS manuals) and maintenance records shall remain on board and accessible to the Owners upon redelivery. Any other technical documentation regarding the Vessel which may be in the Charterers' possession shall promptly after redelivery be forwarded to the Owners at their expense, if they so request. The Charterers may keep the Vessel's log books but the Owners shall have the right to make copies of the same.

11. **Trading Restrictions**

The Vessel shall be employed in lawful trades for the carriage of lawful merchandise within the trading limits stated in Box 14.

The Charterers undertake not to employ the Vessel or allow the Vessel to be employed otherwise than in conformity with the terms of the contracts of insurance (including any warranties expressed or implied therein) without first obtaining the consent of the insurers to such employment and complying with such requirements as to additional premium or otherwise as the insurers may require.

The Charterers will not do or permit to be done anything which might cause any breach or infringement of the laws and regulations of the Flag State, or of the places where the Vessel trades.

Notwithstanding any other provisions contained in this Charter Party it is agreed that nuclear fuels or radioactive products or waste are specifically excluded from the cargo permitted to be loaded or carried under this Charter Party. This exclusion does not apply to radio-isotopes used or intended to be used for any industrial, commercial, agricultural, medical or scientific purposes provided the Owners' prior approval has been obtained to loading thereof.

12. **Contracts of Carriage**

(a) The Charterers are to procure that all documents issued during the Charter Period evidencing the terms and conditions agreed in respect of carriage of goods shall contain a paramount clause which shall incorporate the Hague-Visby Rules unless any other legislation relating to carrier's liability for cargo is compulsorily applicable in the trade. The documents shall also contain the New Jason Clause and the Both-to-Blame Collision Clause.

(b) The Charterers are to procure that all passenger tickets issued during the Charter Period for the carriage of passengers and their luggage under this Charter Party shall contain a paramount clause which shall incorporate the Athens Convention Relating to the Carriage of Passengers and their Luggage by Sea, 1974, and any protocol thereto, unless any other legislation relating to carrier's liability for passengers and their luggage is compulsorily applicable in the trade.

13. **Maintenance and Operation**

(a) Maintenance

The Charterers shall properly maintain the Vessel in a good state of repair, in efficient operating condition and in accordance with good commercial maintenance practice and, at their own expense, maintain the Vessel's Class with the Classification Society stated in Box 4 and all necessary certificates.

(b) New Class and Other Regulatory Requirements

PART II
BARECON 2017 Standard Bareboat Charter Party

(i)*   In the event of any structural changes or new equipment becoming necessary for the continued operation of the Vessel by reason of new class requirements or by compulsory legislation ("Required Modification"), all such costs shall be for the Charterers' account.

(ii)*   In the event of any structural changes or new equipment becoming necessary for the continued operation of the Vessel by reason of a Required Modification, the costs shall be apportioned as follows:

    (1)   if the costs of the Required Modification are less than the amount stated in Box 21(ii), such costs shall be for the Charterers' account;

    (2)   if the costs of the Required Modification are greater than the amount stated in Box 21(ii), the Charterers' portion of costs shall be apportioned using the formula below; all costs other than the Charterers' portion shall be for the Owners' account.

AMT = agreed amount stated in Box 21(ii)

CRM = cost of Required Modification

MEL = modification's expected life in years

VEL = the Vessel's expected remaining life in years stated in Box 21(iii) less the number of years between the date of delivery and the date of the modification.

RPY = remaining charter period in years

(i) If the Required Modification is expected to last for the remaining life of the Vessel, then:

Charterers' portion of costs $= \frac{CRM}{VEL} \, x \, RPY$

(ii) If the Required Modification is not expected to last for the remaining life of the Vessel, then:

Charterers' portion of costs $= \frac{CRM}{MEL} \, x \, RPY$

*Subclauses 13(b)(i) and 13(b)(ii) are alternatives, state alternative agreed in Box 21(i). If Box 21(i) is not filled in, then subclause 13(b)(i) shall apply.

(c)   Financial Security

The Charterers shall maintain financial security or responsibility in respect of third party liabilities as required by any government, including federal, state or municipal or other division or authority thereof, to enable the Vessel, without penalty or charge, lawfully to enter, remain at, or leave any port, place, territorial or contiguous waters of any country, state or municipality in performance of this Charter Party without any delay. This obligation shall apply whether or not such requirements have been lawfully imposed by such government or division or authority thereof. The Charterers shall make and maintain all arrangements by bond or otherwise as may be necessary to satisfy such requirements at the Charterers' sole expense and the Charterers shall indemnify the Owners against all consequences whatsoever (including loss of time) for any failure or inability to do so.

(d)   Operation of the Vessel

The Charterers shall at their own expense crew, victual, navigate, operate, supply, fuel, maintain and repair the Vessel during the Charter Period and they shall be responsible for all costs and expenses whatsoever relating to their use and operation of the Vessel, including any taxes and fees. The Crew shall be the servants of the Charterers for all purposes whatsoever, even if for any reason appointed by the Owners.

PART II
BARECON 2017 Standard Bareboat Charter Party

(e)   Information to Owners

The Charterers shall keep the Owners advised of the intended employment, planned dry-docking and major repairs of the Vessel, as reasonably required by the Owners.

(f)   Flag and Name of Vessel

During the Charter Period, the Charterers shall have the liberty to paint the Vessel in their own colours, install and display their funnel insignia and fly their own house flag. The Charterers shall also have the liberty, with the Owners' prior written consent, which shall not be unreasonably withheld, to change the flag and/or the name of the Vessel during the Charter Period. Painting and re-painting, instalment and re-instalment, registration and re-registration, if required by the Owners, shall be at the Charterers' expense and time.

(g)   Changes to the Vessel

Subject to subclause 13(b) (New Class and Other Regulatory Requirements), the Charterers shall make no structural or substantial changes to the Vessel without the Owners' prior written approval. If the Owners agree to such changes, the Charterers shall, if the Owners so require, restore the Vessel, prior to redelivery of the Vessel, to its former condition.

(h)   Use of the Vessel's Outfit and Equipment

The Charterers shall have the use of all outfit, equipment and spare parts on board the Vessel at the time of delivery, provided the same or their substantial equivalent shall be returned to the Owners on redelivery in the same good order and condition as on delivery as per the inventory (see Clause 8 (Inventories)), ordinary wear and tear excepted. The Charterers shall from time to time during the Charter Period replace such equipment that become unfit for use. The Charterers shall procure that all repairs to or replacement of any damaged, worn or lost parts or equipment will be effected in such manner (both as regards workmanship and quality of materials, including spare parts) as not to diminish the value of the Vessel.

The Charterers have the right to fit additional equipment at their expense and risk but the Charterers shall remove such equipment at the end of the Charter Period if requested by the Owners. Any hired equipment on board the Vessel at the time of delivery shall be kept and maintained by the Charterers and the Charterers shall assume the obligations and liabilities of the Owners under any lease contracts in connection therewith and shall reimburse the Owners for all expenses incurred in connection therewith, also for any new hired equipment required in order to comply with any regulations.

(i)   Periodical Dry-Docking

The Charterers shall dry-dock the Vessel and clean and paint her underwater parts whenever the same may be necessary, but not less than once every sixty (60) calendar months or such other period as may be required by the Classification Society or Flag State.

14.   Inspection during the Charter Period

The Owners shall have the right at any time after giving reasonable notice to the Charterers to inspect the Vessel or instruct a duly authorised surveyor to carry out such inspection on their behalf to ascertain its condition and satisfy themselves that the Vessel is being properly repaired and maintained or for any other commercial reason they consider necessary (provided it does not unduly interfere with the commercial operation of the Vessel).

The fees for such inspections shall be paid for by the Owners. All time used in respect of inspection shall be for the Charterers' account and form part of the Charter Period.

PART II
BARECON 2017 Standard Bareboat Charter Party

The Charterers shall also permit the Owners to inspect the Vessel's class records, log books, certificates, maintenance and other records whenever requested and shall whenever required by the Owners furnish them with full information regarding any casualties or other accidents or damage to the Vessel.

15. **Hire**

(a) The Charterers shall pay hire due to the Owners punctually in accordance with the terms of this Charter Party.

(b) The Charterers shall pay to the Owners for the hire of the Vessel a lump sum in the amount stated in Box 17(i) which shall be payable not later than every thirty (30) running days in advance, the first lump sum being payable on the date and hour of the Vessel's delivery to the Charterers. Hire shall be paid continuously throughout the Charter Period.

(c) Payment of hire shall be made to the Owners' bank account stated in Box 20.

(d) All payments of Charter Hire and any other payments due under this Charter shall be made without any set-off whatsoever and free and clear of any withholding or deduction for, or on account of, any present or future income, freight, stamp or other taxes, levies, imposts, duties, fees, charges, restrictions or conditions of any nature. If the Charterers are required by any authority in any country to make any withholding or deduction from any such payment, the sum due from the Charterers in respect of such payment will be increased to the extent necessary to ensure that, after the making of such withholding or deduction the Owners receive a net sum equal to the amount which it would have received had no such deduction or withholding been required to be made.

(e) If the Charterers fail to make punctual payment of hire due, the Owners shall give the Charterers three (3) Banking Days written notice to rectify the failure, and when so rectified within those three (3) Banking Days following the Owners' notice, the payment shall stand as punctual.

Failure by the Charterers to pay hire due in full within three (3) Banking Days of their receiving a notice from Owners shall entitle the Owners, without prejudice to any other rights or claims the Owners may have against the Charterers, to terminate this Charter Party at any time thereafter, as long as hire remains outstanding.

(f) If the Owners choose not to exercise any of the rights afforded to them by this Clause in respect of any particular late payment of hire, or a series of late payments of hire, under the Charter Party, this shall not be construed as a waiver of their right to terminate the Charter Party.

(g) Any delay in payment of hire shall entitle the Owners to interest at the rate per annum as agreed in Box 19. If Box 19 has not been filled in, the one month interbank offered rate in London (LIBOR or its successor) for the currency stated in Box 17, as quoted on the date when the hire fell due, increased by three (3) per cent, shall apply.

(h) Payment of interest due under subclause 15(g) shall be made within seven (7) running days of the date of the Owners' invoice specifying the amount payable or, in the absence of an invoice, at the time of the next hire payment date.

(i) Final payment of hire, if for a period of less than thirty (30) running days, shall be calculated proportionally according to the number of days and hours remaining before redelivery and advance payment to be effected accordingly.

16. **Mortgage**

(only to apply if Box 22 has been appropriately filled in)

(a)* The Owners warrant that they have not effected any mortgage(s) of the Vessel and that they shall not effect any mortgage(s) without the prior consent of the Charterers, which shall not be unreasonably withheld.

PART II
BARECON 2017 Standard Bareboat Charter Party

(b)*   The Vessel chartered under this Charter Party is financed by a mortgage according to the Financial Instrument. The Charterers undertake to comply, and provide such information and documents to enable the Owners to comply, with all such instructions or directions in regard to the employment, insurances, operation, repairs and maintenance of the Vessel as laid down in the Financial Instrument or as may be directed from time to time during the currency of the Charter Party by the mortgagee(s) in conformity with the Financial Instrument, including the display or posting of such notices as the Mortgagees may require. The Charterers confirm that, for this purpose, they have acquainted themselves with all relevant terms, conditions and provisions of the Financial Instrument and agree to acknowledge this in writing in any form that may be required by the mortgagee(s). The Owners warrant that they have not effected any mortgage(s) other than stated in Box 22 and that they shall not agree to any amendment of the mortgage(s) referred to in Box 22 or effect any other mortgage(s) without the prior consent of the Charterers, which shall not be unreasonably withheld.

    *(Optional, Subclauses 16(a) and 16(b) are alternatives; indicate alternative agreed in Box 22).

17.   **Insurance**

(a)   General

    (i) The value of the Vessel for hull and machinery (including increased value) and war risks insurance is the sum stated in Box 23, or such other sum as the parties may from time to time agree in writing. The party insuring the Vessel shall do so on such terms and conditions and with such insurers as the other party shall approve in writing, which approval shall not be unreasonably withheld, and shall name the other party as co-assured.

    (ii) Notwithstanding that the parties are co-assured, these insurance provisions shall neither exclude nor discharge liability between the Owners and the Charterers under this Charter Party, but are intended to secure payment of the loss insurance proceeds as a first resort to make good the Owners' loss. If such payment is made to the Owners it shall be treated as satisfaction (but not exclusion or discharge) of the Charterers' liability towards the Owners. For the avoidance of doubt, such payment is no bar to a claim by the Owners and/or their insurers against the Charterers to seek indemnity by way of subrogation.

    (iii) Nothing herein shall prejudice any rights of recovery of the Owners or the Charterers (or their insurers) against third parties.

(b)*   Charterers to Insure

    (i) During the Charter Period the Vessel shall be kept insured by the Charterers at their expense against hull and machinery, war, and protection and indemnity risks (and any risks against which it is compulsory to insure for the operation of the Vessel, including maintaining financial security in accordance with subclause 13(c) (Financial Security)).

    (ii) Such insurances shall be arranged by the Charterers to protect the interests of the Owners and the Charterers and the mortgagee(s) (if any), and the Charterers shall be at liberty to protect under such insurances the interests of any managers they may appoint.

    (iii) The Charterers shall upon the request of the Owners, provide information and promptly execute such documents as may be required to enable the Owners to comply with the insurance provisions of the Financial Instrument.

(c)*   Owners to Insure

    (i) During the Charter Period the Vessel shall be kept insured by the Owners at their expense against hull and machinery and war risks. The Charterers shall progress claims for recovery against any third parties for the benefit of the Owners' and the Charterers' respective interests.

PART II
BARECON 2017 Standard Bareboat Charter Party

(ii) During the Charter Period the Vessel shall be kept insured by the Charterers at their expense against Protection and Indemnity risks (and any risks against which it is compulsory to insure for the operation of the Vessel, including maintaining financial security in accordance with subclause 13(c) (Financial Security)).

(iii) In the event that any act or negligence of the Charterers prejudices any of the insurances herein provided, the Charterers shall pay to the Owners all losses and indemnify the Owners against all claims and demands which would otherwise have been covered by such insurances.

*Subclauses 17(b) and 17(c) are alternatives, state alternative agreed in Box 24. If Box 24 is not filled in, then subclause 17(b) (Charterers to Insure) shall apply.

18. **Repairs**

(a) Subject to the provisions of any Financial Instrument, and the approval of the Owners, the Charterers shall effect all insured repairs, and undertake settlement of all miscellaneous expenses in connection with such repairs as well as all insured charges, expenses and liabilities.

To the extent of coverage under the insurances provided for under the provisions of subclause 17(c) (Owners to Insure), the Charterers shall be reimbursed under the Owners' insurances for such expenditures upon presentation of accounts.

(b) The Charterers shall remain responsible for and effect repairs and settlement of costs and expenses incurred thereby in respect of all repairs not covered by the insurances and/or not exceeding any deductibles provided for in the insurances.

(c) All time used for repairs under the provisions of subclauses 18(a) and 18(b) and for repairs of Latent Defects according to Clause 3 (Delivery) above, including any deviation, shall be for the Charterers' account and shall form part of the Charter Period.

19. **Total loss**

(a) The Charterers shall be liable to the Owners by way of damages if the Vessel becomes a Total Loss. Subject to the provisions of any Financial Instrument, if the Vessel becomes a Total Loss, all insurance payments for such loss shall be paid to the Owners who shall distribute the monies between the Owners and the Charterers according to their respective interests, which shall satisfy (but not exclude or discharge) the Charterers' liability to the Owners thereof. The Charterers undertake to notify the Owners and the mortgagee(s), if any, of any occurrences in consequence of which the Vessel is likely to become a Total Loss.

(b) Notwithstanding any other clause herein, it is recognised that the Charterers have a continuing obligation to protect and preserve the Vessel as an asset of the Owners. The Charterers shall have a continuing duty after the termination of the Charter Party to preserve and present claims on behalf of Owners and Charterers and/or any subrogated insurers against any third party held responsible for the Total Loss during the Charter Period and account for any recovery achieved.

(c) The Owners or the Charterers, as the case may be, shall upon the request of the other party, promptly execute such documents as may be required to enable the other party to abandon the Vessel to the insurers and claim a constructive total loss.

20. **Lien**

The Owners shall have a lien upon all cargoes, hires and freights (including deadfreight and demurrage) belonging or due to the Charterers or any sub-charterers, for any amounts due under this Charter Party and the Charterers shall have a lien on the Vessel for all monies paid in advance and not earned.

21. **Non-Lien**

PART II
BARECON 2017 Standard Bareboat Charter Party

The Charterers will not suffer, nor permit to be continued, any lien or encumbrance incurred by them or their agents, which might have priority over the title and interest of the Owners in the Vessel.

22. **Indemnity**

(a) The Charterers shall indemnify the Owners against any loss, damage or expense arising out of or in relation to the operation of the Vessel by the Charterers, and against any lien of whatsoever nature arising out of an event occurring during the Charter Period. This shall include indemnity for any loss, damage or expense arising out of or in relation to any international convention which may impose liability upon the Owners.

(b) Without prejudice to the generality of the foregoing, the Charterers agree to indemnify the Owners against all consequences or liabilities arising from the Master, officers or agents signing bills of lading or other documents.

(c) If the Vessel is arrested or otherwise detained for any reason whatsoever other than those covered in subclause (d), the Charterers shall at their own expense take all reasonable steps to secure that within a reasonable time the Vessel is released, including the provision of bail.

(d) If the Vessel is arrested or otherwise detained by reason of a claim or claims against the Owners, the Owners shall at their own expense take all reasonable steps to secure that within a reasonable time the Vessel is released, including the provision of bail.

In such circumstances the Owners shall indemnify the Charterers against any loss, damage or expense incurred by the Charterers (including hire paid under this Charter Party) as a direct consequence of such arrest or detention.

23. **Salvage**

All salvage and towage performed by the Vessel shall be for the Charterers' benefit and the cost of repairing damage occasioned thereby shall be borne by the Charterers.

24. **Wreck Removal**

If the Vessel becomes a wreck, or any part of the Vessel is lost or abandoned, and is an obstruction to navigation or poses a hazard and has to be raised, removed, destroyed, marked or lit by order of any lawful authority having jurisdiction over the area or as a result of any applicable law, the Charterers shall be liable for any and all expenses in connection with the raising, removal, destruction, lighting or marking of the Vessel and shall indemnify the Owners against any sums whatsoever, which the Owners become liable to pay as a consequence.

25. **General Average**

The Owners shall not contribute to General Average.

26. **Assignment, Novation, Sub-Charter and Sale**

(a) The Charterers shall not assign or novate this Charter Party nor sub-charter the Vessel on a bareboat basis except with the prior consent in writing of the Owners, which shall not be unreasonably withheld, and subject to such terms and conditions as the Owners shall approve.

(b) The Owners shall not sell the Vessel during the currency of this Charter Party except with the prior written consent of the Charterers, which shall not be unreasonably withheld, and subject to the buyer accepting a novation of this Charter Party.

(c) The Owners shall be entitled to assign their rights under this Charter Party.

PART II
BARECON 2017 Standard Bareboat Charter Party

27.   Performance Guarantee

(Optional, to apply only if Box 25 filled in)

The Charterers undertake to furnish, before delivery of the Vessel, a guarantee or bond in the amount of and from the entity stated in Box 25 in a form acceptable to the Owners as guarantee for full performance of their obligations under this Charter Party.

28.   Anti-Corruption

(a)   The parties agree that in connection with the performance of this Charter Party they shall each:

(i) comply at all times with all applicable anti-corruption legislation and have procedures in place that are, to the best of its knowledge and belief, designed to prevent the commission of any offence under such legislation by any member of its organisation and/or by any person providing services for it or on its behalf; and

(ii) make and keep books, records, and accounts which in reasonable detail accurately and fairly reflect the transactions in connection with this Charter Party.

(b)   If either party fails to comply with any applicable anti-corruption legislation, it shall defend and indemnify the other party against any fine, penalty, liability, loss or damage and for any related costs (including, without limitation, court costs and legal fees) arising from such breach.

(c)   Without prejudice to any of its other rights under this Charter Party, either party may terminate this Charter Party without incurring any liability to the other party if:

(i) at any time the other party or any member of its organisation has committed a breach of any applicable anti-corruption legislation in connection with this Charter Party; and

(ii) such breach causes the non-breaching party to be in breach of any applicable anti-corruption legislation.

Any such right to terminate must be exercised without undue delay.

(d)   Each party represents and warrants that in connection with the negotiation of this Charter Party neither it nor any member of its organisation has committed any breach of applicable anti-corruption legislation. Breach of this subclause (d) shall entitle the other party to terminate the Charter Party without incurring any liability to the other.

29.   Sanctions and Designated Entities

(a)   The provisions of this clause shall apply in relation to any sanction, prohibition or restriction imposed on any specified persons, entities or bodies including the designation of specified vessels or fleets under United Nations Resolutions or trade or economic sanctions, laws or regulations of the European Union or the United States of America.

(b)   The Owners and the Charterers respectively warrant for themselves (and in the case of any sub-charter, the Charterers further warrant in respect of any sub-charterers, shippers, receivers, or cargo interests) that at the date of this fixture and throughout the duration of this Charter Party they are not subject to any of the sanctions, prohibitions, restrictions or designation referred to in subclause (a) which prohibit or render unlawful any performance under this Charter Party. The Owners further warrant that the Vessel is not a designated vessel.

(c)   If at any time during the performance of this Charter Party either party becomes aware that the other party is in breach of warranty in this Clause, the party not in breach shall comply with the laws and regulations of any Government to which that party or the Vessel is subject, and follow any orders or directions which may be given by any body acting with powers to compel compliance, including where applicable the Owners' Flag State. In the absence of any such orders, directions, laws or regulations, the party not in breach may, in its option, terminate the Charter Party forthwith in accordance with Clause 31 (Termination).

(d)   If, in compliance with the provisions of this Clause, anything is done or is not done, such shall not be deemed a deviation but shall be considered due fulfilment of this Charter Party.

(e)   Notwithstanding anything in this Clause to the contrary, the Owners or the Charterers shall not be required to do anything which constitutes a violation of the laws and regulations of any State to which either of them is subject.

(f)   The Owners or the Charterers shall be liable to indemnify the other party against any and all claims, losses, damage, costs and fines whatsoever suffered by the other party resulting from any breach of warranty in this Clause.

30.   Requisition/Acquisition

(a)   In the event of the requisition for hire of the Vessel by any governmental or other competent authority at any time during the Charter Period, this Charter Party shall not be deemed to be frustrated or otherwise terminated. The Charterers shall continue to pay hire according to the Charter Party until the time when the Charter Party would have expired or terminated pursuant to any of the provisions hereof. However, if any requisition hire or compensation is received by the Owners for the remainder of the Charter Period or the period of the requisition, whichever is shorter, it shall be payable by the Owners to the Charterers.

(b)   In the event of the Owners being deprived of their ownership in the Vessel by any compulsory acquisition of the Vessel or requisition for title by any governmental or other competent authority (hereinafter referred to as "Compulsory Acquisition"), then, irrespective of the date during the Charter Period when Compulsory Acquisition may occur, this Charter Party shall be deemed terminated as of the date of such Compulsory Acquisition. In such event hire to be considered as earned and to be paid up to the date and time of such Compulsory Acquisition. The Owners shall be entitled to any compensation received for such Compulsory Acquisition.

31.   Termination

(a)   Charterers' Default

The Owners shall be entitled to terminate this Charter Party by written notice to the Charterers under the following circumstances and to claim damages including, but not limited to, for the loss of the remainder of the Charter Party:

(i) Non-payment of hire (see Clause 15 (Hire)).

(ii) Charterers' failure to comply with the requirements of:

(1)   Clause 11 (Trading Restrictions); or

(2)   Subclause 17(b) (Charterers to Insure).

(iii) The Charterers do not rectify any failure to comply with the requirements of subclause 13(a) (Maintenance) as soon as practically possible after the Owners have notified them to do so and in any event so that the Vessel's insurance cover is not prejudiced.

(b)   Owners' Default

PART II
BARECON 2017 Standard Bareboat Charter Party

The Charterers shall be entitled to terminate this Charter Party with immediate effect by written notice to the Owners and to claim damages including, but not limited to, for the loss of the remainder of the Charter Party:

(i) If the Owners shall by any act or omission be in breach of their obligations under this Charter Party to the extent that the Charterers are deprived of the use of the Vessel and such breach continues for a period of fourteen (14) running days after written notice thereof has been given by the Charterers to the Owners; or

(ii) if the Owners fail to arrange or maintain the insurances in accordance with subclause 17(c) (Owners to Insure).

(c) Loss of Vessel

This Charter Party shall be deemed to be terminated, without prejudice to any accrued rights or obligations, if the Vessel becomes lost either when it has become an actual total loss or agreement has been reached with the Vessel's underwriters in respect of its constructive total loss or if such agreement with the Vessel's underwriters is not reached it is adjudged by a competent tribunal that a constructive loss of the Vessel has occurred, or has been declared missing. The date upon which the Vessel is to be treated as declared missing shall be ten (10) days after the Vessel was last reported or when the Vessel is recorded as missing by the Vessel's underwriters, whichever occurs first.

(d) Bankruptcy

Either party shall be entitled to terminate this Charter Party with immediate effect by written notice to the other party if that other party has a petition presented for its winding up or administration or any other action is taken with a view to its winding up (otherwise than for the purpose of solvent reconstruction or amalgamation), or becomes bankrupt or commits an act of bankruptcy, or makes any arrangement or composition for the benefit of creditors, or has a receiver or manager or administrative receiver or administrator or liquidator appointed in respect of any of its assets, or suspends payments, or anything analogous to any of the foregoing under the law of any jurisdiction happens to it, or ceases or threatens to cease to carry on business.

(e) The termination of this Charter Party shall be without prejudice to all rights accrued due between the parties prior to the date of termination and to any claim that either party might have.

32. Repossession

In the event of the early termination of this Charter Party in accordance with the applicable provisions of this Charter Party, the Owners shall have the right to repossess the Vessel from the Charterers at its current or next port of call, or at a port or place convenient to them without hindrance or interference by the Charterers, courts or local authorities. Pending physical repossession of the Vessel, the Charterers shall hold the Vessel as gratuitous bailee only to the Owners. The Owners shall arrange for an authorised representative to board the Vessel as soon as reasonably practicable following the termination of this Charter Party. The Vessel shall be deemed to be repossessed by the Owners from the Charterers upon the boarding of the Vessel by the Owners' representative. All arrangements and expenses relating to the settling of wages, disembarkation and repatriation of the Crew shall be the sole responsibility of the Charterers.

33. BIMCO Dispute Resolution Clause 2017

(a)* This Charter Party shall be governed by and construed in accordance with English law and any dispute arising out of or in connection with this Charter Party shall be referred to arbitration in London in accordance with the Arbitration Act 1996 or any statutory modification or re-enactment thereof save to the extent necessary to give effect to the provisions of this Clause.

The arbitration shall be conducted in accordance with the London Maritime Arbitrators Association (LMAA) Terms current at the time when the arbitration proceedings are commenced.

PART II
BARECON 2017 Standard Bareboat Charter Party

The reference shall be to three arbitrators. A party wishing to refer a dispute to arbitration shall appoint its arbitrator and send notice of such appointment in writing to the other party requiring the other party to appoint its own arbitrator within fourteen (14) calendar days of that notice and stating that it will appoint its arbitrator as sole arbitrator unless the other party appoints its own arbitrator and gives notice that it has done so within the fourteen (14) days specified. If the other party does not appoint its own arbitrator and give notice that it has done so within the fourteen (14) days specified, the party referring a dispute to arbitration may, without the requirement of any further prior notice to the other party, appoint its arbitrator as sole arbitrator and shall advise the other party accordingly. The award of the sole arbitrator shall be binding on both parties as if he had been appointed by agreement.

Nothing herein shall prevent the parties agreeing in writing to vary these provisions to provide for the appointment of a sole arbitrator.

In cases where neither the claim nor any counterclaim exceeds the sum of USD 100,000 (or such other sum as the parties may agree) the arbitration shall be conducted in accordance with the LMAA Small Claims Procedure current at the time when the arbitration proceedings are commenced.

In cases where the claim or any counterclaim exceeds the sum agreed for the LMAA Small Claims Procedure and neither the claim nor any counterclaim exceeds the sum of USD 400,000 (or such other sum as the parties may agree) the arbitration shall be conducted in accordance with the LMAA Intermediate Claims Procedure current at the time when the arbitration proceedings are commenced.

(b)*   This Charter Party shall be governed by U.S. maritime law or, if this Charter Party is not a maritime contract under U.S. law, by the laws of the State of New York. Any dispute arising out of or in connection with this Charter Party shall be referred to three (3) persons at New York, one to be appointed by each of the parties hereto, and the third by the two so chosen. The decision of the arbitrators or any two of them shall be final, and for the purposes of enforcing any award, judgment may be entered on an award by any court of competent jurisdiction. The proceedings shall be conducted in accordance with the SMA Rules current as of the date of this Charter Party.

In cases where neither the claim nor any counterclaim exceeds the sum of USD 100,000 (or such other sum as the parties may agree) the arbitration shall be conducted in accordance with the SMA Rules for Shortened Arbitration Procedure current as of the date of this Charter Party.

(c)*   This Charter Party shall be governed by and construed in accordance with Singapore**/English** law.

Any dispute arising out of or in connection with this Charter Party, including any question regarding its existence, validity or termination shall be referred to and finally resolved by arbitration in Singapore in accordance with the Singapore International Arbitration Act (Chapter 143A) and any statutory modification or re-enactment thereof save to the extent necessary to give effect to the provisions of this Clause.

The arbitration shall be conducted in accordance with the Arbitration Rules of the Singapore Chamber of Maritime Arbitration (SCMA) current at the time when the arbitration proceedings are commenced.

The reference to arbitration of disputes under this Clause shall be to three arbitrators. A party wishing to refer a dispute to arbitration shall appoint its arbitrator and send notice of such appointment in writing to the other party requiring the other party to appoint its own arbitrator and give notice that it has done so within fourteen (14) calendar days of that notice and stating that it will appoint its own arbitrator as sole arbitrator unless the other party appoints its own arbitrator and gives notice that it has done so within the fourteen (14) days specified. If the other party does not give notice that it has done so within the fourteen (14) days specified, the party referring a dispute to arbitration may, without the requirement of any further prior notice to the other party, appoint its arbitrator as sole arbitrator and shall advise the other party accordingly. The award of a sole arbitrator shall be binding on both parties as if he had been appointed by agreement.

PART II
BARECON 2017 Standard Bareboat Charter Party

Nothing herein shall prevent the parties agreeing in writing to vary these provisions to provide for the appointment of a sole arbitrator.

In cases where neither the claim nor any counterclaim exceeds the sum of USD 150,000 (or such other sum as the parties may agree) the arbitration shall be conducted before a single arbitrator in accordance with the SCMA Small Claims Procedure current at the time when the arbitration proceedings are commenced.

**Delete whichever does not apply. If neither or both are deleted, then English law shall apply by default.

(d)* This Charter Party shall be governed by and construed in accordance with the laws of the place mutually agreed by the Parties and any dispute arising out of or in connection with this Charter Party shall be referred to arbitration at a mutually agreed place, subject to the procedures applicable there.

(e) The parties may agree at any time to refer to mediation any difference and/or dispute arising out of or in connection with this Charter Party. In the case of any dispute in respect of which arbitration has been commenced under subclause (a), (c) or (d), the following shall apply:

(i) Either party may at any time and from time to time elect to refer the dispute or part of the dispute to mediation by service on the other party of a written notice (the "Mediation Notice") calling on the other party to agree to mediation.

(ii) The other party shall thereupon within fourteen (14) calendar days of receipt of the Mediation Notice confirm that they agree to mediation, in which case the parties shall thereafter agree a mediator within a further fourteen (14) calendar days, failing which on the application of either party a mediator will be appointed promptly by the Arbitration Tribunal ("the Tribunal") or such person as the Tribunal may designate for that purpose. The mediation shall be conducted in such place and in accordance with such procedure and on such terms as the parties may agree or, in the event of disagreement, as may be set by the mediator.

(iii) If the other party does not agree to mediate, that fact may be brought to the attention of the Tribunal and may be taken into account by the Tribunal when allocating the costs of the arbitration as between the parties.

(iv) The mediation shall not affect the right of either party to seek such relief or take such steps as it considers necessary to protect its interest.

(v) Either party may advise the Tribunal that they have agreed to mediation. The arbitration procedure shall continue during the conduct of the mediation but the Tribunal may take the mediation timetable into account when setting the timetable for steps in the arbitration.

(vi) Unless otherwise agreed or specified in the mediation terms, each party shall bear its own costs incurred in the mediation and the parties shall share equally the mediator's costs and expenses.

(vii) The mediation process shall be without prejudice and confidential and no information or documents disclosed during it shall be revealed to the Tribunal except to the extent that they are disclosable under the law and procedure governing the arbitration.

(Note: The parties should be aware that the mediation process may not necessarily interrupt time limits.)

*Subclauses (a), (b), (c) and (d) are alternatives; indicate alternative agreed in Box 26.

If Box 26 in Part I is not appropriately filled in, subclause (a) of this Clause shall apply. Subclause (e) shall apply in all cases except for alternative (b).

34. Notices

PART II
BARECON 2017 Standard Bareboat Charter Party

All notices, requests and other communications required or permitted by any clause of this Charter Party shall be given in writing and shall be sufficiently given or transmitted if delivered by hand, email, express courier service or registered mail and addressed if to the Owners as stated in Box 30 or such other address or email address as the Owners may hereafter designate in writing, and if to the Charterers as stated in Box 31 or such other address or email address as the Charterers may hereafter designate in writing. Any such communication shall be deemed to have been given on the date of actual receipt by the party to which it is addressed.

35. **Partial Validity**

If by reason of any enactment or judgment any provision of this Charter Party shall be deemed or held to be illegal, void or unenforceable in whole or in part, all other provisions of this Charter Party shall be unaffected thereby and shall remain in full force and effect.

36. **Entire Agreement**

This Charter Party is the entire agreement of the parties, which supersedes all previous written or oral understandings and which may not be modified except by a written amendment signed by both parties.

37. **Headings**

The headings of this Charter Party are for identification only and shall not be deemed to be part hereof or be taken into consideration in the interpretation or construction of this Charter Party.

38. **Singular/Plural**

The singular includes the plural and vice versa as the context admits or requires.

PART III
BARECON 2017 Standard Bareboat Charter Party
PROVISIONS TO APPLY FOR NEWBUILDING VESSELS ONLY
(OPTIONAL, only applicable if Box 27 has been completed)

1. Specifications and Building Contract

(a)   The Vessel shall be constructed in accordance with the building contract between the Builders and the Owners including the specifications and plans incorporated therein ("Building Contract"). The Owners shall provide the Charterers with a copy of the Building Contract to the extent relevant to this Charter Party.

(b)   No variations shall be made to the Building Contract without the Charterers' prior written consent. The Charterers shall be entitled to request change orders in accordance with the Building Contract. Any additional costs or consequences due to Charterers' change orders shall be borne by the Charterers.

(c)   The Owners and the Charterers will liaise and cooperate in all matters regarding the construction of the Vessel and the Building Contract. The Charterers shall have the right to send their representative to the Builders' yard to inspect the Vessel during its construction.

(d)   The Owners shall assign their guarantee rights under the Building Contract to the Charterers, if permitted. If not permitted, the Owners shall exercise their guarantee rights against the Builders for the benefit of the Charterers. The Charterers shall be obliged to accept such sums as the Owners are reasonably able to recover under the guarantee provisions of the Building Contract.

2. Delivery and Cancellation

(a)   (i) Subject to the provisions of Clause 3 (Liquidated Damages) hereunder, the Charterers shall be obliged to accept the Vessel from the Owners, constructed and delivered in accordance with the Building Contract and including buyers' supplies, on the date of delivery by the Builders. The Charterers undertake that having accepted the Vessel they will not thereafter raise any claims against the Owners in respect of the Vessel's performance or specification or defects, if any.

(ii) The date of delivery for the purpose of this Charter shall be the date (the "Delivery Date") when the Vessel is in fact delivered by the Builders to the Owners in accordance with the Building Contract, whether that is before or after the scheduled delivery date under the Building Contract. The Owners shall be under no responsibility for any delay whatsoever in delivery of the Vessel to the Charterers under this Charter Party, except to the extent caused solely by the Owners' acts or omissions resulting in a default by the Owners under the Building Contract. The Owners shall be responsible to the Charterers for any direct losses incurred by the Charterers, if the Vessel is not delivered to the Owners due solely to the Owners' acts or omissions resulting in a default by the Owners under the Building Contract.

(iii) The Owners and the Charterers shall on the Delivery Date sign a Protocol of Delivery and Acceptance evidencing delivery of the Vessel hereunder.

(b)   (i) The Owners' obligation to charter the Vessel to the Charterers hereunder is conditional upon delivery of the Vessel to the Owners by the Builders in accordance with the Building Contract.

(ii) If for any reason other than a default by the Owners under the Building Contract, the Builders become entitled under that Contract not to deliver the Vessel and exercise that right, the Owners shall be entitled to cancel this Charter Party by written notice to the Charterers.

(iii) If for any reason the Owners become entitled to cancel the Building Contract and exercise that right, the Owners shall be entitled to cancel this Charter Party by written notice to the Charterers. If, however, the Owners do not exercise their right to cancel the Building Contract, the Charterers shall be entitled to cancel this Charter Party by written notice to the Owners.

PART III
BARECON 2017 Standard Bareboat Charter Party
PROVISIONS TO APPLY FOR NEWBUILDING VESSELS ONLY
(OPTIONAL, only applicable if Box 27 has been completed)

3.   Liquidated Damages

(a)   Any liquidated damages for physical defects or deficiencies and any costs incurred in pursuing a claim therefor shall be credited to the party stated in Box 27(iv) or if not filled in shall be shared equally between the parties.

(b)   Any liquidated damages for delay in delivery under the Building Contract and any costs incurred in pursuing a claim therefor shall be credited to the party stated in Box 27(v) or if not filled in shall be shared equally between the parties.

PART IV
BARECON 2017 Standard Bareboat Charter Party
PURCHASE OPTION
(OPTIONAL, only applicable if Box 28 has been completed)

1. The Charterers shall have an option to purchase the Vessel (the "Purchase Option") exercisable on each of the dates stated below as follows:

Date (state number of months after delivery of the Vessel)	Purchase Price (the "Purchase Option Price")
Type here (months)	Type here(amount and currency)
Type here	Type here
Type here	Type here

2. To exercise their Purchase Option, the Charterers shall notify the Owners in writing not later than six (6) months prior to the relevant date stated in the table above. Such notification shall not be withdrawn or cancelled.

3. If the Charterers exercise their Purchase Option, the ownership of the Vessel shall be transferred to them on the relevant date. If such date is not a Banking Day, the ownership of the Vessel shall be transferred on the next Banking Day, on a strictly "as is/where is" basis, at the Charterers' sole cost and expense.

4. The Owners shall obtain and provide the Charterers with such documents and take such actions as the Charterers may reasonably request to facilitate the sale and the registration of the Vessel under the flag designated by the Charterers.

5. The Owners warrant that the Vessel at the time of transfer of ownership shall be free of any of Owners' encumbrance or mortgage and that they have not committed any act or omission which would impair title to the Vessel.

6. The Owners make no representation or warranty as to the seaworthiness, value, condition, design, merchantability or operation of the Vessel, or as to the quality of the material, equipment or workmanship in the Vessel, or as to the fitness of the Vessel for any particular trade.

7. In exchange for the transfer of ownership of the Vessel, the Charterers shall pay the Purchase Option Price to the bank account nominated by the Owners together with any unpaid charter hire and other amounts due and payable under this Charter Party.

8. Upon payment and transfer of ownership in accordance with Clause 7 above, this Charter Party and all rights and obligations of the parties shall terminate without prejudice to all rights accrued due between the parties prior to the date of termination and any claim that either party might have.

PART V
BARECON 2017 Standard Bareboat Charter Party
PROVISIONS TO APPLY FOR VESSELS REGISTERED IN A BAREBOAT CHARTER REGISTRY
(OPTIONAL, only to apply if expressly agreed and stated in Box 29)

1.   Definitions

"Bareboat Charter Registry" shall mean the registry stated in Box 29(ii) whose flag the Vessel will fly and in which the Charterers are registered as the bareboat charterers during the period of this Charter Party.

"Underlying Registry" shall mean the registry stated in Box 29(i) in which the Owners of the Vessel are registered as Owners and to which jurisdiction and control of the Vessel will revert upon termination of the Bareboat Charter registration.

2.   The Owners have agreed to and the Charterers shall arrange for the Vessel to be registered under the Bareboat Charter Registry. The Charterers shall be responsible for all costs thereof.

3.   Upon termination of this Charter Party for any reason whatsoever the Charterers shall immediately arrange for the deletion of the Vessel from the Bareboat Registry.

4.   In the event of the Vessel being deleted from the Bareboat Charter Registry due to any default by the Owners, the Charterers shall have the right to terminate this Charter forthwith and without prejudice to any other claim they may have against the Owners under this Charter Party.

VIII. SUPPLEMENTAL CASE MATERIALS

CHAPTER 4

VESSELS AND JURISDICTION

Insert after page 151:

Lozman v. The City of Riviera Beach, Florida

Supreme Court of the United States, 2013.
568 U.S. 115, 133 S.Ct. 735, 184 L.Ed.2d 604, 2013 A.M.C. 1.

■ JUSTICE BREYER delivered the opinion of the Court.

The Rules of Construction Act defines a "vessel" as including "every description of watercraft or other artificial contrivance used, or capable of being used, as a means of transportation on water." 1 U.S.C. § 3. The question before us is whether petitioner's floating home (which is not self-propelled) falls within the terms of that definition.

In answering that question we focus primarily upon the phrase "capable of being used." This term encompasses "practical" possibilities, not "merely . . . theoretical" ones. *Stewart v. Dutra Constr. Co.*, 543 U.S. 481, 496, 125 S.Ct. 1118, 160 L.Ed.2d 932 (2005). We believe that a reasonable observer, looking to the home's physical characteristics and activities, would not consider it to be designed to any practical degree for carrying people or things on water. And we consequently conclude that the floating home is not a "vessel."

I

In 2002 Fane Lozman, petitioner, bought a 60-foot by 12-foot floating home. App. 37, 71. The home consisted of a house-like plywood structure with French doors on three sides. *Id.*, at 38, 44. It contained a sitting room, bedroom, closet, bathroom, and kitchen, along with a stairway leading to a second level with office space. *Id.*, at 45–66. An empty bilge space underneath the main floor kept it afloat. *Id.*, at 38. (See Appendix, *infra*, for a photograph.) After buying the floating home, Lozman had it towed about 200 miles to North Bay Village, Florida, where he moored it and then twice more had it towed between nearby marinas. In 2006 Lozman had the home towed a further 70 miles to a marina owned by the city of Riviera Beach (City), respondent, where he kept it docked. Brief for Respondent 5.

After various disputes with Lozman and unsuccessful efforts to evict him from the marina, the City brought this federal admiralty lawsuit *in rem* against the floating home. It sought a maritime lien for dockage fees and damages for trespass. See Federal Maritime Lien Act, 46 U.S.C.

§ 31342 (authorizing federal maritime lien against vessel to collect debts owed for the provision of "necessaries to a vessel"); 28 U.S.C. § 1333(1) (civil admiralty jurisdiction). See also *Leon v. Galceran,* 11 Wall. 185, 20 L.Ed. 74 (1871); *The Rock Island Bridge,* 6 Wall. 213, 215, 18 L.Ed. 753 (1867).

Lozman, acting *pro se,* asked the District Court to dismiss the suit on the ground that the court lacked admiralty jurisdiction. See 2 Record, Doc. 64. After summary judgment proceedings, the court found that the floating home was a "vessel" and concluded that admiralty jurisdiction was consequently proper. Pet. for Cert. 42a. The judge then conducted a bench trial on the merits and awarded the City $3,039.88 for dockage along with $1 in nominal damages for trespass. *Id.,* at 49a.

On appeal the Eleventh Circuit affirmed. *Riviera Beach v. That Certain Unnamed Gray, Two-Story Vessel Approximately Fifty-Seven Feet in Length,* 649 F.3d 1259 (2011). It agreed with the District Court that the home was a "vessel." In its view, the home was "capable" of movement over water and the owner's subjective intent to remain moored "indefinitely" at a dock could not show the contrary. *Id.,* at 1267–1269.

Lozman sought certiorari. In light of uncertainty among the Circuits about application of the term "capable" we granted his petition. Compare *De La Rosa v. St. Charles Gaming Co.,* 474 F.3d 185, 187 (C.A.5 2006) (structure is not a "vessel" where "physically," but only "theoretical[ly]," "capable of sailing," and owner intends to moor it indefinitely as floating casino), with *Board of Comm'rs of Orleans Levee Dist. v. M/V Belle of Orleans,* 535 F.3d 1299, 1311–1312 (C.A.11 2008) (structure is a "vessel" where capable of moving over water under tow, "albeit to her detriment," despite intent to moor indefinitely). See also 649 F.3d, at 1267 (rejecting views of Circuits that " 'focus on the intent of the shipowner' ").

II

At the outset we consider one threshold matter. The District Court ordered the floating home sold to satisfy the City's judgment. The City bought the home at public auction and subsequently had it destroyed. And, after the parties filed their merits briefs, we ordered further briefing on the question of mootness in light of the home's destruction. 567 U.S. ___, 132 S.Ct. 1543, 182 L.Ed.2d 160 (2012). The parties now have pointed out that, prior to the home's sale, the District Court ordered the City to post a $25,000 bond "to secure Mr. Lozman's value in the vessel." 1 Record, Doc. 20, p. 2. The bond ensures that Lozman can obtain monetary relief if he ultimately prevails. We consequently agree with the parties that the case is not moot.

III

A

We focus primarily upon the statutory phrase "capable of being used . . . as a means of transportation on water." 1 U.S.C. § 3. The Court of Appeals found that the home was "capable" of transportation because it could float, it could proceed under tow, and its shore connections (power cable, water hose, rope lines) did not " 'rende[r]' " it "practically incapable of transportation or movement." 649 F.3d, at 1266 (quoting *Belle of Orleans,* supra, at 1312, in turn quoting *Stewart,* 543 U.S., at 494, 125 S.Ct. 1118). At least for argument's sake we agree with the Court of Appeals about the last-mentioned point, namely that Lozman's shore connections did not " 'render' " the home " 'practically incapable of transportation.' " But unlike the Eleventh Circuit, we do not find these considerations (even when combined with the home's other characteristics) sufficient to show that Lozman's home was a "vessel."

The Court of Appeals recognized that it had applied the term "capable" broadly. 649 F.3d, at 1266. Indeed, it pointed with approval to language in an earlier case, *Burks v. American River Transp. Co.,* 679 F.2d 69 (C.A.5 1982), in which the Fifth Circuit said:

> " 'No doubt the three men in a tub would also fit within our definition, and one probably could make a convincing case for Jonah inside the whale.' " 649 F.3d, at 1269 (brackets omitted) (quoting *Burks, supra,* at 75).

But the Eleventh Circuit's interpretation is too broad. Not *every* floating structure is a "vessel." To state the obvious, a wooden washtub, a plastic dishpan, a swimming platform on pontoons, a large fishing net, a door taken off its hinges, or Pinocchio (when inside the whale) are not "vessels," even if they are "artificial contrivance[s]" capable of floating, moving under tow, and incidentally carrying even a fair-sized item or two when they do so. Rather, the statute applies to an "artificial contrivance . . . capable of being used . . . *as a means of transportation on water.*" 1 U.S.C. § 3 (emphasis added). "[T]ransportation" involves the "conveyance (of things or persons) from one place to another." 18 Oxford English Dictionary 424 (2d ed. 1989) (OED). Accord, N. Webster, An American Dictionary of the English Language 1406 (C. Goodrich & N. Porter eds. 1873) ("[t]he act of transporting, carrying, or conveying from one place to another"). And we must apply this definition in a "practical," not a "theoretical," way. *Stewart, supra,* at 496, 125 S.Ct. 1118. Consequently, in our view a structure does not fall within the scope of this statutory phrase unless a reasonable observer, looking to the home's physical characteristics and activities, would consider it designed to a practical degree for carrying people or things over water.

B

Though our criterion is general, the facts of this case illustrate more specifically what we have in mind. But for the fact that it floats, nothing about Lozman's home suggests that it was designed to any practical degree to transport persons or things over water. It had no rudder or other steering mechanism. 649 F.3d, at 1269. Its hull was unraked, *ibid.,* and it had a rectangular bottom 10 inches below the water. Brief for Petitioner 27; App. 37. It had no special capacity to generate or store electricity but could obtain that utility only through ongoing connections with the land. *Id.,* at 40. Its small rooms looked like ordinary nonmaritime living quarters. And those inside those rooms looked out upon the world, not through watertight portholes, but through French doors or ordinary windows. *Id.,* at 44–66.

Although lack of self-propulsion is not dispositive, *e.g., The Robert W. Parsons,* 191 U.S. 17, 31, 24 S.Ct. 8, 48 L.Ed. 73 (1903), it may be a relevant physical characteristic. And Lozman's home differs significantly from an ordinary houseboat in that it has no ability to propel itself. Cf. 33 CFR § 173.3 (2012) ("Houseboat means a *motorized* vessel . . . designed primarily for multi-purpose accommodation spaces with low freeboard and little or no foredeck or cockpit" (emphasis added)). Lozman's home was able to travel over water only by being towed. Prior to its arrest, that home's travel by tow over water took place on only four occasions over a period of seven years. *Supra,* at 739. And when the home was towed a significant distance in 2006, the towing company had a second boat follow behind to prevent the home from swinging dangerously from side to side. App. 104.

The home has no other feature that might suggest a design to transport over water anything other than its own furnishings and related personal effects. In a word, we can find nothing about the home that could lead a reasonable observer to consider it designed to a practical degree for "transportation on water."

C

Our view of the statute is consistent with its text, precedent, and relevant purposes. For one thing, the statute's language, read naturally, lends itself to that interpretation. We concede that the statute uses the word "every," referring to "*every* description of watercraft or other artificial contrivance." 1 U.S.C. § 3 (emphasis added). But the term "contrivance" refers to "something contrived for, or employed in contriving to effect a purpose." 3 OED 850 (def.7). The term "craft" explains that purpose as "water carriage and transport." *Id.,* at 1104 (def.V(9)(b)) (defining "craft" as a "vesse[l] . . . for" that purpose). The addition of the word "water" to "craft," yielding the term "watercraft," emphasizes the point. And the next few words, "used, or capable of being used, as a means of transportation on water," drive the point home.

For another thing, the bulk of precedent supports our conclusion. In *Evansville & Bowling Green Packet Co. v. Chero Cola Bottling Co.,* 271 U.S. 19, 46 S.Ct. 379, 70 L.Ed. 805 (1926), the Court held that a wharfboat was *not* a "vessel." The wharfboat floated next to a dock; it was used to transfer cargo from ship to dock and ship to ship; and it was connected to the dock with cables, utility lines, and a ramp. *Id.,* at 21, 46 S.Ct. 379. At the same time, it was capable of being towed. And it was towed each winter to a harbor to avoid river ice. *Id.,* at 20–21, 46 S.Ct. 379. The Court reasoned that, despite the annual movement under tow, the wharfboat "was not used to carry freight from one place to another," nor did it "encounter perils of navigation to which craft used for

356

transportation are exposed." *Id.*, at 22, 46 S.Ct. 379. (See Appendix, *infra*, for photograph of a period wharfboat).

The Court's reasoning in *Stewart* also supports our conclusion. We there considered the application of the statutory definition to a dredge. 543 U.S., at 494, 125 S.Ct. 1118. The dredge was "a massive floating platform" from which a suspended clamshell bucket would "remov[e] silt from the ocean floor," depositing it "onto one of two scows" floating alongside the dredge. *Id.*, at 484, 125 S.Ct. 1118. Like more traditional "seagoing vessels," the dredge had, *e.g.*, "a captain and crew, navigational lights, ballast tanks, and a crew dining area." *Ibid.* Unlike more ordinary vessels, it could navigate only by "manipulating its anchors and cables" or by being towed. *Ibid.* Nonetheless it did move. In fact it moved over water "every couple of hours." *Id.*, at 485, 125 S.Ct. 1118.

We held that the dredge was a "vessel." We wrote that § 3's definition "merely codified the meaning that the term 'vessel' had acquired in general maritime law." *Id.*, at 490, 125 S.Ct. 1118. We added that the question of the "watercraft's use 'as a means of transportation on water' is . . . practical," and not "merely . . . theoretical." *Id.*, at 496, 125 S.Ct. 1118. And we pointed to cases holding that dredges ordinarily "served a waterborne transportation function," namely that "in performing their work they carried machinery, equipment, and crew over water." *Id.*, at 491–492, 125 S.Ct. 1118 (citing, *e.g.*, *Butler v. Ellis*, 45 F.2d 951, 955 (C.A.4 1930)).

As the Court of Appeals pointed out, in *Stewart* we also wrote that § 3 "does not require that a watercraft be used *primarily* for that [transportation] purpose," 543 U.S., at 495, 125 S.Ct. 1118; that a "watercraft need not be in motion to qualify as a vessel," *ibid.*; and that a structure may qualify as a vessel even if attached—but not "permanently" attached—to the land or ocean floor. *Id.*, at 493–494, 125 S.Ct. 1118. We did not take these statements, however, as implying a universal set of sufficient conditions for application of the definition. Rather, they say, and they mean, that the statutory definition *may* (or may not) apply—not that it *automatically must* apply—where a structure has some other *primary* purpose, where it is stationary at relevant times, and where it is attached—but not permanently attached—to land.

After all, a washtub is normally not a "vessel" though it does not have water transportation as its primary purpose, it may be stationary much of the time, and it might be attached—but not permanently attached—to land. More to the point, water transportation was not the *primary purpose* of either *Stewart's* dredge or *Evansville's* wharfboat; neither structure was "in motion" at relevant times; and both were sometimes attached (though not permanently attached) to the ocean bottom or to land. Nonetheless *Stewart's* dredge fell within the statute's definition while *Evansville's* wharfboat did not.

The basic difference, we believe, is that the dredge was regularly, but not primarily, used (and designed in part to be used) to transport workers and equipment over water while the wharfboat was not designed (to any practical degree) to serve a transportation function and did not do so. Compare *Cope v. Vallette Dry-Dock Co.,* 119 U.S. 625, 7 S.Ct. 336, 30 L.Ed. 501 (1887) (floating drydock not a "vessel" because permanently fixed to wharf), with *Jerome B. Grubart, Inc. v. Great Lakes Dredge & Dock Co.,* 513 U.S. 527, 535, 115 S.Ct. 1043, 130 L.Ed.2d 1024 (1995) (barge sometimes attached to river bottom to use as a work platform remains a "vessel" when "at other times it was used for transportation"). See also *ibid.* (citing *Great Lakes Dredge & Dock Co. v. Chicago,* 3 F.3d 225, 229 (C.A.7 1993) ("[A] craft is a 'vessel' if its purpose is to some reasonable degree 'the transportation of passengers, cargo, or equipment from place to place across navigable waters' ")); *Cope, supra,* at 630, 7 S.Ct. 336 (describing "hopper-barge," as potentially a "vessel" because it is a "navigable structure[,] used for the purpose of transportation"); cf. 1 Benedict on Admiralty § 164, p. 10–6 (7th rev. ed.2012) (maritime jurisdiction proper if "the craft is a navigable structure intended for maritime transportation").

Lower court cases also tend, on balance, to support our conclusion. See, *e.g., Bernard v. Binnings Constr. Co.,* 741 F.2d 824, 828, n. 13, 832, n. 25 (C.A.5 1984) (work punt lacking features objectively indicating a transportation function not a "vessel," for "our decisions make clear that the mere capacity to float or move across navigable waters does not necessarily make a structure a vessel"); *Ruddiman v. A Scow Platform,* 38 F. 158 (S.D.N.Y.1889) (scow, though "capable of being towed ... though not without some difficulty, from its clumsy structure" just a floating box, not a "vessel," because "it was not designed or used for the purpose of navigation," not engaged "in the transportation of persons or cargo," and had "no motive power, no rudder, no sails"). See also 1 T. Schoenbaum, Admiralty and Maritime Law § 3–6, p. 155 (5th ed.2011) (courts have found that "floating dry-dock[s]," "floating platforms, barges, or rafts used for construction or repair of piers, docks, bridges, pipelines and other" similar facilities are not "vessels"); E. Benedict, American Admiralty § 215, p. 116 (3d rev. ed. 1898) (defining "vessel" as a " 'machine adapted to transportation over rivers, seas, and oceans' ").

We recognize that some lower court opinions can be read as endorsing the "anything that floats" approach. See *Miami River Boat Yard, Inc. v. 60' Houseboat,* 390 F.2d 596, 597 (C.A.5 1968) (so-called "houseboat" lacking self-propulsion); *Sea Village Marina, LLC v. A 1980 Carlcraft Houseboat,* No. 09–3292, 2009 WL 3379923, *5–*6 (D.N.J., Oct. 19, 2009) (following *Miami River Boat Yard*); *Hudson Harbor 79th Street Boat Basin, Inc. v. Sea Casa,* 469 F.Supp. 987, 989 (S.D.N.Y.1979) (same). Cf. *Holmes v. Atlantic Sounding Co.,* 437 F.3d 441 (C.A.5 2006) (floating dormitory); *Summerlin v. Massman Constr. Co.,* 199 F.2d 715 (C.A.4 1952) (derrick anchored in the river engaged in building a bridge is a vessel). For the reasons we have stated, we find such an approach inappropriate and inconsistent with our precedents.

Further, our examination of the purposes of major federal maritime statutes reveals little reason to classify floating homes as "vessels." Admiralty law, for example, provides special attachment procedures lest a vessel avoid liability by sailing away. 46 U.S.C. §§ 31341–31343 (2006 ed. and Supp. IV). Liability statutes such as the Jones Act recognize that sailors face the special " 'perils of the sea.' " *Chandris, Inc. v. Latsis,* 515 U.S. 347, 354, 373, 115 S.Ct. 2172, 132 L.Ed.2d 314 (1995) (referring to " 'vessel[s] in navigation' "). Certain admiralty tort doctrines can encourage shipowners to engage in port-related commerce. *E.g.,* 46 U.S.C. § 30505; *Executive Jet Aviation, Inc. v. Cleveland,* 409 U.S. 249, 269–270, 93 S.Ct. 493, 34 L.Ed.2d 454 (1972). And maritime safety statutes subject vessels to U.S. Coast Guard inspections. *E.g.,* 46 U.S.C. § 3301.

Lozman, however, cannot easily escape liability by sailing away in his home. He faces no special sea dangers. He does not significantly engage in port-related commerce. And the Solicitor General tells us that to adopt a version of the "anything that floats" test would place unnecessary and undesirable inspection burdens upon the Coast Guard. Brief for United States as *Amicus Curiae* 29, n. 11.

Finally, our conclusion is consistent with state laws in States where floating home owners have congregated in communities. See Brief for Seattle Floating Homes Association et al. as *Amici Curiae* 1. A Washington State environmental statute, for example, defines a floating home (for regulatory purposes) as "a single-family dwelling unit constructed on a float, that is moored, anchored, or otherwise secured in waters, and is not a vessel, even though it may be capable of being towed." Wash. Rev.Code Ann. § 90.58.270(5)(b)(ii) (Supp.2012). A California statute defines a floating home (for tax purposes) as "a floating structure" that is "designed and built to be used, or is modified to be used, as a stationary waterborne residential dwelling," and which (unlike a typical houseboat), has no independent power generation, and is dependent on shore utilities. Cal. Health & Safety Code Ann. § 18075.55(d) (West 2006). These States, we are told, treat structures that meet their "floating home" definitions like ordinary land-based homes rather than like vessels. Brief for Seattle Floating Homes Association 2. Consistency of interpretation of related state and federal laws is a virtue in that it helps to create simplicity making the law easier to understand and to follow for lawyers and for nonlawyers alike. And that consideration here supports our conclusion.

D

The City and supporting *amici* make several important arguments that warrant our response. First, they argue against use of any purpose-based test lest we introduce into "vessel" determinations a subjective element—namely, the owner's intent. That element, they say, is often "unverifiable" and too easily manipulated. Its introduction would "foment unpredictability and invite gamesmanship." Brief for Respondent 33.

We agree with the City about the need to eliminate the consideration of evidence of subjective intent. But we cannot agree that the need requires abandonment of all criteria based on "purpose." Cf. *Stewart,* 543 U.S., at 495, 125 S.Ct. 1118 (discussing transportation purpose). Indeed, it is difficult, if not impossible, to determine the use of a human "contrivance" without some consideration of human purposes. At the same time, we have sought to avoid subjective elements, such as owner's intent, by permitting consideration only of objective evidence of a waterborne transportation purpose. That is why we have referred to the views of a reasonable observer. *Supra,* at 739. And it is why we have looked to the physical attributes and behavior of the structure, as objective manifestations of any relevant purpose, and not to the subjective intent of the owner. *Supra,* at 741–742. We note that various admiralty treatises refer to the use of purpose-based tests without any suggestion that administration of those tests has introduced too much subjectivity into the vessel-determination process. 1 Benedict on Admiralty § 164; 1 Admiralty and Maritime Law § 3–6.

Second, the City, with support of *amici,* argues against the use of criteria that are too abstract, complex, or open-ended. Brief for Respondent 28–29. A court's jurisdiction, *e.g.,* admiralty jurisdiction, may turn on application of the term "vessel." And jurisdictional tests, often applied at the outset of a case, should be "as simple as possible." *Hertz Corp. v. Friend,* 559 U.S. 77, ___, 130 S.Ct. 1181, 1186, 175 L.Ed.2d 1029 (2010).

We agree with the last-mentioned sentiment. And we also understand that our approach is neither perfectly precise nor always determinative. Satisfaction of a design-based or purpose-related criterion, for example, is not always sufficient for application of the statutory word "vessel." A craft whose physical characteristics and activities objectively evidence a waterborne transportation purpose or function may still be rendered a nonvessel by later physical alterations. For example, an owner might take a structure that is otherwise a vessel (even the *Queen Mary)* and connect it permanently to the land for use, say, as a hotel. See *Stewart, supra,* at 493–494, 125 S.Ct. 1118. Further, changes over time may produce a new form, *i.e.,* a newly designed structure—in which case it may be the new design that is relevant. See *Kathriner v. Unisea, Inc.,* 975 F.2d 657, 660 (C.A.9 1992) (floating processing plant was no longer a vessel where a "large opening [had been] cut into her hull").

Nor is satisfaction of the criterion always a necessary condition, see Part IV, *infra.* It is conceivable that an owner might *actually use* a floating structure not designed to any practical degree for transportation as, say, a ferry boat, regularly transporting goods and persons over water.

Nonetheless, we believe the criterion we have used, taken together with our example of its application here, should offer guidance in a significant number of borderline cases where "capacity" to transport over water is in doubt. Moreover, borderline cases will always exist; they require a method for resolution; we believe the method we have used is workable; and, unlike, say, an "anything that floats" test, it is consistent with statutory text, purpose, and precedent. Nor do we believe that the dissent's approach would prove any more workable. For example, the dissent suggests a relevant distinction between an owner's "clothes and personal effects" and "large appliances (like an oven or a refrigerator)." *Post,* at 752 (opinion of SOTOMAYOR, J.). But a transportation function need not turn on the size of the items in question, and we believe the line between items being transported from place to place (*e.g.,* cargo) and items that are mere appurtenances is the one more likely to be relevant. Cf. Benedict, American Admiralty § 222, at 121 ("A ship is usually described as consisting of the ship, her tackle, apparel, and furniture . . .").

Finally, the dissent and the Solicitor General (as *amicus* for Lozman) argue that a remand is warranted for further factfinding. See *post,* at 753–755; Brief for United States as *Amicus Curiae* 29–31. But neither the City nor Lozman makes such a request. Brief for Respondent 18, 49, 52. And the only potentially relevant factual dispute the dissent points to is that the home suffered serious damage during a tow. *Post,* at 753–754. But this would add support to our ultimate conclusion that this floating home was not a vessel. We consequently see nothing to be gained by a remand.

IV

Although we have focused on the phrase "*capable* of being used" for transportation over water, the statute also includes as a "vessel" a structure that is *actually* "used" for that transportation. 1 U.S.C. § 3 (emphasis added). And the City argues that, irrespective of its design, Lozman's floating home was *actually* so used. Brief for Respondent 32. We are not persuaded by its argument.

We are willing to assume for argument's sake that sometimes it is possible actually to use for water transportation a structure that is in no practical way designed for that purpose. See *supra,* at 744–745. But even so, the City cannot show the actual use for which it argues. Lozman's floating home moved only under tow. Before its arrest, it moved significant distances only twice in seven years. And when it moved, it carried, not passengers or cargo, but at the very most (giving the benefit of any factual ambiguity to the City) only its own furnishings, its owner's personal effects, and personnel present to assure the home's safety. 649 F.3d, at 1268; Brief for Respondent 32; Tr. of Oral Arg. 37–38. This is far too little *actual* "use" to bring the floating home within the terms of the statute. See *Evansville,* 271 U.S., at 20–21, 46 S.Ct. 379 (wharfboat not a "vessel" even though "[e]ach winter" it "was towed to [a] harbor to protect it from ice"); see also *Roper v. United States,* 368 U.S. 20, 23, 82 S.Ct. 5, 7 L.Ed.2d 1 (1961) ("Unlike a barge, the S.S. *Harry Lane* was not moved in order to transport commodities from one location to another"). See also *supra,* at 741–744.

V

For these reasons, the judgment of the Court of Appeals is reversed.

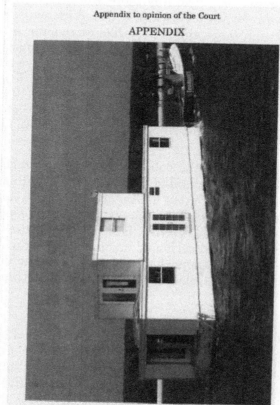

Appendix to opinion of the Court

APPENDIX

Petitioner's floating home. App. 69.

Appendix to opinion of the Court

50- by 200-foot wharf boat in Evansville, Indiana, on Nov. 13, 1918.
H. R. Doc. No. 1521, 65th Cong., 3d Sess., Illustration No. 13 (1918).

■ JUSTICE SOTOMAYER, with whom JUSTICE KENNEDY joins, dissenting.

I agree with much of the Court's reasoning. Our precedents fully support the Court's reasoning that the Eleventh Circuit's test is overinclusive; that the subjective intentions of a watercraft's owner or designer play no role in the vessel analysis of 1 U.S.C. § 3; and that an objective assessment of a watercraft's purpose or function governs whether that structure is a vessel. The Court, however, creates a novel and unnecessary "reasonable observer" reformulation of these principles and errs in its determination, under this new standard, that the craft before us is not a vessel. Given the underdeveloped record below, we should remand. Therefore, I respectfully dissent.

I

The relevant statute, 1 U.S.C. § 3, "sweeps broadly." *Stewart v. Dutra Constr. Co.,* 543 U.S. 481, 494, 125 S.Ct. 1118, 160 L.Ed.2d 932 (2005). It provides that "[t]he word 'vessel' includes every description of watercraft or other artificial contrivance used, or capable of being used, as a means of transportation on water." This broad phrasing flows from admiralty law's long recognition that vessels come in many shapes and sizes. See E. Benedict, American Admiralty § 218, p. 121 (1870 ed.)

("[V]essel, is a general word, many times used for any kind of navigation"); M. Cohen, Admiralty Jurisdiction, Law, and Practice 232 (1883) ("[T]he term 'vessel' shall be understood to comprehend every description of vessel navigating on any sea or channel, lake or river . . .").

Our test for vessel status has remained the same for decades: "Under § 3, a 'vessel' is any watercraft practically capable of maritime transportation. . . ." *Stewart*, 543 U.S., at 497, 125 S.Ct. 1118; see also *Evansville & Bowling Green Packet Co. v. Chero Cola Bottling Co.*, 271 U.S. 19, 22, 46 S.Ct. 379, 70 L.Ed. 805 (1926); *Cope v. Vallette Dry-Dock Co.*, 119 U.S. 625, 627, 7 S.Ct. 336, 30 L.Ed. 501 (1887). At its core, vessel status has always rested upon the objective physical characteristics of a vessel (such as its structure, shape, and materials of construction), as well as its usage history. But over time, several important principles have guided both this Court and the lower courts in determining what kinds of watercraft fall properly within the scope of admiralty jurisdiction.

Consider the most basic of requirements. For a watercraft to be "practically capable" of maritime transportation, it must first be "capable" of such transportation. Only those structures that can simultaneously float and carry people or things over water are even presumptively within § 3's reach. Stopping here, as the Eleventh Circuit essentially did, results in an overinclusive test. Section 3, after all, does not drag every bit of floating and towable flotsam and jetsam into admiralty jurisdiction. Rather, the terms "capable of being used" and "practical" have real significance in our maritime jurisprudence.

"[A] water craft is not 'capable of being used' for maritime transport in any meaningful sense if it has been permanently moored." *Stewart*, 543 U.S., at 494, 125 S.Ct. 1118. So, to take an obvious example, a floating bridge over water does not constitute a vessel; such mooring is clearly permanent. Cf. *The Rock Island Bridge*, 6 Wall. 213, 216, 18 L.Ed. 753 (1867). Less dramatically, a watercraft whose objective physical connections to land "evidence a permanent location" does not fall within § 3's ambit. See, *e.g.*, *Evansville*, 271 U.S., at 22, 46 S.Ct. 379 ("[The wharfboat] served at *Evansville* as an office, warehouse and wharf, and was not taken from place to place. The connections with the water, electric light and telephone systems of the city evidence a permanent location"); *Dunklin v. Louisiana Riverboat Gaming Partnership*, 260 F.3d 621, ___, n. 1, No. 00–31455, 2001 WL 650209, *1, n. 1 (C.A.5, May 22, 2001) (*per curiam*) (describing a fully functional casino boat placed "in an enclosed pond in a cofferdam"). Put plainly, structures "permanently affixed to shore or resting on the ocean floor," *Stewart*, 543 U.S., at 493–494, 125 S.Ct. 1118, have never been treated as vessels for the purposes of § 3.

Our precedents have also excluded from vessel status those watercraft "rendered practically incapable of transportation or movement." *Id.*, at 494, 125 S.Ct. 1118. Take the easiest case, a vessel whose physical characteristics have been so altered as to make waterborne transportation a practical impossibility. *Ibid.* (explaining that a "floating processing plant was no longer a vessel where a 'large opening [had been] cut into her hull,' rendering her incapable of moving over the water") (quoting *Kathriner v. UNISEA, Inc.,* 975 F.2d 657, 660 (C.A.9 1992)). The longstanding admiralty exception for "dead ships," those watercraft that "require a major overhaul" for their "reactivation," also falls into this category. See *Roper v. United States,* 368 U.S. 20, 21, 82 S.Ct. 5, 7 L.Ed.2d 1 (1961) (finding that a liberty ship "deactivated from service and 'mothballed'" is not a "vessel in navigation"); see generally Rutherglen, Dead Ships, 30 J. Maritime L. & Comm. 677 (1999).[1] Likewise, ships that "have been withdrawn from the water for extended periods of time" in order to facilitate repairs and reconstruction may lose their status as vessels until they are rendered capable of maritime transport. *Stewart,* 543 U.S., at 496, 125 S.Ct. 1118. Cf. *West v. United States,* 361 U.S. 118, 120, 122, 80 S.Ct. 189, 4 L.Ed.2d 161 (1959) (noting that "the *Mary Austin* was withdrawn from any operation whatever while in storage with the 'moth-ball fleet'" and that "[t]he *Mary Austin,* as anyone could see, was not in maritime service. She was undergoing major repairs and complete renovation . . .").

Finally, our maritime jurisprudence excludes from vessel status those floating structures that, based on their physical characteristics, do not "transport people, freight, or cargo from place to place" as one of their purposes. *Stewart,* 543 U.S., at 493, 125 S.Ct. 1118. "Purpose," in this context, is determined solely by an objective inquiry into a craft's function. "[N]either size, form, equipment nor means of propulsion are determinative factors upon the question of [vessel status]," though all may be considered. *The Robert W. Parsons,* 191 U.S. 17, 30, 24 S.Ct. 8, 48 L.Ed. 73 (1903). Moreover, in assessing a particular structure's function, we have consistently examined its past and present activities. *Stewart,* 543 U.S., at 495, 125 S.Ct. 1118; *Cope,* 119 U.S., at 627, 7 S.Ct. 336. Of course, a seaborne craft is not excluded from vessel status simply because its "primary purpose" is not maritime transport. *Stewart,* 543 U.S., at 497, 125 S.Ct. 1118. We held as much in *Stewart* when we concluded that a dredge was a vessel notwithstanding that its "primary purpose" was "dredging rather than transportation." *Id.,* at 486, 495, 125 S.Ct. 1118. So long as one purpose of a craft is transportation, whether of cargo or people or both, § 3's practical capability requirement is satisfied.

Certainly, difficult and marginal cases will arise. Fortunately, courts do not consider each floating structure anew. So, for example, when we were confronted in *Stewart* with the question whether a dredge is a § 3

---

[1] The converse category of ships "not yet born" is another historical exclusion from vessel status. See *Tucker v. Alexandroff,* 183 U.S. 424, 438, 22 S.Ct. 195, 46 L.Ed. 264 (1902) ("A ship is born when she is launched, and lives so long as her identity is preserved. Prior to her launching she is a mere congeries of wood and iron—an ordinary piece of personal property—as distinctly a land structure as a house, and subject only to mechanics' liens created by state law and enforceable in the state courts").

vessel, we did not commence with a clean slate; we instead sought guidance from previous cases that had confronted similar structures. See *id.,* at 490, and n. 5, 125 S.Ct. 1118; see also *Norton v. Warner Co.,* 321 U.S. 565, 571–572, 64 S.Ct. 747, 88 L.Ed. 931 (1944) (likewise surveying earlier cases).

In sum, our precedents offer substantial guidance for how objectively to determine whether a watercraft is practically capable of maritime transport and thus qualifies as a § 3 vessel. First, the capacity to float and carry things or people is an obvious prerequisite to vessel status. Second, structures or ships that are permanently moored or fixed in place are not § 3 vessels. Likewise, structures that are practically incapable of maritime transport are not vessels, whether they are ships that have been altered so that they may no longer be put to sea, dead ships, or ships removed from navigation for extended periods of time. Third, those watercraft whose physical characteristics and usage history reveal no maritime transport purpose or use are not § 3 vessels.

II

The majority does not appear to disavow the legal principles described above. The majority apparently accepts that permanent mooring suffices to take a ship out of vessel status, *ante,* at 742, 744,[2] and that "[a] craft whose physical characteristics and activities objectively evidence a waterborne transportation purpose or function may still be rendered a nonvessel by later physical alterations," *ante,* at 745.[3] No one argues that Lozman's craft was permanently moored, see App. 32 (describing the "deteriorated" ropes holding the craft in place), or that it had undergone physical alterations sufficient to take it out of vessel status, see Tr. of Oral Arg. 13 (Lozman's counsel arguing that the craft was never a vessel in the first place). Our precedents make clear that the Eleventh Circuit's "anything that floats" test is overinclusive and ignores that purpose is a crucial factor in determining whether a particular craft is or is not a vessel. Accordingly, the majority is correct that determining whether Lozman's craft is a vessel hinges on whether that craft had any maritime transportation purpose or function.

The majority errs, though, in concluding that the purpose component of the § 3 test is whether "a reasonable observer, looking to the [craft]'s physical characteristics and activities, would not consider it to be

---

[2] In discussing permanent mooring, as well as *Stewart*'s rejection of primary-purpose and state-of-transit tests for vessel status, *Stewart v. Dutra Constr. Co.,* 543 U.S. 481, 495, 125 S.Ct. 1118, 160 L.Ed.2d 932 (2005), the majority states that our holdings "say, and they mean, that the statutory definition [given by § 3] *may* (or may not) apply—not that it *automatically must* apply—where a structure has some other *primary* purpose, where it is stationary at relevant times, and where it is attached—but not permanently attached—to land." *Ante,* at 742. This must mean, by negative implication, that a permanently moored structure never falls within § 3's definition.

[3] Presumably, this encompasses those kinds of ships "otherwise rendered practically incapable of transportation or movement." *Stewart,* 543 U.S., at 494, 125 S.Ct. 1118. That is, ships which have been altered so they cannot travel the seas, dead ships, and ships removed from the water for an extended period of time. *Supra,* at 749–750.

designed to any practical degree for carrying people or things on water." *Ante,* at 739. This phrasing has never appeared in any of our cases and the majority's use of it, despite its seemingly objective gloss, effectively (and erroneously) introduces a subjective component into the vessel-status inquiry.

For one thing, in applying this test the majority points to some characteristics of Lozman's craft that have no relationship to maritime transport, such as the style of the craft's rooms or that "those inside those rooms looked out upon the world, not through water-tight portholes, but through French doors or ordinary windows." *Ante,* at 741. The majority never explains why it believes these particular esthetic elements are important for determining vessel status. In fact, they are not. Section 3 is focused on whether a structure is "used, or capable of being used, as a means of transportation on water." By importing windows, doors, room style, and other esthetic criteria into the § 3 analysis, the majority gives our vessel test an "I know it when I see it" flavor. *Jacobellis v. Ohio,* 378 U.S. 184, 197, 84 S.Ct. 1676, 12 L.Ed.2d 793 (1964) (Stewart, J., concurring). But that has never been nor should it be the test: A badly designed and unattractive vessel is different from a structure that lacks any "practical capacity" for maritime transport. In the majority's eyes, the two appear to be one and the same.

The majority's treatment of the craft's past voyages is also strange. The majority notes that Lozman's craft could be and was, in fact, towed over long distances, including over 200 miles at one point. *Ante,* at 739–742. But the majority determines that, given the design of Lozman's craft, this is "far too little *actual* 'use' to bring the floating home within the terms of the statute." *Ante,* at 746. This is because "when it moved, it carried, not passengers or cargo, but at the very most (giving the benefit of any factual ambiguity to the City) only its own furnishings, its owner's personal effects, and personnel present to assure the home's safety." *Ante,* at 745–746.

I find this analysis confusing. The majority accepts that the record indicates that Lozman's craft traveled hundreds of miles while "carrying people or things." *Ante,* at 739. But then, in the same breath, the majority concludes that a "reasonable observer" would nonetheless conclude that the craft was not "designed to any practical degree for carrying people or things on water." *Ibid.* The majority fails to explain how a craft that apparently did carry people and things over water for long distances was not "practically capable" of maritime transport.

This is not to say that a structure capable of such feats is necessarily a vessel. A craft like Lozman's might not be a vessel, for example, if it could only carry its owner's clothes and personal effects, or if it is only capable of transporting itself and its appurtenances. *Jerome B. Grubart, Inc. v. Great Lakes Dredge & Dock Co.,* 513 U.S. 527, 535, 115 S.Ct. 1043, 130 L.Ed.2d 1024 (1995) ("[M]aritime law . . . ordinarily treats an 'appurtenance' attached to a vessel in navigable waters as part of the vessel itself"). But if such a craft can carry large appliances (like an oven or a refrigerator) and all of the other things we might find in a normal home in addition to the occupants of that home, as the existing record suggests Lozman's craft may have done, then it would seem to be much more like a mobile home (and therefore a vessel) than a firmly rooted residence. The simple truth is that we know very little about the craft's capabilities and what did or did not happen on its various trips. By focusing on the little we do know for certain about this craft (*i.e.*, its windows, doors, and the style of its rooms) in determining whether it is a vessel, the majority renders the § 3 inquiry opaque and unpredictable.

Indeed, the little we do know about Lozman's craft suggests only that it was an unusual structure. A surveyor was unable to find any comparable craft for sale in the State of Florida. App. 43. Lozman's home was neither obviously a houseboat, as the majority describes such ships, *ante,* at 741–742, nor clearly a floating home, *ante,* at 743–744. See App. 13, 31, 79 (sale, lease, and surveying documents describing Lozman's craft as a "houseboat"). The only clear difference that the majority identifies between these two kinds of structures is that the former are self-propelled, while the latter are not. *Ante,* at 741–742. But even the majority recognizes that self-propulsion has never been a prerequisite for vessel status. *Ante,* at 741 (citing *The Robert W. Parsons,* 191 U.S., at 31, 24 S.Ct. 8); see *Norton,* 321 U.S., at 571, 64 S.Ct. 747. Consequently, it is unclear why Lozman's craft is a floating home, why all floating homes are not vessels,[4] or why Lozman's craft is not a vessel. If windows, doors, and other esthetic attributes are what take Lozman's craft out of vessel status, then the majority's test is completely malleable. If it is the craft's lack of self-propulsion, then the majority's test is unfaithful to our longstanding precedents. See *The Robert W. Parsons,* 191 U.S., at 30–31, 24 S.Ct. 8. If it is something else, then that something is not apparent from the majority's opinion.

Worse still, in straining to find that Lozman's craft was a floating home and therefore not a vessel, the majority calls into question the conclusions of numerous lower courts that have found houseboats that lacked self-propulsion to be § 3 vessels. See *ante,* at 743–744 (citing *Miami River Boat Yard, Inc. v. 60' Houseboat,* 390 F.2d 596, 597 (C.A.5 1968); *Sea Village Marina, LLC v. A 1980 Carlcraft Houseboat,* No. 09–3292, 2009 WL 3379923, *5–*6 (D.N.J., Oct. 19, 2009); *Hudson Harbor 79th Street Boat Basin, Inc. v. Sea Casa,* 469 F.Supp. 987, 989 (S.D.N.Y.1979)). The majority incorrectly suggests that these cases applied an " 'anything that floats' " test. *Ante,* at 743. These cases suggest

---

4 To be clear, some floating homes are obviously not vessels. For example, some floating homes are structures built upon a large inverted pyramid of logs. Brief for Seattle Floating Homes Assn. et al. as *Amici Curiae* 14. Cf. App. 38 (Lozman's craft was buoyed by an empty bilge space). These kinds of floating homes can measure 4,000 or 5,000 square feet, see Brief for Seattle Floating Homes Assn. et al. as *Amici Curiae* 4, and may have connections to land that require the aid of divers and electricians to remove, *ibid.* These large, immobile structures are not vessels and have physical attributes directly connected to their lack of navigational abilities that suggest as much. But these structures are not before us; Lozman's craft is.

something different. Many of these decisions in assessing the crafts before them looked carefully at these crafts' structure and function, and determined that these ships had capabilities similar to other long-established vessels, suggesting a significant maritime transportation function. See *Miami River Boat Yard,* 390 F.2d, at 597 (likening houseboat at issue to a "barg[e]"); *Sea Village Marina,* 2009 WL 3379923, *7 ("According to the available evidence, [the houseboats in question] float and can be towed to a new marina without substantial effort . . ."); *Hudson Harbor,* 469 F.Supp., at 989 (houseboat "was capable of being used at least to the extent that a 'dumb barge' is capable of being used" and comparable to a "yach[t]"). Their holdings are consistent with older cases, see, *e.g., The Ark,* 17 F.2d 446, 447 (S.D.Fla.1926), and the crafts at issue in these cases have been widely accepted as vessels by most treatises in this area, see 1 S. Friedell, Benedict on Admiralty § 164, p. 10–6, n. 2 (7th ed. rev.2012); 1 T. Schoenbaum, Admiralty & Maritime Law § 3–6, p. 153, n. 10 (5th ed.2011); 1 R. Force & M. Norris, The Law of Seamen § 2:12, p. 2–82 (5th ed.2003). The majority's suggestion that rejecting the Eleventh Circuit's test necessitates jettisoning these other precedents is simply wrong. And, in its rejection, the majority works real damage to what has long been a settled area of maritime law.[5]

III

With a more developed record, Lozman's craft might be distinguished from the houseboats in those lower court cases just discussed. For example, if Lozman's craft's previous voyages caused it serious damage, then that would strongly suggest that it lacked a maritime transportation purpose or function. There is no harm in remanding the case for further factfinding along the lines described above, cautioning the lower courts to be aware that features of Lozman's "incomparable" craft, see App. 43, may distinguish it from previous precedents. At most, such a remand would introduce a relatively short delay before finally ending the years-long battle between Lozman and the city of Riviera Beach.

On the other hand, there is great harm in stretching the facts below and overriding settled and likely correct lower court precedents to reach the unnecessary conclusion that Lozman's craft was not a vessel. Without an objective application of the § 3 standard, one that relies in a predictable fashion only on those physical characteristics of a craft that are related to maritime transport and use, parties will have no *ex ante*

---

[5] The majority's invocation of two state environmental and tax statutes as a reason to reject this well-established lower court precedent is particularly misguided. See *ante,* at 744–745. We have repeatedly emphasized that the "regulation of maritime vessels" is a "uniquely *federal* are[a] of regulation." *Chamber of Commerce of United States of America v. Whiting,* 563 U.S. ___, ___, 131 S.Ct. 1968, 1983, 179 L.Ed.2d 1031 (2011) (plurality opinion) (emphasis added); see also *United States v. Locke,* 529 U.S. 89, 99, 120 S.Ct. 1135, 146 L.Ed.2d 69 (2000) (explaining that "the federal interest [in regulating interstate navigation] has been manifest since the beginning of our Republic and is now well established"). Our previous cases did not turn to state law in determining whether a given craft is a vessel. There are no good reasons to do so now.

notion whether a particular ship is a vessel. As a wide range of *amici* have cautioned us, numerous maritime industries rely heavily on clear and predictable legal rules for determining which ships are vessels.[6] The majority's distorted application of our settled law to the facts of this case frustrates these ends. Moreover, the majority's decision reaches well beyond relatively insignificant boats like Lozman's craft, *id.*, at 79 (listing purchase price of Lozman's craft as $17,000), because it specifically disapproves of lower court decisions dealing with much larger ships, see *ante*, at 744 (questioning *Holmes v. Atlantic Sounding Co.*, 437 F.3d 441 (C.A.5 2006) (finding a 140-foot-long and 40-foot-wide dormitory barge with 50 beds to be a § 3 vessel)).

IV

It is not clear that Lozman's craft is a § 3 vessel. It is clear, however, that we are not in a good position to make such a determination based on the limited record we possess. The appropriate response is to remand the case for further proceedings in light of the proper legal standard. See Brief for United States as *Amicus Curiae* 29–31. The Court resists this move and in its haste to christen Lozman's craft a nonvessel delivers an analysis that will confuse the lower courts and upset our longstanding admiralty precedent. I respectfully dissent.

NOTE

As the Court in *Lozman* notes, some post-*Stewart* lower court opinions could be read as endorsing the "anything that floats" approach to vessel status. The Court casts doubt on those prior decisions because it finds "such an approach inappropriate and inconsistent with our precedents." As a result, after *Lozman*, courts have declined to assign vessel status to structures similar to those that were found to be vessels under *Stewart*. For example, in Martin v. Fab-Con, Inc., 9 F.Supp. 3d 642, 2014 A.M.C. 1280 (E.D. La. 2014), the court concluded that a floating structure used to house

---

[6] For example, without knowing whether a particular ship is a § 3 vessel, it is impossible for lenders to know how properly to characterize it as collateral for a financing agreement because they do not know what remedies they will have recourse to in the event of a default. Brief for National Marine Bankers Assn. as *Amicus Curiae* 14–15. Similarly, cities like Riviera Beach provide docking for crafts like Lozman's on the assumption that such crafts actually are "vessels," App. 13–21 (Riviera Beach's wet-slip agreement referring to Lozman's craft as a "vessel," "boat," or "houseboat"), that can be "remove[d]" upon short notice, *id.*, at 17 (requiring removal of the craft on three days' notice). The majority makes it impossible for these marinas to know whether the "houseboats" that fill their slips are actually vessels and what remedies they can exercise in the event of a dispute. See *id.*, at 15 ("In addition to any other remedies provided for in this Agreement, the Marina, as a provider of necessities to this *vessel*, has a maritime lien on the *vessel* and may bring a civil action *in rem* under 46 United States Code 31342 in Federal Court, to arrest the *vessel* and enforce the lien . . ." (emphasis added)). Lozman's behavior over the years is emblematic of this problem. For example, in 2003, prior to his move to Riviera Beach, Lozman had his craft towed from one marina to another after a dispute arose with the first marina and he was threatened with eviction. App. 76–78. The possibility that a shipowner like Lozman can depart so easily over water and go beyond the reach of a provider of necessaries like the marina in response to a legal dispute is exactly the kind of problem that the Federal Maritime Lien Act, 46 U.S.C. § 31342, was intended to address. See *Dampskibsselskabet Dannebrog v. Signal Oil & Gas Co. of Cal.*, 310 U.S. 268, 272–273, 60 S.Ct. 937, 84 L.Ed. 1197 (1940).

crew members (described as a "floating hotel") was not a vessel despite the fact that structure was nearly indistinguishable from the quarterbarge considered in Holmes v. Atlantic Sounding Co. 437 F.3d 441 (5th Cir. 2006) (crew's quarterbarge, in essence a floating dormitory," was a vessel).

Likewise, in Sea Village Marina, LLC v. A 1980 Carlcraft Houseboat, 2013 WL 1501789 (D.N.J. Apr. 11, 2013), the court reversed its prior ruling that admiralty jurisdiction existed over an in rem action against four houseboats. Based on *Lozman*, the court held that it lacked subject matter jurisdiction over the case "because the Lozman case established that floating homes which do not transport passengers or cargo" are not vessels. See also Armstrong v. Manhattan Yacht Club, Inc., 2013 WL 1819993 (E.D.N.Y. Apr. 30, 2013) (holding that a floating clubhouse was not a vessel because "[i]ts primary purpose (and, as the evidence demonstrates, its only use) [was] to serve as a viewing platform" for individuals to watch sailboat races).

Is the issue of vessel status a question of law to be decided by the court or a question of fact to be decided either by the court on summary judgment or a jury at trial? In *Martin*, supra, the court concluded it was a matter of law. In *Armstrong*, supra, the court reviewed the factual materials submitted in support of and in opposition to a motion for summary judgment and concluded "that a reasonable observer, looking to the Clubhouse's physical characteristics and activities, would not consider it to be designed to any practical degree for carrying people or things on water." Another example of a case in which the court concluded that the issue was a question of fact for the jury is Dune Energy, Inc. v. Frogco Amphibious Equipment, LLC., 2013 WL 185608 (E.D. La. 2013). In Dune Energy the court declined to determine as a matter of law whether an amphibious back hoe, also known as a marsh buggy excavator, was a vessel. The court found that the *Lozman* test was highly fact dependent and that there were materials facts in dispute concerning the marsh buggy's status as a vessel. Therefore, the court denied the defendant's motion for summary judgment.

CHAPTER 5

ADMIRALTY JURISDICTION AND FEDERALISM

D. REMOVAL JURISDICTION

Insert on page 189 before the NOTE:

Boudreaux v. Global Offshore Resources, LLC

United States District Court, Western District Louisiana, 2015.
2015 WL 419002.

■ C. MICHAEL HILL, United States Magistrate Judge.

Pending before the undersigned is the Motion to Remand filed by plaintiffs, Mark Boudreaux ("Boudreaux") and John Guidry ("Guidry"), on September 5, 2014. . . . Defendant, Global Offshore Resources, LLC ("Global"), filed opposition on September 26, 2014. . . . Following oral argument I took the motion under advisement. . . .

For the following reasons, the motion is **GRANTED.**

Background

Plaintiffs, Boudreaux and Guidry, were employed by Global. On November 4, 2013, Boudreaux was assigned to the Hornbeck Offshore Services ("Hornbeck") vessels *Voyager* and *Sweetwater,* while Guidry was assigned to the Hornbeck vessel *Stormridge*. On that date, plaintiffs were en route to a safety meeting hosted by Global, when a third-party automobile caused an accident resulting in plaintiffs' alleged injuries.

On July 15, 2014, plaintiffs filed a lawsuit against Global in the 15th Judicial District Court for the Parish of Lafayette, State of Louisiana, asserting claims under the general maritime law and the Jones Act, 46 U.S.C. §§ 30104–30105 (formerly 46 U.S.C.App. § 688), as well as for maintenance and cure.[1] Plaintiffs invoked the "savings to suitors" clause under 28 U.S.C. § 1333 and requested a jury trial. . . .

On August 18, 2014, Global removed the action to this Court pursuant to 28 U.S.C. §§ 1331[2] and 1441(a). Global asserted that this case was removable on the basis of federal question jurisdiction because plaintiffs had asserted general maritime claims, specifically for maintenance and cure benefits.

On September 5, 2014, plaintiffs filed the instant Motion to Remand on the grounds that actions brought in state court under the general

---

[1] At the hearing, plaintiff counsel withdrew his claims under the Jones Act.
[2] Section 1331 provides: "The district courts shall have original jurisdiction of all civil actions arising under the Constitution, laws, or treaties of the United States."

maritime law are not removable. . . . Global argues that this case is removable under the holding in *Ryan v. Hercules Offshore,* 945 F.Supp.2d 772 (S.D.Tex.2013), and its progeny.

Analysis

This motion presents the Court with a hotly contested issue— whether general maritime claims are removable after the 2011 amendment to 28 U.S.C. § 1441. *Butler v. RLB Contracting, Inc.,* 2014 WL 1653078, *1 (S.D.Tex. Apr. 24, 2014). To date, the Fifth Circuit has not directly addressed this question, and the trial courts are sharply divided.

Global removed this case on the grounds of federal question jurisdiction under §§ 1331 and 1441(a). Under 28 U.S.C. § 1441(a), any state court civil action over which the federal courts would have original jurisdiction may be removed. Jurisdiction over a claim for maintenance and cure is based upon the general maritime law, over which the federal courts have jurisdiction. *Billiot v. Cenac Towing Co.,* 2009 WL 1458265, *1 (E.D.La. May 22, 2009) (*citing Fitzgerald v. U.S. Lines Co.,* 374 U.S. 16, 17 (1963)).

When considering a motion to remand, the removing party bears the burden of showing that federal jurisdiction exists and that removal was proper. *Manguno v. Prudential Prop. & Cas. Ins. Co.,* 276 F.3d 720, 723 (5th Cir.2002); *Scarlott v. Nissan North America, Inc.,* ___ F.3d ___, 2014 WL 4920255 (5th Cir. Sept. 30, 2014) (*citing Mumfrey v. CVS Pharmacy, Inc.,* 719 F.3d 392, 397 (5th Cir.2013)). Because removal raises significant federalism concerns, the removal statutes are strictly and narrowly construed, with any doubt resolved against removal and in favor of remand. *Gutierrez v. Flores,* 543 F.3d 248, 251 (5th Cir.2008). In short, any doubts regarding whether removal jurisdiction is proper should be resolved against federal jurisdiction. *Vantage Drilling Co. v. Hsin-Chi Su,* 741 F.3d 535, 537 (5th Cir.2014) (*quoting Acuna v. Brown & Root Inc.,* 200 F.3d 335, 339 (5th Cir.), *cert. denied,* 530 U.S. 1229, 120 S.Ct. 2658, 147 L.Ed.2d 273 (2000)).

In this case, plaintiffs filed suit in state court invoking the "saving to suitors clause" as well as asserting a claim for maintenance and cure. Defendants removed this case on the grounds that after the 2011 amendment to 28 U.S.C. § 1441, general maritime claims are removable.

Prior to the amendment in December, 2011, 28 U.S.C. § 1441 provided:

> (a) *Except as otherwise expressly provided by Act of Congress,* any civil action brought in a State court of which the district courts of the United States have original jurisdiction, may be removed by the defendant or the defendants, to the district court of the United States for the district and division embracing the place where such action is pending. For purposes

of removal under this chapter, the citizenship of defendants sued under fictitious names shall be disregarded.

(b) Any civil action of which the district courts have original jurisdiction *founded on a claim or right arising under the Constitution, treaties or laws of the United States* shall be removable without regard to the citizenship or residence of the parties. Any other such action shall be removable only if none of the parties in interest properly joined and served as defendants is a citizen of the State in which such action is brought.

(emphasis added).

Before the amendment, the general rule in the Fifth Circuit was that maritime claims were not removable absent a basis of jurisdiction outside of admiralty. *Tennessee Gas Pipeline v. Houston Cas. Ins. Co.*, 87 F.3d 150, 153 (5th Cir.1996) (maritime claim is not removable under the first sentence of § 1441(b) by falling within the admiralty jurisdiction of the federal courts, but is removable when original jurisdiction is based on something other than admiralty); *In re Dutile*, 935 F.2d 61, 63 (5th Cir.1991) (admiralty and maritime claims may be removed to federal court only by non-forum defendants and only where there is complete diversity of citizenship). *Dutile* reasoned that because admiralty and general maritime claims are not "founded on a claim or right arising under the Constitution, treaties or laws of the United States," such claims were subject to the in-state-defendant bar to removal found in section 1441(b). Thus, admiralty and maritime claims could be removed to federal court "only by non-forum defendants and only where there [wa]s complete diversity of citizenship." *Dutile*, 935 at 63.

However, the 2011 amendment to § 1441 created a split among the trial courts as to whether admiralty and maritime claims are now removable. The Federal Courts Jurisdiction and Venue Clarification Act of 2011 revised § 1441 as follows:

(a) **Generally.**—Except as otherwise expressly provided by Act of Congress, any civil action brought in a State court of which the district courts of the United States have original jurisdiction, may be removed by the defendant or the defendants, to the district court of the United States for the district and division embracing the place where such action is pending.

(b) **Removal based on diversity of citizenship.**—(1) In determining whether a civil action is removable on the basis of the jurisdiction under section 1332(a) of this title, the citizenship of defendants sued under fictitious names shall be disregarded.

(2) A civil action otherwise removable solely on the basis of the jurisdiction under section 1332(a) of this title may not be removed if any of the parties in interest properly

joined and served as defendants is a citizen of the State in which such action is brought.

28 U.S.C. § 1441. Although § 1441(a) remained basically the same, Congress removed the "original jurisdiction" and "other such action" language from § 1441(b).

Global argues that the 2011 amendment to the statute now permit removal of general maritime claims, regardless of the citizenship of the parties, citing *Ryan* and its progeny. . . . The court in *Ryan* reasoned that when Congress amended § 1441, it deleted the text upon which courts in the Fifth Circuit had previously interpreted as precluding removal of admiralty cases. *Id.* at 777. Thus, *Ryan* concluded, because Section 1333 (saving to suitors clause) also grants jurisdiction to the federal courts over admiralty and maritime matters, general maritime law claims have become removable. *Id.; see Gregoire v. Enterprise Marine Services., LLC,* ___ F.Supp.2d ___, 2014 WL 3866589, *3 (E.D.La. Aug. 6, 2014) (Duval, J) (analyzing *Ryan*).

This issue has sharply divided the district courts within the Fifth Circuit and courts outside of this Circuit. *See Cassidy v. Murray,* ___ F.Supp.2d ___, 2014 WL 3723877, *5 (D.Md. July 24, 2014) ("The Court is not inclined to reject decades of well-established law to adopt an unsettled attempt to alter the course of removal procedures without clear, binding, precedent"); *In re Foss Maritime Co.,* ___ F.Supp.2d ___, 2014 WL 2930860, *4 (W.D. Ky. June 27, 2014) (rejecting *Ryan's* conclusion that the December 2011 amendment altered the removability of maritime claims); *Pierce v. Parker Towing Co.,* 2014 WL 2569132, *7 (S.D. Ala. June 9, 2014) (remanding maritime claim on grounds that "not only would Plaintiffs be deprived of their forum of choice, but importantly, they would be deprived of their right to pursue non-maritime remedies, a right the savings clause 'protects' "); *Coronel v. AK Victory,* 1 F.Supp.3d 1175, 1188 (W.D.Wash.2014) (recognizing that removal would "deprive the plaintiff of his long-recognized choice of remedies, including, potentially, his right to a jury trial").

Courts in the Eastern and Western Districts of Louisiana and in the Southern and Eastern Districts of Texas have held that the 2011 amendments did not change the Fifth Circuit's longstanding rule that maritime claims are not removable absent a basis of jurisdiction outside of admiralty. *See Parker v. U.S. Environmental Services, LLC,* 2014 WL 7338850, *5 (S.D. Texas Dec. 22, 2014) (Ellison, J); *Serigny v. Chevron U.S.A., Inc.,* 2014 WL 6982213, *3 (W.D.La. Dec. 9, 2014) (Drell, J); *Harbor Docking & Towing, LLC v. Rolls Royce Marine North America, Inc.,* 2014 WL 6608354, *3 (W.D.La. Nov. 19, 2014) (Kay, J); *Rutherford v. Breathwite Marine Contractors, Ltd.,* ___ F.Supp.3d ___, 2014 WL6388786, *3 (S.D. Texas Nov. 12, 2014) (Gilmore, J); *Yavorsky v. Felice Navigation, Inc.,* 2014 WL 5811699, *5 (E.D.La. Nov. 7, 2014)2014 WL 5811699, *5 (E.D.La. Nov. 7, 2014) (Lemmon, J); *Henry J. Ellender Heirs, LLC v. Exxon Mobil Corp.,* ___ F.Supp.2d ___, 2014 WL 4231186,

*6 (E.D.La. Aug. 26, 2014) (Fallon, J); *Bisso Marine Co., Inc. v. Techcrane Intern., LLC*, 2014 WL 4489618, *4 (E.D.La. Sep. 10, 2014) (Feldman, J); *Riley v. Llog Exploration Co. LLC*, 2014 WL 4345002, *3 (E.D.La. Aug. 28, 2014) (Milazzo, J); *Gregoire, supra* (Duval, J); *Grasshopper Oysters, Inc. v. Great Lakes Dredge & Dock, LLC*, 2014 WL 3796150, *2 (E.D.La. July 29, 2014) (Berrigan, J); *Porter v. Great Am. Ins. Co.*, 2014 WL 3385148, *1 (W.D.La. July 9, 2014) (Walter, J); *Gabriles v. Chevron USA., Inc.*, 2014 WL 2567101, *4 (W.D. La. June 5, 2014) (Haik, J); *Perrier v. Shell Oil Co.*, 2014 WL 2155258, *3 (E.D.La. May 22, 2014) (Zainey, J); *see also Figueroa v. Marine Inspection Services*, ___ F.Supp.2d ___, 2014 WL 2958597, *4 (S.D. Texas July 1, 2014) (Ramos, J) (disagreeing with *Ryan*); *Alexander v. Seago Consulting, LLC*, 2014 WL 2960419, *1 (S.D. Texas June 23, 2014) (Hoyt, J) (disagreeing with *Ryan*); *Hamerly v. Tubal-Cain Marine Servs., Inc.*, ___ F.Supp.2d ___, 2014 WL 5149752, *5 (E.D. Tex. June 12, 2014) (Crone, J); *Rogers v. BBC Chartering America, LLC*, 2014 WL 819400 at *1 (S.D.Tex. March 3, 2014) (Hoyt, J) ("maritime cases filed in state court cannot be removed to federal court unless an independent basis for federal jurisdiction exists.").

However, the Middle District of Louisiana and other courts in the same Texas district in which *Ryan* was decided have followed *Ryan*, holding that the 2011 amendment makes these cases removable. *Exxon Mobil Corp. v. Starr Indem. & Liab. Co.*, 2014 WL 2739309, *2 (S.D. Tex. June 17, 2014) (Atlas, J), *remanded on other grounds on reconsideration*, 2014 WL 4167807 (S.D.Tex. Aug. 20, 2014); *Provost v. Offshore Service Vessels, LLC*, 2014 WL 2515412, *3 (M.D. La. June 4, 2014) (Dick, J); *Garza v. Phillips 66 Company*, 2014 WL 1330547, *4 (M.D. La. April 1, 2014) (Dick, J); *Carrigan v. M/V AMC AMBASSADOR*, 2014 WL 358353, *2 (S.D.Tex. Jan. 31, 2014) (Werlein, J); *Bridges v. Phillips 66 Co.*, 2013 WL 6092803, *5 (M.D.La. Nov. 19, 2013) (Brady, J); *Wells v. Abe's Boat Rentals Inc.*, 2013 WL 3110322, *3 (S.D. Tex. June 18, 2013) (Rosenthal, J); *but see Perise v. Eni Petroleum*, 2014 WL 4929239, *5 (M.D.La. Oct. 1, 2014) (Dick, J) (noting that the district judge had not considered the argument that the "saving to suitors" clause bars removal of general maritime actions, in the absence of an independent ground for the court's original jurisdiction, where the plaintiff requested a jury trial in state court).[3]

Recently, Judge DeGravelles of the Middle District followed the majority view holding that general maritime claims are not removable, despite the changes to 28 U.S.C. § 1441. *Harrold v. Liberty Ins. Underwriters*, 2014 WL 5801673, *3 (M.D.La. Nov. 7, 2014). Additionally, Judge Brady adopted Magistrate Judge Bourgeois' recommendation to remand a case where plaintiff had alleged Jones Act and general maritime law claims. *Bartel v. Alcoa Steamship Co., Inc.*, 2014 WL

---

[3] Judge Dick adopted the Report and Recommendation of Magistrate Judge Bourgeois, who indicated, *in dicta*, that plaintiff's maritime claims would warrant remand under the savings to suitors clause because of his jury demand. *Perise at* *5.

6879012, *5 (M.D.La. Dec. 4, 2014); *Bartel v. American Export Isbrandtsen,* 2014 WL 6879027, *5 (M.D.La. Dec. 4, 2014).

The Fifth Circuit has yet to directly address whether the current version of 28 U.S.C. § 1441 permits the removal of general maritime claims. In *Barker v. Hercules Offshore, Inc.,* 713 F.3d 208 (5th Cir.2013), the Court interpreted the updated version of § 1441(b) as a "clarification," rather than an amendment. *Id.* at 223 *(citing* H.R.Rep. No. 112–10 "explaining that the updated version is a clarification, as opposed to an amendment, of the original statute"). Thus, the Court found, the citizenship requirement in § 1441(b) only applies when a case is removed on the basis of diversity jurisdiction. The Court, relying on *Dutile,* further noted that "cases invoking admiralty jurisdiction under 28 U.S.C. § 1333 *may* require complete diversity prior to removal." (emphasis added). *Id.* at 223.

In *Gregoire, supra,* Judge Duval observed that *Barker,* which was decided under the pre-2011 version of Section 1441, "may be interpreted as simply reiterating *Dutile's* holding and recognizing no substantive change in removal jurisdiction as it pertains to maritime cases." 2014 WL 3866589, *8 *(citing Perrier, supra;* 14A Charles A. Wright, Arthur R. Miller, & Edward H. Cooper, *Federal Practice and Procedure* note 2, § 3674 (4th ed.2014)). Other courts, including *Ryan,* have regarded *Barker's* discussion of the 2011 amendments as mere *dictum,* noting that *Barker* did not directly address the issue. *See Maturin v. Commerce & Indus. Ins. Co.,* 2014 WL 2567150, *2 (W.D. La. June 6, 2014) (Haik, J) (noting *Barker, in dicta,* reasoned that the amendments in 1441(b) showed "Congress only meant the diversity requirement to apply to cases removed on the basis of diversity jurisdiction").

Until the Fifth Circuit definitively decides this issue, I am disinclined to hold that Congress intended to make such a major substantive change to § 1441, which would, in effect, upset centuries of well-established precedent by denying plaintiffs their right to a jury trial.

Article III, Section 2 of the United States Constitution vests federal courts with jurisdiction over "all cases of admiralty and maritime jurisdiction." *Coronel,* 1 F.Supp.3d at 1181 *(citing* U.S. Const. art. III, § 2). Section 9 of the Judiciary Act of 1789 originally codified this jurisdictional grant as follows:

> That the district courts shall have, exclusively of the courts of the several States . . . exclusive original cognizance of all civil causes of admiralty and maritime jurisdiction . . . within their respective districts as well as upon the high seas; *saving to suitors, in all cases, the right of a common law remedy, where the common law is competent to give it.*

(emphasis added). *Id.* (citing Ch. 20, § 9, 1 Stat. 73).

The last passage, known as the saving to suitors clause, now states:

> The district courts shall have original jurisdiction, exclusive of the courts of the States, of: (1) Any civil case of admiralty or maritime jurisdiction, *saving to suitors in all cases all other remedies to which they are otherwise entitled.*

(emphasis added). 28 U.S.C. § 1333.

The saving to suitors clause reserves to admiralty claimants all remedies that would be available at common law. *Lewis v. Lewis & Clark Marine, Inc.*, 531 U.S. 438, 454, 121 S.Ct. 993, 1004 (2001) (*citing The Hine v. Trevor*, 4 Wall. 555, 18 L.Ed. 451 (1866)). In short, the clause reserves to plaintiffs all remedies traditionally available at common law via *in personam* proceedings. *Id.* (*citing Lewis*, 531 U.S. at 455, 121 S.Ct. 993). Thus, the federal courts' admiralty jurisdiction "is 'exclusive' only as to those maritime causes of action begun and carried on as proceedings *in rem*, that is, where a vessel or thing is itself treated as the offender and made the defendant by name or description in order to enforce a lien." *Coronel* at 1181 (*citing Madruga v. Superior Court of State of Cal. in and for San Diego County*, 346 U.S. 556, 560, 74 S.Ct. 298, 301, 98 L.Ed. 290 (1954)). State courts are " 'competent' to adjudicate maritime causes of action in proceedings 'in personam,' that is, where the defendant is a person, not a ship or some other instrument of navigation." *Id.* (*quoting Madruga* at 560–61).

The saving to suitors clause has always been understood to preserve the remedy, not the forum. *Bisso* at *4. Thus, admiralty cases filed in state court that fall within the federal court's jurisdiction under an independent, non-admiralty doctrine, such as diversity, have always been removable. *Id.* For centuries, the savings clause has provided a maritime plaintiff with three options: (1) sue in admiralty in federal court under admiralty jurisdiction, (2) sue at law in state court, or (3) sue at law in federal court "if he can make proper parties to give that court jurisdiction of his case." *Id.* (*quoting The Belfast*, 74 U.S. 634, 644 (1868)).

As to procedure, historically, the federal courts maintained separate dockets and separate rules of procedure for cases under admiralty and law jurisdiction. *Coronel*, 1 F.Supp.3d at 1183 (*citing Wilmington Trust v. U.S. Dist. Court for Dist. of Hawaii*, 934 F.2d 1026, 1029 (9th Cir.1991); Erastus C. Benedict, *Benedict on Admiralty* § 133 (2013)). In 1966, the separate dockets were merged and the Federal Rules of Procedure were made applicable to admiralty claims. *Id.* (*citing Benedict, supra*, § 133; *Wilmington Trust*, 934 F.2d at 1029; Fed.R.Civ.P. 1). Thus, a plaintiff can bring a maritime suit in federal court either in admiralty or at law. *Bisso* at *5.

The differences between claims brought in admiralty and at law are procedural. *Bisso* at *5 (*citing* Fed.R.Civ.P. 14(c) (third party practice), 38(e) (no jury trial), and 82 (lack of venue restriction)); *Coronel* at 1183. Probably the most salient distinction is the right to a jury trial. *Coronel* at 1183 (*citing Lewis,* 531 U.S. at 455, 121 S.Ct. 993). The Seventh Amendment right to a jury trial does not apply to cases brought in admiralty. *Id.* (*citing Fitzgerald v. U.S. Lines Co.,* 374 U.S. 16, 20 (1963)); *see also Bisso* at *5.

Here, plaintiffs filed their petition in state court invoking the saving to suitors clause and requested a trial by jury. Allowing removal to this Court would "require the Court to disregard hundreds of years of admiralty tradition" by stripping plaintiffs of their right to a jury trial. *Riley* 2014 WL 4345002 at *4. For this reason, the undersigned rejects the holding of the court in *Ryan,* and adopts Judge Milazzo's very sound reasoning in *Riley.*

In *Riley,* plaintiff, a commercial fisherman filed a maritime negligence action in state court, alleging that he was injured when his shrimp net struck an unmarked underwater pipe in the open waters of Plaquemines Parish, causing his boat to unexpectedly stop and throw him backwards. Defendants, the owners of the pipe and the lessor of the land on which the pipe was placed, removed the case to federal court on the grounds that the amended removal statute permitted removal of admiralty claims. Plaintiff opposed, arguing that removal of admiralty cases in state court offends the saving to suitors clause of 28 U.S.C. § 1333.

Judge Milazzo assumed, without deciding, that defendants' analysis of the removal statute was correct. *Id.* at 3. Then, she proceeded to plaintiffs' argument: that the saving to suitors clause was an Act of Congress operating to prevent removal of the case. Relying "largely by the manner in which federal courts have historically treated admiralty claims," she concluded that plaintiff was correct.

In her analysis, Judge Milazzo cited *Romero v. International Terminal Operating Co.,* 358 U.S. 354, 79 S.Ct. 468, 3 L.Ed.2d 368 (1959), in which the Supreme Court held that admiralty claims could not be brought on the law side of federal courts unless the claims also fell within a statutory grant of jurisdiction such as §§ 1331 or 1332.[4] In light of *Romero,* she noted that three things were clear: (1) plaintiff's case must proceed either at law or in admiralty, (2) the case could only proceed at law if there was a jurisdictional basis outside of section 1333, and (3) the only possible jurisdictional basis for the suit was section 1333. Thus, the Court could only exercise jurisdiction over the case if it could do so in admiralty.

In urging the court to uphold removal, defendants argued that the court had the power to grant plaintiff a jury trial even if the case proceeded in admiralty, citing *Fitzgerald* and *Luera v. M/V Alberta,* 635 F.3d 181 (5th Cir.2011). After distinguishing these cases, Judge Milazzo rejected defendant's argument, reasoning as follows:

---

[4]   This holding has been consistently followed by the Fifth Circuit. *Barker,* 713 F.3d at 219; *In re Dutile,* 935 F.2d at 63; *Tennessee Gas Pipeline,* 87 F.3d at 153.

Defendants have cited no case where a federal court presented only with claims arising under the general maritime law has granted the parties a jury trial. Indeed, to do so would require the Court to disregard hundreds of years of admiralty tradition, something this Court is not prepared to do.

Considering the foregoing, the Court is left with the firm conviction that the savings clause of section 1333 prohibits this case from proceeding in admiralty. To be sure, courts have long held that the saving-to-suitors clause is not an independent bar to removal. The savings clause preserves a plaintiff's right to pursue common law remedies but not a right to a non-federal forum. The clause does, however, require that a plaintiff's choice between proceeding at law or in admiralty be honored. It is similarly well settled that, because federal courts possess exclusive admiralty jurisdiction, state court suits are necessarily brought at law. Thus, when a plaintiff files suit in state court he has affirmatively elected to proceed at law and his suit may only be removed to the law side of federal court. As explained *supra,* there is no ground on which this Court can exercise jurisdiction over this case at law. Accordingly, the only at-law forum available to the parties is state court and that is where this suit must be litigated.

Id. at *4–5.

Here, the plaintiffs specifically invoked the saving to suitors clause and requested a jury trial in state court. By affirmatively electing to proceed at law, their suit can only be removed based on an independent ground for this Court's original jurisdiction, such as diversity. Unless and until the Fifth Circuit addresses this issue, this Court will join the reasoning set forth by the judges of this District (*see Porter* and *Gabriles, supra*) and Judge Milazzo in finding that plaintiffs' claims remain unremovable.

Conclusion

For the foregoing reasons, the Motion to Remand is **GRANTED.**

NOTE

As the court in *Boudreaux* notes, Ryan v. Hercules Offshore, 945 F.Supp. 2d 772 (S.D. Tex. 2013), is the leading case supporting the minority view that make admiralty claims filed in state court removable to federal court. The Seventh Circuit addressed the issue in Lu Junhong v. Boeing Co., 792 F.3d 805 (7th Cir. 2015). The court, however, did not cite *Ryan* or any of the other cases supporting the minority view. Instead the Seventh Circuit concluded that even if the saving-to-suitors clause gave plaintiffs the right to remain in state court, plaintiffs could and did waive that right by not mentioning the saving-to-suitors clause. So far, no other court of appeals has addressed the impact of the 2011 amendments to § 1441 on the removal of admiralty cases from state courts.

CHAPTER 19

MARITIME LAW OF INDUSTRIAL ACCIDENTS

A. SEAMEN

4. THE WARRANTY OF SEAWORTHINESS

c. DAMAGES

Insert on page 1042 before Horsley v. Mobil Oil Corp.:

The Dutra Group v. Batterton
Supreme Court of the United States, 2019.
139 S.Ct. 2275, 204 L.Ed.2d 692, 2019 A.M.C. 1521.

■ JUSTICE ALITO delivered the opinion of the Court.

By granting federal courts jurisdiction over maritime and admiralty cases, the Constitution implicitly directs federal courts sitting in admiralty to proceed "in the manner of a common law court." *Exxon Shipping Co. v. Baker*, 554 U.S. 471, 489–490, 128 S.Ct. 2605, 171 L.Ed.2d 570 (2008). Thus, where Congress has not prescribed specific rules, federal courts must develop the "amalgam of traditional common-law rules, modifications of those rules, and newly created rules" that forms the general maritime law. *East River S. S. Corp. v. Transamerica Delaval Inc.*, 476 U.S. 858, 864–865, 106 S.Ct. 2295, 90 L.Ed.2d 865 (1986). But maritime law is no longer solely the province of the Federal Judiciary. "Congress and the States have legislated extensively in these areas." *Miles v. Apex Marine Corp.*, 498 U.S. 19, 27, 111 S.Ct. 317, 112 L.Ed.2d 275 (1990). When exercising its inherent common-law authority, "an admiralty court should look primarily to these legislative enactments for policy guidance." *Ibid.* We may depart from the policies found in the statutory scheme in discrete instances based on long-established history, see, *e.g.*, *Atlantic Sounding Co. v. Townsend*, 557 U.S. 404, 424–425, 129 S.Ct. 2561, 174 L.Ed.2d 382 (2009), but we do so cautiously in light of Congress's persistent pursuit of "uniformity in the exercise of admiralty jurisdiction." *Miles, supra,* at 26, 111 S.Ct. 317 (quoting *Moragne v. States Marine Lines, Inc.*, 398 U.S. 375, 401, 90 S.Ct. 1772, 26 L.Ed.2d 339 (1970)).

This case asks whether a mariner may recover punitive damages on a claim that he was injured as a result of the unseaworthy condition of the vessel. We have twice confronted similar questions in the past several decades, and our holdings in both cases were based on the particular claims involved. In *Miles*, which concerned a wrongful-death claim under the general maritime law, we held that recovery was limited to pecuniary damages, which did not include loss of society. 498 U.S. at 23, 111 S.Ct. 317. And in *Atlantic Sounding*, after examining centuries of relevant case law, we held that punitive damages are not categorically barred as part of the award on the traditional maritime claim of maintenance and cure. 557 U.S. at 407, 129 S.Ct. 2561. Here, because there is no historical basis for allowing punitive damages in unseaworthiness actions, and in order to promote uniformity with the way courts have applied parallel statutory causes of action, we hold that punitive damages remain unavailable in unseaworthiness actions.

I

In order to determine the remedies for unseaworthiness, we must consider both the heritage of the cause of action in the common law and its place in the modern statutory framework.

A

The seaman's right to recover damages for personal injury on a claim of unseaworthiness originates in the admiralty court decisions of the 19th century. At the time, "seamen led miserable lives." D. Robertson, S. Friedell, & M. Sturley, Admiralty and Maritime Law in the United States 163 (2d ed. 2008). Maritime law was largely judge-made, and seamen were viewed as "emphatically the wards of the admiralty." *Harden v. Gordon*, 11 F.Cas. 480, 485 (No. 6,047) (CC Me. 1823). In that era, the primary responsibility for protecting seamen lay in the courts, which saw mariners as "peculiarly entitled to"—and particularly in need of—judicial protection "against the effects of the superior skill and shrewdness of masters and owners of ships." *Brown v. Lull*, 4 F.Cas. 407, 409 (No. 2,018) (CC Mass. 1836) (Story, J.).[1]

Courts of admiralty saw it as their duty not to be "confined to the mere dry and positive rules of the common law" but to "act upon the enlarged and liberal jurisprudence of courts of equity; and, in short, so far as their powers extend[ed], they act[ed] as courts of equity." *Ibid.* This Court interpreted the Constitution's grant of admiralty jurisdiction to the Federal Judiciary as "the power to . . . dispose of [a case] as justice may require." *The Resolute*, 168 U.S. 437, 439, 18 S.Ct. 112, 42 L.Ed. 533 (1897).

Courts used this power to protect seamen from injury primarily through two causes of action. The first, maintenance and cure, has its roots in the medieval and renaissance law codes that form the ancient

---

[1] Riding circuit, Justice Story described mariners in markedly paternalistic terms: "Seamen are a class of persons remarkable for their rashness, thoughtlessness and improvidence. They are generally necessitous, ignorant of the nature and extent of their own rights and privileges, and for the most part incapable of duly appreciating their value. They combine, in a singular manner, the apparent anomalies of gallantry, extravagance, profusion in expenditure, indifference to the future, credulity, which is easily won, and confidence, which is readily surprised." Brown, 4 F.Cas. at 409.

foundation of maritime common law.[2] The duty of maintenance and cure requires a ship's master "to provide food, lodging, and medical services to a seaman injured while serving the ship." *Lewis v. Lewis & Clark Marine, Inc.*, 531 U.S. 438, 441, 121 S.Ct. 993, 148 L.Ed.2d 931 (2001). This duty, "which arises from the contract of employment, does not rest upon negligence or culpability on the part of the owner or master, nor is it restricted to those cases where the seaman's employment is the cause of the injury or illness." *Calmar S. S. Corp. v. Taylor*, 303 U.S. 525, 527, 58 S.Ct. 651, 82 L.Ed. 993 (1938) (citations omitted).

The second claim, unseaworthiness, is a much more recent development and grew out of causes of action unrelated to personal injury. In its earliest forms, an unseaworthiness claim gave sailors under contract to sail on a ship the right to collect their wages even if they had refused to board an unsafe vessel after discovering its condition. See, *e.g., Dixon v. The Cyrus,* 7 F.Cas. 755, 757 (No. 3,930) (Pa. 1789); *Rice v. The Polly & Kitty,* 20 F.Cas. 666, 667, (No. 11754) (Pa. 1789). Similarly, unseaworthiness was a defense to criminal charges against seamen who refused to obey a ship master's orders. See, *e.g., United States v. Nye,* 27 F.Cas. 210, 211, (No. 15906) (CC Mass. 1855); *United States v. Ashton,* 24 F.Cas. 873, 874–875, (No. 14470) (CC Mass. 1834). A claim of unseaworthiness could also be asserted by a shipper to recover damages or by an insurer to deny coverage when the poor condition of the ship resulted in damage to or loss of the cargo. See *The Caledonia,* 157 U.S. 124, 132–136, 15 S.Ct. 537, 39 L.Ed. 644 (1895) (cataloging cases).

Only in the latter years of the 19th century did unseaworthiness begin a long and gradual evolution toward remedying personal injury. Courts began to extend the cases about refusals to serve to allow recovery for mariners who were injured because of the unseaworthy condition of the vessel on which they had served.[3] These early cases were sparse, and they generally allowed recovery only when a vessel's owner failed to exercise due diligence to ensure that the ship left port in a seaworthy condition. See, *e.g., The Robert C. McQuillen,* 91 F. 685, 686–687 (Conn.

---

[2] A right resembling maintenance and cure appears in the Laws of Oleron, promulgated by Eleanor of Aquitaine around 1160, in the 13th-century Laws of Wisbuy, in the Laws of the Hanse Towns, published in 1597, and in the Marine Ordinances of Louis XIV, published in 1681. See 30 F. Cas. 1169 (collecting sources). The relevant passages are the Laws of Oleron, Arts. VI and VII, 30 F.Cas. at 1174–1175; the Laws of Wisbuy, Arts. XVIII, XIX, and XXXIII, 30 F.Cas. at 1191–1192; the Laws of the Hanse Towns, Arts. XXXIX and XLV, 30 F.Cas. at 1200; the Marine Ordinances of Louis XIV, Tit. IV, Arts. XI and XII, 30 F.Cas. at 1209.

[3] Most of these cases allowed recovery for personal injury in "erroneous reliance" on certain passages in *Dixon v. The Cyrus,* 7 F.Cas. 755 (No. 3,930) (Pa. 1789). Tetreault, Seamen, Seaworthiness, and the Rights of Harbor Workers, 39 Cornell L. Q. 381, 390 (1954) (Tetreault). These cases misread *The Cyrus* as resting on an implied warranty of seaworthiness. Tetreault 390. But *The Cyrus* is more fairly read to turn on a theory of true implied condition. While a warranty would provide a basis for damages if the breach caused an injury, an implied condition would only allow the mariner to escape performance without surrendering the benefit of the contract. In other words, "[t]he manifest unseaworthiness of the vessel at the commencement of the voyage would excuse non-performance by the mariners but did not constitute a basis for damages." Tetreault 390.

1899); *The Lizzie Frank*, 31 F. 477, 480 (SD Ala. 1887); *The Tammerlane*, 47 F. 822, 824 (ND Cal. 1891).

Unseaworthiness remained a suspect basis for personal injury claims until 1903, when, in dicta, this Court concluded that "the vessel and her owner are . . . liable to an indemnity for injuries received by seamen in consequence of the unseaworthiness of the ship." *The Osceola*, 189 U.S. 158, 175, 23 S.Ct. 483, 47 L.Ed. 760 (1903). Although this was the first recognition of unseaworthiness as a personal injury claim in this Court, we took pains to note that the claim was strictly cabined. *Ibid.* Some of the limitations on recovery were imported from the common law. The fellow-servant doctrine, in particular, prohibited recovery when an employee suffered an injury due to the negligent act of another employee without negligence on the part of the employer. *Ibid.*; see, *e.g.*, *The Sachem*, 42 F. 66 (EDNY 1890) (denying recovery based on fellow-servant doctrine). Because a claimant had to show that he was injured by some aspect of the ship's condition that rendered the vessel unseaworthy, a claim could not prevail based on "the negligence of the master, or any member of the crew."[4] *The Osceola, supra*, at 175, 23 S.Ct. 483; see also *The City of Alexandria*, 17 F. 390 (SDNY 1883) (no recovery based on negligence that does not render vessel unseaworthy). Instead, a seaman had to show that the owner of the vessel had failed to exercise due diligence in ensuring the ship was in seaworthy condition. See generally *Dixon v. United States*, 219 F.2d 10, 12–14 (C.A.2 1955) (Harlan, J.) (cataloging evolution of the claim).

B

In the early 20th century, then, under "the general maritime law . . . a vessel and her owner . . . were liable to an indemnity for injuries received by a seaman in consequence of the unseaworthiness of the ship and her appliances; but a seaman was not allowed to recover an indemnity for injuries sustained through the negligence of the master or any member of the crew." *Pacific S. S. Co. v. Peterson*, 278 U.S. 130, 134, 49 S.Ct. 75, 73 L.Ed. 220 (1928); see also *Plamals v. S. S. "Pinar Del Rio,"* 277 U.S. 151, 155, 48 S.Ct. 457, 72 L.Ed. 827 (1928) (vessel was not unseaworthy when mate negligently selected defective rope but sound rope was available on board). Because of these severe limitations on recovery, "the seaman's right to recover damages for injuries caused by unseaworthiness of the ship was an obscure and relatively little used remedy." G. Gilmore & C. Black, The Law of Admiralty § 6–38, p. 383 (2d ed. 1975) (Gilmore & Black).

---

[4] To be sure, in some instances the concept of "unseaworthiness" expanded to embrace conditions that resulted from the negligence of fellow servants, see, *e.g.*, *Carlisle Packing Co. v. Sandanger*, 259 U.S. 255, 259, 42 S.Ct. 475, 66 L.Ed. 927 (1922) (vessel was rendered unseaworthy when it left port with gasoline in a container labeled "coal oil"); see also G. Robinson, Handbook of Admiralty Law in the United States § 37, p. 305–307 (1st ed. 1939) (collecting cases). But it was only after the passage of the Jones Act that negligence by a fellow mariner provided a reliable basis for recovery. See Part I-B, *infra*.

Tremendous shifts in mariners' rights took place between 1920 and 1950. First, during and after the First World War, Congress enacted a series of laws regulating maritime liability culminating in the Merchant Marine Act of 1920, § 33, 41 Stat. 1007 (Jones Act), which codified the rights of injured mariners and created new statutory claims that were freed from many of the common-law limitations on recovery. The Jones Act provides injured seamen with a cause of action and a right to a jury. 46 U.S.C. § 30104. Rather than create a new structure of substantive rights, the Jones Act incorporated the rights provided to railway workers under the Federal Employers' Liability Act (FELA), 45 U.S.C. § 51 *et seq.* 46 U.S.C. § 30104. In the 30 years after the Jones Act's passage, "the Act was the vehicle for almost all seamen's personal injury and death actions." Gilmore & Black § 6–20, at 327.

But the Jones Act was overtaken in the 1950s by the second fundamental change in personal injury maritime claims—and it was this Court, not Congress, that played the leading role. In a pair of decisions in the late 1940s, the Court transformed the old claim of unseaworthiness, which had demanded only due diligence by the vessel owner, into a strict-liability claim. In *Mahnich v. Southern S. S. Co.*, 321 U.S. 96, 64 S.Ct. 455, 88 L.Ed. 561 (1944), the Court stated that "the exercise of due diligence does not relieve the owner of his obligation" to provide a seaworthy ship and, in the same ruling, held that the fellow-servant doctrine did not provide a defense. *Id.*, at 100, 101, 64 S.Ct. 455. *Mahnich*'s interpretation of the early cases may have been suspect, see Tetreault 397–398 (*Mahnich* rests on "startling misstatement" of relevant precedents), but its assertion triggered a sea-change in maritime personal injury. Less than two years later, we affirmed that the duty of seaworthiness was "essentially a species of liability without fault . . . neither limited by conceptions of negligence nor contractual in character. It is a form of absolute duty owing to all within the range of its humanitarian policy." *Seas Shipping Co. v. Sieracki*, 328 U.S. 85, 94–95, 66 S.Ct. 872, 90 L.Ed. 1099 (1946) (citations omitted). From *Mahnich* forward, "the decisions of this Court have undeviatingly reflected an understanding that the owner's duty to furnish a seaworthy ship is absolute and completely independent of his duty under the Jones Act to exercise reasonable care." *Mitchell v. Trawler Racer, Inc.*, 362 U.S. 539, 549, 80 S.Ct. 926, 4 L.Ed.2d 941 (1960). As a result of *Mahnich* and *Sieracki*, between the 1950s and 1970s "the unseaworthiness count [was] the essential basis for recovery with the Jones Act count preserved merely as a jury-getting device."[5] Gilmore & Black § 6–20, at 327–328.

The shifts in plaintiff preferences between Jones Act and unseaworthiness claims were possible because of the significant overlap between the two causes of action. See *id.*, § 6–38, at 383. One leading

---

[5] The decline of Jones Act claims was arrested, although not reversed, by our holding that some negligent actions on a vessel may create Jones Act liability without rendering the vessel unseaworthy. See *Usner v. Luckenbach Overseas Corp.*, 400 U.S. 494, 91 S.Ct. 514, 27 L.Ed.2d 562 (1971); see also 1B Benedict on Admiralty § 23, p. 3–35 (7th rev. ed. 2018).

treatise goes so far as to describe the two claims as "alternative 'grounds' of recovery for a single cause of action." 2 R. Force & M. Norris, The Law of Seamen § 30:90, p. 30–369 (5th ed. 2003). The two claims are so similar that, immediately after the Jones Act's passage, we held that plaintiffs could not submit both to a jury. *Plamals, supra,* at 156–157, 48 S.Ct. 457 ("Seamen may invoke, at their election, the relief accorded by the old rules against the ship, or that provided by the new against the employer. But they may not have the benefit of both"). We no longer require such election. See *McAllister v. Magnolia Petroleum Co.,* 357 U.S. 221, 222, n. 2, 78 S.Ct. 1201, 2 L.Ed.2d 1272 (1958). But a plaintiff still cannot duplicate his recovery by collecting full damages on both claims because, "whether or not the seaman's injuries were occasioned by the unseaworthiness of the vessel or by the negligence of the master or members of the crew, . . . there is but a single wrongful invasion of his primary right of bodily safety and but a single legal wrong." *Peterson,* 278 U.S. at 138, 49 S.Ct. 75; see also 2 Force, *supra,* §§ 26:73, 30:90.

II

Christopher Batterton worked as a deckhand and crew member on vessels owned and operated by the Dutra Group. According to Batterton's complaint, while working on a scow near Newport Beach, California, Batterton was injured when his hand was caught between a bulkhead and a hatch that blew open as a result of unventilated air accumulating and pressurizing within the compartment.

Batterton sued Dutra and asserted a variety of claims, including negligence, unseaworthiness, maintenance and cure, and unearned wages. He sought to recover general and punitive damages. Dutra moved to strike Batterton's claim for punitive damages, arguing that they are not available on claims for unseaworthiness. The District Court denied Dutra's motion, 2014 WL 12538172 (CD Cal., Dec. 15, 2014), but agreed to certify an interlocutory appeal on the question, 2015 WL 13752889 (CD Cal., Feb. 6, 2015).

The Court of Appeals affirmed. 880 F.3d 1089 (C.A.9 2018). Applying Circuit precedent, see *Evich v. Morris,* 819 F.2d 256, 258–259 (C.A.9 1987), the Court of Appeals held that punitive damages are available for unseaworthiness claims. 880 F.3d at 1096. This holding reaffirmed a division of authority between the Circuits. Compare *McBride v. Estis Well Serv., L. L. C.,* 768 F.3d 382, 391 (C.A.5 2014) (en banc) (punitive damages are not recoverable), and *Horsley v. Mobil Oil Corp.,* 15 F.3d 200, 203 (C.A.1 1994) (same), with *Self v. Great Lakes Dredge & Dock Co.,* 832 F.2d 1540, 1550 (C.A.11 1987) ("Punitive damages should be available in cases where the shipowner willfully violated the duty to maintain a safe and seaworthy ship . . ."). We granted certiorari to resolve this division. 586 U.S. ___, 139 S.Ct. 627, 202 L.Ed.2d 454 (2018).

III

Our resolution of this question is governed by our decisions in *Miles* and *Atlantic Sounding*. *Miles* establishes that we "should look primarily to . . . legislative enactments for policy guidance," while recognizing that we "may supplement these statutory remedies where doing so would achieve the uniform vindication" of the policies served by the relevant statutes. 498 U.S. at 27, 111 S.Ct. 317. In *Atlantic Sounding*, we allowed recovery of punitive damages, but we justified our departure from the statutory remedial scheme based on the established history of awarding punitive damages for certain maritime torts, including maintenance and cure. 557 U.S. at 411–414, 129 S.Ct. 2561 (discussing cases of piracy and maintenance and cure awarding damages with punitive components). We were explicit that our decision represented a gloss on *Miles* rather than a departure from it. *Atlantic Sounding, supra*, at 420, 129 S.Ct. 2561 ("The reasoning of *Miles* remains sound"). And we recognized the importance of viewing each claim in its proper historical context. " '[R]emedies for negligence, unseaworthiness, and maintenance and cure have different origins and may on occasion call for application of slightly different principles and procedures.' " 557 U.S. at 423, 129 S.Ct. 2561.

In accordance with these decisions, we consider here whether punitive damages have traditionally been awarded for claims of unseaworthiness and whether conformity with parallel statutory schemes would require such damages. Finally, we consider whether we are compelled on policy grounds to allow punitive damages for unseaworthiness claims.

A

For claims of unseaworthiness, the overwhelming historical evidence suggests that punitive damages are not available. Batterton principally relies on two cases to establish that punitive damages were traditionally available for breach of the duty of seaworthiness. Upon close inspection, neither supports this argument.

The Rolph, 293 F. 269, 271 (ND Cal. 1923), involved a mate who brutally beat members of the crew, rendering one seaman blind and leaving another with impaired hearing. The central question in the case was not the form of damages, but rather whether the viciousness of the mate rendered the vessel unseaworthy. *The Rolph*, 299 F. 52, 54 (C.A.9 1924). The court concluded that the master, by staffing the vessel with such an unsuitable officer, had rendered it unseaworthy. *Id.*, at 55. To the extent the court described the basis for the damages awarded, it explained that the judgment was supported by testimony as to "the expectation of life and earnings of these men." 293 F. at 272. And the Court of Appeals discussed only the seamen's entitlement "to recover an indemnity" for their injuries. 299 F. at 56. These are discussions of compensatory damages—nowhere does the court speak in terms of an exemplary or punitive award.[6]

The Noddleburn, 28 F. 855, 857–858 (Ore. 1886), involved an injury to a British seaman serving on a British vessel and was decided under English law. The plaintiff in the case was injured when he fell to the deck after being ordered aloft and stepping on an inadequately secured line. *Id.,* at 855. After the injury, the master neglected the man's wounds, thinking the injury a mere sprain. *Id.,* at 856. The leg failed to heal and the man had to insist on being discharged to a hospital, where he learned that he would be permanently disabled. *Ibid.* As damages, the court awarded him accrued wages, as well as $ 1,000 to compensate for the loss in future earnings from his disability and $ 500 for his pain and suffering. *Id.,* at 860. But these are purely compensatory awards—the only discussion of exemplary damages comes at the very close of the opinion, and it is clear that they were considered because of the master's failure to provide maintenance and cure. *Ibid.* (discussing additional award "in consideration of the neglect and indifference with which the libelant was treated by the master *after his injury*" (emphasis added)).

Finally, Batterton points to two other cases, *The City of Carlisle,* 39 F. 807 (Ore. 1889), and *The Troop,* 118 F. 769 (Wash. 1902). But these cases, like *The Noddleburn,* both involve maintenance and cure claims that rest on the willful failure of the master and mate to provide proper care for wounded sailors after they were injured. 39 F. at 812 ("master failed and neglected to procure or provide any medical aid or advice . . . and was contriving and intending to get rid of him as easily as possible"); 118 F. at 771 (assessing damages based on provision of Laws of Oleron requiring maintenance). Batterton characterizes these as unseaworthiness actions on the theory that the seamen *could have* pursued that claim. But, because courts award damages for the claims a plaintiff actually pleads rather than those he could have brought, these cases are irrelevant.

The lack of punitive damages in traditional maritime law cases is practically dispositive. By the time the claim of unseaworthiness evolved to remedy personal injury, punitive damages were a well-established part of the common law. *Exxon Shipping,* 554 U.S. at 491, 128 S.Ct. 2605. American courts had awarded punitive (or exemplary) damages from the Republic's earliest days. See, *e.g., Genay v. Norris,* 1 S. C. L. 6, 7 (1784); *Coryell v. Colbaugh,* 1 N.J.L. 77, 78 (1791). And yet, beyond the decisions discussed above, Batterton presents no decisions from the formative years of the personal injury unseaworthiness claim in which exemplary damages were awarded. From this we conclude that, unlike maintenance

---

[6] Even if this case did involve a *sub silentio* punitive award, we share the Fifth Circuit's reluctance to "rely on one dust-covered case to establish that punitive damages were generally available in unseaworthiness cases." *McBride v. Estis Well Serv., L. L. C.,* 768 F.3d 382, 397 (2014) (Clement, J., concurring). Absent a clear historical pattern, *Miles v. Apex Marine Corp.,* 498 U.S. 19, 111 S.Ct. 317, 112 L.Ed.2d 275 (1990), commands us to seek conformity with the policy preferences the political branches have expressed in legislation.

and cure, unseaworthiness did not traditionally allow recovery of punitive damages.

B

In light of this overwhelming historical evidence, we cannot sanction a novel remedy here unless it is required to maintain uniformity with Congress's clearly expressed policies. Therefore, we must consider the remedies typically recognized for Jones Act claims.

The Jones Act adopts the remedial provisions of FELA, and by the time of the Jones Act's passage, this Court and others had repeatedly interpreted the scope of damages available to FELA plaintiffs. These early decisions held that "[t]he damages recoverable [under FELA] are limited . . . strictly to the financial loss . . . sustained."[7] *American R. Co. of P. R. v. Didricksen*, 227 U.S. 145, 149, 33 S.Ct. 224, 57 L.Ed. 456 (1913); see also *Gulf, C. & S. F. R. Co. v. McGinnis*, 228 U.S. 173, 175, 33 S.Ct. 426, 57 L.Ed. 785 (1913) (FELA is construed "only to compensate . . . for the actual pecuniary loss resulting" from the worker's injury or death); *Michigan Central R. Co. v. Vreeland*, 227 U.S. 59, 68, 33 S.Ct. 192, 57 L.Ed. 417 (1913) (FELA imposes "a liability for the pecuniary damage resulting to [the worker] and for that only"). In one particularly illuminating case, in deciding whether a complaint alleged a claim under FELA or state law, the Court observed that if the complaint "were read as manifestly demanding exemplary damages, that would point to the state law." *Seaboard Air Line R. Co. v. Koennecke*, 239 U.S. 352, 354, 36 S.Ct. 126, 60 L.Ed. 324 (1915). And in the years since, Federal Courts of Appeals have unanimously held that punitive damages are not available under FELA. *Miller v. American President Lines, Ltd.*, 989 F.2d 1450, 1457 (CA6 1993); *Wildman v. Burlington No. R. Co.*, 825 F.2d 1392, 1395 (C.A.9 1987); *Kozar v. Chesapeake & Ohio R. Co.*, 449 F.2d 1238, 1243 (C.A.6 1971).

Our early discussions of the Jones Act followed the same practices. We described the Act shortly after its passage as creating "an action for compensatory damages, on the ground of negligence."[8] *Peterson*, 278 U.S. at 135, 49 S.Ct. 75. And we have more recently observed that the Jones Act "limits recovery to pecuniary loss." *Miles*, 498 U.S. at 32, 111 S.Ct. 317. Looking to FELA and these decisions, the Federal Courts of Appeals have uniformly held that punitive damages are not available under the Jones Act. *McBride*, 768 F.3d at 388 ("[N]o cases have awarded punitive damages under the Jones Act"); *Guevara v. Maritime Overseas Corp.*, 59 F.3d 1496, 1507, n. 9 (C.A.5 1995) (en banc); *Horsley*, 15 F.3d at 203;

---

[7] Treatises from the same period lend further support to the view that "in all actions under [FELA], an award of exemplary damages is not permitted." 2 M. Roberts, Federal Liabilities of Carriers § 621, p. 1093 (1918); 1 *id.*, § 417, at 708; 5 J. Berryman, Sutherland on Damages § 1333, p. 5102 (4th ed. 1916) (FELA "provid[es] compensation for pecuniary loss or damage only").

[8] We also note that Congress declined to allow punitive damages when it enacted the Death on the High Seas Act. 46 U.S.C. § 30303 (allowing "fair compensation for the pecuniary loss sustained" for a death on the high seas).

Miller, supra, at 1457 ("Punitive damages are not . . . recoverable under the Jones Act"); *Kopczynski v. The Jacqueline,* 742 F.2d 555, 560 (C.A.9 1984).

Batterton argues that these cases are either inapposite or wrong, but because of the absence of historical evidence to support punitive damages—evidence that was central to our decision in *Atlantic Sounding*—we need not reopen this question of statutory interpretation. It is enough for us to note the general consensus that exists in the lower courts and to observe that the position of those courts conforms with the discussion and holding in *Miles.* Adopting the rule urged by Batterton would be contrary to *Miles*'s command that federal courts should seek to promote a "uniform rule applicable to all actions" for the same injury, whether under the Jones Act or the general maritime law. 498 U.S. at 33, 111 S.Ct. 317.

C

To the extent Batterton argues that punitive damages are justified on policy grounds or as a regulatory measure, we are unpersuaded. In contemporary maritime law, our overriding objective is to pursue the policy expressed in congressional enactments, and because unseaworthiness in its current strict-liability form is our own invention and came after passage of the Jones Act, it would exceed our current role to introduce novel remedies contradictory to those Congress has provided in similar areas. See *id.,* at 36, 111 S.Ct. 317 (declining to create remedy "that goes well beyond the limits of Congress' ordered system of recovery"). We are particularly loath to impose more expansive liabilities on a claim governed by strict liability than Congress has imposed for comparable claims based in negligence. *Ibid.* And with the increased role that legislation has taken over the past century of maritime law, we think it wise to leave to the political branches the development of novel claims and remedies.

We are also wary to depart from the practice under the Jones Act because a claim of unseaworthiness—more than a claim for maintenance and cure—serves as a duplicate and substitute for a Jones Act claim. The duty of maintenance and cure requires the master to provide medical care and wages to an injured mariner in the period after the injury has occurred. *Calmar S. S. Corp.,* 303 U.S. at 527–528, 58 S.Ct. 651. By contrast, both the Jones Act and unseaworthiness claims compensate for the injury itself and for the losses resulting from the injury. *Peterson, supra,* at 138, 49 S.Ct. 75. In such circumstances, we are particularly mindful of the rule that requires us to promote uniformity between maritime statutory law and maritime common law.[9] See *Miles, supra,* at

---

[9]   The dissent, *post* at 2292, and n. 7 (opinion of GINSBURG, J.), suggests that because of the existing differences between a Jones Act claim and an unseaworthiness claim, recognizing punitive damages would not be a cause of disparity. But, as the dissent acknowledges, much of the expanded reach of the modern unseaworthiness doctrine can be attributed to innovations made by this Court following the enactment of the Jones Act. See *post* at 2292, and n. 6; *supra,* at 2281–2282. Although Batterton and the dissent would continue this evolution by recognizing

27, 111 S.Ct. 317. See also *Mobil Oil Corp. v. Higginbotham*, 436 U.S. 618, 625, 98 S.Ct. 2010, 56 L.Ed.2d 581 (1978) (declining to recognize loss-of-society damages under general maritime law because that would "rewrit[e the] rules that Congress has affirmatively and specifically enacted").

Unlike a claim of maintenance and cure, which addresses a situation where the vessel owner and master have "just about every economic incentive to dump an injured seaman in a port and abandon him to his fate," in the unseaworthiness context the interests of the owner and mariner are more closely aligned. *McBride, supra*, at 394, n. 12 (Clement, J., concurring). That is because there are significant economic incentives prompting owners to ensure that their vessels are seaworthy. Most obviously, an owner who puts an unseaworthy ship to sea stands to lose the ship and the cargo that it carries. And if a vessel's unseaworthiness threatens the crew or cargo, the owner risks losing the protection of his insurer (who may not cover losses incurred by the owner's negligence) and the work of the crew (who may refuse to serve on an unseaworthy vessel). In some instances, the vessel owner may even face criminal penalties. See, *e.g.*, 46 U.S.C. § 10908.

Allowing punitive damages on unseaworthiness claims would also create bizarre disparities in the law. First, due to our holding in *Miles*, which limited recovery to compensatory damages in wrongful-death actions, a mariner could make a claim for punitive damages if he was injured onboard a ship, but his estate would lose the right to seek punitive damages if he died from his injuries. Second, because unseaworthiness claims run against the owner of the vessel, the ship's owner could be liable for punitive damages while the master or operator of the ship—who has more control over onboard conditions and is best positioned to minimize potential risks—would not be liable for such damages under the Jones Act. See *Sieracki*, 328 U.S. at 100, 66 S.Ct. 872 (The duty of seaworthiness is "peculiarly and exclusively the obligation of the owner. It is one he cannot delegate").

Finally, because "[n]oncompensatory damages are not part of the civil-code tradition and thus unavailable in such countries," *Exxon Shipping*, 554 U.S. at 497, 128 S.Ct. 2605, allowing punitive damages would place American shippers at a significant competitive disadvantage and would discourage foreign-owned vessels from employing American seamen. See Gotanda, Punitive Damages: A Comparative Analysis, 42 Colum. J. Transnat'l L. 391, 396, n. 24 (2004) (listing civil-law nations

---

damages previously unavailable, *Miles* dictates that such innovation is the prerogative of the political branches, our past expansion of the unseaworthiness doctrine notwithstanding.

Of course, *Miles* recognized that the general maritime law need not be static. For example, our decision in *Moragne v. States Marine Lines, Inc.*, 398 U.S. 375, 90 S.Ct. 1772, 26 L.Ed.2d 339 (1970), smoothed a disjunction created by the imperfect alignment of statutory claims with past decisions limiting maritime claims for wrongful death. But when there is no disjunction—as here, where traditional remedies align with modern statutory remedies—we are unwilling to endorse doctrinal changes absent legislative changes.

that restrict private plaintiffs to compensatory damages). This would frustrate another "fundamental interest" served by federal maritime jurisdiction: "the protection of maritime commerce." *Norfolk Southern R. Co. v. James N. Kirby, Pty Ltd.*, 543 U.S. 14, 25, 125 S.Ct. 385, 160 L.Ed.2d 283 (2004) (internal quotation marks omitted; emphasis deleted).

Against this, Batterton points to the maritime doctrine that encourages special solicitude for the welfare of seamen. But that doctrine has its roots in the paternalistic approach taken toward mariners by 19th century courts. See, *e.g.*, *Harden*, 11 F.Cas. at 485; *Brown*, 4 F.Cas. at 409. The doctrine has never been a commandment that maritime law must favor seamen whenever possible. Indeed, the doctrine's apex coincided with many of the harsh common-law limitations on recovery that were not set aside until the passage of the Jones Act. And, while sailors today face hardships not encountered by those who work on land, neither are they as isolated nor as dependent on the master as their predecessors from the age of sail. In light of these changes and of the roles now played by the Judiciary and the political branches in protecting sailors, the special solicitude to sailors has only a small role to play in contemporary maritime law. It is not sufficient to overcome the weight of authority indicating that punitive damages are unavailable.

IV

Punitive damages are not a traditional remedy for unseaworthiness. The rule of *Miles*—promoting uniformity in maritime law and deference to the policies expressed in the statutes governing maritime law—prevents us from recognizing a new entitlement to punitive damages where none previously existed. We hold that a plaintiff may not recover punitive damages on a claim of unseaworthiness.

We reverse the judgment of the United States Court of Appeals for the Ninth Circuit and remand the case for further proceedings consistent with this opinion.

■ JUSTICE GINSBURG, with whom JUSTICE BREYER and JUSTICE SOTOMAYER join, dissenting.

In *Exxon Shipping Co. v. Baker*, 554 U.S. 471, 128 S.Ct. 2605, 171 L.Ed.2d 570 (2008), the Court recognized that punitive damages normally are available in maritime cases. *Id.*, at 489–490, 502, 508, n. 21, 128 S.Ct. 2605. Relying on *Miles v. Apex Marine Corp.*, 498 U.S. 19, 111 S.Ct. 317, 112 L.Ed.2d 275 (1990), the Court today holds that unseaworthiness claims are an exception to that general rule. Respondent Christopher Batterton, defending the Ninth Circuit's decision in his favor, relies on the Court's more recent decision in *Atlantic Sounding Co. v. Townsend*, 557 U.S. 404, 129 S.Ct. 2561, 174 L.Ed.2d 382 (2009). In my view, the Ninth Circuit correctly determined that *Atlantic Sounding* is the controlling precedent. See 880 F.3d 1089, 1095–1096 (2018) (case below). I would therefore affirm the judgment of the

Court of Appeals, cogently explained in Senior Circuit Judge Kleinfeld's opinion.

I

Batterton was employed as a deckhand for petitioner The Dutra Group, a dredging and marine construction company. As Batterton worked on a Dutra vessel, fellow crewmembers pumped pressurized air into a below-decks compartment. The build up of pressurized air blew open a hatch cover that crushed Batterton's hand, permanently disabling him. The accident could have been prevented, Batterton alleges, by a valve to vent excess air from the compartment, something to hold the hatch cover open, or simply better warnings or supervision.

Batterton filed a civil action asserting one claim of negligence under the Jones Act[1] and two claims under general maritime law: one for breach of the duty to provide a seaworthy vessel and one for breach of the duty to provide maintenance and cure.[2] As to his unseaworthiness claim, Batterton sought punitive damages, alleging that Dutra's breach was wanton and willful.

Dutra moved to strike or dismiss Batterton's punitive damages request. The District Court denied the motion, 2014 WL 12538172, *2 (CD Cal. Dec. 15, 2014), and the Ninth Circuit, accepting an interlocutory appeal, affirmed, 880 F.3d 1089. Longstanding Ninth Circuit precedent, the court observed, recognized the availability of punitive damages in seamen's actions for unseaworthiness. *Id.*, at 1091 (citing *Evich v. Morris*, 819 F.2d 256, 258 (1987)). *Miles*, 498 U.S. at 29–33, 111 S.Ct. 317, which held that loss-of-society damages are not available in survivors' actions for unseaworthiness resulting in a seaman's wrongful death, the court observed, did not undermine that precedent. 880 F.3d at 1093–1096. "Whatever room might [have] be[en] left to support broadening *Miles* to cover punitive damages" sought by a seaman, the Ninth Circuit said, "was cut off by [this] Court's decision in *Atlantic Sounding*," in which this Court, recognizing that "historically, punitive damages have been available and awarded in general maritime actions," held that such damages are available in seamen's suits for maintenance and cure. *Id.*, at 1095. (quoting *Atlantic Sounding*, 557 U.S. at 407, 129 S.Ct. 2561; alteration omitted). Punitive damages, the Ninth Circuit concluded, are similarly available when a seaman sues for unseaworthiness under general maritime law.

---

[1] The Jones Act provides: "A seaman injured in the course of employment or, if the seaman dies from the injury, the personal representative of the seaman[,] may elect to bring a civil action at law, with the right of trial by jury, against the employer. Laws of the United States regulating recovery for personal injury to, or death of, a railway employee apply to an action under this section." 46 U.S.C. § 30104.

[2] "Maintenance and cure" is the right of "the seaman, ill or injured in the service of the ship without willful misbehavior on his part [to] wages to the end of the voyage and subsistence, lodging, and medical care to the point where the maximum cure attainable has been reached." 2 R. Force & M. Norris, The Law of Seamen § 26:1, p. 26–4 (5th ed. 2003).

II

I turn now to an examination of *Miles* and *Atlantic Sounding* closer than the attention accorded those decisions by the Court.

Miles, decided in 1990, addressed this question: In a wrongful-death action premised on unseaworthiness, may a deceased seaman's parent recover damages for loss of society? 498 U.S. at 21, 111 S.Ct. 317. As the Court explained in *Miles*, historically, general maritime law did not recognize a cause of action for wrongful death. *Id.*, at 23, 111 S.Ct. 317 (citing *The Harrisburg*, 119 U.S. 199, 7 S.Ct. 140, 30 L.Ed. 358 (1886)). But since the late 19th century, every State had adopted a statutory wrongful-death cause of action. *Miles*, 498 U.S. at 23, 111 S.Ct. 317. And in two statutes, Congress had provided for wrongful-death recoveries in maritime cases. *Ibid.* First, the Jones Act, 46 U.S.C. § 30104, provided a right of action for the survivor of a seaman killed in the course of his employment. Second, the Death on the High Seas Act (DOHSA), 46 U.S.C. § 30301 *et seq.*, provided a right of action for the survivor of anyone killed "by wrongful act, neglect, or default . . . on the high seas." § 30302; *Miles*, 498 U.S. at 24, 111 S.Ct. 317. But the Jones Act and DOHSA left some wrongful deaths at sea without a remedy. See *Miles*, 498 U.S. at 25–26, 111 S.Ct. 317.[3] To fill gaps in this statutory regime, and in light of legislative abrogation of the common-law disallowance of wrongful-death claims, the Court in *Moragne v. States Marine Lines, Inc.*, 398 U.S. 375, 409, 90 S.Ct. 1772, 26 L.Ed.2d 339 (1970), recognized a general maritime cause of action for the wrongful death of a longshoreman. See also *Miles*, 498 U.S. at 26–30, 111 S.Ct. 317 (claim for wrongful death is also available to seamen's survivors).

After recounting this history, the *Miles* Court addressed the damages relief available for maritime wrongful death. Because "Congress and the States ha[d] legislated extensively in" the field of maritime law, the Court stated, "admiralty court[s] should look primarily to these legislative enactments for policy guidance." *Id.*, at 27, 111 S.Ct. 317. Congress had expressly limited damages recoverable under DOHSA to "pecuniary loss" sustained by the decedent's survivor. *Id.*, at 31, 111 S.Ct. 317 (citing 46 U.S.C. App. § 762, recodified at § 30303). And the Jones Act adopted the substantive provisions of the Federal Employers Liability Act, 45 U.S.C. § 51 *et seq.*, which the Court construed to confine wrongful-death damages to "pecuniary loss." *Miles*, 498 U.S. at 32, 111 S.Ct. 317. The *Miles* Court reasoned that loss-of-society damages were

---

[3]   These were the unprovided-for cases: "First, in territorial waters, general maritime law allowed a remedy for unseaworthiness resulting in injury, but not for death. Second, DOHSA allowed a remedy for death resulting from unseaworthiness on the high seas, but general maritime law did not allow such recovery for a similar death in territorial waters. Finally, . . . in those States whose statutes allowed a claim for wrongful death resulting from unseaworthiness, recovery was available for the death of a longshoreman due to unseaworthiness, but not for the death of a Jones Act seaman. This was because wrongful death actions under the Jones Act are limited to negligence, and the Jones Act pre-empts state law remedies for the death or injury of a seaman." *Miles v. Apex Marine Corp.*, 498 U.S. 19, 26, 111 S.Ct. 317, 112 L.Ed.2d 275 (1990) (citation omitted).

nonpecuniary, that such damages could not be recovered under DOHSA or the Jones Act, and that it would "be inconsistent with [the Court's] place in the constitutional scheme ... to sanction more expansive remedies" under general maritime law. *Miles*, 498 U.S. at 31–33, 111 S.Ct. 317.[4]

Some 19 years after *Miles*, in *Atlantic Sounding*, this Court held that punitive damages are available in actions for maintenance and cure under general maritime law. 557 U.S. at 408, 129 S.Ct. 2561. *Atlantic Sounding*'s reasoning had four components. First, the Court observed, punitive damages had a long common-law pedigree. *Id.*, at 409–410, 129 S.Ct. 2561. Second, the "general rule that punitive damages were available at common law extended to claims arising under federal maritime law." *Id.*, at 411, 129 S.Ct. 2561; see *id.*, at 411–412, 129 S.Ct. 2561. Third, "[n]othing in maritime law undermine[d] the applicability of this general rule in the maintenance and cure context," notwithstanding slim evidence that punitive damages were historically awarded in maintenance and cure actions. *Id.*, at 412, 129 S.Ct. 2561; see *id.*, at 412–415, 129 S.Ct. 2561, and n. 4. Finally, neither the Jones Act nor any other statute indicated that Congress sought to displace the presumption that remedies generally available under the common law are available for maritime claims. While the Jones Act armed seamen with a statutory action for negligence attributable to a vessel operator, that remedy, *Atlantic Sounding* noted, did not curtail pre-existing maritime causes of action and remedies. *Id.*, at 415–418, 129 S.Ct. 2561. The *Atlantic Sounding* Court rejected as "far too broad" the argument that the remedies available under general maritime law were confined to those available under the Jones Act or DOHSA. *Id.*, at 418–419, 129 S.Ct. 2561.

The *Atlantic Sounding* inquiries control this case. As in *Atlantic Sounding*, "both the general maritime cause of action"—here, unseaworthiness—"and the remedy (punitive damages) were well established before the passage of the Jones Act." 557 U.S. at 420, 129 S.Ct. 2561; *Mitchell v. Trawler Racer, Inc.*, 362 U.S. 539, 544, 80 S.Ct. 926, 4 L.Ed.2d 941 (1960); *The Osceola*, 189 U.S. 158, 175, 23 S.Ct. 483, 47 L.Ed. 760 (1903). And, unlike the maritime wrongful-death action at issue in *Miles*, Batterton's claim of unseaworthiness resulting in personal injury was not created to fill gaps in a statutory scheme. See *Atlantic Sounding*, 557 U.S. at 420, 129 S.Ct. 2561; *Miles*, 498 U.S. at 27, 36, 111 S.Ct. 317. The damages available for Batterton's unseaworthiness claim,

---

[4] The *Miles* Court relied on comparable reasoning in denying the deceased seaman's estate, which had brought a survival action, the right to recover future earnings. See *id.*, at 33–37, 111 S.Ct. 317. Under "the traditional maritime rule," "there [wa]s no survival of unseaworthiness claims." *Id.*, at 34, 111 S.Ct. 317. The Court declined to decide whether to recognize a general maritime survival right, however, because, even if such a right were recognized, it would not support recovery of lost future income. *Ibid.* This damages limitation followed from the Jones Act, DOHSA, and most States' laws, which did not permit recovery of such damages. See *id.*, at 35–36, 111 S.Ct. 317.

Atlantic Sounding therefore signals, need not track those available under the Jones Act. See 557 U.S. at 424, n. 12, 129 S.Ct. 2561.

III

Applying *Atlantic Sounding*'s test, see *supra*, at 2290, punitive damages are not categorically barred in unseaworthiness actions. *Atlantic Sounding* itself answers the first two inquiries. See *supra*, at 2290. "Punitive damages have long been an available remedy at common law for wanton, willful, or outrageous conduct." 557 U.S. at 409, 129 S.Ct. 2561; see *id.*, at 409–410, 129 S.Ct. 2561. And "[t]he general rule that punitive damages [are] available at common law extended to claims arising under federal maritime law." *Id.*, at 411, 129 S.Ct. 2561; see *id.*, at 411–412, 129 S.Ct. 2561. As next explained, the third and fourth components of *Atlantic Sounding*'s test are also satisfied.

A

Atlantic Sounding asks, third, whether anything in maritime law "undermines the applicability [to the maritime action at issue] of th[e] general rule" that punitive damages are available under general maritime law. *Id.*, at 412, 129 S.Ct. 2561. True, there is no evidence that courts awarded punitive damages for unseaworthiness before the mid-20th century. See *ante*, at 2283–2285. But neither is there evidence that punitive damages were *unavailable* in unseaworthiness actions. Tr. of Oral Arg. 17.

Contrary to the Court's assertion, evidence of the availability of punitive damages for maintenance and cure was not "central to our decision in *Atlantic Sounding*." *Ante*, at 2285. Far from it. "[A] search for cases in which punitive damages were awarded for the willful denial of maintenance and cure . . . yields very little." *Atlantic Sounding*, 557 U.S. at 430, 129 S.Ct. 2561 (ALITO, J., dissenting). The Court in *Atlantic Sounding* invoked historical evidence about punitive damages in maintenance and cure actions, "strikingly slim" though it was, *id.*, at 431, 129 S.Ct. 2561, only to underscore this point: Without a showing that punitive damages were unavailable, the generally applicable common-law rule allowing punitive damages should not be displaced. See *id.*, at 412–415, 129 S.Ct. 2561 (majority opinion). Here, too, the absence of evidence that punitive damages were unavailable in unseaworthiness cases supports adherence to the general common-law rule permitting punitive damages.

B

Atlantic Sounding asks fourth: Has Congress "enacted legislation departing from th[e] common-law understanding" that punitive damages are generally available? See. Dutra contends that unseaworthiness claims and claims under the Jones Act are "simply two paths to compensation for the same injury." Brief for Petitioner 19–20 (emphasis deleted). Positing that punitive damages are unavailable under the Jones

Act,[5] Dutra concludes they are likewise unavailable in unseaworthiness suits. *Id.*, at 17, 125 S.Ct. 385. See also *ante*, at 2284–2286. Dutra's argument is unavailing, for the Jones Act does not preclude the award of punitive damages in unseaworthiness cases.

As noted, the Jones Act provides a cause of action for a seaman injured by his or her employer's negligence. 46 U.S.C. § 30104. Congress passed the Act "primarily to overrule *The Osceola*, [189 U.S. 158, 23 S.Ct. 483, 47 L.Ed. 760,] in which this Court prohibited a seaman or his family from recovering for injuries or death suffered due to his employers' negligence." *Atlantic Sounding*, 557 U.S. at 415, 129 S.Ct. 2561. The Jones Act was intended to "enlarge th[e] protection" afforded to seamen, "not to narrow it." *The Arizona v. Anelich*, 298 U.S. 110, 123, 56 S.Ct. 707, 80 L.Ed. 1075 (1936). Accordingly, the Jones Act did not provide an "exclusive remedy" for seamen's injuries; instead, it "preserve[d]" and supplemented "common-law causes of action." *Atlantic Sounding*, 557 U.S. at 416–417, 129 S.Ct. 2561. As *Miles* itself recognized, the Jones Act "d[id] not disturb seamen's general maritime claims for injuries resulting from unseaworthiness." 498 U.S. at 29, 111 S.Ct. 317.

When the Jones Act was enacted, unseaworthiness and negligence were "discrete concepts": Unseaworthiness related "to the structure of the ship and the adequacy of [its] equipment and furnishings," while negligence concerned "the direction and control of operations aboard ship." G. Gilmore & C. Black, Law of Admiralty § 6–3, p. 277 (2d ed. 1975). Because these actions were distinct, it is improbable that, by enacting the Jones Act, Congress meant to limit the remedies available in unseaworthiness cases. Though unseaworthiness and Jones Act negligence now "significant[ly] overlap," *ante*, at 2281–2282, that overlap resulted primarily from mid-20th-century judicial decisions expanding the scope of unseaworthiness liability. See *Mitchell*, 362 U.S. at 547–550, 80 S.Ct. 926.[6] Those decisions do not so much as hint that Congress, in enacting the Jones Act, intended to cabin the relief available for unseaworthiness. Even today, unseaworthiness and Jones Act negligence are "not identical." 2 R. Force & M. Norris, The Law of Seamen § 27:25, p. 27–61 (5th ed. 2003).[7] The persistent differences between

---

[5] This Court has not decided whether punitive damages are available under the Jones Act. See *Atlantic Sounding Co. v. Townsend*, 557 U.S. 404, 424, n. 12, 129 S.Ct. 2561, 174 L.Ed.2d 382 (2009) (reserving the question).

[6] In particular, this Court held that a shipowner's duty to provide a seaworthy vessel was "absolute," thereby rendering unseaworthiness a strict-liability tort. *Seas Shipping Co. v. Sieracki*, 328 U.S. 85, 94–95, 66 S.Ct. 872, 90 L.Ed. 1099 (1946); *Mahnich v. Southern S. S. Co.*, 321 U.S. 96, 100–101, 64 S.Ct. 455, 88 L.Ed. 561 (1944); see 1B Benedict on Admiralty § 23, pp. 3–12 to 3–16 (7th rev. ed. 2018). In addition, courts broadened the range of conditions that could render a vessel unseaworthy. *Id.*, § 23, at 3–16 to 3–19.

[7] Unseaworthiness is a strict-liability tort, *ante*, at 2281–2282; the Jones Act requires proof of negligence, *Lewis v. Lewis & Clark Marine, Inc.*, 531 U.S. 438, 441, 121 S.Ct. 993, 148 L.Ed.2d 931 (2001). Unseaworthiness claims run against the vessel's owner, *Mahnich*, 321 U.S. at 100, 64 S.Ct. 455; Jones Act claims are brought against the seaman's "employer," § 30104. Injury caused by the negligent act or omission of a fit fellow crewmember may be actionable under the Jones Act but is not ground for an unseaworthiness suit. 1B Benedict on Admiralty § 23, at 3–34 to 3–38; see *Usner v. Luckenbach Overseas Corp.*, 400 U.S. 494, 91 S.Ct. 514, 27

unseaworthiness and Jones Act claims weigh against inserting into general maritime law damages limitations that may be applicable to Jones Act suits. See *supra*, at 2291, n. 5.[8]

The Court observes that a plaintiff may not recover twice for the same injury under the Jones Act and unseaworthiness. *Ante*, at 2282. True enough. But the Court does not explain why a bar to double recovery of compensatory damages should affect the availability of a single award of punitive damages. Notably, punitive damages are not awarded to compensate the plaintiff; their office is to punish the defendant and deter misconduct. See *Exxon*, 554 U.S. at 492, 128 S.Ct. 2605; W. Keeton, D. Dobbs, R. Keeton, & D. Owen, Prosser and Keeton on Law of Torts § 2, p. 9 (5th ed. 1984). There is thus no tension between preventing double recovery of compensatory damages and allowing the recovery, once, of punitive damages.

IV

Finally, the Court takes up policy arguments against the availability of punitive damages in unseaworthiness actions. *Ante*, at 2285–2287. The Court, however, has long recognized the general availability of punitive damages under maritime law. *E.g.*, *Atlantic Sounding*, 557 U.S. at 411–412, 129 S.Ct. 2561; *Exxon*, 554 U.S. at 489–490, 128 S.Ct. 2605; *The Amiable Nancy*, 3 Wheat. 546, 558, 4 L.Ed. 456 (1818).

Punitive damages serve to deter and punish "lawless misconduct." *Ibid.* The imperative of countering a "heightened threat of harm," *Exxon*, 554 U.S. at 490, 128 S.Ct. 2605, is especially pressing with regard to sailors, who face unique "hazards in the ship's service," *Harden v. Gordon*, 11 F.Cas. 480, 483 (No. 6,047) (CC Me. 1823) (Story, J.). These dangers, more than paternalistic 19th-century attitudes towards sailors, see *ante*, at 2287, account for the Court's " 'special solicitude' " for "those who undertake to 'venture upon hazardous and unpredictable sea voyages.' " *Air & Liquid Systems Corp.* v. *DeVries*, 586 U.S. ___, ___, 139 S.Ct. 986, 995, 203 L.Ed.2d 373 (2019) (quoting *American Export Lines, Inc.* v. *Alvez*, 446 U.S. 274, 285, 100 S.Ct. 1673, 64 L.Ed.2d 284 (1980)).

Dutra and the Court warn that allowing punitive damages in unseaworthiness actions could impair maritime commerce. Brief for Petitioner 33–34; *ante*, at 2286–2287. But punitive damages have been available in maintenance and cure cases in all Circuits for the last decade, *Atlantic Sounding*, 557 U.S. 404, 129 S.Ct. 2561, 174 L.Ed.2d

---

L.Ed.2d 562 (1971). And a vessel owner is liable for unseaworthiness only when the unseaworthy condition proximately caused the plaintiff's injury; under the Jones Act, a plaintiff can prevail upon showing the "slight[est]" causal connection between the defendant's conduct and the plaintiff's injury. 2 Force & Norris, The Law of Seamen § 27:25, at 27–62 to 27–63. See also *id.*, § 27:2, at 27–7, and n. 6 (the duty to provide a seaworthy vessel may run to "seamen" who do not qualify as such under the Jones Act).

8   The Court recognizes "that the general maritime law need not be static," but would confine changes in that law to those needed to align it with statutory law. *Ante*, at 2286 n. 9. As just stated, however, *supra*, at 2291–2292, the Jones Act was intended to augment, not to cabin, relief available to seamen.

382, and in unseaworthiness cases in some Circuits for longer, see *Self v. Great Lakes Dredge & Dock Co.*, 832 F.2d 1540, 1550 (C.A.11 1987); *Evich*, 819 F.2d at 258. No tidal wave has overwhelmed commerce in those Circuits.

Permitting punitive damages for unseaworthiness, the Court further urges, would create "bizarre disparities." *Ante*, at 2286–2287. I see no "bizarre disparit[y]" in allowing an injured sailor to seek remedies unavailable to survivors of deceased seamen. See Keeton, *supra*, § 127, at 949, 951 (state wrongful-death statutes frequently limit survivors' recoveries to pecuniary damages). Nor is it "bizarre" to permit recovery of punitive damages against a shipowner "for injuries due to unseaworthiness of the vessel." *The Arizona*, 298 U.S. at 120, 56 S.Ct. 707. Exposure to such damages helps to deter wrongdoing, particularly when malfeasance is "hard to detect." *Exxon*, 554 U.S. at 494, 128 S.Ct. 2605. If there is any "bizarre disparit[y]," it is the one the Court today creates: Punitive damages are available for willful and wanton breach of the duty to provide maintenance and cure, but not for similarly culpable breaches of the duty to provide a seaworthy vessel.

* * *

For the reasons stated, I would affirm the Court of Appeals' judgment.

NOTE

In a footnote in Atlantic Sounding Co., the Court reserved the question of whether punitive damages are available under the Jones Act. Atlantic Sounding Co. v. Townsend, 557 U.S. 404, 424 n.12, 129 S.Ct. 2561, 174 L.Ed.2d 382 (2009). In *Dutra Group*, the dissent reiterates this point. See n.5, supra. Does the majority's decision in *Dutra Group* effectively end any argument that punitive damages are available under the Jones Act? Are punitive damages available in cases brought by maritime workers under the general maritime law? For example, can a longshore or harbor worker who is injured while working on a vessel (not the worker's employer) sue the vessel under the general maritime law and seek to recover punitive damages? Are punitive damages available to non-seafarers/passengers for injuries caused by cruise ships? See Archer v. Carnival Corporation and PLC, 2020 WL 7314847 (S.D. Cal., 2020) (refusing to dismiss claims for punitive damages made by cruise ship passengers who were exposed to COVID-19). See also Calhoun v. Yamaha Motor Corp., 216 F.3d 338 (3d Cir. 2000) (issue of punitive damages for the death of a non-seafarer who died in a jet ski accident determined by the laws of Puerto Rico, where the accident occurred, rather than Pennsylvania, where the plaintiffs resided).